The REAL Wisdom Hunter Story

The REAL Wisdom Hunter Story

A Journey Of Faith, Danger,
and Storytelling Across Five Decades

An Autobiography

by

Randall Arthur

The REAL Wisdom Hunter Story
A Journey Of Faith, Danger, and Storytelling
Across Five Decades

By Randall Arthur

www.RandallArthur.com

Copyright © 2023, 2026 – Randall Arthur

All rights reserved. This book or parts thereof may not be reproduced in any form, stored in any retrieval system, or transmitted in any form by any means – electronic, mechanical, photocopy, recording, or otherwise – without prior written permission of the publisher.

Scripture quotations are taken from the Holy Bible,
New Living Translation,
copyright © 1996, 2004, 2015 by Tyndale House Foundation.
Used by permission of Tyndale House Publishers, Inc., Carol Stream, Illinois 60188.
All rights reserved.

Published by
Life Image Publishers
www.LifeImagePublishers@gmail.com

ISBN 978-0-9850257-9-3

Printed in the United States of America

Cover design by Fiverr/Sadia

1 2 3 1 2 5

Other Books by Randall Arthur
www.RandallArthur.com

Fiction
Wisdom Hunter
Jordan's Crossing
Brotherhood of Betrayal
Forgotten Road
A Quiet Roar

Nonfiction
46 Stones

Children's Book
ABCs On The Move

NOTES FROM THE AUTHOR

Dedicated to
My three children
My grandchildren
My great grandchildren to be
My great great grandchildren to be

Inspired by King Solomon
who compiled the Proverbs
as a gift to his biological children

This volume is an anthology of the adventures, traumas, and lessons—occurring over a fifty year period—that helped give birth to the content of my five novels - *Wisdom Hunter, Jordan's Crossing, Brotherhood of Betrayal, Forgotten Road,* and *A Quiet Roar*. It was written primarily for my kids as a collection of their father's personal exploits, as well as for those Randall Arthur fans who are hungry to know the stories behind the stories.

Every story in this book is true.
Nothing is made up.

Throughout the book I include conversations from decades past. I obviously don't remember those conversations verbatim. However, I do remember the basics of those conversations. And that's what I've recorded.

Some names—of mission agencies, mission board directors, editors, counselors, and pastors—have been changed to respect the privacy of those individuals and to honor their perspectives which might be different than mine. An asterisk will be used when the aliases are used for the first time.

CONTENTS

Foreword		1
Prologue		3
PART I	Wisdom Hunter	7
PART II	Jordan's Crossing	351
PART III	Brotherhood of Betrayal	403
PART IV	Forgotten Road	481
PART V	A Quiet Roar	585
Epilogue		653
Acknowledgments		657

FOREWORD

After reading every page of the first draft of my father's autobiography—twice the size of this volume—I highly recommended that a Foreword be written to ensure that people truly understand him. I quickly volunteered to take on the assignment. So here it is.

My dad can be stubborn. He's been hurt, and at times, he's hidden from the consequences of his own choices. As you read the stories in this book, you might cringe, feel embarrassed, or even shake your head in disbelief at some of his decisions. I know I did. But these are his stories, and through every single one, God has been guiding him.

Beyond his tough exterior and adrenaline-seeking ways, my dad has always been driven by a deep passion to make a difference in the lives of others. He stands up for the underdog and shares God's love in ways that often surprise people. Though he's stubborn, it's his fear of stagnation that has pushed him to move, to challenge boundaries, and to seek new ways to live out his faith. For my dad, God has never been just a concept—He's been a real Father when my dad's own father wasn't there, a steady guide when church leaders failed him, and a source of grace and mercy when he needed it most.

This book isn't just about struggles or mistakes. It's also filled with the heart-touching ways God has shown up and blessed Randy, sometimes beyond explanation. From moments of grace to perfectly timed blessings, God's presence is woven through every chapter of his life. My dad's journey is raw, messy, and reflective. It's filled with hard lessons and deep insights. My hope is that through his story, you'll see a glimpse of God's relentless grace, and understand that no matter how lost or stubborn we are, we are never beyond the reach of His love.

—Heidi
Randall's oldest "say-it-like-it-is" child.

PROLOGUE
Fall 1990

"Hello, is this missionary Randy Dodd in Munich, Germany?"

"Yeah, that's me."

"Randy, my name is *Allen Dust. I'm the senior editor at Questar Publishers in Oregon. I'm calling in regard to the *Wisdom Hunter* manuscript you sent to us."

I gulped and tried to breathe. "Okay."

"Well, I just want to let you know that I and everyone on the executive staff here has read the story. And we all love it. We believe it could fill a real niche in the marketplace right now. So we would like to offer you a contract to publish the book nationwide here in the U.S. as well as in Canada, the United Kingdom, Australia, and South Africa. We would start the editing process next month and have the book ready for an April release next year. How does that sound to you?"

"Uh...wow...Allen," I stammered. "I'm nearly speechless here." An avalanche of worst-case scenarios regarding my status with my legalistic mission board instantly cascaded through my head, sweeping away all elements of pragmatism. "But to be honest...I'm not sure I want the book to go to press."

Now Allen verbally stumbled. "I'm sorry... what?" he asked. "That doesn't make sense. People submit manuscripts,

3

hoping and praying they'll be published. So why would you send us a manuscript and then turn down our offer to put the book into print? Of the hundreds of manuscripts mailed to us every month, we only select a precious few to publish. There are many writers right now that would give their right arm to receive this offer. So help me understand why you're even the least bit hesitant."

I took a deep breath. "Well...first of all, I'm more than grateful for the offer. I'm truly honored. I really am. But if the book goes to press my Independent Baptist mission board will fire me. And I'm just not sure I'm ready for that. I..."

"What? Fire you? Why in the world would your mission board fire you? I'm not sure I understand that one either."

"Well, as you know, the main character in my story—Jason Faircloth—is a very mean pastor at the beginning of the book. He's heartless, dictatorial, and extremely judgmental. He's never been merciful to anybody a day in his life. Believe it or not, Allen, Jason Faircloth is stereotypical of many of the pastors and leaders inside my Independent Baptist denomination. And, as you know, the story of *Wisdom Hunter* demonstrates in a true-to-life drama just how destructive these types of leaders can be." I hesitated, then decided to forge onward. "My wife and I are currently supported by seventy-five Independent Baptist churches. And probably sixty of those churches are pastored by a Jason Faircloth."

"So," Allen again interrupted, "you're telling me that Jason Faircloth in your story is not just a one-off case of extremism?"

"That's exactly what I'm telling you. There are literally thousands of Jason Faircloths in my denomination. It's not pretty, Allen."

"For some reason," Allen retorted, "I find this hard to

believe. I'm not saying you're intentionally exaggerating the situation, but I've never heard of a denomination with this type of all-around abusive leadership."

"Well, welcome to my world. Maybe this kind of leadership isn't so prolific in the northwest where you are. But it's common in the southeast. I mean I've literally been in the middle of it for twenty years. It's the pain inflicted by this way of life that motivated me to write the book. The *Wisdom Hunter* story is my journey out of hardline legalism. I've experienced it, Allen. That's how I've been able to write about it. And in this story, I'm trying to show my peers just how ugly it is."

"And you honestly think the president of your mission board will fire you if the book is published."

"I know he will."

"Does he even know you've written the book?"

"No, he doesn't."

"And none of your supporting pastors know?"

"Only one of them knows. But he is not one of the authoritarians."

"I'm still just having a hard time believing the mission board will fire you. I just can't get my mind around that."

"Well again, welcome to my world." Substantial silence followed over the phone line. "As a matter of fact," I finally spoke up, "I'll tell you just how bad it would be. You said the book would be published in April of next year; right?"

"That's right."

"Well, we're not scheduled to finish out our term and turn our church over to new leadership until August of next year. This has been the plan all along. We've built our life around this time table. But if *Wisdom Hunter* was released to the marketplace next April and our mission board found out about it, they would fire us the same month. They wouldn't allow our oldest daughter to finish out her school year. They wouldn't allow us to serve out our rental lease in our house. They wouldn't give us the time we need to transition our church over to new leadership. They simply wouldn't give us the time to bring proper closure to our life here in this community. They would call us home immediately, regardless of the chaos it would create for me, my wife, our two daughters, and all the families in our church. And we sacrificed everything to plant this church and make it healthy. So, there you go. That's why I'm so hesitant."

"I'm just...what can I say...I'm stunned to think all this could even be remotely true."

After two more minutes of conversation, I hung up, not committing to the offer.

I lingered for a few moments in solitude. A legitimate publishing house with national clout had just called and offered me a contract. I could hardly believe it. A part of me felt giddy on the inside. Another part felt utterly sick. I couldn't help but wonder if the deal—a once-in-a-lifetime opportunity—would slip through my fingers because of my hesitancy.

PART I

WISDOM HUNTER

Chapter 1

As the first of my mom's two kids, I was born Thursday night, December 3, 1953 at Crawford Long Hospital in downtown Atlanta. The winter temperature that particular night in the Georgia capital hovered around 47 degrees. Dwight Eisenhower had just completed his first year as America's president. And America was roaring economically in the aftermath of World War II.

My father, Toy Arthur Dodd, was a surviving soldier of the war. He had fought in the D-Day invasion and in the Battle of the Bulge. With only a third-grade education, he had upon his return from the war fortunately landed a decent job with Southern Railroad.

My mother, Flora Dean Fields, had been pulled permanently from school in the seventh grade to help work the family farm following the untimely death of her mom. Now, as a married woman—it was her second marriage; her first husband had abandoned her—my mother earned a supplemental income as a blue-collar laborer at Williams Printing in downtown.

My mother was a dedicated Christian, church-goer, and prayer warrior. My father was none of those.

My mother, who was told by doctors that, medically, she would never have children, made sure I was in church every Sunday. This was her way of "thanking" God for giving her a child against all odds.

The first ten years of my life were lived out at 362 Augusta Avenue. Our house was a medium-sized duplex located a block and a half from Grant Park, the home of Atlanta's one and only zoo.

My very first memories are of my mother walking me as a 4-year-old to the W.F. Slaton Kindergarten, two blocks from our house. She walked me to the three-story brick building the first day of school, introduced me to the teachers, then left.

Every day thereafter, up through the fifth grade, I walked to the school building, and returned home, on my own.

On-my-own; this seemingly became the pattern of my childhood. I never saw it as neglect, though.

My mother, who was a 'goer,' would always take me with her on her plethora of social runs, but once at our destination, I was left alone to entertain myself; left alone to wander, investigate, and reconnoiter. And to make my own friends.

Thus, at an early age, I became an explorer, an adventurer, even a risk taker.

Those particular traits went into overdrive when my father moved our family in December 1963—the middle of my fifth-grade year—to a rural setting in Henry County, Georgia, twenty miles outside Atlanta. Our new house, a three-bedroom brick home constructed in the middle of two acres of land, was at 898 Panola Road. My walking and biking parameters expanded significantly. The undeveloped countryside promised adventures galore.

These adventures became so all-consuming that, to my deep regret and shame, I totally ignored my only sibling, a sister five years younger than me, also a miracle child. Because of our household dynamics, she—like me—learned to figure out life on her own.

Our "new" church, chosen immediately after our move, was Mt. Vernon Baptist. Mother took me with her every Sunday morning, Sunday night, and Wednesday night. She never permitted me to skip any of the meetings. But once at church, I was again left to intermingle "on my own" while mother socialized with multiple friends before and after the services. And intermingle I did. I was never shy.

Throughout my elementary and high school years—all in Henry County—a school bus picked me up every weekday morning and delivered me back to the house every afternoon. The entirety of those academic semesters, and all the summers in between, were spent, it seems, with very little parental enterprising socially, emotionally, mentally, or intellectually. In their defense, my father and mother both labored long hours. They devotedly provided food, shelter, clothes, and a few play things. I knew I was loved. But, I don't have a single memory of either of them attending a PTA meeting, reading a book to me, helping me with homework, introducing me to new music, attending any of my sandlot activities, giving me any social guidance, teaching me to garden, or teaching me to cook. They did, at a basic level, attempt to teach me right from wrong. And they did discipline me on occasions. They simply loved me the best they knew how. This was the template of 'parenting' they had been given when growing up. Of course, mother regularly took me to church, but left all the Bible teaching to the pastors and Sunday school teachers. I suspect mother's and dad's minimal education, at least in the formal sense, was a factor in their lack of confidence to teach and train their own children at any depth.

Regardless, my adolescent years—due to my own initiatives—were filled with an abundance of friendships and adrenalin-filled exploits. I became the creator of my own world. And I loved it.

My pubescent and early teen years were spent damming up creeks, climbing and swinging from trees, riding horses, building forts, speeding down dirt roads on bicycles, wrestling with buddies, teasing girls, hanging out with neighbors, shooting BB guns, overnighting with best friends, playing all the major sandlot sports, and riding minibikes.

Ah, yes...minibikes. My mom and dad would never know just how far outside their landmark boundaries my best friend and I traveled on those machines. Those were some great adventures indeed.

And then...at the age of thirteen, I made a decision that brought indescribable joy to my mother's heart. In one of the final mornings of a week-long summer Vacation Bible School at our church, I paused for the very first time in all my church-going years and mentally analyzed the Gospel presentation. And to my young mind, the New Testament claims about Jesus, affirmed by hundreds of New Testament eyewitnesses, seemed completely logical. So I decided that very day to trust that Jesus was the Savior of the world and to become one of his followers. I shared my decision publicly that morning from the front of the church auditorium, with my pastor standing at my side.

I was baptized three weeks later in front of a large Sunday night audience.

I had absolutely no inkling as to how these faith-filled decisions would forever alter the course of my life.

Chapter 2

The spring I was fifteen, my pastor invited the teenagers in our congregation to participate in a ten-day summer mission trip to Juarez, Mexico. The trip—in six-weeks time—would be coordinated by an Independent Baptist mission agency headquartered in Chattanooga, Tennessee. Young people had been invited from select churches across a four-state area. The journey would commence in Chattanooga. The mode of transportation would be a retired Greyhound bus. The cost for the trip would be $95 per person. The price would cover the expense of the roundtrip bus journey, the meals, and the lodging. The temporary residence while in Mexico would be at an old Catholic compound—with a few bunkhouses and a dining hall – that was exceedingly bare and rustic, and blistered by the desert sun.

Having the heart of an adventurer, I immediately got excited about the prospects of such an epic mission. At that point in my life I had never traveled beyond Georgia, Florida, Tennessee, and North Carolina. And here was an opportunity to add four more States—Alabama, Mississippi, Louisiana, and Texas, along with Mexico—to my repertoire of visited regions.

I immediately started begging my mom and dad to provide the $95 so that I could secure my place on the team. For financial reasons they were reluctant, and strongly so. But I so badly wanted to go that I selfishly pleaded day after day until their feelings of guilt could no longer bear my pain-filled desperation.

The day they produced the money was truly one of the most exciting days of my young life. During the weeks building up to the trip, I was literally filled with over-the-top anticipation.

In the end, four young men from our church—with the help of gracious parents—came up with the finances. We joined a group of twenty-one other guys and gals, along with four adult chaperones, from Virginia, Kentucky, Tennessee, and Georgia.

On the June morning that we all rendezvoused in Chattanooga, the summer air was hot and sticky. That is when we were told the bus's air conditioning unit had stopped working.

When my one piece of luggage was stowed in the bus's cargo bin I boarded the giant vehicle and proceeded to one of the back rows. I was one of the first people to climb aboard.

In a playful and anxious mood I started fiddling with the seat in front of me and quickly discovered that when pulled backward to a reclining position, the seat—obviously broken—would lay flat in my lap. But the locking mechanism wouldn't hold the seat in place. When I took my hands off the seat, it would violently spring forward to its upright position.

As a fifteen-year-old boy, I found this intriguing. And, of course, the situation seemed to invite some type of mischief. An idea quickly came to me when I spotted a scrap piece of paper that had been left in the seat pocket in front of me. I tore off a tiny segment, wadded it into a ball, and—defying all measures of hygiene—stuck it in my mouth. I rolled it around with my tongue, swished it in saliva, and made a spit ball. I promptly pulled the seat in front of me all the way back, placed the balled-up paper on the head rest, and waited. At the opportune moment I launched the projectile at passengers headed down the aisle in my direction. I missed all my targets. I repeated the experiment a few more times until I finally hit someone. The person I hit was maneuvering into their seat a few rows ahead. A couple of people laughed. Some looked at me with disgust.

Those who were disgusted quickly labeled me as the immature teen from Georgia. And not without merit. At that early stage of my Christianity, my desire for fun and attention far superseded my desire for a "godly" or respectful reputation.

And in all honesty, my motive for being on the trip was to rack up adventures more than anything else. And I was determined to have as much fun as possible.

But a few days into the trip—and after initiating more distasteful pranks at restaurants and at our bunkhouses—I was approached angrily at our desert compound by one of the adult chaperones. "You're ruining the trip for everyone," the man scolded. "This is a mission trip, not a spend-the-night party. Try to think about other people for once."

The gentleman's words actually registered with me, but only because I had already noticed the "think-about-other-people" behavior demonstrated brilliantly by one of the teen boys from Virginia. The boy's name was Leland. Leland's demeanor, from the minute he had boarded the bus in Chattanooga, had been so out of the ordinary it had secretly captivated my attention. He had gone out of his way to be helpful to everyone. He had yielded to all the quiet times by sitting restfully, and reading. And I had witnessed over and over again that the only reading material he possessed was his Bible. Every page, it seemed, was covered with handwritten notes. And his focus on God's Word didn't appear to be pretentious. That particular observation was made clear when he shared his first of several devotionals on the trip. I had never been around a Christian—young or old—who was so immersed in the Scriptures. To me, Leland's devotionals, and the spiritual depth behind them, were absolutely mesmerizing. His love for his Savior hung on his every word. His passion was equally manifested as he led the way every afternoon when our group knocked on doors, distributed fliers, and invited people to nightly evangelistic meetings.

So, to become a more tempered team player, I tried to behave more like Leland. But by the end of the trip I had failed miserably and had indeed spoiled the trip for a lot of people, including our host missionary who was sacrificing everyday to serve the poor people in his village.

The return trip to Chattanooga, for me, consequently became a 24-hour period of deep reflection. Why had I been so self serving? So inconsiderate? So immature? I couldn't shake the questions. The self-examination, mixed with all the impactful aspects of cross-cultural ministry that I had witnessed, hounded me for three long months.

Leland's Christianity had shown me a template for true discipleship. The mission field had introduced me to a purpose higher than myself. So, what was I going to do with these real-life insights? In some ethereal fashion that I couldn't explain I felt God calling me. Seriously calling me. Calling me to abandon my youthful dream of becoming a major league baseball player, track star, or gymnast. Calling me to rise up and say, "I'll sacrifice everything for You. Here I am. Send me."

The "call" was relentless and overpowering.

So at the age of fifteen I swallowed hard and said, "I'm yours. I'm surrendering now to become a disciple, a preacher, a missionary. I'll give in to your wishes for my life. Now and forever."

It was the most intense, most tearful, most absorbing, most transformative decision I had ever made.

My life would never be the same.

And my unbelieving dad would despise me for it.

Chapter 3

"His decision won't last," I heard my dad say angrily to my mother right after I had made my decision publicly at the church. His fatherly expressions over the following few days conveyed feelings that my career choice of becoming a minister was a disgrace to the family and a sad and monumental waste of my life. He was truly despondent. His sentiments only seemed to harden over the ensuing months.

But for me, I had never felt more alive, more purposeful, more focused. My whole approach to life seemingly morphed overnight.

All fun momentarily ceased. Developing an insatiable desire for God's Word, I distanced myself from my friends and began gorging every evening on radio sermons, especially chapel sermons from Bob Jones University, an institution of higher learning renowned for its elite spirituality.

I started avidly memorizing Bible verses, a minimum of one a day.

And I quickly bonded with my high school history teacher who was openly vocal about his relationship with Christ. At his request—as the adult leader of the school's

Christian Union Club—I added my name to the club's membership role and became an assistant. In a sense the man became my unspoken mentor for a few months, encouraging me, teaching me, and supporting me.

And then...Mike Bove came into my life.

Mike was the first youth pastor ever hired at our hundred-year-old church. He was 28, married, and had three young boys.

He was hired, I believe, for $300 a month.

He was originally from Minnesota, had served as a soldier at Fort Bliss, Texas, and had worked for a while as a Billy Graham crusade counsellor.

Mike wasted no time once our church employed him. There were no guidance books in the late 60's about how to build a youth ministry. So Mike asked himself, "How did Jesus build his church?" Mike set out to find the answer in the Gospels. What he discovered was that instead of selecting hundreds or thousands of people to be his foundation stones, Jesus instead focused primarily on just twelve men; they would become the base of his structure; they would be trained to reach the hundreds and thousands. So Mike decided, "That's the approach I'll take."

Soon, thereafter, Mike handpicked twelve young people from our church to take under his wing. I was fortunate enough to be one of the twelve, not because Mike saw any potential in me, but simply because I was one of only twelve in the youth group at the time. I and the other eleven were clueless regarding Mike's personal theological discovery, or that we had been "chosen" as the "foundation stones" for a youth ministry. We only knew that we now had a youth director.

With a fixed plan, Mike began immediately interacting one-on-one with each of us, to ascertain where we were in our spiritual growth and understanding. He asked each of us to tell him our story of coming to Christ for salvation. After deciphering our hearts through myriad questions, and after building us up with God's Word, he later nudged us to share our testimonies in front of the youth group, and eventually before the entire church congregation of 500 people.

During this same period, he patiently trained us to share the Gospel with individuals in general. Every Sunday afternoon he would pile us into one of the church buses and drive us to subdivisions, shopping centers, and inner-city parks where we would be dropped off in pairs to share the Good News with housewives, construction workers, bankers, attorneys, business owners, other teens, minorities, gang members, druggies, the homeless – anybody and everybody.

During the beginning stages of this process, I asked God one day to give me my first opportunity, all alone without a partner, to present the Gospel to at least one of my high school classmates – any of them; it didn't matter.

The next day, I shuffled to my desk in my third-period art class and heard the teacher announce, "This morning I'm going to give you a free period. I need to catch up on a backlog of administrative work. So as long as you keep your noise to a minimum you're welcome to move around, whisper, sleep, read, or study. You can do whatever you like; just don't cause a disturbance. I'll be sitting here. If you need me, just come to my desk."

Absolutely delighted with the teacher's decision I settled into my desk, looked around, and tried to decide how to spend my time.

My focus was instantly hijacked when my eyes landed on the person in front of me – one of the high school's coolest and most popular jocks who happened to be one of the most intimidating extroverts I had ever met. His name was Joey.

Here's the opportunity you asked for, I seemingly heard God announce.

I immediately tensed up. You've got to be kidding, I mumbled.

And then...it was as though an invisible hand, totally ignoring my reluctancy, shoved me in Joey's direction.

Come on, not Joey! I nearly cried. *Not for my first attempt at school. Please, I'm trying to be available here. At least give me someone easier to start with.*

At that moment, Joey folded his arms and lowered his head to his desktop.

I can't now, I stammered. *He's trying to sleep. I shouldn't bother him. You see that, don't you?*

I imagined the Almighty blasting my lame excuse with a hard stare.

Okay, okay, but if I mess this up, it's your fault, I blasted back. Psyching myself, I took a deep breath, swallowed hard, and slowly, slowly tapped Joey on the shoulder.

Joey raised his head and half turned in my direction. "Yeah, what do you need?" he blathered in a deadpan voice.

I had never before spoken to Joey. He was simply out of my league socially. He knew it. I knew it.

"I...uh...apologize for bothering you. My name is Randy...I..."

"Yeah, I know who you are."

"Oh...okay...well...I go to Mt. Vernon Baptist Church over in Fairview. And we just got a new youth director. And he's really good. So, I thought I'd invite you...."

"Nope. Don't like church. And I certainly don't like church people." Without a second's worth of pause, Joey turned and lowered his head back to his desk.

See, what did I tell you! I nearly shouted at the heavens. *He's not going to listen to anything I have to say. And I just made a fool of myself. So...*

You didn't share the Gospel, came the stedfast stance.

Didn't share the...! I was pushed to anger. This insistence felt like an absolute injustice. I closed my eyes and huffed. *All right...all right! Just give me a minute.* After a long second or two I reached forward and tapped Joey's shoulder again.

"What do you want, man?" Joey snapped as he turned to look at me a second time. "I already told you; I'm not interested in church."

"I understand," I replied, going into an automatic mode. "But, is it okay if I share something else with you?"

"Well, it looks like I'm not going to get any sleep," he spouted sarcastically. "So, what is it? Please tell me."

"Can I draw you a picture?"

"A picture?"

"Yeah, a picture."

His eyes, looking half agitated, said, Well, get on with it then.

I pulled a single sheet of paper from my notebook and picked up a pen from atop the desk. "It's a picture of God's love," I said, trying not to throw up. I honestly expected Joey to slap me at that point. But instead, a look of intrigue surfaced on his face. I paused. He gestured with his hand for me to continue.

Totally stupefied, I followed the instructions Mike Bove had given us in the youth group, instructions on how to explain John 3:16 word for word using a combination of illustrative drawings. Joey watched and listened. When I reached the phrase "so loved the world" I substituted the word "world" with Joey's name.

And then the most bizarre thing happened. Joey shed a tear. He sniffled and wiped at his nose. The look on his countenance was suddenly a heartfelt blend of doubt and hope.

Oh my...what have I done? I wondered. This fueled my nervousness even further.

"Wait a minute," Joey interjected. "Are you telling me that God honestly loves ME? Me?"

"That's what the Bible says, Joey."

"I've never heard that before."

I went over the verse again, this time highlighting the crucifixion – the way in which God irrevocably proved his love for us. I could almost see the gears inside Joey's head going into motion.

"And you're saying he died for me?"

"Yes, as the God of the universe, he punished himself for your sins – your bad behavior, thoughts, and choices. That's how much he loves you. And if you grasp that, and run to him, he will forgive you and embrace you with all the love you can stand. He will become your Savior, your teacher, your best friend."

The partial doubt on Joey's expression gave way to hope.

I shared for another ten minutes or more as Joey gave his rapt attention. Then, as Mike had trained us, I extended the invitation. "So, would you like to accept God's gift of eternal life?" I posed with a shaky voice. At that point I didn't know what else to ask.

Joey just looked at me for a few seconds, then finally responded. "Yeah...if God loves me like you say he does, then...yeah...I'd like to take his gift."

I was floored. I would never have anticipated such a quick and eager response, especially from someone with Joey's status of a playboy-in-the-making. And now, according to Mike's outline, I was suppose to lead Joey in a prayer of "acceptance." I quickly looked around. Subdued conversations and focused activities circled us in every direction.

Did I dare pray with Joey out loud in front of our classmates and teacher? "Joey," I said, "Is it okay if we get up and go into the dark room where we can talk in private for a few more minutes?"

Looking a bit confused, Joey squinted his eyes and said, "Sure; I guess."

I stood up and led the way. Once we were inside the dark room I switched on the light and closed the door.

"All right," I spoke softly, "you say you want to take his gift. So let's tell him. I'll pray first. And then I'd like for you to pray a simple prayer telling God you believe he gave his son for you and that you accept his gift of salvation."

Joey looked a little dazed and unsure.

Before anything else could be said or done, I closed my eyes and prayed. "God, I thank you that you so loved me and Joey that you gave your only son to die in our place and that if we believe in you, you will forgive us of our sins and give us eternal life. Thank you that Joey believes and wants to accept your gift. Amen." I looked up at Joey who was now staring at me. "Okay," I said, "Now it's your turn. Just tell God that you want him to save you." I closed my eyes before Joey could say anything else, and held my breath.

A few seconds lapsed until I heard Joey mildly clear his throat. "Okay, God," he prayed. "This is Joey, Joey from Stockbridge, Georgia. If you can hear me, then I want to thank you for loving me. This is all new to me, the fact that you would die for me. So if what I've heard this morning is true, then I want to open my heart and accept your love. And I want to take your gift of eternal life. I want you to save me."

When I heard no additional words, I opened my eyes. Joey opened his.

"Well?" he asked.

"Well, did you mean everything you said?"

"I did. I absolutely did."

"Then God says you're saved. You now have eternal life."

"Just like that?

"Just like that."

Before I could blink, a huge smile spread across Joey's face. At that very moment the dismissal bell rang. A look of urgency, mixed with an unbelievable smile, exploded in Joey's eyes. He immediately lurched out of the room.

I followed.

Joey grabbed the books from his desk and ran out of the classroom. I collected my books and followed, bewildered as to why Joey was in such a hurry.

Out in the hallway, now overrun with hundreds of students changing classes, I saw Joey up ahead pushing his way through the crowd. I then saw him raise his hand and wave frantically. Across the mass of moving bodies I heard Joey then shout, "Pam! Pam! Over here! Pam, I just got saved! I just got saved!"

Pam was Joey's girlfriend at the time.

Shocked by Joey's fearless and boisterous declaration in the packed hallway I stopped and backed up against a wall. I froze in place, unable to fully grasp all that had happened during the last forty minutes.

Over the next weeks, it was apparent that Joey's prayer couldn't have been more sincere. His life was truly transformed. Everyone who knew him could see it. He began sharing his spiritual discovery with anyone who would listen.

This overall encounter of watching God's Spirit completely

upend a person's life and place them on a new and joyous path—all because I was willing to open my mouth and share the Gospel—emboldened me to the nth degree. It soon, thereafter, became my goal, and the goal of the entire youth group, to clearly and intelligently present God's Good News to every student and every teacher at Stockbridge High.

Attacking this goal with vigor, my confidence as a one-on-one evangelist started to soar. And then...one day while running an errand with Mike, I saw him look at me from the driver's seat of his car and ask, "What has God been teaching you from his Word this week?"

It was a question he posed frequently to those of us he was discipling. So I wasn't caught off guard.

"Colossians chapter two, verse six," I told him. Naturally I elaborated on the fine points I had been mulling over - the meaning of the words 'as,' 'receive,' 'walk,' and 'in.'

Mike presented a few questions, provoking me to view aspects of the verse from different angles. We then enjoyed a great moment of analyzing, debating, and discussing all the various nuances of the verse. As we were reaching our destination, Mike asked me to recap, and list, the top three truths we learned. I did.

"Great," he said when he pulled into a parking lot and turned off the car engine, "I'm scheduled to preach next Sunday night at Mercer Avenue Baptist Church. But I'm going to call the pastor this evening and tell him you will be preaching in my place and that your text will be Colossians chapter two, verse six."

"Wait...what...no...no...I'm not ready for..."

"It's too late; I've already made up my mind."

"But I've never preached before!"

"Sorry, no turning back now."

Chapter 4

Preparing and outlining my first sermon over the next few days drove me to a new measure of anxiety and excitement.

The closer the hours counted down to the Sunday night presentation, the more tense I became. Yet, oddly at the same time, I was somewhat eager to stand and deliver.

When I was finally introduced to the Sunday night audience of about thirty people I was only able to approach the podium and remain standing because of the presence of my mentor, Mike, and a few of the young people from our youth group. Their smiling faces told me everything was going to be manageable.

I had been given a time allotment of twenty to twenty-five minutes. I feared I couldn't stretch my thoughts, or notes, far enough to fill the time slot. Yet, I ended up sermonizing for a solid forty minutes. I'm sure I repeated myself, detoured onto numerous rabbit trails, and spoke so speedily that most of my listeners received little, if anything, worth hearing. I'm guessing the only person receiving a blessing that evening was me.

But...I was immediately ready to preach again. And

that's the reason Mike thrust me, against my will, in the first place to speak in his stead.

I, however, wasn't the only one being mobilized in the youth group. Mike nudged every one into trial runs of leading, evangelizing, teaching, and preaching to see what latent gifts would surface.

And, man, did gifts start to emerge.

The youth group became a spiritual bootcamp for raising up a young army of pastors, teachers, deacons, and missionaries. Because of Mike's dynamic impact, one couple would years later serve as long-term missionaries in Japan, two couples in Africa, one couple in Alaska, one couple in Brazil, one couple in Italy, one couple in Paraguay, one pastoral couple in West Virginia, one single pastor in Georgia, one couple as worship leaders in Florida, and three couples as Christian school teachers in Georgia. Sherri and I—the girl I would marry out of the youth group—would be among that number. But that's a story for later.

Back in high school, one of my youth group buddies and I, in our ever growing spiritual development, soon founded and led a daily Bible study during the school's midday fifteen-minute break. Twenty to thirty students—freshmen, sophomores, juniors, and seniors—attended and participated five days a week. Joey, the jock I had helped lead to Christ, was among that number.

To phrase it mildly, my junior and senior years were unquestionably dominated by my Christian life – not my family life, my academic life, or my social life. I was totally preoccupied with teaching, preaching, and evangelizing – in youth meetings, in schools, in churches, and in market places everywhere.

With utter certainty, it was Mike's full devotion to his

ministry, and to us his young people, that had hoisted me to such a height of spiritual interest. Mike, by far, became the most influential person in my life. Fortunately for all of us under his wing, he wasn't the kind of spiritual leader who drew an imaginary line of spiritual maturity out in front of us and screamed that "this is where you should be." Rather he met us where we were—and we were all at different stages of growth—and helped us take our next step. And the next. And the next. He extended grace extraordinaire. And, of course, as teenagers we still needed it. Regardless of our earnestness as God's young disciples, we still had moments when our behavior would have made the most cynical-free person cringe. But Mike's patience with us was limitless.

One hot Saturday morning, for example, Mike took me and Billy along on a ministry run to visit a few young people who, because of personal struggles, needed encouragement. Billy, the other teen in the car, was a paramount figure in the youth group. Like me, he had surrendered to serve as a preacher of God's Word. And his transformation had been beyond the scale of most. It was never discussed openly, but it was assumed Billy had been adopted. His parents were caucasian, but Billy himself looked to be of Indian descent, and his dark skin had through the years made him a victim of racial slurs and social rejection. Consequently, Billy had developed a tough demeanor and a you-can't-beat-me attitude. He was the most fearless person I had ever met. He wasn't intimidated by anyone – young or old, big or small. He and I got along well, unless I crossed him, which occasionally happened. En route that day to our first stop, for instance, I strongly disagreed with Billy's conclusion about an important youth group matter.

Billy, sitting in the front passenger seat, turned to face

me in the back seat. "Are you calling me a liar?" he half growled, stretching my comments way out of context.

"I'm saying you are completely wrong; that's all."

"You ARE calling me a liar, then," Billy snorted. "Take it back or I'll jump back there and make you take it back."

Billy regularly issued threats to those he perceived as trying to shame him. Most people would back down. If they didn't, Billy would almost always follow through on his promise. I knew this, of course, but I always felt Billy's volatile temper was uncalled for. I wasn't his judge, but I wasn't going to be his lackey either.

"Sorry," I said, "You're still wrong."

Like a pit bull on edge, Billy launched himself over the bench seat of the old car with his fist raised.

Just as quickly, I slid down so that my face was out of range of his knuckles and propelled my feet upward. My feet connected with Billy's chest and drove him into the roof of the car where I pinned him.

He started swinging his fists downward, barely missing my head.

At that point Mike leveled a few words such as "come on, guys," "immature," and "we're pulling into Ronnie's driveway."

Billy, though, wouldn't stop throwing punches.

My survival instinct, as strong as anyone's, caused me to ignore everything Mike was saying. I pushed my feet deeper into Billy's chest. Billy and I both were breathing hard, extremely hard. But we were both too bullheaded to give in.

Growing weary, I thrust my shoulders upward in between an avalanche of pummeling fists and grabbed two handfuls of Billy's thick, jet-black hair and yanked downward. My feet, though, were still buried in his chest.

Billy yelped.

My move, understandably, put Billy's hands within easy reach of my face. Instinctively, he grabbed two handfuls of my hair and pulled upward.

As we were panting and groaning we heard Mike get out of the car and close the door. We had arrived at our first stop.

By the time Mike returned to the car, after visiting for a few minutes at the front door of Ronnie's house, Billy and I had fought to exhaustion. We were both hyperventilating—Billy collapsed in the front seat; I in the back seat. We were both covered in blood, with dazed looks in our eyes.

Mike never said a word about the argument that turned explosive. He simply started the car and headed for our next visit.

Yes, his patience with us—with every teenager in the group—was endless. Around Mike we always felt understood and forgiven. He made it safe for us to blunder and still carry on.

And carry on, we did. It seemed that nothing could completely derail us. Life couldn't have been better.

As a plus, my final two years in the youth group—my junior and senior years of school—happened to coincide with an explosion in the growth of every ministry at Mt. Vernon Baptist. It was an unprecedented season of joy and excitement, for me and for everyone in the church. It seemed that every church gathering—whatever the day or for whatever the reason—was absolutely electric. Lives were being changed everywhere. From my limited perspective, Mt. Vernon Baptist, at the time, seemed like one of the greatest churches in the world.

Indeed, the dynamics of the church's ministry were heralded far and wide. The church started attracting attention from prominent Christian leaders around the entirety of the southeast.

And then, to add greater prestige to the church, *Wally was brought on staff.

Unanticipated by anyone, Wally's inclusion at the church would be Mt. Vernon's first descent into hardcore legalism.

And I would blindly follow.

Chapter 5

Wally was from the north. For years he had circulated in the orbit of, and been a staunch supporter of, the pastor of the largest congregation in America. That renowned pastor, with his church in Hammond, Indiana, was such a strong and charismatic leader that he had garnered the respect, admiration, and envy of thousands of church leaders across the nation. To teach these pastors how to be like him, he and his church hosted a pastors' conference every year, a conference that drew veteran pastors and newly-ordained pastors from all corners of the continent. The attendees took notes on everything the man taught; they memorized and preached his sermons; they adopted his authoritative and dictatorial style of leadership; and, perhaps most of all, they enthusiastically embraced his list of dos and don'ts that, according to him and his esteemed pastoral peers, showed one's true spirituality. For thousands of churches across America, this list became the absolute standard for judging one's standing with God.

The list was thorough and unrelenting:

- No pants on women. Dresses only. And the

hems could not be more than an inch above the knees.
- No long hair on men. The hair couldn't touch the ears.
- No piercings.
- No tattoos.
- No dancing.
- No mixed swimming.
- No attending movie theaters.
- No dice and card games.
- No alcohol consumption.
- No smoking.
- No chewing tobacco.
- No using snuff.
- No questioning the pastor, the "man of God."

These were the blanket rules imposed on every church in this denomination. Of course, individual churches and pastors within the community always added a few extra mandates they believed were pertinent.

If a church member violated one of these rules, he or she was classified as "carnal" and stood in need of a pastoral rebuke or maybe even church discipline. If a church member disregarded several of the edicts, he or she was deemed a spurious "Christian" and was verbally blacklisted and condemned.

None of the items on the list were negotiable.

Inside the denomination, this was not called legalism. It was called "no compromise" devotion.

This was the mindset that defined Wally, the celebrity Christian from the north, when he joined our congregation. Our pastor—who was not a legalist—was simply flattered that such a renowned personality would be drawn to our church. But, being that Wally was a national figure who traveled around the country conducting his own massive conferences, his presence at the church started attracting new staff and new members who shared his hardline views. Over time, this group's "no compromise" list of dos and don'ts began seeping into the church services and started reshaping everyone's understanding of spirituality.

We were just simple country folk, but were being set straight by the biggest names in American fundamentalism.

Mike, our youth leader, was a critical thinker and thus proceeded with caution.

But me? Wanting to please Jesus more than anything else in life, I quickly climbed aboard the "no compromise" train. I became so solidified in this new way of thinking that during my final semester as a senior at Stockbridge High I became a merciless judge condemning everyone who didn't share my beliefs and standards. At the same time I began looking for a Bible College that had a likeminded perspective.

After researching multiple schools I placed Bob Jones University in Greenville, South Carolina at the top of my list. Tennessee Temple Bible College in Chattanooga, Tennessee was a distant second. Piedmont Bible College in Winston-Salem, North Carolina was next.

I assessed all my options carefully. And finally made my choice.

I was a day away from applying to Bob Jones University when Mike strongly recommended that I select Tennessee Temple instead. I don't exactly remember Mike's reasoning. It could have been that two couples from our church were already enrolled there, majoring in missions, and would thus provide some back-home company. But because of Mike's investment in my life, and the fact that I held him in such high regard, I was persuaded at his counsel to redirect. So I applied at Tennessee Temple. And was accepted.

Unbeknownst to me—and to Mike—I was about to be immersed into the deeper, darker, more dangerous waters of radical legalism.

Chapter 6

The founder and president of Tennessee Temple—comprised of the college, Bible school, and seminary—was Dr. Lee Roberson. Dr. Roberson was a physically intimidating figure. He was tall with broad shoulders and spoke with a husky voice that demanded immediate attention. He exploited his boss-like persona without compunction. Even his wife, at least in public, addressed him by the title of "Dr."

At orientation, Dr. Roberson emphasized stringently that Tennessee Temple was superior to other Bible colleges due to the fact that it was local-church based, under the direct auspices of the famous Highland Park Baptist Church – of which Dr. Roberson was the pastor.

Euphoric at how privileged I was to be a student there, as well as being a new member of Highland Park Baptist Church, I could hardly wait to commence my studies as a Theology major.

During my first days on campus, all the school rules were laid out for first-year students. I wholeheartedly applauded them, even the rule that allowed Temple students to listen to only one radio station – WDYN, the school-sponsored station. Not only were all pop stations off limits, so was the local affiliate station of Moody Bible Institute out of Chicago. Moody after all was a "dangerous, compromising, neo-evangelical" organization.

With fervor I quickly settled into my new life. During the morning and early afternoon hours, I sat under the tutelage of my professors and hungrily and ferociously took notes. In the late afternoons, I worked on the school's work-scholarship program as a custodian at the Tennessee Temple High School where I vacuumed, mopped, emptied trash, and cleaned toilets. In the evenings I researched, studied, and completed homework assignments.

On the weekends, as required of all first-year students—I attended all the services at the Highland Park church. The church was independent, not belonging to any national network or convention. The church services, both Sunday morning and Sunday evening, were filled with around 5,000 people.

In addition to the church services, the Bible college conducted chapel services every Monday, Wednesday, and Friday mornings. Thus, as students, we were saturated weekly with sermons from revered pastors, evangelists, and missionaries from around the world.

On top of these meetings was the annual week-long Bible conference in the fall and the annual week-long missions conference in the spring.

Since my ultimate calling was to serve as a foreign missionary, the missions conference, to me, was the most intriguing and inspiring series of meetings during my freshman year. For eight full days I was able to meet and interact with hundreds of missionaries that collectively served on all continents of the globe and in every conceivable capacity. My mind was pumped with stories, statistics, and facts beyond my imagination. I was thoroughly stimulated with all the possibilities in front of me. It was like discovering for the first time the bigger part of the iceberg, the part not seen on the surface.

The question now was: Where outside America would I serve and in what capacity?

As I navigated my first year at the school I also discovered—as part of my ongoing spiritual enlightenment—that to be sanctioned by God as a decent Christian, I, as a man, had to wear a suit and tie to all church services, and had to display a clean-shaven face at all times. Beards, mustaches, and goatees were a sign of a heart-gone-astray. Men and women alike had to be clean, well-groomed, and professional looking from morning till night. We were also taught that all syncopated music, or any music that caused the body to move, was "born in hell and perpetrated by communism in a covert effort to destroy one's morals." Thus, all such music was categorized as the "devil's music" and was forbidden. We also learned that the King James Version of the Bible was the one and only true voice of God. All other English translations of the Bible were works of Satan to lure people from truth. And to sanctify us even further, it was impressed upon us that we should never fellowship with "Christians" from other denominations—even Southern Baptists. They were most likely not genuinely redeemed anyway. And then, in order to keep us really pure, we were not allowed to fellowship with anyone who DID fellowship with Christians from other denominations. This was called "second-degree separation."

To prove our commitment to Christ, and to the school authorities, every student—in the college, Bible school, and seminary—had to sign an accountability sheet every Monday morning in chapel, stating we had abided by all the rules during the previous week. Any infraction of the rules—whether one was caught or told on—was punishable by an accumulation of demerits. At a certain maximum, the student would be suspended.

To help steep us—as future pastors, missionaries, and evangelists—in these godly values, and to give us real-life platforms for rehearsing all that we were learning theologically and practically, the school offered a plentiful array of controlled service opportunities. The Highland Park church, for example, operated over thirty buses, each with its own designated route, that ventured out every Sunday morning to bring in "lost sheep" – kids and adults alike. Each bus had to be supplied with a "bus captain" and several assistants to present music, games, and devotions to the riders en route to the Sunday morning service. The church also supervised over forty chapels, or "mini churches," scattered across a hundred-mile radius. Each of the chapels had to have a pastor, a music leader, a youth worker, and as many assistants as possible. The Temple college, Bible school, and seminary, of course, were the primary sources for all these volunteer workers.

Zealous to put into practice all I was learning, I volunteered my first year to work as an assistant on one of the bus routes. As it happened, I worked with Pete and Jean, the bus captains, who were one of the couples from my home church in Stockbridge. It was inspiring for me to witness this couple moving ever and ever closer to their calling to serve as church planters in Japan.

By the end of my first year, I had become absolutely pompous in my outlook. Tennessee Temple was the Mecca of Christianity and I, a country boy from Georgia, had walked its halls and partook of its knowledge and experience, things that I was convinced could rarely be enjoyed anywhere else on earth. I was sure that theologically I was well on my way to "knowing it all."

I was feeling good.

Chapter 7

Hello Honey,
This afternoon has been so long, knowing I wouldn't get to see you. If you were only here I'd be happy! I miss you! Hope you have a wonderful weekend. I can hardly wait til we can be together again.
                                Love you always,
                                        Sherri

    Sherri was three and a half years younger than me, but was extremely intelligent and mature for her age, and had also surrendered to serve one day as a foreign missionary. She had come up through the ranks of the Mt. Vernon youth group. Mike, the youth pastor, had often paired us as witnessing partners during the Sunday afternoon evangelistic outreach events. Sherri had even attended the daily Bible studies I had led in high school. During our summer door-to-door evangelistic efforts I had been placed in an unusually close setting with her. And to say I was impressed would be underplaying my feelings.
    I actually enjoyed her company so much that as an eighteen

year old I went to her father during my first summer break back in Georgia and said, "Is it okay if I date your daughter?"

Sherri's dad couldn't believe the question. He looked at me with a look of dismay. "Randy," he half snarled, half derided, "Of course you cannot date my daughter. She's only fourteen. What are you thinking? You'll have to wait til she's fifteen."

Frustrated, I felt the man was being unreasonable. But a few weeks later on Sherri's fifteenth birthday, I was permitted by her parents to pick her up and, without a chaperone, spend an entire day—from morning till night—with her on a "first date."

To impress me that day—and she succeeded—Sherri made a dress for the occasion and also prepared fried chicken, potato salad, and homemade biscuits for a picnic lunch. We spent six or more hours at the famous Stone Mountain state park. Capturing each other's hearts that day, we both fell in love.

Well into my junior year of Bible college, I was missing her. We had been writing letters to each other at least once a week, sometimes more. A fire for one another was building in our hearts and spirits.

I was discovering all the intense layers of boy/girl love and trying as much as possible to maintain my academic focus. I somehow managed to finish my third year at Temple with more determination than ever. And against the wishes of a few key people, I was about to change a young lady's life.

"Will you marry me?" I asked Sherri the night she graduated from high school. She had been able, because of her academic achievements, to advance a grade. The youngest in her class by far, she still walked the stage as the valedictorian for the senior class.

"Yes!" she cried in jubilation, following the ceremony. "Yes, yes, You know I will!"

I was not terribly appreciated by Sherri's mother. Her mother told her more than once *You don't have to marry the first guy you liked.*

Yet, Sherri and I felt our marriage was ordained of God and destined to be. We quickly set a wedding date. It would be fourteen months away, a few weeks after my college graduation.

Three days later, with an engagement ring on her finger, Sherri moved into a girls' dorm in Chattanooga and began her first semester of Bible college during Tennessee Temple's summer session. Her goal was to proceed through her college education as quickly as possible to help expedite our entry into the world of missions.

I remained in Georgia for the summer and earned money as a surveyor's assistant to help pay the tuition for my final year.

By the time I returned to campus in the fall, Sherri—carrying a maximum number of courses—had aced two full semesters of summer classes. I was so proud of her.

The goal I set for myself for my senior year was three-fold. First, I wanted to foster the love relationship with Sherri. But this would be no easy exercise considering all the draconian dating rules imposed on Temple students. Second, I aspired to earn my Bachelor of Theology degree with high marks. I had managed with pure discipline to merit a place on the Dean's list every semester for the three previous years. I wanted to continue that streak. My high school grades, due to a lack of interest in school at the time, had been predominantly C's and D's. I now wanted to demonstrate to myself that I possessed a mind that, if taxed, could compete with the intelligent students. And lastly, I hoped to gain some guidance as to where Sherri and I should serve as cross-cultural missionaries. That question was still far from being answered.

As one month quickly rolled into the next, these goals materialized bit by bit.

Sherri and I—when we were allowed to be together–enjoyed just strolling and conversing. Additionally, we regularly discussed our wedding plans – the bridesmaids, their dresses, the groomsmen, their suits and ties, the rehearsal meal, the vows, the wedding cake, the reception, and, of course, the honeymoon.

Academically, I barely managed to secure the A's I was wanting. Greek II presented the greatest challenge and nearly upset my run. But I slowly became the victor.

When the school's annual mission conference came around I had an epiphany regarding my and Sherri's possible place of service. I had already established—due I'm sure to my adventurous nature—that I wanted to serve where no other missionaries were serving. I initially thought this would be in some remote tribal village. But over the years of meeting, and reading about, hundreds of missionaries I realized that very few missionaries from North America were working in Europe. Most of the missionaries it seemed were ministering in the Caribbean, Central America, South America, Asia, India, or Africa. The few who were operating in Europe had settled in the southern part of the continent around the Mediterranean - in Spain, France, and Italy. I had never met a single missionary working in Switzerland, Belgium, Austria, Holland, Denmark, Sweden, Finland, or Norway. So I began to look closely at those regions of the world.

But how would I know with any degree of certainty where God wanted us to serve? Did God utilize a universal step-by-step procedure to lead his followers? I researched the Scriptures, both Old and New Testaments, to find God's modus operandi for guiding his followers. It soon became clear to me that God didn't use a one-size-fits-all approach. To some of his followers He spoke audibly. To some He spoke through angels. To some through animals. To some through dreams. To some through visions. To some through nature. To some through prophets. To some through apostles. To some through miracles. To some through letters. And to some there was only silence.

And then, I took notice of a particular missionary, actually the most famous missionary in all of Christendom—the Apostle Paul. On three well documented missionary journeys, Paul left a trail of newly planted churches all across Asia Minor, churches that have been immortalized in Scripture. So, how did Paul sense God's leading as he moved from one region to another, from one city to another? Well, instead of waiting for guidance that was perceived as divine or heavenly, he used his God-given logic to decide. He simply selected a destination according to his preference and trusted God to close the door if he was heading in a wrong direction.

Yet, it seemed all too common for many Christians to persistently wait in life, in a type of spiritual cocoon, hoping that God—with some type of can't-miss sign—would miraculously open a door for them.

Paul, though, was purely proactive. There is no indication anywhere in the New Testament of Paul praying and asking God where he should go next. Paul simply moved into action and trusted God to close doors.

I decided to follow Paul's example. Since my missionary reveries had funneled my attention to Western Europe, that's where I would maintain my focus.

A few weeks later while vacuuming a geography classroom, I stared at a large globe atop a corner table. I slowly rotated the orb until I was gazing at the European continent, then rested a finger tip on that part of the world. I closed my eyes and moved my finger in small circles. I finally halted the movement and opened my eyes. I was touching the landmass of Norway, the northernmost country in Europe. As a totally inexperienced world traveler I knew absolutely nothing about Norway's history, culture, language, or people. Yet, reveling in the Apostle Paul's example, I said to myself and to God, "That's it. We'll start moving in that direction. If You keep the doors open, we'll go to Norway." In that one instant I sealed my and Sherri's destiny. We would be moving to an arctic country, the land of the ancient and feared Vikings.

Chapter 8

Before the school year came to a close, Sherri and I, as an engaged couple, filled out applications to serve as missionaries under the auspices of a well-known Independent Baptist mission agency called *Independent Baptist World Outreach, or better known as *IBWO. IBWO, headquartered in Chattanooga, was the natural mission agency of choice for Temple students entering the world of cross-cultural missions. IBWO's world view and doctrinal statement was the exact same as Tennessee Temple's. Over one-thousand missionaries were part of the IBWO family at the time, and the majority of those were Tennessee Temple graduates.

Filled with excitement galore Sherri and I—in view of our applications—were interviewed, evaluated, and in February 1975 were officially accepted as members of the IBWO organization. Sherri was seventeen. I was twenty-one. We were still weeks away from being married.

To our utter surprise, we were informed around the same time by IBWO staff that another couple—*Brian and Celeste—had recently arrived in Norway as IBWO missionaries. They were about five years older than Sherri and me. We learned they were starting children's clubs. Our goal would be different than theirs, so we would probably never work together, but we could at least provide one another with likeminded fellowship. It wasn't but a few weeks later, after I contacted Brian via mail, that he sent me a dozen slides of beautiful Oslo landmarks.

Sherri and I, like all newly appointed IBWO missionaries, were responsible for raising our own monthly financial support from churches and individuals. So, I immediately started scheduling weekend speaking engagements where I would preach, show the Oslo slides, and present Sherri and myself as "missionaries to Norway," hoping the churches would vote to support us with $25, $50, or $75 a month.

As Sherri's and my wedding was fast approaching on July 27, I was anticipating that by the end of the school year I could raise enough money to at least afford monthly apartment rent. But by late April, a few weeks before my scheduled graduation, I had failed to raise a sufficient number of dollars.

Then on a Wednesday evening in early May I encountered something that bolstered my faith beyond imagination. I was gathering my Bible and note-taking materials following the dismissal of the midweek service at Highland Park Baptist Church when I heard someone say, "Randy, you forgot your keys."

I turned to look behind me. Bobby, with his wife Louise at his side, was holding up a ring of keys. Bobby and Louise were another couple out of Mt. Vernon Baptist Church back home. They would be graduating from the Bible College within the month and making a long-term move to Africa as church planters.

I checked my pants. My keys were nestled safely in my front pocket. "Those aren't my keys, Bobby," I told him.

"They belong to someone else." I turned and started to walk away.

"Randy," I heard Bobby call my name again, "You're walking away without your keys."

"Bobby," I said, pivoting, "those aren't my keys. I have mine right here." I removed my keys from my pocket so he could see he had made a mistake.

Bobby sighed. "Randy, I'm telling you, these are your keys."

"Bobby, I don't under…" I halted in mid-sentence, mentally stumbled, then backtracked. "Am I missing something here?" I half whispered.

Bobby pulled his wife closer to his side and half-grinned. "Louise and I have been so blessed over the years here in Chattanooga, we've decided we want to be a major blessing to someone else before we leave."

A car! my mind explosively speculated with absolute enthusiasm. *They're going to give me a car! I can't believe it!*

"So," Bobby proceeded, "we know you're getting married in a couple of months. And you'll need a place to live. So," he emphasized as he again extended the keys to me, "enjoy it. Enjoy it as much as we have."

The expression on my countenance must have been one of total bewilderment.

"Our mobile home, Randy. We're giving you and Sherri our mobile home. Along with the appliances. We'll be out of the house in three weeks. And it will be all yours."

He handed the keys to me. Was I dreaming?

"It's completely paid for," Bobby added while I stood in stunned silence. "There is a $35 dollar-a-month rental fee you'll have to pay the trailer park for the use of their property."

"You're giving...me...your...house?" I finally managed to stammer.

Bobby and Louise looked at each other, looked at me, grinned, and nodded in sublime pleasure.

I threw myself into their embrace and cried for the longest time.

What a stupefying moment!

I ended my four years at Temple in the spring of 1975 with a proudly-earned Bachelor of Theology Degree, simultaneously keeping my name on the Dean's list right up to the very end, for eight straight semesters.

Two weeks following my graduation—as Sherri delved into the first semester of summer school—I was officially ordained and commissioned as a gospel minister at Mt. Vernon Baptist, back home in Stockbridge.

And then on Sunday evening, July 27—following Sherri's one semester of summer-school that year—Sherri, at 18, and I, at 21, became Mr. and Mrs. Dodd. The elaborate wedding ceremony was intertwined with Mt. Vernon's weekly Sunday night worship service. Over three-hundred people, along with five bridesmaids and five groomsmen, witnessed our vows. The reception was outdoors on the church property in beautiful 80 degree weather.

Following a joyous and relaxing three-day honeymoon in Morganton, Georgia, on Blue Ridge Lake, Sherri and I promptly set up household at our new place of residency. Our gifted mobile home was located in a trailer park in North Georgia, right across the Tennessee/Georgia state line. And next door to a drag strip.

The mobile home was a perfect setup for a newlywed couple like ourselves who were on a modest budget. Several of the other trailer park tenants were poor Temple students as well, so we felt genuinely comfortable with the surroundings.

We spent the final five weeks of summer—before Sherri returned to classes in the fall—organizing the house, becoming acquainted with our neighbors, and speaking in church services to raise our missionary support.

Rolling through the fall and into the winter, Sherri and I quickly found a pace of life that became our "norm." She attended classes during the day, again carrying a maximum load of classroom hours, and worked on her school assignments in the evening. I mainly traveled and preached, immersed in the task of building our monthly financial support. I was out of town nearly every week from Friday to Monday.

Every day, though, seemed to be a good day in our minds; even initially when we were so poor that we had to drive to the downtown Gospel Mission in Chattanooga and accept grocery bags of charitable food items; even when we resorted to cutting down a 24-inch spriggly pine from the nearby woods for our first Christmas tree; or even later when a leak sprung in one of the bathroom pipes and flooded the trailer from end to end with an inch of water. We were simply too young, too in love, and too focused to surrender to discouragement.

And then to add to the intensity of our life and faith, another phenomenal thing happened that we've never, not even to this day, been able to explain.

Chapter 9

On a Sunday night in early fall I had a speaking engagement in Georgia, near our parents' homes. Sherri joined me on this particular trip.

When we arrived at the church, I took note that our car's fuel gauge showed only a quarter of a tank of gas. I knew from my extensive traveling that the remaining fuel would afford us only another seventy-five miles or so. From the church we were visiting to our mobile home back at the Tennessee state line was a hundred-and-fifty miles. Neither Sherri nor I had cash to purchase extra gas. But I wasn't concerned. The church where I was about to preach would give us a love offering. This was standard protocol whenever a missionary was a guest speaker. As a matter of fact, the love offerings I regularly received helped me and Sherri pay our bills every month.

Following the church service that night I waited around for the pastor or treasurer to forward the cash to me that had been collected in the special offering. The pastor finally approached me when he managed to break free of church members needing to talk. He shook my hand and thanked me for my message. But there were no promises of forthcoming support, and no money that was placed in my hand by him, the treasurer, or anyone else at the church that evening.

When Sherri and I returned to our car, we were certainly a little disappointed. We had driven three hours to honor the speaking engagement, and yet the church did not provide a meal or an honorarium. This absence of any show-of-support was simply not normal.

Sherri and I decided, contrary to our original plans, to stop by my mom and dad's house for a few minutes to say "hi" and hopefully receive a five or ten dollar bill that my mom typically slipped into my pocket. That night, however, she gave us two bags of groceries—for which we were grateful—but no money.

We then decided to drive a few miles out of the way and briefly visit Sherri's parents. Surely they would feel impressed to give us a few dollars that we could use as gas money.

Sherri had to attend classes early the next morning, so we had no choice but to return to Chattanooga that night. "If dad doesn't offer you any money, then ask for some," Sherri told me outright before we knocked on the door. "I can assure you, dad had rather you ask him for a few dollars now than to receive a call in the middle of the night telling him we are stranded in the middle of nowhere Georgia."

Even though we visited for fifteen minutes or so, I simply couldn't bring myself to solicit any cash. I decided deep in my spirit before we said "good-bye" that I would just trust God. He, after all, thoroughly understood our plight. So, he would just have to take care of us.

Yes, my faith as a young man was childlike and even smacked of foolishness. So, understandably, Sherri was upset when we returned to the car and headed northward into the night. We simply rode in silence as the gas gauge started to drop. We were not even half way back to Chattanooga when the needle on the gauge fell below "E."

After a few more miles, the needle truly couldn't move any farther to the left. I sighed. I felt like an idiot. Sherri's biological clock normally eased her into a state of sleep around 10:00 PM. It was now 10:30. She was wide-eyed. She stared at me. She stared at the needle. We were north of Cartersville entering a long stretch of countryside where there were only a few houses. Would I really have to walk up to some stranger's front door at that time of night and beg for gasoline that would probably have to be siphoned out of a vehicle? I sighed again.

By the time we reached Adairsville, another twenty miles up the road, we could hardly believe the car engine was still firing. Sherri remained fully awake. But, we had another fifty miles left before we reached home.

The car kept rolling.

A little after midnight, we pulled into our driveway. We just sat in the car and cried. Had angels pushed our car up the darkened highways? Had God somehow replenished the fuel?

Sherri hitched a ride the next morning with another Temple student that lived in the trailer park. I borrowed a five-dollar bill from a neighbor and went and sat in our car. I turned the ignition. To my shock, the car started right up. I drove one mile to the nearest gas station. When I entered the gas station property, on a downward slope, the car engine died. I literally coasted to the gas pump.

Sherri and I, who were both eyewitnesses to what happened, will never be convinced there was a logical explanation. For us, it was simply our Heavenly Father demonstrating compassion for his little ones in an extraordinary act of intervention. That one experience reinforced our faith in God's majestic abilities for a lifetime.

Ever growing in my faith journey, I would attend a missions conference in Florida in the upcoming new year that would for the first time, however, make me question the legitimacy of my legalistic mindset. And for me, considering my steadfast loyalty to the spiritual convictions of Tennessee Temple, this would be alarming.

Chapter 10

Normally I booked my own fundraising engagements. Rarely did IBWO arrange any of my church bookings. In the spring of 1976, however, the IBWO home office asked me to participate as the only IBWO representative at a huge three-day missions conference in St. Petersburg, Florida. I heartily accepted.

Even though my fundraising ventures had taken me to fifteen states over a fourteen month period I had never been to the city of St. Pete. And I always enjoyed exploring new towns. Plus, our monthly income was rising rapidly and had reached 65% of our preset goal. I was eager to procure the remaining 35%. So I accepted any and all speaking engagements that came my way.

When I arrived at the St. Pete church I was immediately impressed by the size of the facilities. It was larger by far than most churches I had visited.

It was obvious from the start that the conference was going to be well organized and exciting. At a welcoming orientation, the visiting missionaries were introduced to the church staff and briefed on the church's history. An all-inclusive schedule for the three days of meetings, meals, and activities was then distributed and clarified. Then, right before the two dozen or so missionaries were acknowledged one-by-one, I saw on the schedule that the key speaker for the conference was a visiting pastor from Wisconsin named Stuart Briscoe. I had never heard of the man, but was certain IBWO knew all about him and approved of his character, convictions, and beliefs.

During the introduction of the missionaries, I was completely mesmerized in an unexpected, but thrilling, way when a tall husky man was introduced and recognized as a missionary to Sweden where he taught at a Bible institute. The institute had been founded by a group of American missionaries serving with an agency called Greater European Mission. The man was the first North American, other than Brian and Celeste, with IBWO, that I had heard of who ministered in Scandinavia. I memorized his name. I definitely intended to meet him one-on-one. And then to my further elation, the missionary-to-Sweden motioned for four young gentlemen, who accompanied him, to stand. "These guys are Scandinavian students at the Bible school where I teach," he explained. "This is their first visit to America. As representatives of Greater European Mission and the Scandinavian Bible Institute we'll be preaching, singing, and testifying in churches all across the country over the next several weeks. We're promoting ourselves as The Northern Lights." I could hardly wait to engage the group in conversation. So at dinner time, in the church fellowship hall, I joined the group for the evening meal.

As the teacher/missionary introduced me to his four students, my thoughts and emotions instantly became sidetracked and laser focused when I learned that one of the students was Norwegian. This was my first ever face-to-face encounter with a Norwegian national. The meeting produced an emotional and mental high that was hard to explain.

For the next forty minutes I absentmindedly ignored the others and conversed exclusively with the Norwegian. I was totally engrossed in the exchange. I even tried, and failed, about twenty times to correctly pronounce the guy's five-letter name – GISLE. There was a particular vowel sound I couldn't mimic. I secretly wondered if this was a foretaste of some inability on my part to learn languages. This repeated failure was both embarrassing and disconcerting. So was the young man's expression when I told him my goal was to plant an "independent fundamental Bible-believing King-James-only Baptist church for his people in Oslo." He understood my words and meaning, but didn't share my enthusiasm. And then, all too soon, our chat came to a close as we were given just a few minutes to relocate to the church auditorium in preparation for the evening meeting.

On my way to the auditorium I made a mental note to reengage Gisle at an opportune time and pose a few additional questions about his beliefs.

Entering the sanctuary I sat in the balcony on the front pew, right at the rail. The seat would give me a grand overview of the crowd. I sat down, opened my briefcase, and pulled out my Bible, a notebook and pen, along with the program for the ninety-minute meeting. I spread everything out beside me on the pew, then relaxed and waited. I was thinking about my conversation with the Norwegian when the opening song commenced.

The songs, testimonies, and mission reports that followed were uplifting and vision-filled. But, I was eager to hear the mission-oriented sermon. I hoped it would validate the "bigness" of the conference. Finally the key speaker,

Stuart Briscoe, was introduced. It was pointed out that he was a British national transplanted in the US. I suspected that one of the pastoral-looking gentlemen sitting on the platform was Mr. Briscoe. But when the introduction was complete, a man stood up from the pews near the front of the church and made his way up the steps to the podium.

I squinted and did a visual retake. Were my eyes playing tricks? The man who entered the sacred pulpit was dressed like a rich pleasure seeker going out to eat on a Friday night. He wasn't wearing a suit. Rather, he was sporting a brown leather jacket with an open-collared shirt and no tie, casual pants, and a pair of suede-looking loafers. His hair was thick and long, definitely covering his ears. The man was irrefutably worldly in his outward appearance. And his relaxed demeanor told me he didn't care one iota. I immediately concluded that he was a disgrace to the cause of Christ.

If this is the key speaker, I thought, *I can't participate in the conference. It's that simple. Obviously IBWO knows nothing about this man, or they wouldn't have sanctioned the meeting by sending me here as one of their missionaries.*

I looked down and started collecting my belongings when the speaker presented his introductory remarks. His British accent was not disinteresting. I had only heard a few British accents in my life and always found them intriguing and intelligent-sounding. But, to my further dismay, by the time I'd placed all my items in my briefcase, the man announced he would be reading his sermon text, Acts chapter one, from the recently released New International Version.

This man is a complete charlatan! I surmised without hesitation. How could he even pretend to be a voice of God when he was reading from one of Satan's counterfeit bibles?

I looked around. There were people on both sides of me. I

was trying to determine the best route of escape when Mr. Briscoe introduced the book of Acts. My knowledge of the book of Acts, I thought, was quite good. Nevertheless, Mr. Briscoe opened with a few exegetical insights that, against my will, grabbed my attention. In all my Book-of-Acts classes, the notations Briscoe was highlighting had been totally overlooked, or at least untaught, by my Tennessee Temple professors. Yet…the points Briscoe was making seemed at the offset to be critical to a full and accurate comprehension of the book.

I was mildly upset. Why had I not heard these details before? I was upset enough to listen to Briscoe teach for a few additional minutes. And before I picked up my briefcase to exit the property, I realized Briscoe was bringing his message to a close. I had sat captivated for nearly three-quarters of an hour.

I was now honestly confused.

I was earlier convinced Briscoe was the proverbial wolf in sheep's clothing. But, how could I explain that I had just been edified, nourished, and motivated by the man, and had gained a greater appreciation for the book of Acts and its author, Luke? What was I missing here? My head, based on all the teachings I had embraced as a Temple student, told me the man was a fraud. My soul, based on the personal experience I had just savored in real time, told me the man was a true student of God's word with a genuine heart for God.

I still wanted to be cautious. And I would be. But feeling pressed to probe deeper into this mystery I decided to stay for the rest of the three-day conference. It was that simple solitary decision to stay that would conceive inside me my first ever embryo of critical thought. Briscoe would ultimately go on to convince me that he was actually a genuine soldier of the cross and not a pawn of devilish forces. Not only that, but my ongoing conversations with Gisle, the Norwegian, would half persuade me that as a Lutheran he was not a lost sheep either.

But these were dangerous thoughts inside the world of Independent Baptists where there was no allowance for compromise. So, I was compelled to keep these "wayward" thoughts to myself, even from Sherri. I would have to pretend, for awhile at least, that I was a solid rock – unmovable and impenetrable. But the first seeds of doubt regarding my Tennessee Temple indoctrination had just been planted.

Chapter 11

Within a few weeks, Sherri graduated from Temple at the age of 18 with a three-year Graduate-of-Theology degree. Having taken maximum class loads and plowing through summer-school semesters, she had acquired her college degree in only two years.

I couldn't have been more proud of her. Neither could her parents. After all, Sherri was the first one in her family to ever attend college. A few weeks later, we celebrated her 19th birthday. At that point in our year-long marriage, I had been away from home an estimated six months. But now, to my joy, Sherri was free to travel with me as we endeavored to raise the final 25% of our needed support.

And travel we did. It was a prestigious feeling to stand before congregations, large and small, and say as a 22-year-old and 19-year-old, "We're moving to Europe as missionaries." The anticipation of standing on Norwegian soil and serving as full-time missionaries filled us with nearly uncontrollable excitement.

That "spiritual high" remained fully intact as we journeyed hand-in-hand to multiple churches between July and November presenting our vision and showing our Norwegian slides. Finally...finally, we managed to garner 100% of the monthly income we needed. We floated on the jubilation, then gave away our prized mobile home to another young couple from Mt. Vernon who were moving to Chattanooga as newly-enrolled Temple students.

It seemed we were living in a dream...until...the day of our US departure.

When my bride and I at long last stood at the jetway at the Atlanta airport on Monday, December 27, 1976, ready to board our overseas flight, our excitement strangely disappeared. We, instead, were overcome by a spirit of solemnity. A huge crate, 8' X 4' X 4', containing all our earthly possessions was already on a cargo ship making its journey across the Atlantic. So was an automobile we had purchased. Moving to Norway was suddenly no longer a fantasy. As the reality of our situation set in, we were no longer laughing, no longer smiling. Like most missionaries we knew, we had made a commitment to serve at our foreign post for a lifetime. We were standing there saying what we believed could be our final good-byes, maybe for all time, to Sherri's parents and one sister, and to my mom and one sister. My dad had refused to be there. He had accused me of not loving him or mom. "If he truly loved us," he had stated emphatically, "he wouldn't leave us like this." He had also declared to my face that he would never spend his money to come and visit us.

As Sherri and I, with tear stained faces, made the irreversible walk through the jetway and into the plane, we were too overwrought with emotion to say anything else. We just sat in our seats and yielded helplessly to the unimaginable weight of what we were doing. The enthusiasm that had propelled us for two years quickly abandoned us without warning. The only detail that afforded us even the tiniest bit of reassurance was that IBWO missionaries Brian and Celeste would be on the other end to greet us.

I'm not sure who at IBWO booked our airline tickets, but the itinerary would be divided into five legs - (1) from Atlanta to Buffalo, New York, (2) from Buffalo to Toronto, Canada, (3) from Toronto to Amsterdam, Holland, (4) from Amsterdam to Gothenburg, Sweden, and finally (5) from Gothenburg into Oslo, Norway.

This would be my first ever commercial flight. It would be Sherri's second. Years earlier she had flown one time to Chicago.

When our plane lifted off the Atlanta runway, the weather in the metropolitan area was around 45 °F. When we arrived in Buffalo, we touched down in the middle of a blizzard. There were three-and-four-foot snow drifts outlining the landing strip. Even though Sherri and I stayed on the plane for that particular stop, the biting cold outside seemed to penetrate the fuselage and mock us with its intimidation. Staring dumbfounded out the window, it was my first time to see more than an inch of snow. I was suddenly reminded: *We're moving to an arctic country.* The fun, excitement, and sense of adventure that had encapsulated our lives over the previous two years died right there on the spot. I looked at Sherri. The growing loneliness in our hearts rendered us speechless. We both wanted to turn around and go home.

The moment we entered Canadian airspace on the next leg of our flight, I thought seriously, *Why don't we just get off in Toronto. We don't actually have to cross the ocean to be foreign missionaries.* But we were bound now to our supporters. It was Norway or nothing.

The overnight transatlantic journey to Holland seemed to

seal our destiny. In 1976, the continent of Europe—distance wise—felt like the other side of the planet. When we landed in Amsterdam the next morning and deplaned, Sherri and I for the first time in our young lives were the "foreigners." All the signs throughout the airport were in Dutch, a language we had never heard before. The language, being uttered all around us, sounded like gibberish. And the people! They all looked so tall, so unusually tall. In order to keep moving, we had to squelch the uncomfortableness assaulting our souls. Thankfully, the flight information for our next flight—the flight number, departure gate, and departure time—were all posted in regular numbers we could read.

When we made our next stopover—in Gothenburg, Sweden—it was close to 3:15 PM. The sun was already setting. The ominous winter darkness was already imprisoning the day. We were intellectually aware that inside the arctic circle the sun never rose above the horizon for three months during the winter season, but somehow we had failed to register the fact that just a few hundred miles south of the arctic circle—where both Gothenburg and Oslo were positioned—the winter daylight hours dwindled to as little as six hours a day. We were so weary, and still in shock, at this point. We were just thankful the layover was brief.

We were utterly exhausted by the time our last plane came to a stop and parked on the Oslo tarmac. When the fuselage door was opened, a cold blast of arctic wind—unlike anything our bodies had ever felt—swept through the cabin with such intensity that every muscle in our bodies tightened in a reflexive knot. Sherri was wearing a polyester dress, pantyhose, and a "winter" coat she had purchased in Georgia. I was wearing a lightweight jacket. We felt like we were wearing no clothes at all.

Walking down the aisle to disembark, we were shivering

uncontrollably. When we stepped out of the aircraft onto the portable stairway, the ambient cold was even more brutal. The wind felt like it reached all the way to the bone. Even though the sun had long since disappeared below the horizon, the lights of the airport, along with the brilliance of the moon, illuminated the infinite snow – snow on the tarmac, snow on the buildings, snow on the ground, snow on the fences, snow on the car tops. Piles of it. Everywhere. Everything, literally everything was buried beneath the white mounds of frozen ice particles.

The thirty-yard scramble from the bottom of the stairway to the opening of an underground corridor leading to the terminal was a scramble-of-shock—both physically and mentally—that we would never forget.

Once inside at the passport-control area, we couldn't be thankful enough for the bit of warmth that touched our skin, but inside our heads we were convinced we had made the biggest mistake of our lives.

Chapter 12

As planned, IBWO missionaries Brian and Celeste were inside the Oslo airport waiting eagerly to welcome us.

When Sherri and I cleared customs and entered the arrival hall, Brian was holding a sign that read, "Welcome Randy and Sherri." He and Celeste were both smiling. Sherri and I walked into their embrace and feigned a bit of positivity. We were just grateful at that moment for Brian and Celeste's back-home "southern" presence.

The thirty-minute drive across town to their house was laden with conversations about our flight, the Norwegian winters, and our stay with them over the next three weeks while we waited for the apartment they had secured for us to come available.

Once at their tiny row-house, Celeste showed us our bedroom – literally the size of an American walk-in closet. We would be sleeping on a twin mattress on the floor. She then fed us dinner. Beyond fatigued, Sherri and I then retired to our tiny room where we literally cried ourselves to sleep in each other's arms.

Over the next three days, while in the initial throes of

severe culture shock and jet lag, Sherri and I wondered out loud with each other if we could ever adjust to such a bleak, frigid, landscape. We had approached our run-up to Norway, honestly believing we might be Norway's only hope spiritually. But now we were crying ourselves to sleep each night wondering if we would even stay in the country. We seriously discussed the idea of getting on a plane and moving immediately back to the US. "We can explain to our supporters," I confided to Sherri, "that our decision to come to Norway was premature, that the decision was made out of youthful zeal and that we now understand we're too young for such a heavy responsibility. We can ask them to forgive us and to please realize we need a few more years of life experience, and then maybe we can try again."

But several key elements were already in motion that would prohibit such a reversal of plans – (1) Brian and Celeste had already signed a lease agreement for the apartment we would be moving into, (2) our crate containing all our earthly possessions was en route by sea, (3) our car was aboard a different ship crossing the North Atlantic, and finally, (4) our bank account had been drained to the point that we simply didn't have enough money to purchase return airline tickets. We were stranded, like it or not, in one of the northernmost capitals on the planet, and there was absolutely nothing we could do about it.

While on a lonely walk to a grocery kiosk on day four, I lifted my face to the frost-glazed heavens and whined, "Well, I hope you're happy! You tell your followers to take the Gospel to the uttermost parts of the earth. Well, we're here! It sure would be nice if you would help us to like the place!"

I noticed about that time that a couple of Norwegians, layered in their winter garb, were tying not to stare at me. I wondered if it was because I was so poorly dressed for the nearly zero-degree weather. I tried to dismiss the matter until I entered the little store and witnessed three or more individuals fighting not to gawk at me. I knew there had to be a reason. One of the quick gazes from a lady caused me to look down at my pants. What's so odd....? And then the answer hit me. I looked at the few Norwegians around me. They were all clad from head to toe in dark browns, deep-olive greens, navy blues, and multiple shades of black. I looked down at my pants again. They were a bright burgundy, and made of polyester. Back home in Georgia, my pants were stylish. But obviously in Norway, the pants stood out like a clown's costume. I walked immediately back to the house, took off the burgundy pants, and never wore them again.

The subject of "pants" surfaced again in the next day or two when Brian asked, "Do you want to go out and learn to ski?" Scandinavia, of course, is the birthplace of skiing. We learned it was a popular saying in Norway that "Norwegians are born with skis on their feet." And it was not an exaggeration to say that Sherri and I had already seen dozens, if not hundreds, of Norwegians traverse a cross-country ski trail every day just fifty yards from Brian and Celeste's house. So, naturally the topic of skiing came up regularly in conversations.

"Yeah, of course, I'd like to try," I told Brian. If I was going to live in Norway—as much as I was now struggling with the idea—I needed to start engaging with the culture, especially the adventurous elements I thought I could enjoy.

"And what about you, Sherri?" Brian asked. "Do you want to go out and give it a try?"

Sherri and I looked at each other with raised eyebrows. How was she going to go outside in freezing weather and take a ski lesson in deep snow while wearing a dress? The suggestion bordered on ridiculousness. Our IBWO standards forbade IBWO ladies from wearing pants...ever...for any reason. Pants were considered immoral for a lady. They highlighted her female curves and, thus, promoted sexual provocation. Sherri had not donned a pair of slacks since becoming a dedicated believer five years earlier.

"I don't have any culottes," Sherri explained to Brian, "so I don't know how I would manage." The Independent Baptists did allow ladies to ski, but only if they wore baggy culottes. These specialty items were even marketed and advertised in Independent Baptist periodicals.

"You'd definitely have to wear a pair of pants, then," Brian conceded.

Sherri and I were somewhat shocked. Here was a devoted IBWO missionary making an exception to a IBWO rule. The Stuart Briscoe episode back in Florida less than a year in the past had planted questions in my spirit that I still hadn't voiced out loud to anyone, questions that still persisted. I wondered if Brian had been questioning the spiritual legitimacy of IBWO's hardcore restrictions as well. I honestly didn't know. It was a subject we didn't talk about. I just quickly assumed that Celeste wore pants when skiing. It was a fact that all Norwegian ladies wore pants when participating in the sport. As a matter of fact, Sherri and I had not seen one Norwegian female, indoors or outdoors, wearing a dress, period. If Sherri slipped into a pair of pants, she definitely wouldn't be considered worldly by anyone...except by us. And in this climate, in these temperatures, would God really hold it against her? Brian obviously didn't believe so. I swallowed hard and told Sherri I thought it would be okay...just for skiing, though.

I could tell by Sherri's countenance that she had now seen an unexpected weakness in my resolve. Dressing in a pair of Brian's ski pants, she took on a lot of guilt, and I was responsible. And unbeknownst to us, we both had just stepped out onto the topside of a long, steep "slippery slope."

In three week's time—after learning to ski—Sherri and I, as scheduled, moved out of Brian and Celeste's place into a tiny two-bedroom apartment of our own. Brian and Celeste graciously continued to assist us during our setup phase. Brian helped me navigate the bureaucratic protocol necessary to take possession of our car once it arrived at the Oslo port. He and Celeste helped us transport all our belongings from the harbor to our apartment when our crate was offloaded at the waterfront docks. Over a several week period, they even introduced us to four or five couples, two of which were missionary couples, to help give us a "starter" network of friends.

And then they left. They returned to the states for a planned six-month furlough.

And suddenly...Sherri and I were on our own.

Within a day or two we realized our mission board had not given us one bit of cultural, psychological, or social training for overseas living; only their long list of dos and don'ts for spiritual acceptance. We were now four-thousand, three-hundred miles from our families, home church, mission headquarters, supporters, and colleagues.

We had truly been left out in the cold, both literally and figuratively.

Chapter 13

During our fundraising period in the states, Sherri and I had informed our audiences that we would be attending the University of Oslo for our Norwegian-language studies. So, following the Christmas and New Year's holidays we went to the registrars office at the university, as planned, to enroll as new students. But, there in the office we learned to our utter shock that there had been a breakdown in the information we had received. The university would accept our academic credits if we had graduated from the Tennessee Temple College, but not from the Tennessee Temple **Bible School**. And there was no leeway for exceptions.

Embarrassed by the setback, we scrambled to find an alternative for learning the Norwegian language. Thankfully we heard about the Friundervisningen, a state sponsored institution that offered free Norwegian-language classes five days a week.

We promptly registered and within a week or so began classes. Oslo has an extensive inner-city subway system, along with a profusion of regional and national passenger trains. Fortunately, our new apartment was only a ten-minute walk from one of the subway stations, so we started using public transportation almost exclusively for our excursions to our language classes downtown. These thirty-minute rides to and from the school gave us relaxing moments to people watch, to pick up tidbits of data about the culture, and, of course, to prep for and finish homework assignments.

Once we were headway into the classes, my fear from a year earlier—when meeting Gisle in Florida and being unable to correctly pronounce his name—proved to be true. I just didn't seem to have the innate ability to learn a foreign language. I listened carefully and took notes in every class, but I simply couldn't pick up the unique sounds that were unknown to my American tongue. Sherri, on the other hand, quickly deciphered and assimilated all aspects of the language – the pronunciation, grammar, vocabulary, and comprehension. I was both amazed and, to be honest, a little jealous.

Plus, whenever I tried to use my rudimentary Norwegian, it didn't help my confidence when the Norwegians would hurriedly become frustrated and say, "Just speak English."

What I did learn quickly, though, and capitalize on, was that at least seventy-five percent of the Norwegians could speak English quite fluently. For Norway to compete in the international marketplace, the burden of communication was theirs. Quite simply, other nations such as Germany, France, and the U.S. were not going to learn Norwegian, one of the smallest language groups in Europe. So, the Norwegian schools taught multiple languages such as German and French, but especially English. Almost all Norwegians were bilingual. And many could speak three and four languages.

So, without quitting my Norwegian lessons, I started using English more and more with the nationals. Plus, I realized I didn't have to wait until I was proficient in

Norwegian to start evangelizing. So, I created a ten-question survey in English and started visiting door-to-door in our neighborhood. Seven of the survey questions pertained to current events, both national and international. The final three questions centered around religion. It was those final three questions I used as a springboard to share the Gospel. When I started knocking on doors, I was truly amazed at how many Norwegians—men and women alike—would give me, a foreigner, ten to fifteen minutes of their time to take part in a survey, and then to engage in a conversation about the validity of the Bible, the person of Christ, and salvation from sin. What saddened me, though, was the realization that the majority of Norwegians didn't think they had a need for God. After all, they reminded me with passion, they lived in a country that had one of the highest living standards in the world, had the cleanest air, the purest water, the lowest crime rate, the highest literacy rate, the longest life span, the best social justice system, the most comprehensive health care program, and the most expansive and generous welfare arrangement on the planet. Everyone was financially secure from the cradle to the grave. "So why do I need God?" they asked. "What can God give me that I don't already have?" When I broached the subject of sin and the need for forgiveness, most would rebuff the idea. With passion, they would declare, "We're not sinners. We are good and generous people, some of the most generous people in the world." They simply could not, or would not, grasp the Bible truth that all men are born with a sinful, selfish heart, in need of a Savior.

 After months of knocking on literally hundreds of doors in frigid weather, I was secretly feeling discouraged. I had only made a connection with three individuals – a young single lady, a middle-aged mother, and an elderly widow.

These three ladies, each with a mild interest, started coming to our apartment for Bible studies. But how long would it take, harvesting attention at this glacial pace, to win and disciple enough converts to establish a vibrant and productive congregation? Back home in Bible school, when I was surrounded by thousands of highly energized ministers-in-training, the vision of planting such a church seemed extremely straightforward, if not downright simple. But live on the field, the idea—especially with my poor language skills—was seeming more and more like a lifelong undertaking. I was willing to give it my all, but the realization that it might take a lifetime was demoralizing.

Irrespective of my struggle to learn the language and my inability to win the Norwegians over to my Christian views, my mood did start to brighten a little as spring arrived and the ever-present snow melted. As the protracted daylight hours of the new season ushered in copious amounts of sunshine and warmth, a collective giddiness swept across the national psyche. And it was contagious. Relief and revelry swept through the city of Oslo as greenery exploded everywhere with sweet-smelling blossoms, combined with the scent of the sea that cascaded in from the Oslo fjord. It was a glorious time of year.

The temperature started to reach into the high 70's. Life in the city moved predominantly outdoors to make the most of the eighteen-hour days. The streets, parks, cafes, trains, and harbor fronts were all packed with people moving to and fro and basking in the sunlight. This elevated my spirits even higher.

Apart from the spiritual dispassion that seemed to permeate the society, I actually started to like the place. A nation of only four-million people, the country—with it's mountains, glaciers, waterfalls, fjords, rivers, salmon, reindeer, and fit-and-blonde people—seemed more and more indeed like an idyllic wonderland.

To add to the pleasure of that first summer, along with all its many revelations, we found a new place to live across town as the eight-month lease to our apartment was soon coming to a close. The new place was bigger, less expensive, and had more bedrooms for hosting guests and for housing an at-home office. Plus, it was just a ten-minute walk from a bank, a post office, a grocery store, and a subway station. The new location even included a designated parking space inside a huge parking deck for our car.

When we made the move a few weeks later, the three ladies who had been attending our in-home Bible studies were not willing at that point to travel such a distance for a one-hour meeting. So, evangelistically, to our chagrin, we had to start over again at square one.

Once we were settled into the new apartment, and before I became serious about evangelizing in the new community, I took a break and went downtown one afternoon to explore.

While there I ended up making an unexpected purchase, a purchase that would push me a little farther down the slippery slope of "compromise," a purchase that would further jar Sherri's confidence in me as a spiritual leader.

Chapter 14

I had walked into a music store in downtown Oslo. I was shopping for a cassette of easy-listening instrumentals. While flipping through the cassettes I heard a song over the store's speaker system that brought me to a standstill. It was a soft-pop song, the kind of music I had been conditioned to despise. And normally, I did despise it. But the voice filling the small store space was the purest, most perfect singing voice I had ever heard.

I walked over to the store clerk. "Excuse me," I said in English. "Do you know the name of the person singing?" I pointed to the wall-mounted speakers.

"Absolutely," the man answered, "It's Karen Carpenter. Have you never heard of her. She's from your country. She's American."

"No, I haven't," I told him, trying not to sound embarrassed. "It's not the kind of music I listen to."

The man responded with a lift of his eyes, as if to say, *Really? That's weird.*

I returned to the tapes that were displayed in alphabetical order on table tops and searched the "C's" until I found one of the Carpenter's recordings. I stood there staring at the cassette while listening to Karen's voice sing to me over the in-store speakers. I continued to be mesmerized by the clarity of her voice. For the first time since I was fifteen, I was intentionally listening to "Pop" music, and was actually finding pleasure in it. My conscience reprimanded me. Yet, I continued to be swayed by the sheer "feel good" effect of the music.

I picked up the cassette, held it in my hand, and felt guilty. But I was over four-thousand miles from my Independent Baptist community. And there was no one around to pronounce judgment on me. Suppressing my conscience I did something I never thought I would do. I paid money to own a recording of pop music. I placed the tape in a shopping bag, not for the ease of carrying it, but for the purpose of hiding it—maybe even "hiding" it from myself.

With intense nervousness, I showed Sherri the tape when I returned home. She could hardly believe what I had done. Even though I tried to persuade her to listen to one of the songs, she wouldn't. She wanted me to return the cassette immediately. I refused, which produced even more guilt on my part. But in an effort to placate her, I promised, "I'll keep it hidden. No visitor will ever see it." And for months, not a single guest who ever came into our apartment came close to discovering that I was the owner of a pop music tape. I had to ask myself if my conscience was being seared, or if it was being freed? I wanted to believe the latter. But I honestly wasn't sure.

However, meeting a new American missionary couple to Oslo soon thereafter helped appease my inner voice a bit. The man's name was *Neil. His wife was *Remi. They were serving under the auspices of a different mission agency, but one that was still in the Independent Baptist camp. I quickly approved of Neil's appearance and his beliefs, and thus became a serious friend. Sherri and I promptly started fellowshipping with them on a regular basis, both in our home and in theirs. It wasn't until we were seriously knitted together as friends that I learned that Neil used the New International Version of the Bible for his daily reading. I was stunned when Neil confessed that it was true.

As Pastor Stuart Briscoe back in St. Pete, Florida had created a conundrum for me, so now did Neil. Neil was a genuine believer. He loved God, loved God's Word, and loved people. These truths were written all over his life. So, how could I judge him as someone less spiritual, or worse, spiritually destitute for simply reading a version of the Bible that wasn't the King James Version? I mean, I loved God, yet, I was the owner of a Karen Carpenter tape. Not only did I not condemn Neil for this grave Independent Baptist violation, but I found that his comfort level with the NIV gave me the courage to dare pick up a copy for the first time and actually read it. When I sat down and slowly and willingly digested the syntax of the Scripture in contemporary English, it was another turning point in my life. The ease of reading and comprehending the NIV, compared to the KJV, was beyond noteworthy; it was transformative. I quickly found myself gorging on the modern translation. What was happening to me? Was I slipping? Or was I growing? The question still haunted me.

To justify the violation of reading the "devil's" Bible, I did my own extensive research. Contrary to what I had heard from a hundred boisterous voices in the Independent Baptist camp, the NIV—when compared side-by-side with the KJV—did not diminish one doctrine, one principle, or one truth. It was the same Scripture, Scripture that had been translated fully, honestly, and accurately from the Hebrew and Greek texts. The more I read the NIV, the more I cherished it, and the more I strained to understand why the so-called scholars in my denomination condemned it. Was I missing something? Or were a lot of pastors and teachers in my camp simply echoing the skewed opinion of a few power-wielding, shallow-thinking, legalists?

Sherri wasn't asking the same questions, so I didn't feel free to share my disturbing musings with her. We did, though, continue to share a mutual desire for sowing evangelistic seeds. So, I was excited when Sherri told me she was going to bake a cake and go door-to-door in the stairwell of our new apartment, introduce herself to the neighbors, and in the Norwegian language invite them to our place for cake, coffee, and conversation. I was looking forward to meeting the people in our building. But on the day Sherri knocked on the doors, she returned in tears.

"No one would accept my invitation," she wept. "Did I do something wrong? I don't understand." The reserved, exclusive nature of the Norwegian community that we had witnessed so often outright proved itself more and more. How were we ever going to reach these people?

The next day, Sherri tried again. This time she invited a young preteen girl to join her in the kitchen for some of the homemade cake. To her delight, the girl accepted, and even brought a friend. By this time, Sherri was speaking fluent Norwegian. She was thrilled to interact with the kids' in their native tongue. The young girls found Sherri, as an American, to be fascinating. They posed question after question. Sherri and the girls had such an enjoyable time that the girls wanted to come back again and bring friends. Within a few weeks,

Sherri had successfully and ecstatically started a weekly Bible club in Norwegian for a dozen boys and girls ranging from ages 9 to 12.

The question then arose: would this become our long-range approach for planting a church? This was not our original plan, but we were definitely open to a change of direction. Since we were feeling the constant pressure to produce for our monthly donors, we concluded that trying a new approach would be far better than floundering.

Of course, life wasn't always so serious. We valued fun and downtime as much as anyone. For example, during our first Christmas at the new apartment, we hosted an American missionary family—another family in our Independent Baptist camp—from Bergen, eight hours away on the country's west coast. Anticipating the five-day visit from the parents with their three daughters filled our lives with an extra boost of joy and energy. In preparation for the family's Christmas stay, Sherri was perhaps overcome with too much energy. She ended up baking for five days straight. Using thirty pounds of flour and twenty-five pounds of sugar, she made cookies, cakes, and breads aplenty so that there would be no lack of Christmas goodies. And what a visit it was! The conversations, games, meals, and rambunctious outings on sleds provided long overdue laughter. The visit was unforgettable.

After enjoying my first excursions on a sled, I was invited a few weeks later by Neil, my missionary friend in Oslo, to make my first attempt at downhill skiing. Oslo is surrounded by moderate-sized mountains. So downhill ski courses were plentiful throughout the region. Neil loaned me his wife's skis and took me north of the city to a very steep run. I would learn later it was a "black diamond" run, the kind used by advanced athletes where there are more hazards, rocky areas, and narrow slopes.

Standing for the first time at the top of the hill was intimidating for me, but at the same time invigorating. I had all the confidence in the world I could master it. It took me seven runs, dozens and dozens of hard falls, and one broken pair of skis, but on my seventh run I bombed the course without falling. I was on my way to becoming a more-than-decent downhill skier. I was always a good athlete, with excellent dexterity, balance and speed. I was just frustrated that my evangelistic abilities didn't measure up to my athletic ones.

But all of that was about to change with one phone call.

Chapter 15

"Randy, my name is *Peyton Black. I'm calling from Stavanger on the west coast where I serve as a missionary with Bible Baptist Fellowship. I'm pastoring a church for the Americans that are here training the Norwegians in the oil industry. I'm getting ready for our church to host its first ever missions conference, and I'm wondering if you would have an interest in being one of our speakers?" He gave me the date of the conference, and added a few more details. "Of course, we'll provide food and lodging, and cover the cost of transportation for you and your wife."

I didn't know Peyton—he was a relative newcomer to Norway—but I was familiar with Bible Baptist Fellowship. It was an older and more strict sister organization to IBWO. After hearing Peyton's answers to a few of my questions, I accepted his invitation. "I'll be glad to," I told him. "Sherri will too."

In a few weeks time, Sherri and I were jubilant when we got off the train in Stavanger and met Peyton and his wife for the first time. Almost before we could unpack our suitcase, Peyton had us in his car, enthusiastically giving us a tour of the area and educating us a bit regarding the oil industry in the area. We learned that Norway—after discovering large deposits of off-shore oil in the 60's—had hired thousands of Americans seasoned in off-shore exploration, drilling, and production to help mentor Norway in those major sectors. Peyton highlighted that most of those Americans, by far, were residing in and around Stavanger, the location of the Statoil headquarters. As a matter of fact, there was such a heavy concentration of Americans in the area that the Americans had opened their own grocery stores—importing favorite foods not available in the Norwegian markets—and had started their own churches. Peyton's church—that rented a local school building for their gatherings—was one of those.

On Sunday morning when the conference began, Sherri and I met the congregation, about a hundred and fifty strong. For us, after being without a church for more than a year, the experience of worshipping with such a large and likeminded group was more than thrilling; it was inspiring, re-energizing, and reassuring. And downright heavenly.

Following the final meeting of the conference, which passed way too quickly, one of the couples in the church approached me. "We really enjoyed listening to you speak," they enthused. "So we have a proposal for you. In two weeks from now, we'll be traveling to Oslo on a business trip. Another couple from the church will be joining us. We'll be there over a weekend. We know you don't have a church yet. But we're wondering if you would conduct a Sunday morning service for us in your home?"

I didn't even have to think about it. "Yes, absolutely I'll do it," I promised. "It'll be my pleasure."

Two weeks later, Sherri and I hosted what we thought would be the one and only church service ever held in our home. To make it a fun event, we had invited everyone we knew in the city to join us, along with the two couples from Stavanger, for the special occasion.

When we commenced the meeting that morning, there were fourteen adults sitting around our living room. One of the couples was Danish. One couple was American, working at the NATO base outside Oslo. One was Neil and Remi, the local missionary couple. One was Brian and Celeste, our IBWO compatriots who had returned from their furlough in the US. And, of course, there were the two couples from Stavanger.

The service was truly encouraging, even more than I had anticipated. At the end of the program—which I really wanted to prolong indefinitely, because I was enjoying it so much—I asked if anyone was inclined to add anything else before we dismissed for lunch.

The American serving with NATO said, "Yeah...let's do this again at some point." There was a minuscule pause, and then I saw nods quickly fill the room, along with some hearty "Amens."

Taken somewhat off guard, but excited by the idea, I replied, "Well, while we're together, should we go ahead and plan a date?"

"What about next Sunday," the man from NATO offered nonchalantly.

"Really?" I replied. I'm sure my voice revealed the element of surprise that I suddenly felt.

"Yeah, why not?" came the enthusiastic response.

"Well...sure...I guess." I cleared my throat. "How many of you would have an interest?" To my further surprise, everyone in the room, except understandably the two couples from out of town, lifted their hand. "Sure...okay...let's do it, then," I announced. "Next Sunday. Same time. Same place. And, of course, feel free to invite anyone else who might want to join in."

Over the following week, I couldn't help but wonder if the next gathering would be a pop-and-fizzle type event, or if it might lead to something unexpected.

The next gathering, however, was just as rich and just as special as the first one. Christians in the country, it seemed, were so few in number that any assembly of believers was like a small taste of heaven.

"If you have the time and interest, let's just start meeting every Sunday," was the plea that came my way following the meeting.

A few weeks later, the petition changed to "let's just start a church and make it official."

Things were moving so fast it secretly made me a bit nervous. Sherri and I had raised funds under the premise that we were coming to Norway to plant a Norwegian church. Yet, the group that was meeting in our home, that now wanted to become a church plant, was an eclectic group representing America, Norway, Denmark, Germany, and England. And all the services were in English. I asked Brian, my colleague with IBWO, if he would do some of the Sunday preaching. I was trying tactfully to detach myself from any notion of taking on an official or permanent position. "I'll occasionally preach," Brian let me know, "but I'll not take on a pastoral role. I'm committed right now to my own work."

So, all the cards were on the table. If we continued to gather in perpetuity—and all the attendees hungered to do so—I would have to accept the leadership role, at least for a while. So, without a lot of fanfare, I became the de facto pastor. But the question kept looming; was I willing to become the permanent full-time pastor if we officially organized and registered with the State? I struggled with that decision for several weeks. Would I be betraying our supporters who had sent us to plant a Norwegian church in the Norwegian language? Or would they graciously accept our change of direction?

The pressure quickly mounted as the number of gatherers soon outgrew our apartment. As the recognized leader, and the only one with enough spare time, I assumed the responsibility to search for a new meeting place. During the weeks that I was scouring the city for a rental facility our group could afford, Sherri and I learned she was pregnant. We were elated. At the same time, I found a tennis club, geographically centered in the city, that contractually agreed to let our Sunday group use their meeting hall for twenty US dollars a week. I and one of the other men in the group signed the contract. It looked more and more like Sherri and I were getting ready to give birth, both to our first child and our first church.

But before I yielded fully to the soaring expectation to officially organize a church—with a name, a constitution, a set of bylaws, and a roster of officers—I wanted to do one more thing; needed to do one more thing.

Chapter 16

I had heard that Dr. Billy Graham, America's famous Gospel evangelist, was coming to Oslo for a one-afternoon crusade meeting. He had been invited by a few Norwegian Lutheran churches to stop by en route to Stockholm, Sweden where he was scheduled to lead a multi-day crusade.

It had been asserted at Tennessee Temple Bible School that Dr. Graham was a worldwide detriment to the cause of Christ, that he was one of the great compromisers of the faith. Even though a part of me believed the assessment—since that's what I had been told repeatedly by my trusted professors—I, nevertheless, wanted to see how the Norwegians would respond to this world renowned preacher. Could Dr. Graham, with his years of evangelistic know-how, manage to reach the hearts and minds of the Norwegian people? If he succeeded, then perhaps I should abandon the English-speaking Sunday group and refocus totally on the Norwegian community. I mean, if Dr. Graham, as a compromising so-called teacher of the Gospel, could reach them, then over time, I, as a preacher with more loyalty to Bible truth, could certainly learn to do so.

When the day of the Oslo crusade arrived, Sherri and I

didn't tell a single soul where we were going. We didn't want our reputation in anyway to be soiled because of an association, even in passing, with Dr. Graham or his organization. When we arrived at the Ullevaal Stadium, the largest event venue in Oslo at the time, we hung our heads and slunk our way to the upper level where we perched ourselves overlooking the whole stadium.

When it was time for the meeting to begin, I was somewhat amazed that the stadium was less than half filled. Weren't Billy Graham crusade meetings usually packed out? Despite the sparse crowd, a Norwegian choir—Lutherans, I guessed—began singing. Cliff Barrows soon took over and led the choir and the audience in a few songs. A couple of Lutheran pastors made some introductory remarks, and then Dr. Graham was introduced. When Dr. Graham stepped up to the podium, all bedlam broke loose. A group of fifty people sitting in stadium seats right behind the huge makeshift platform jumped to their feet and started shouting in English, "Billy, go home! Billy, go home! Billy, go home! Billy, go home!" They wouldn't stop, and didn't stop, until their voices faded with exertion. And then another group of fifty stood—to take the first group's place—and continued the harassment, "Billy, go home! Billy, go home!" Dr. Graham paused and politely asked the shouters to show respect for everyone else who had come to hear his message. The request only egged on the crowd. Another group of people, almost on cue it seemed, started blowing horns from various locations inside the arena. They would blow and sustain a single note as long as their lungs would permit. Then others would take over and continue the blaring. One man climbed a tall light pole and unfettered a giant banner that read, "Billy, we don't want you here." Another man jumped over the railing at ground level and ran out onto the field with a long scarf fluttering behind him. Immediately, a security guard with a large dog appeared, chasing the runner around the field. The meeting had been reduced to total chaos.

Dr. Graham predictably cut his message short. The people simply would not respect the message or the messenger, no matter how seriously and kindly Graham pleaded with them to do so. When the public invitation was given to walk forward and embrace the Christian message and become a follower of Christ, only the appointed counselors moved to the front to take their positions. No one that we could detect walked the aisle to seek salvation.

I was stunned.

If Dr. Graham could not garner the spiritual interest of the people—not even a few—then I was certain I couldn't either. My mind immediately reverted back to my so-called dilemma with the Sunday morning group. Would I stay? Or would I walk? I decided on the spot to stay and build a church with the people God had placed in my hands. Sherri agreed.

A few weeks later, in October, our Sunday morning circle had a charter service where we officially organized as the Free Baptist Assembly of Taasen, Taasen being the city district where the tennis facility was located. Instead of becoming a Norwegian church, we would become an English-speaking international church, an international church that would hopefully some day reach a few Norwegians. At 25 years old, I would serve as the founding pastor. And my 21-year-old wife would serve at my side.

But once instated as the legitimate pastor, I was quickly handed a problem I wasn't sure how to tackle. Several of the new people attending the church could speak English well enough as a second language, but struggled to understand the archaic English of the King James Bible. The KJV just wasn't a good pulpit Bible for our congregation, pure and simple. It was an issue that became more and more pressing until I was forced to make a decision – to keep using the KJV and watch people walk away from the church in frustration, or adopt a modern translation that the people could easily understand, such as the New International Version.

I had established a routine of mailing out a newsletter to our financial donors every six weeks, giving them regular updates about our life and ministry. And it was time to compose a new one. I had already planned to tell about our new church, with its international focus. I figured three or four churches would drop our support anyway when they read we had gone the English-speaking-international-church route, but I seriously suspected that more might withdraw their support if they learned I was on the verge of replacing the KJV. So, I decided I would not mention my dilemma to anyone back home, unless asked. But for the sake of my young congregation, I eventually chose to ignore everything I had been taught about King James onlyism. Under my leadership, our church appropriated the NIV as its standard text.

I also made another decision that I would not reveal to my peers back home, unless asked. I grew a closely cropped beard. In my Bible-belt Independent Baptist culture, facial hair on a man was considered a sign of rebellion.

So, I guess I was rebelling after all – with allowing Sherri to wear pants while skiing, with owning a pop music cassette, with embracing the NIV, and now with sporting a beard. I battled with guilt because of these "transgressions." But there was no one at IBWO I could talk to about it, without being condemned. Yet, in Europe, inside Christendom—and inside our Sunday morning group—none of these practices were given a second thought. They were as harmless and inoffensive as a butterfly sunbathing on an old man's shoulder.

As Sherri and I nervously shepherded the new-born congregation and watched it take its first glorious steps, we were simultaneously blessed with the birth of our first child, an eight-pound tow-headed daughter who we named Heidi.

Everyone in our back-home network was thrilled with the news of Heidi's birth. Our parents were more than thrilled; they were euphoric. Sherri's parents, because of Heidi, flew over a few months later for a ten-day stay. The visit was absolutely therapeutic for Sherri. It had been more than two years since she had seen her parents or felt the blessing of their hugs.

After one day on the ground, multiple conversations, and hours of cuddling with Heidi, Sherri's mom wanted to know all about the birthing care in Norway. Sherri happily gave her a litany of all the positives : (1)the state-of-the-art hospitals, (2)the encouragement toward natural births, (3)the fact that midwives delivered the babies unless a life-threatening situation arose, (4)that if a delivery doctor was needed, it would be the doctor on duty who was not fatigued and who wouldn't perform a c-section in order to hurry up for a tee-time, (5)that mothers were kept in the hospital for five days, or so, until the baby started gaining weight, and the mother started producing milk, (6)that new mothers were taught in the hospital how to handle, bathe, dress, and nurse their baby, (7)that a nurse visited the new mother in her home following the delivery to provide extra help if needed, and (8)that all those services were paid for out of the nation's tax coffers that every tax-paying citizen contributed to.

As I heard Sherri tell her mother about all the merits of

the Norwegian system, I knew that the constant and supportive attention Sherri had received from the medical community had endeared her to Norway to a greater measure. I was utterly pleased, because I too was falling in love with Norway more and more. We just hoped Sherri's parent's, as their visit unfolded, would come to see that their daughter was truly in a stable, clean, and healthy country, and that they could relay the comforting news to our friends back home.

And indeed, their impressions of Norway did evolve positively throughout their time with us. As a mom and dad, they were feeling better and better about their daughter's and granddaughter's life in this country called Norway. But, two nights before their departure, an unexpected phone call nearly ruined everything. We were sitting around the dinner table enjoying one of our final meals together when the call came through. Sherri answered the phone. "Yes...yes...," I heard her say. And then with a shrug, she looked at me. "It's for you, hon."

Chapter 17

I cleared my throat and took the phone. "Hello. Randy speaking."

"Randy Dodd, the pastor of the International Baptist Church?"

"That's me."

"Mr. Dodd, my name is Steve. I'm the youth pastor downtown at the American Lutheran Church. I'm calling because I need some help."

"Okay...what can I do to help you, Steve?"

"A teenage girl from the U.S. needs some immediate attention. She came to the church office two days ago seeking help. But our pastor is away on a business trip. And I'm honestly not comfortable dealing with the situation. The girl is single. I'm single. The girl's a runaway and a prostitute. I just don't feel qualified to give her the kind of help she needs. And I'm running out of options. Would you be willing to speak to her? And maybe help her? She's in a pretty desperate situation."

For a split second I looked around the room at my wife and in-laws. How could I possibly help a prostitute? I wasn't sure I felt qualified either. This was definitely beyond my realm of experience and expertise. But if the girl was desperate, then perhaps I should at least try. But how much of the 'urgency' aspect was even true?

"Does the girl know you're reaching out to me?" I queried.

"No, I haven't told her. I first wanted to see if you were available."

"All right," I quickly improvised, "I'm willing to talk to her, but only if it's her decision. Let her know I'm available. If she's interested, give her my phone number and tell her to call me."

When I hung up, I of course had to tell Sherri and her parents what the call was about. I purposely omitted the part about the girl being a prostitute.

Before we finished our meal, the phone rang again. It was Steve. "She says she wants to meet you. Tonight if possible. She sounds more frantic than ever."

My mind quickly went into overdrive. I looked around the room again. This was crazy. Where in town could I meet a prostitute in a public setting this late in the day, or should I even relent to such a request? I squeezed the bridge of my nose. "All right, Steve, tell her I'll meet her at the airport. Let's say in the restaurant area, in an hour and a half from now. How about that?"

"Sounds good. I'll tell her," Steve said, sounding thoroughly relieved.

At the appointed time, I walked nervously into the airport. When I entered the restaurant, I was looking for a teenage girl sitting alone. I had told Steve to tell her I would be wearing a brown french beret. The restaurant was not crowded at that time of night. So, the girl and I spotted each other quickly. Other than her utterly empty and hopeless-looking eyes, the girl could have been a model. She had long dark hair, and looked trim and fit. She was beautiful.

"Are you the pastor of the Baptist church?" she asked as I approached the booth where she was sitting. Her voice sounded distraught, unimaginably so. Maybe Steve hadn't exaggerated.

"Yeah...that's me. My name is Randy." I extended my hand. She didn't respond. So, awkwardly I sat across the booth from her.

Before I could get settled into the seat, the girl, with immeasurable grimness draining her voice, muttered, "You're my last hope. If you can't help me, I WILL leave here, and I WILL kill myself." Her eyes left no doubt she meant it.

With adrenalin instantly hitting my brain, I took a deep breath and said, "Okay...uh...tell me what's going on."

Colleen was her name. She was eighteen. She disclosed openly, with no emotional protection, that her biological father had raped her when she was fifteen. That same night she ran away from home. She fled two states away, to Illinois, to live temporarily with an older cousin on her mother's side of the family. The cousin was a single lady estranged from all family relations. The cousin welcomed Colleen into her home and promised she would never reveal Colleen's location. Wrestling with the atrocity of what her father had done to her, Colleen tried to bury the explosive thoughts and feelings ravaging her soul, and made an effort to carry on with life the best she knew how. She enrolled at the local high school and pressed onward in her final semester as a sophomore where she turned sixteen. Within a month or so, she was befriended by an older girl, a junior. After a few weeks of friendship, the girl asked Colleen if she wanted to make a lot of money.

Colleen at that point was strapped for cash, so of course she was interested. "All you have to do," the girl told her, "is to go to bachelor parties and do a quick striptease." She would earn over a hundred dollars for a four or five minute dance. The girl assured Colleen that because of Colleen's beauty she could easily wield power over her male audience and squeeze even more money out of them. At first, Colleen was repulsed. But, she carried a heavy load of anger directed at the primary male in her life, her dad. Were all men as depraved as him? If most, or all, men were so perverted that they would give up their hard-earned income just to see a woman do a quick dance unclothed, then maybe she should take advantage of every one of the fools. In this way, she could strike back at the male gender and "strip" them of their needed cash. Then she could laugh sadistically all the way to the bank.

"If the job is still available," she confided to her friend a couple of weeks later, "then I'd like to get more information."

Within twenty-four hours, Colleen was introduced to a rough-looking, but charismatic and handsome man in his early thirties. The man would be her "arranger." He would make all the contacts, set the appointments, coordinate the logistics, and provide her with security. Of course, he would take a portion of Colleen's earnings for his work.

Within days, Colleen was earning easy money just like her friend had promised. She felt dirty, but at least her need for revenge was being satiated. Men indeed were pathetic and deserved every single loss that she, as one of their victims, could inflict on them. She felt empowered every second she was siphoning dollars from their billfolds, dollars they needed for car payments, health insurance, and house payments. The fools!

When what she was doing became too easy, her

"arranger" told her she could double her money if she would consent to letting the men at the parties touch her.

She eventually did.

And from there her tolerances quickly loosened until one day as a junior she moved into her own apartment and crossed the line from being an entertainer to being a prostitute. At that point, she was passed off to a different "arranger"—a pimp—and a whole new network of girls.

Somewhere along the way, though, she came to understand that, in all truthfulness, her life was on a trajectory that might one day become irreversible, and that if she did reach that point of no return, she would be the fool. So, if for no other reason than to save herself, she decided to back away from her off-the-rails campaign. The day that she planned to tell her pimp she was not going to prostitute herself anymore is the day she heard that one of the girls in her network had been beaten and hospitalized the previous night by the pimp for fleeing to a neighboring state and trying to escape. Using his sources, the pimp had hired someone to track her down and bring her back. The pimp had then beaten her nearly senseless.

With discreet questioning, Colleen had learned that this show of "ownership" had happened to several of the girls. Realizing she had perhaps already reached a place of total imprisonment, Colleen, over the following months, resorted to alcohol to help medicate her hopelessness. And finally, during the summer break before her senior year, when she was unable to bear the weight of life anymore, she called home for the first time since she had run away. She told her mom what her dad had done to her at the age of fifteen and asked if she could come home. Her mom didn't believe her. When Colleen pleaded, her mom—in anger—said, "Colleen, who?" and hung up on her. That night, Colleen took a razor blade and slit both her wrists.

But someone had found her before she bled out.

When she woke up, she was in a strange apartment, in the presence of her pimp. She received a severe beating. The pimp then threatened to break major bones in her body if she ever refused for any reason to service her appointments.

Colleen knew then that the only way to fully escape her plight was to flee to a different country. She had heard years ago that she had a distant relative who lived in Oslo. With a little research, she found the man's name. She contacted him. She lied and told him she was moving to Norway as an exchange student for the initial semester of her senior year and wondered if she could live with him instead of being placed in the home of a complete stranger. The man graciously said, "yes." So several weeks ago she had dropped out of school, run away to Norway and moved in with the relative. During the day when she was suppose to be in school, she had gotten a job as a nanny and was babysitting two small children under the age of two. And she hated it. Life no longer held any meaning for her, absolutely none. She had reached her limit of coping. She had gone desperately to the American Lutheran Church seeking help, any kind of help. And they had now shuffled her off to me.

When she wrapped up her story, the emptiness that ruled her countenance had not changed one iota. She closed her eyes tightly as if daring not to hope for anything positive.

I sat for a second or two in silence. Her story had indeed rendered me, a naive 25-year-old preacher, almost speechless. Quickly trying to gather my wits, I pulled a compact New Testament from my shirt pocket and turned to John 3:16.

"Colleen," I offered gently, "I want to show you here in

the Bible that regardless of what you've done, or how worthless you might think you are, God loves you with all his heart. There's never been a moment when he hasn't loved you. His love is so…"

WHAM!

My whole body recoiled as Colleen rose to her full height, slapped the table violently, and growled, "Don't dare talk to me about a loving God!" She sidestepped until she was free of the booth. "There is no God! And there is no love! Period!" She blew out a strong puff of air. "I can see I've wasted my time! You and your God are a pathetic joke! Life's over! I'm finished!"

I cringed as I watched her turn to rush away.

"Wait! Wait!" I begged her.

She turned to look at me one more time.

What I did next would change my life. And hers.

Chapter 18

"All right," I said, breathing heavily, "I won't talk about God's love anymore. I think you just need a place to stay for a while, a place where you don't have to work or even get out of bed, a place where you'll be safe, where you can rest as long as you want." At that point, I saw Colleen take a deep breath as if my words were a long lost key that had suddenly been found, a key that had just unlocked an outer door to her heart. "Hold on," I told her, "let me call my wife. I want to open our home to you, but I first have to let my wife know what's happening. So, please...sit down and give me a moment."

I ran to a pay phone and called Sherri. I told her an abbreviated version of Colleen's story and asked if she would permit Colleen to move in with us.

"For how long?" Sherri mumbled under the sudden heaviness of what I was asking.

"Indefinitely," I whispered.

"But, Randy, she's a prostitute."

"I know," I heard my voice quiver. "But if I let her leave here alone, I really believe she'll kill herself. I honestly do."

"But what about my parents? How are they going to react? What are they going to say?"

"They're leaving tomorrow. Does it really matter what they think or say?"

Almost through the phone lines I could see the gears turning inside my young wife's heart and mind. "All right," she finally exhaled. "If you think this is what God wants, I'll try to prepare mom and dad."

Within two hours—after collecting her suitcase and penning a note to her relative that she would be away for a few days—Colleen walked into the front door of my and Sherri's apartment. Sherri greeted her with a hug and assured her that she was genuinely welcome. Sherri then showed Colleen to her designated bedroom.

Colleen would never know that Sherri's parents, as they returned to the states the next day, were totally bewildered by our decision. The teenager slept for nearly two days. When she finally surfaced and came out of her room, Sherri's parents were already back in Georgia. We introduced Colleen to our daughter Heidi who was nine months old and let her know she was now a part of our family and was welcome to utilize our home as a place of refuge for as long as she needed.

I informed our young international church about Colleen, explained how we were trying to help her, and asked them to pray diligently for her wellbeing.

For a week or so, Colleen shuffled around the house, ate like she was famished, slept in excess, and was relatively quiet. And then one morning, she divulged she was most likely pregnant. She had no idea who the father might be. And immediately she started talking about having an abortion if she was indeed carrying a child.

"If you're pregnant, you can stay with us during the entire pregnancy," we prodded. "Just keep the baby. We'll give you all the support you need. And if you have a baby girl, we'll give you Heidi's baby clothes."

A few days later, Colleen left the house for the day. When she returned, she was visibly shaken and withdrawn.

"Are you okay," Sherri reached out to her.

"I'm fine," came the numb, almost inaudible, reply.

Sherri and I respectfully backed off at that point and gave Colleen the space to fight her own demons in her own way. That evening she collected Heidi in her arms and slowly and wordlessly rocked her to sleep. When we put Heidi to bed, Colleen announced sullenly, "It was confirmed today that I was pregnant, so I had an abortion."

Abortions in Norway were easily available and free.

Our hearts ached for her.

Over the next several days, Colleen just sat and cradled Heidi in her embrace, and hummed.

I knew about a ministry in Texas that took in girls like Colleen who had been abused, and gave them a family structure, an education, and a disciplined work ethic. Hundreds of young girls in Colleen's shoes had been transformed under the safekeeping of that particular ministry. I told Colleen about the home and asked her if she would like to place herself under their care. She wasn't sure. But, even if she did have an interest, she didn't have the money for a plane ticket.

I immediately contacted the men of our church, gave them an update on Colleen, told them about the Texas home-for-girls, and wondered if the church would be willing to take up an offering to cover the cost of a plane ticket from Oslo to Corpus Christi, Texas. The men didn't hesitate with their answer. "Absolutely, we'll do it," they said. "Let us know what she wants."

After several more days and several more conversations, Colleen announced she would like to relocate to the Texas home. So I called the ministry leader and told him all about Colleen. "Yes," he said, "We'll make room for her. Give us the flight information when you have it."

We quickly purchased a plane ticket.

On the morning, a week or so later, when Sherri and I were driving Colleen to the airport, Colleen broke the news that she had changed her mind. She wasn't going to the Texas home after all. She would get off the plane in New York at her connecting hub.

"What will you do in New York?" we asked in total shock.

"I don't know," she uttered, sounding completely lost all over again. "I'll just have to figure it out."

Our hearts were completely shattered, but there was nothing we could do to persuade her differently. We tried, and failed. We simply wept with her as she prepared to board her flight out of Oslo.

We would eventually hear from Colleen one final time. That communication would come nearly two years later, in the form of a postcard.

During that nearly-two-year period before Colleen broke her silence, I—as a pastor—decided to step outside the lines of my "pastoral role" of always being the one up front during Sunday church services. I remembered the preaching opportunities afforded me and my buddies when we were in the Mt. Vernon youth group. Those experiences literally changed the course of our lives. I chose to give the men in my church the same opportunities. So, I approached several of the guys individually and asked them to preach on a Sunday morning at least once. Most of the men were reluctant. They cited "feelings of inadequacy" as the primary reason. I brushed off the excuse and explained they would have ample time to prepare. Five of the men finally conceded. And what a joy! It gave the church family an opportunity to hear the hearts and minds of our men. Plus, the exercise proved to be invaluable. Latent gifts of teaching rose to the forefront. Several of the men received so much affirmation from the congregation and so many requests to teach again that they jumped at every invitation thereafter. One of the men, a NATO officer just five years shy of retirement, along with a retirement pension, even started talking about walking away from his military service, enrolling in Bible college, and training for full-time ministry. He asked me for my counsel. I was honestly afraid to encourage him either way. I didn't want him to miss out on the extravagant joy of using one's spiritual gifts full-time to effect change. At the same time, I didn't want to be personally blamed for causing him to lose his and his family's financial security for the remainder of life. I was actually shocked when the man, a few months later, decided he was not going to extend his military contract. Almost immediately, he sent enrollment applications to three or four Bible colleges. He was overjoyed when he received an acceptance letter from the institute that had been his number one pick. Even though the fleshly side of me wondered if he shouldn't serve his country for five more years and qualify for his substantial lifelong pension, there was still my spiritual side that felt like a proud papa. I had to trust that God would honor the man's decision and would provide for him and his family going forward. It was good that I adopted that mindset, because unbeknownst to me several of the men in our church would go on to repeat the same pattern – quit their secular job, study theology, and then serve as a pastor, teacher, missionary, evangelist, elder, or nonprofit leader. Our international church quickly became an unplanned bootcamp, training and mobilizing male and female soldiers for God's kingdom. And I couldn't have been more thrilled.

I had certainly failed earlier to reach Colleen, but I had at least found one of my strengths as a ministry leader.

And then Colleen's postcard arrived in the mail.

The note on the postcard was short and to the point.

> "Dear Randy and Sherri. When I first met you, I told you I didn't believe in God. And it's true; I didn't. But while living with you for six weeks, I saw God. I saw him speaking and reaching out to me through your loving words and actions. I have now become a believer. Please pray for me. Next month I will be traveling to Mexico on my first ever mission trip. Your Christian sister, Colleen."

Sherri and I were profoundly impacted by Colleen's words. For two days we teared up whenever we saw the postcard lying on our dining room table. And that was often. We immediately wanted to reconnect with Colleen, by letter or by phone, but her card didn't include a return address or a phone number. Even the postmark was smudged and indecipherable.

As it so happened, we would never hear from Colleen again. But as a young pastor, I learned a lifelong lesson from the whole Colleen story. The lesson was driven home to me in a deep-rooted way that my ability to reach someone's heart with the message of Christ was not dependent on a flawless presentation of the Gospel. Or even a thorough presentation. And it certainly wasn't resting on my skills of verbal persuasion. I learned that love and grace—shown both in words and actions—were the most powerful amplifiers of the Gospel, bar none.

Chapter 19

Shortly after receiving the postcard, which was totally unexpected, my focus immediately shifted to a new issue that demanded my attention. The lease to my and Sherri's apartment was reaching its termination date, with no possibility for an extension. So I had to find a new place for us to live.

Our church had just relocated from the small tennis-club facility in central Oslo to a much larger building in a southwestern suburb called Sandvika. Sandvika was selected because it was centrally located among all our church attendees —now around sixty-five people from twenty different nations.

So Sherri and I sought for, and found, a "new" house that was only fifteen minutes—as opposed to forty minutes—away from the church's new gathering spot.

As the church continued to grow in number and morale, I—as the young pastor—began to realize more and more just how beautiful, extraordinary, and potential-packed the international congregation was, compared to homogenous congregations. The medley of world cultures that assembled every week added a cadre of traditions, insights, and questions that enriched and challenged all of us beyond measure.

Fortunately, I stepped back and gave the church free rein to evolve and to speak. Because of the spiritual, social, and mental contributions the people made to my life, and everyone else's in the assembly, I was progressively convinced that God was not as narrow-minded as my previous understanding of things, that he especially wasn't as narrow-minded as the Independent Baptist's understanding of things, my Bible college's understanding of things, or even America's understanding of things. These mental concessions were not easy for me. But I simply could not close my mind to what I was seeing with my physical, spiritual, and cerebral eyes. Things were becoming too clear for me, at that point, to deny.

For example, I asked a young man from India to teach a Sunday Bible class one week. He taught on the subject of "God's Chain of Authority." He listed, in order of hierarchy – the triune God, angels, men, women, and children. When he expounded on "children"—his final point—he emphasized that children should obey and honor their parents, according to Ephesians 6:1-2. Virtually everyone in the congregation, representing multiple countries and at least four continents, nodded their concurrence. The young man went on to elaborate. He heralded that children must obey their parents for as long as their parents are alive. "Even if you're in your forties and your parents are in their sixties," he expounded, "you're obligated under God to obey them. If they tell you, for example, 'you can't make that career change, or you can't make that geographical move,' then you must obey them. God expects no less."

Immediately the Europeans and Americans throughout the room glanced at each other and lifted their eyebrows as if to say, *What in the world is he talking about?*

"All right, are there any questions, comments, or

additional thoughts?" the Indian posed during the closing minutes of his lesson.

A European father, without pause, raised his hand. "Yeah...I just want to say that the last point you made about children obeying their parents for as long as their parents are living is actually not a Bible mandate. It sounds more like a cultural tradition that's part of your Indian heritage, a tradition you've somehow twisted into your theology."

"No, no, it's a Biblical principle. That's why Christians in my country teach it and practice it."

"I'm sorry, but it's not a Biblical principle," the European retorted, graciously taking a few minutes to substantiate his viewpoint.

Other individuals spoke up at that point and took sides with the European father. The Indian man was left flustered that he was unable to sway the crowd to his side of the argument. I sat in silence and listened. It was obvious to me that the Indian was indeed confusing his cultural tradition with a Biblical principle, that he was interpreting the Scripture through the eyes of his culture.

I was suddenly aghast.

Was this the same thing my Independent Baptist denomination back in the U.S. was doing—interpreting Scripture through the eyes of our southern, Bible-belt culture, and then recklessly imposing our prized, Christian traditions on everybody, all in the name of God?

This pertinent question was answered conclusively a few weeks later in one of our church house meetings. What I learned in that particular home gathering became a life-changing lesson that I would carry with me forever.

Chapter 20

I distributed a pen and a blank sheet of paper to everyone in the room. "Draw a line down the middle of the sheet, creating two columns," I instructed the twenty or so people. "Label one column *external*. Label the other *internal*. Each of you, whether you've been a believer for years, or for only a few weeks, probably have a mental image of what you think the ideal Christian should look like. Take that image that's in your head and describe him/her in words. Fill in the two columns on your sheet of paper. Tell me what that ideal Christian looks like on the inside, and on the outside."

Committing to the exercise, the people took about ten minutes and completed their lists. I then asked each person to read out loud what they had written. They all did.

When the last person finished reading their descriptions, a man from Australia immediately raised his hand and said, "Pardon me for interrupting. But I just have to point this out before we go any further. I noticed, and you can fact-check me if you want, that every American in the room, and only the Americans, described the ideal Christian as one who, on the outside, is neat...clean...well groomed...professional looking...not shabby. This is fascinating to me. As you all know, I'm from down under. I've only been a Christian for less than a year. And as you can see, I'm not well groomed or neat looking. I'm pretty sloppy really. And you Americans are pretty knowledgeable about the Bible. So, if God wants me to cut my shaggy hair, take a shower every day, and look more professional, then I'm ready to make those changes. But I first need to know; where in the Bible does God tell his people to look clean and neat in their external appearance?"

Bingo! This, of course, was my planned agenda for the evening – to help those in the church understand that, as Christians, we should always be intentional about looking neat and respectful in our public appearance, that we constantly wanted to leave a good impression among those who were spiritually lost. Besides, I had known the Australian for a few months. He wasn't being sarcastic. He was being serious. It was an honest challenge. I smiled inwardly. The nine or ten Americans in the room immediately huddled together to collectively bring to the floor all the Bible verses that promoted the "clean and neat" doctrine.

One of the ladies in the powwow leaned forward and whispered, "What about the verse that says *cleanliness is next to godliness?*"

I cringed, but tried not to show it. "That's not a Bible verse," I told her. "It's just an old American saying." To give assistance to the group, I then quoted Romans 12:1-2 as some of the verses we were looking for - "Offer your bodies," I emphasized, "as a living sacrifice, holy and pleasing to God—this is your true and proper worship. Do not conform to the patterns of this world, but be transformed by the renewing of your mind. Then you will be able to test and approve what God's will is – his good, pleasing, and perfect will."

Another person, from a fundamentalist background like myself, read First John 2:15 – "Do not love the world or anything in the world. If anyone loves the world, the love of the father is not in him."

Another person offered James 4:4 – "Don't you know that friendship with the world means enmity against God? Therefore, anyone who chooses to be a friend of the world becomes an enemy of God."

Everyone in the small American group nodded their head as we compiled our litany of verses. I was feeling good. Pastors, evangelists, and professors alike in my denomination had always used these verses as a direct conveyance of God's will that Christians should adamantly refrain from looking like the world, with long hair, tight clothes, and casual attire to the point of looking unkempt. After all, we should always look our best for God. That's what I had been taught all my life. It was a teaching I had never questioned. I remembered a church meeting years earlier when a pastor, preaching on carnality, paused in his sermon when a visiting couple walked in late and sat near the front of the auditorium. The pastor just stared. Both the man and the woman were wearing leathers, as if they had ridden to church on a motorcycle. The lady's leather pants were rather snug. And the man had long hair. Both the man and the woman were sporting visible tattoos on their arms. When the pastor finally spoke, he pointed to the couple and said into the microphone, "If you want to see a sample of carnality, there it is. It just walked in."

Of course, in my current state of "slightly rebelling" against a few of the legalistic things I had been taught, I was not wanting to be belligerent as a teacher, but rather gentle and gracious. So, as the American huddle broke up, I asked a couple of the American guys to share our verses with the rest of the group - made up that evening of Europeans, South Americans, Asians, and the Australian.

The verses were all read aloud, with everybody in the room following along in their Bibles.

"Yeah, but not one of those verses, when read in context, focuses on one's neatness of apparel or one's physical cleanliness," a European, steeped in the Scriptures, cited. It was a man I highly respected.

As the pastor and moderator, I wanted to stress that the "clean and neat" doctrine, if not exactly specified in the verses, was certainly inferred. But was I perhaps missing something in the passages that the European was seeing? Doubt momentarily held me hostage. I suddenly remembered Stuart Briscoe, the pastor I had heard years earlier in Florida, who at the time had appeared worldly in my eyes with his long hair and overly casual attire for a church service, but obviously had a solid relationship with Christ. That memory suddenly stunted my momentum for the evening. Before I debated the European's point, I said, "Let's go back and hear what everyone outside the American group listed in their external column.

"Hands that help others," "ears that graciously listen," "a tongue that encourages" were the types of descriptions that were reread. Those answers, which were a hundred percent Scriptural, caused me to mentally stumble even further. Was my denomination not only in error regarding Christian women wearing slacks, Christian men growing beards, and Christians using other English translations of the Bible other than the KJV – were they also wrong regarding the aggressive precept that "Christians should always look their best for God?" Had I been so young, so naive, and so respectful that I had believed literally everything my pastors, teachers, and professors had taught me? Why, I wondered, had I never questioned any of those men face to face? Had I just assumed they were all theological experts and could neither believe nor teach anything that was doctrinally off? Obviously I had. But, as far as I could remember, I had never been encouraged or invited a single time to challenge, debate, disagree with, or oppose any of my teachers. *Critical thinking* had never been part of my vocabulary, had never been discussed in any of my educational settings. I hadn't even known such an exercise existed until I moved to Europe. Questioning the pastors, teachers, and professors in my denomination had always been sharply condemned as "disrespectful," "divisive," and "a blatant show of ignorance." It was becoming more and more obvious by the day, and embarrassingly so, that I had only been taught *what* to think, and never taught *how* to think. I was suddenly feeling inadequate as a Bible teacher.

The evening Bible study ended in a stalemate. My agenda had backfired. Just like the Indian who had mistaken his cultural tradition of *children obeying their parents for a lifetime* as a Bible edict, it seemed that we Americans were teaching the "neat and clean" dictum in the name of God when in reality it might be nothing more than just a manmade tradition. Had we in the U.S. somehow wrongfully entangled our Bible-belt preference with our Christianity?

I vowed to look at the Romans, First John, and James verses anew and in depth, especially in their contexts.

In the ensuing couple of days, I overheard another conversation that pinged my thinking regarding these issues. It was mentioned that the color red was believed, in Romania, to be the Devil's color and was, therefore, taught from church pulpits as a forbidden color for followers of Christ. It was a legalistic teaching that people fought over. Here again was yet another example of a manmade tradition being forced on people in the name of God. I was beginning to see it more and more clearly. I actually came to the conclusion that when

Christianity thrives in a particular culture for multiple generations, at some point it becomes difficult to completely divide some of the "good" cultural practices from the divine teachings of Jesus. Consequently, we end up preaching those "good" manmade traditions in the name of God and needlessly handcuffing people in a way that is legalistic and unhealthy.

Sherri and I, for example, started talking regularly about the "appearance culture" that permeated our own Independent Baptist denomination. Appearing professional. Appearing strong. Appearing invulnerable. Appearing well-groomed. Appearing knowledgable. Appearing confident. Appearing to be perfect. We concluded that the whole idea of appearing acceptable was stifling. And it was definitely tradition based, not Bible based. Plus, it detracted from being real. To live according to this expectation, a person had to always pretend. Pretend. Pretend. Pretend. It was absolutely tiring, and seemingly far beyond the Biblical criteria for true spirituality. We asked if "true spirituality" and "pretension" could even coexist in the same heart?

It seemed we were discovering more truth about the Christian life in our first years in Norway than we had acquired in all our years of Bible college. Maybe, just maybe, we were finally taking some baby steps in learning *how* to think. Perhaps honest questioning and critical thinking were indeed necessary for genuine growth.

Even though I was convinced my eyes were being opened, I wasn't ready yet to share any of my newly-formed insights with my constituents back in the U.S. I strongly suspected they would condemn me outright, just for my questioning heart alone, not to mention my few compromises.

But a few months later—whether ready or not—Sherri and I would be forced once again to confront the stifling

Independent Baptist ideology head-on when we returned to the States for a required missionary-training refresher course and a required twelve-month visit to give a ministry report to our sixty-plus supporting churches.

And it would be one of the few times I would see my young wife nearly overcome with anger.

Chapter 21

As we prepared to return to the States, Sherri and I felt hammered with mixed emotions. We had adjusted so well to living in Norway, especially to leading the international church, that a large portion of our hearts didn't want to leave our post. Another portion of our hearts, though, were eager to report our ministry milestones to our supporting churches, and to engage with our extended families.

Our international congregation in Oslo, we were convinced, would thrive just fine during our twelve-month absence. A new missionary in Norway, serving with Bible Baptist Fellowship, had agreed to fill our position while we were away and had even consented to live in our house and pay rent so that we wouldn't lose our contract.

So, after four years, we packed away our NIVs, I shaved my beard, Sherri packed away her pants, and we boarded the plane with our daughter, Heidi—almost three years old—and flew back to the U.S. But, having been influenced philosophically and spiritually in prominent ways by our "Norwegian" experience, we returned to the States with an evolving mindset that, for the time being, we would keep to ourselves.

One of the first items on our agenda, after the welcomed reunion with our families and our home church, was to attend the required missionary-training-refresher-course in Chattanooga, hosted by our mission board. We anticipated the event would be encouraging and affirming, and would offer a significant amount of camaraderie with a large group of missionary colleagues.

The three-day event finally arrived.

The camaraderie aspect indeed proved to be wonderful as we interacted with new missionaries going overseas for the first time, as well as a host of veteran missionaries who had been serving all over the world in multiple capacities. The conversations and stories, especially among the veterans, were absolutely mesmerizing. Sherri and I truly felt like members of an elite special-forces group that had been given a mission to change the world. The impact of this group on multiple continents was immeasurable.

It was the IBWO leadership, however, that produced monumental disappointment, along with irrepressible anger. One after another, the directors for Asia, Africa, South America, North America, Europe, the Caribbean, and the executive board stood and addressed us. We had been led to believe the meetings would impart encouragement, insight, and overall substantial training. Instead, all we received were lectures on the importance of a responsible work ethic, a disciplined and daily devotional time, an organized ledger to keep our ministry expenses separated from our personal expenses, a punctual lifestyle that would consistently earn respect, and, of course, the unquestionable importance of IBWO's long list of dos and don'ts. There was absolutely nothing about culture shock and how to approach it and survive it. Nothing about the likelihood of struggling on the field with one's feelings of inadequacy, one's marriage, one's faith, or one's team - or WHO at the mission headquarters would be available to offer confidential help in such cases. Nothing about the course of action one should take if their ministry plans, for which they garnered support, failed to come to fruition. Nothing about the multiplicity of things a new missionary would possibly encounter that were not imagined or expected. Nothing about the inevitable struggle of re-entry and reverse culture shock. Nothing, absolutely nothing, that encouraged or offered hope. Nothing that could be categorized as serious or legitimate missionary training. Sherri and I couldn't have been more disheartened. That is, until...she attended the "ladies only" session one morning led by the wife of one of IBWO's directors.

When all the sessions—including the "ladies only" group—broke for lunch that morning, and the husbands were reunited with their wives, I found Sherri bawling.

"What's going on?" I whispered with urgency. "What happened?"

"I can't talk here," she screeched in a stifled cry. We quickly found a room where we could talk in private. "I'm so angry right now, I could scream!" Sherri shrieked.

My pulse accelerated. "Go on," I implored.

Sherri couldn't stand still. She was pacing in short distances. "We need to leave IBWO," she bellowed. "This is insane. I'm...I'm...just standing here in total disbelief." She shook her head as if trying to dislodge a massive load of confusion. "I still can't believe it. Mrs. *Sykes just spent a whole hour facing a room full of new missionary wives, and all she did was talk utter nonsense. She actually looked the ladies in the eye and told them the important goals for a missionary wife were to make sure their blouse was always tucked into their panty hose, to make sure they never chewed gum in public, and to make sure they were dressed early in the mornings, with makeup on, just in case someone showed up at their door unexpected. It was all about appearances. It's just...outright stupid. I mean...is this for real?" Sherri carried on with her tirade for another five minutes or more. She was seriously hurt. She couldn't stop crying and venting.

I was angry as well. I was also now in a precarious situation. Sherri and I were unquestionably seeing the implementation of missions very differently than IBWO. And our differences were seemingly becoming greater. But should we walk away? This was the question that haunted me. Our differences with IBWO pertained only to certain practices, not the fundamental doctrines of the faith. Would it be worth losing the financial support that had taken us a year and a half to raise, just because of a disagreement over a few non-essential practices? All I knew at the moment was that IBWO's oversight of their missionaries, it seemed, was mostly "out of sight, out of mind." If no supporting church was leveling a complaint against us, and if our home church wasn't dissatisfied with our overseas performance, the IBWO directors, it appeared, all but forgot we were part of the organization. In our first four years on the field, for example, not a single IBWO director had ever called us or visited us. The inference seemed to be, "if no one is complaining, we're not watching." So, did they really believe the draconian and legalistic standards of their own banner? Or did they lift high their rules just to satiate the five-thousand legalistic churches that trusted and supported the IBWO name? I honestly wasn't sure. And I certainly didn't believe I would learn the truth in a one-on-one conversation with any of the leaders. So, right or wrong, I decided we would stick with IBWO and simply "play the game" whenever we were around IBWO staff and supporters. Besides, I knew of several other IBWO missionaries who were doing the same. Plus, I had already put together a full schedule to visit our supporting churches, and I wanted those congregations to hear firsthand the great report of what we had achieved with their help in such a short period of time.

So, when the three-day "training" event was over, and we had calmed down a bit, it was time to traverse the country and make our in-person visits. And that's what we did. We built a bed in the back of a Chevy van and set out to honor our schedule that encompassed nearly every Sunday morning, Sunday night, and Wednesday night.

Once we were on the road, the busyness of traveling around the country—with all the meetings, conversations, and in-home meals—turned out to be a good distraction for us, at least in a small way. But, we honestly missed Norway more than we had imagined. It didn't help that, compared to Norway, the U.S. appeared to have no deep, meaningful, and textured culture. From our point of view, behind the wheel of the van, the American culture looked as if it were irrevocably defined by the Interstate system, displayed pitifully in the thousands of cookie-cutter exits, all hosting the same identical gas stations, hotels, restaurants, and malls, whether in Georgia, Illinois, Missouri, or anywhere in between. The culture of my own home nation felt superfluous, almost artificial. And for the first time we struggled to appreciate it.

To add to the complexity of the whole ordeal, the exhausting schedule proved to be too much for our daughter, Heidi. Even though she was already an extrovert by her third birthday, being in a different city and a different church three times a week simply presented too much stimulation. Within two months of enduring endless hours on America's highways, Heidi would start screaming uncontrollably every time Sherri or I would maneuver the van onto an Interstate entry ramp.

Yet, we had to keep pushing.

Heidi's restlessness, though, did provide a few memorable moments that Sherri and I will never forget. For example, I was preaching at a supporting church on a Sunday morning. Sherri was sitting with Heidi midway in the auditorium, next to a window aisle. For whatever reason, Heidi would not sit still and behave. Sherri reprimanded her three or four times, instructing her to stop wiggling and to stop poking the person beside her.

Heidi didn't obey.

Sherri, as a mother, reached her limit for tolerance. She pulled Heidi to her side and whispered in her ear, "If you misbehave one more time, I will take you outside, and I will spank you. Do you understand?"

Heidi nodded that she understood, then immediately stretched out on the pew and gently kicked the adult sitting beside her.

Without hesitation, Sherri stood up, placed Heidi over her shoulder, and headed down the outside aisle, toward the foyer. I was in the middle of my sermon. From the podium, I heard Heidi blurt out, "Everybody pray for me. My mother's taking me out to spank me."

In another church service, in a different town, Heidi exclaimed shamelessly to the whole congregation, "I just pooped in my pants."

After a few months of nonstop traveling, not only was Heidi losing her stamina, Sherri and I were starting to lose ours as well, but in a spiritual sense. Behaviors of church leaders inside the Independent Baptist community—behaviors we once would have considered heroic—were starting to appear absurd, even destructive.

One of those exploits unfolded when I made a solo trip to Virginia to report to a supporting church.

Chapter 22

Prior to the church service, I was standing in the foyer of the Virginia church talking to the pastor and one of his deacons when a young boy about nine-years-old buzzed past.

"Hi, brother Eric!" the boy jovially greeted the pastor as he flew by.

In a split second, the pastor pounded his hands together in a single bombastic clap. "Hey!" he snapped.

The kid stopped dead in his tracks, turned, and looked at the pastor with a countenance of shock and fear.

The pastor clapped hard again. "Don't ever...," he raised his voice in outright meanness. "I repeat! Don't ever call me brother! I am not your brother! Do you understand! I am your pastor! Your God-ordained pastor! From now on you will address me with respect. You will call me Pastor *Eric! Pastor! Not brother! Understand?"

The young boy stood gobsmacked. And scared speechless.

"Do you understand?" the pastor shouted.

The kid nodded with confusion.

The pastor waved him away with a wide brush of his hand. The boy turned and darted off. The pastor promptly rejoined our conversation with a civil demeanor, as if everything was normal.

In years gone by, I would have applauded the man. But now, I found what he did to be repulsive. I wanted to chase down the kid, hug him tightly, and tell him the pastor was an idiot. I'm ashamed that I didn't. I can only imagine that the young boy never wanted to attend church again. I was starting to dislike my denomination, and its leaders, more and more.

My distaste was only heightened a few weeks later, following one of my Sunday night presentations, this time in Brunswick, Georgia. The pastor of the church came to me immediately after the service.

"I want to see you tomorrow morning before you leave town."

I could tell by the tone of his voice that whatever was on his mind was not pleasant. The following morning, I met him for breakfast at the appointed time and location.

"The length of your hair bothers me," he declared assertively when we were seated.

Oh no, here we go, I thought.

"It's indicative of something gone wrong in your heart," he stated sharply.

Granted, my hair was slightly over my ears and long enough in the back to touch my collar. But...

"So, do you know what happened last night?" he quizzed as if I should know the answer.

I remained silent to let him finish what was clearly going to be a stern rebuke.

"I'll tell you what happened. In the twenty-one years that I've served this church as pastor, I have never, not once, allowed any man with hair as long as yours to stand in my pulpit and minister from behind my sacred desk. But last night I did. And it was a mistake. And my people will now think I'm a compromiser. So, if you want our church to keep supporting you, here's what you'll do. When you get back to Atlanta, you will get a decent haircut. And then you'll have three pictures made. One from the right side of your head. One from the left side. And one from the back. You will mail those pictures to me, pronto. When I get them, I'll pin them on our church bulletin board so that everyone who was here last night will see them. And they'll realize that when you were here, you were just overdue for a haircut, and that what they saw last night was not normal."

I nodded. The message was clear. I made no verbal promise, though, that I would comply.

I stewed all the way back to Atlanta. My confidence in my denominational leaders was slowly eroding.

Four weeks later, the Brunswick pastor saw me at the Southwide Baptist Fellowship, a huge annual conference attended by Independent Baptist pastors from all over America. The pastor spotted me across an exhibit-hall floor. He saw that I had not complied with his demand to get a haircut, not even a trim. With an irate expression buckling his face, he stared at me from across the room and raked his finger across his neck, symbolizing that his church would immediately cut their support to our ministry. And they did.

More and more, Sherri and I were eager to get back to Norway, to reconnect with our grace-filled international church, and to get as far away as possible from the legalistic leaders and toxic culture of our denomination. But over the following weeks, before our return flight to Europe, another display of toxicity, this time from one of the most celebrated pastors in the Independent Baptist circles, further shook my world and created even more perplexity inside my head, along with a hefty amount of loathing.

The offending pastor—with a church of 10,000 or more people—was a national icon in Independent Baptist circles. The man was so idolized that he hosted and led an annual pastors' conference attended by thousands of hero-worshipping pastors, deacons, evangelists, and missionaries. As a skilled orator, the man had captured the ears and admiration of nearly every pastor I knew. The man was quoted constantly. So, I was totally shocked when I heard one of his newly recorded sermons—from the pastors' conference—pushing the King James agenda to new extremes. His announced text was I Peter 1:23 which says, "Being born again, not of corruptible seed, but of incorruptible by the word of God, which liveth and abideth forever." The man-of-the-hour stated emphatically that the incorruptible seed is the King James Version of the Bible. He declared that all other English translations are the corruptible seed. Therefore, he hammered home that one can only be born again if he comes to Christ through the preaching of the King James Version, the incorruptible seed. He said, "If you are listening to me today and you say you are born again, and you came to Christ through the preaching of another translation such as the New International Version, the corruptible seed, then you're not born again. You're fooling yourself."

The man's misinterpretation of the text—intentional or unintentional, I wasn't sure—was simply egregious beyond measure. The man's teaching had no substance whatsoever. I thought about all the English-speaking followers of Christ who lived before King James had authorized the translation that would carry his name. They had been reading from the Geneva Bible. I guess they were shocked when they stood before God and heard Him say, 'I never knew you, being that you preceded the King James translation."

Disturbing, absolutely disturbing. The offending pastor at that moment lost all credibility in my eyes. So did all the Christian leaders who quoted him and blindly believed him. I would return to Norway with less dedication than ever to my Independent Baptist roots. Subconsciously, I was slowly and progressively being set adrift.

And Sherri wasn't far behind.

Chapter 23

This time, our flight into Oslo was an unmitigated joyous occasion. We were more than thrilled to move back into our Norwegian house and reengage with our congregation that now included a multiplicity of new families, along with several new singles. The interim pastor had done an outstanding job shepherding and expanding the flock in our absence. We couldn't have been more appreciative.

As I settled back into my role as pastor of the international congregation, I decided, based on my faith journey of the previous five years, that prestige—something so lauded in the independent Baptist camp—was not something I wanted or prioritized any longer. Rather, I needed friends. I needed friends that would feel totally comfortable and unjudged around me, friends that would grant me the same freedom and authenticity. I no longer gave credence to the Bible college training I received which stressed over and over that I, as a pastor, should always keep a social and psychological distance from my congregants lest they discover I was a normal, flawed human being, not worthy of being placed on a pedestal. It was simply another legalistic teaching, I realized, that had no basis in Scripture. So, I gladly added it to my ever growing list of extra-Biblical teachings that could be permanently discarded.

So, as we commenced our second term on the field, I not only made a commitment to do a better job at teaching the people, but to also do a better job at playing alongside and befriending the people. And that's what I did.

I learned there was an earthen bobsled run built for the 1952 winter Olympics—almost hidden away in a mountain forest outside the city—that was still useable and open for public use. So, during our first winter back in Oslo, I invited the men of the church to go bobsledding. Seven or eight jumped at the invitation. We all bought, or else built our sleds —plastic sleds, tricycle sleds, inner-tube sleds, steel-runner sleds, and luge-style sleds.

Our debut run was on a Saturday afternoon before sunset. Once at the site, we saw that the earthen course banked and weaved downward and disappeared into a thick forest. From the launch area, we could only see about thirty yards down the run. Beyond that, we had no idea how many turns there were, how high or dangerous the banks were, how long the track was, or how fast.

I volunteered to be the first in our group to make the descent. I stepped into the launch zone and placed my plastic sled on the hard packed snow. I dropped down into a sitting position on the sled and used my gloved hands as outriggers.

"All right," I shouted, "let's do it!" I pushed off. As I swept into the first bank at 20 to 25 miles-per-hour, using my hands as rudders, the adrenalin rush hit hard. Into the second bank, I found myself up on the wall, perpendicular to the ground. The adrenalin surging through my veins kept me gasping desperately through every subsequent turn, sweep, and straight away. By the time I reached the final run-off, I was laughing so hard I couldn't stand up. I had to roll out of the sled and off the track.

As the men, following me, came to a sliding stop one by one, their animated body gestures and wild facial expressions were priceless. When everyone reached the bottom uninjured, the knee slapping, unbridled laughter, and nonstop story-telling created a memory we would each take to the grave. We sledded down the course three more times before dark that evening. We, of course, became more and more familiar with the layout of the lines with each run. This cumulative knowledge equipped us with total fearlessness for all subsequent runs. And there would be many. Enjoying the bobsled run became almost a weekly event during that particular winter. We even invited the wives to join us on a few occasions. The first time Sherri made the run, she lost control of the sled in the second or third sweeping bank and shot right out of the chute into the woods. She sailed over the rim, flew between two trees, and landed in the snow. She was fortunate that she walked away with only a few bruises and a great story to tell.

One overcast night when just the men were participating, we brought the sledding to a close when it became too dark to safely negotiate the run. We packed our sleds into a couple of vans and headed down the mountain, sharing all the wild escapades that had taken place in the chute. A quarter of the way down the mountainside, we approached the famous Holmenkollen ski jump, also used in the 1952 Winter Olympics. It was a celebrated piece of architecture that was perched on the mountain overlooking Oslo. It could be seen from nearly everywhere in the city. For Norwegians, it was the equivalent to Paris' Eiffel Tower, Rome's Coliseum, London's Big Ben, Sydney's Opera House, and New York's Empire State

Building. On this particular night, the shrouded moonlight, just for a second or two, split the clouds and spotlighted the giant twenty-story structure as if even the heavens were impressed with it. It was a sight that captured the attention of every man in both vehicles. I was sitting up front in the lead van. And I was suddenly whammied with an idea.

"Bill," I said breathlessly to the driver. "Let's drive up to the ski jump. I want to see something."

Bill looked over at me, squinched his face, then switched on his turn signal.

Within minutes, all the men in our group, from both vans, were standing beneath the edge of the takeoff ramp. In those days, there were no security barriers or security cameras anywhere on site. I motioned for the men to follow me. I led them out onto the top of the 400 foot landing hill. On a cold and cloudy night, we all for the first time stood directly in the line of the ski jumper, with the jump tower looming above us and the landing hill dipping below us. We were momentarily speechless at the sheer size of it all. From our location we couldn't even see to the bottom of the landing zone. The earth bowed outward immediately in front of us into a convex curvature and then dropped the length of one and a third American football fields.

"Do you think we can sled down it?" I said, revealing my reason for bringing us to the spot.

There was a slight pause. And then came the reactions.

"Are you serious?"

"Oh my gosh! I'd nev…"

"I think we can do it!"

"It could literally kill us!"

"You're crazy; not me."

"Do you think anyone has ever tried it?"

"It's too dark, guys!"

"I can't believe this!"

But within minutes, we were all gathered there again, this time with our sleds. We continued to be both mesmerized and petrified by what we were contemplating.

"If you lose control of the sled, or fall off the sled," one of the men stated nervously, "you could literally tumble with such velocity that you could break an arm, a leg, your neck, your back. Is this something we really want to try?"

No one rushed to mount his sled.

"What if we don't use a sled?" I suggested. "What if we just lay down on our back?"

"Are we sure the slope is smooth all the way down?" one of the guys queried. "If not, it could be as dangerous as falling off the sled and tumbling head over heels."

"Wouldn't a smooth surface be an absolute priority for the maintenance team?" another pitched in. "I mean, you know, for the safety of the skiers."

"Yeah, that should be an absolute given," someone else spoke up.

"Then let's veto the sleds and try it on our back," another voice said. "Let's do it."

"So, who's going to be first?" came the verbal challenge.

I wanted to volunteer, but simply couldn't muster the courage to be the proverbial guinea pig. The hill, with all its uncertainties, especially in the dark, was simply too daunting. It would be like sliding down the outside of a leaning 35-story building. Maybe this was a bad idea after all.

"I'll do it," came a sudden declaration. The speaker was Bill. He was an American soldier serving in Norway with NATO. He was physically the biggest man in the group, by far.

"Are you sure?" I stressed, clearly wanting to give him a chance to change his mind.

"No pain, no gain," he proclaimed. He walked slowly out to the crest of the slope and positioned himself on his back, with his feet out in front of him.

While the rest of us were trying to get our mind around what was happening, Bill disappeared over the curvature of the hill. Everybody went silent. Ten seconds passed. Fifteen seconds. Was Bill okay? Twenty seconds ticked off. How was I, as the pastor of the church and the instigator of the stunt, going to explain all this if Bill had to be taken away in an ambulance? Just when I was on the cusp of panicking, loud hoots of victory echoed from the bottom of the giant slope. We all turned to each other and laughed.

I quickly laid on my back and pushed myself over the crest. The next twenty seconds were the most heart-stopping moments of my life, at least to that point. Speeding downward, I literally fought to breathe, and was convinced for a second or two that I might suffocate. With my feet splayed, I had mistakenly configured my body like a scoop. As I zoomed down the hill, the snow piled up between my legs and then flew up to my face, completely covering my mouth and nostrils. My hands, instead of wiping the snow from my face, were at my side, like wings, fighting to keep my body on a straight trajectory, fighting to not whirl sideways, or even upside down.

The moment I reached the bottom, I frantically went to my knees and cleared my nose and mouth and coughed and gasped until I could breathe again. Taking in deep breaths, I laid back down in the snow and sighed, just glad to be alive and in one piece. What a trip! Incredible!

Bill quickly rushed to my side, grabbed my gloved hand,

and pulled me to my feet. "YES!" he hollered. "Oh MY GOSH, can you believe this?" His face lit up. "We've got to do it again. This is the most amazing thing ever!"

As Bill raved, we suddenly saw and heard the next man flying down the hill, a flume of spray highlighting his speeding path. We jumped aside as the man slid to where we were standing. The hoots and hollers erupted all over again.

When all the men were standing safely at the bottom, we knew we had done something spectacular. We wondered if anyone else had ever done it, or if we were the first. The men voted immediately to make the long, steep hike up the side steps and slide down again. We were now hooked.

On my second descent, I crossed my ankles and cupped both hands over my nose and mouth. This, I learned, was the optimal position for a faster and easier-to-breathe run.

Sliding down the Holmenkollen slope became an event we repeated four or five more times that winter. And once again some of the wives joined us on one of those occasions. Sherri was included in that number. She requested on her maiden attempt that I lay down beside her, hold her hand, and make our descent side by side. We would be the first to do a paired-up run. As we pushed off, we were immediately pulled apart and thrown into out-of-control spins. Only when we reached the bottom unscathed could we laugh about it. Otherwise, it had been a breathtaking and frightening drop. Of course, our experiment only spurred the guys to try a three-man, four-man, and even a five-man side-by-side descent.

Those momentous adventures that winter, along with serious snowball fights, king-of-the-snow-mound battles, camping trips, cross-country ski trips, weekend retreats, heart-to-heart interactive Bible studies, and one-horse open sleigh rides—yes, with deer skins, torches, and bells—produced the best friends I had ever known. And I loved every minute of it. For me, the belief that the pastor should never be a close friend with his congregants proved to be a complete fallacy. And an absurd one at that.

To dare go a step further and engage the community outside the church, I joined a NATO softball league where I played in the outfield for two seasons. I also joined a fitness studio owned and operated by Sjur Hall, a runner-up in both the Mr. Europe and Mr. Universe bodybuilding competitions. Sjur even became my fitness coach.

I was 29-years old. I was fit. I had the best wife and best daughter in the world. I had the dearest friends. I was leading a fruitful ministry that many would envy.

Yet, contrary to my historical devotion to God, something switched in my heart that I never would have expected in a hundred years. And little did I know that it would define much of my life for the next four years.

Chapter 24

Maybe it was my ever-growing disillusionment regarding my Independent Baptist orientation. Maybe it was my progressive abandonment of the legalistic rules that for so long had been an anchor in my life. Maybe it was a premature midlife crisis brought on by the hedonistic Norwegian culture. Maybe it was all three. Maybe it was something completely different. But I somehow started to venture beyond the parameters of emotional and mental safety. And in so doing, I found myself in a strange place where I started losing my heart for trying to be a model husband, father, missionary, and pastor. I started struggling to simply perform everyday responsibilities. In opposition to everything I had ever been taught and believed, I slowly became obsessed with a hidden desire to abandon everyone and everything and…just run.

The temptation became greater and greater by the week. I tried really hard, with a limited amount of success, to distract myself with "safe" and engaging initiatives.

For example, I concentrated diligently on trying to shepherd a new church member, a young liberal from New York named Freddie, who was actually refreshing, for me, to be around.

Freddie was a communication specialist at the NATO base just outside Oslo. He was also a relatively young believer. He had become a follower of Christ during a military stint in Italy. He was single and full of passion. And music was a constant backdrop in his life; it was one of his mainstays. As I built a friendship with Freddie, he introduced me to a few of his favorite bands like Genesis and Yes. He introduced me as well to extraordinary musicians and composers like Tangerine Dream and Vangelis. Because of his taste in music, Freddie was never impressed or moved by the music found in traditional hymnals. So, together, he and I learned of Christian groups that were pioneering Christian rock, groups like Petra and WhiteHeart. Freddie enjoyed these bands. They reached his heart. I was likewise drawn to their music. Their nontraditional music satisfied some of the rebellion rising in my soul.

During this same period, I made plans for our church to have a weekend retreat at a campsite on the edge of one of the country's famous fjords located five hours away on the west coast. As plans were being finalized, Freddie approached me and asked if I could baptize him in the fjord during the church retreat.

"Absolutely," I resounded. Even though I was warring with my own heart, I still rejoiced when others were taking profitable steps in their faith journey. I especially enjoyed baptisms. At that point in my ministry, I had baptized converts in lakes, rivers, and indoor swimming pools. But this would be my first opportunity to baptize someone in a fjord, one of the beautiful inlets of the infamous North Sea.

"And can the Blade Runner soundtrack be playing in the background when I'm baptized?" Freddie asked. "Maybe from a car stereo at the water's edge."

"Uh...sure," I conceded. "I guess that'll be okay." I was

just glad no one from my legalistic network in the states would be present for the occasion.

Eight or nine families eventually signed up to take part in the three-day event. I was mildly surprised, since we would be camping in tents.

The sun was shining for the baptismal service on Sunday morning. The baptism, with the Blade Runner soundtrack resounding melodramatically through the valley and across the fjord, was one of the most beautiful baptisms I'd ever performed. It was an absolutely spectacular moment. And the music, I might add, only heightened the ethereal "feel" of the whole experience, regardless of what my legalistic peers would have thought.

Back in Oslo—even with the restless heart that was hamstringing me—I still tried with the last bits of resolve left in me to provide an element of acceptable leadership for my congregation. Even though I was slowly losing my own grip on life, I still wanted the best for my people. I wanted them to be strong. Out of our congregation, three men—all from the U.S.—had already gone into full-time ministry. I felt it was time to mobilize some of the newer members in the congregation. Plus, doing so would give me an occasional break from the pulpit. So, I went to twelve men and asked them to preach or teach at least once in the unfolding year. As was typical, I had to gently nudge, but eventually ten of the men capitulated.

I scheduled all ten men to speak during the next six month period. Eight of those men—three Norwegians, two Brits, one Scotsman, and two Americans—discovered they had the gift of teaching and ended up in full or part-time ministry. The church continued to function as a spiritual incubator, sending out church leaders all around the world.

In the secret parts of my heart, I attributed this fruit to my inclusive leadership style, and carried a certain amount of pride about it all.

Yet, at the same time, I was feeling more and more isolated and more and more distrustful of almost everything I had ever been taught by my stateside mentors. There were just too many verses they had taken out of context to propagate misleading things in the name of God, things I had initially embraced without question, things I now found both repulsive and disturbing. So, what else had I been taught in the name of God that was outright bogus? The virgin birth of Christ? The deity of Christ? The inspiration of Scripture? Heaven and hell? I was growing less and less confident about what I could believe or teach with any semblance of assurance.

And it showed.

Even my own daughter, now five, could see it.

On a Sunday night, for example, I was leading an interactive Bible study and was expecting the crowd to carry most of the discussion. But they didn't. Every one that night, for some reason, was tired and non engaging. So, like it or not, I had to fill the minutes. I wasn't sufficiently prepared, so I ad libbed. About ten minutes into my babbling, Heidi raised her hand. Good, I thought. Maybe I had provoked a question about the text we were considering.

'Yes," I said, acknowledging my daughter.

"Dad," Heidi blurted out shamelessly, "since you're not saying anything anyway, can we kids go out and play?"

As a church planter, I had been gifted with a winning formula: (1) a host country that was first-class and safe, (2) a wide open door to an ever growing expat community that staffed embassies, universities, oil companies, military compounds, and business conglomerates, (3) a conveniently located and affordable rental building that could seat a hundred and fifty people, and (4) a complete absence of competition. At the time, there was only one other English-speaking international church in the city, and it was a high-church Lutheran assembly, unlike our church which was informal and perhaps more authentic. Our church had developed organically from a perfect combination of elements, including the element of a pastor—myself—who saw its dynamic potential and who intentionally nurtured it. At the time, I wasn't aware of another international church anywhere on the European continent. I honestly felt like I was helping pioneer a new breed of church. Secretly, I took great pride in my ministerial accomplishment. Yet, I felt like I was dying alone on the inside. I was hurting. I was confused. I was afraid.

I stood in my home office one afternoon staring at my library, a collection of a hundred books displayed on a five-shelf bookcase. I was angry; more than angry. I had been misled, intentionally or unintentionally I wasn't sure, but misled nevertheless. Fourteen years earlier, as an innocent teen, I had gullibly embraced the doctrine of a single American-based Christian denomination, a denomination steeped in hardline legalism. I had hungrily listened to the denomination's nationally-respected pastors, teachers, evangelists, professors, and missionaries. And I had believed, as they repeatedly taught me, that "we" had a monopoly on truth, that we had developed Christianity to its maximum potential, that we were right and everybody—literally everybody—else was wrong.

But now, I had gradually come to see that a significant portion of those teachings on which I had built my life was nothing more than a pitiful and flimsy house of cards, an extravagant list of manmade dos and don'ts concocted and preached as the only benchmark for winning and retaining God's approval.

As I slowly shifted my gaze from one theology book to

another, I read the names of the authors. Ninety-five percent of the authors represented in my library, I realized, were men inside my denomination. And their radical ideas about Christian living had years earlier molded my teenage heart into that of a merciless judge. I had been forged as a young man into a self-righteous, narrow-minded, obnoxious minister. In my initial years of ministry, I had probably offended more people than I had helped.

But now, thanks to the gracious and patient people in my Oslo congregation—people representing more than thirty different nations—my eyes had been opened to the destructive fanaticism that had held me in its grip. And the house of cards had finally collapsed, subsequently taking me down with it.

So now, as a Christian leader, who was I? What did I believe any longer about God? The Bible? The Christian life? About anything my pompous, judgmental mentors had taught me?

I sighed. I felt emotionally sick.

The books in my library were now not only worthless, they were, in my opinion, subversive. I removed two volumes from a commentary set and stared intently at the covers for a few seconds. And then I loaded my arms with a few more volumes and walked them to a burn barrel in the backyard. I drenched the books in paraffin and set them ablaze.

After several roundtrips to my office, I was relieved that the bookcase in my study finally stood empty.

Back at the burn barrel, I poked and jabbed and watched smoke rise into the sky for more than an hour as a ten-year collection of books containing thousands and thousands of pages was forever destroyed.

Eventually stepping away from the smoke, I inhaled deeply and decided it was time I learned "how" to think.

I vowed then and there as a teacher of the Bible that I

would never again blindly believe or easily parrot another Christian leader.

The evening after I burned my library, I went for a late-night stroll in a forest outside the city. Alone on a moon-lit trail, I was lost in my thoughts of devastation when my world was suddenly interrupted by the sound of exploding tree branches and the pounding of giant's feet. I halted in my tracks, instantly held motionless by fear and uncertainty. Then I heard a deep, rough snorting fast approaching in my direction. Before I could process an additional thought or feeling, a gargantuan moose shot across my path at a break-neck speed. He missed me by three feet. Had he collided with me, I would have been killed on the spot. And strangely, I was somewhat sad that I had survived the close-call. That's how conflicted I was in my soul and spirit. I just wasn't sure anymore who I was or what I believed. I was almost too tired spiritually to keep going.

There was only one lingering thing that I knew with absolute certainty. Legalism as an extreme expression of Christianity was both hideous and repulsive. If personified, legalism would be the ultimate short-tempered eccentric professor who psychologically seduced and brainwashed his students with his self-delusional belief that he was the smartest man in his career field, and could believe no wrong, and refused to subject himself to any correction.

It was during this time when *Wisdom Hunter*, my first novel, was conceived. I deeply wanted to pull off the mask that I typically wore when in the presence of my stateside legalistic leaders, sit across a table from them, and have an honest-to-God civilized debate about the dangers of legalism, especially the extreme judgmental and self-righteous attitudes that accompanied it. But I knew from an insider's perspective that those leaders would not grant me even a minimal discussion. In their eyes I would no longer be perceived as a credible thinker. I would be an enemy, not worthy of their time or conversation.

So I decided to try a different approach. I decided to convey my discovered insights through a novel. If I could create a story that was adventurous enough and compelling enough, maybe my legalistic colleagues would read the pages, get caught up in the plot, and then be unexpectedly blindsided with the dramatic sections that illustrated the putridness of their ideology. I had no literary training or experience, yet with a new-found purpose I devoted enormous amounts of mental energy trying to put together a story that would produce the desired effect.

And finally, I came up with the plot line that's now found in *Wisdom Hunter*. It's the story of a prominent legalistic pastor who, because of his hard-nosed commitment to nonsensical rules drives away his daughter and his wife. He's eventually able to redeem himself with his granddaughter when he repents of his closed-mindedness and humbly becomes a proactive seeker of wisdom.

In the backdrop of creating the story, I also repented of my closed-mindedness, overblown piety, and reckless judgmental attitude. I set out to become a genuine wisdom hunter myself. Or, at least, I wanted to.

Chapter 25

Picking up pen and paper, I wrote for six months in my spare time, learning how to describe my feelings and thoughts along the way. I completed two-hundred-and-sixty typed pages, then regretfully gave up. I could no longer bridle my thirst for running away and being free. It was all I could think about. I was now mentally off balance. My church started to suffer. My marriage started to suffer. Emotionally, I started shutting down as a pastor, father, and husband. Sherri begged me multiple times to go with her to a marriage counselor.

"And just what's a marriage counselor going to tell us that we don't already know?" I spouted defensively. "Besides, what would happen if IBWO found out we were going to a counselor? Oh wait; I'll tell you what would happen! Our ministry would be over in a heartbeat! That's what would happen!"

"What ministry?" Sherri retorted with a broken and confused heart. "Nobody even knows where your heart is these days! You're a ghost in your own home! You're a ghost in your own church!"

Unaware of the war that I was fighting inside my head

and heart, an unbelieving man who attended our church at the time invited me to sail with him from Oslo to Copenhagen. As an executive with NCR—National Cash Register—the man was being relocated to the company's headquarters in Denmark. All his family's household goods would be trucked and ferried to the new location. But he would personally sail his 35-foot yacht the 280 nautical miles through the North Sea. Would I join him and his nineteen-year-old son? They needed one more crew member. The trip would take about three days.

I jumped at the invitation. I didn't even consult Sherri. The trip would give me a chance to escape my pastoral and family duties, at least for a few days.

On the morning of our departure from the harbor, the sky was deeply overcast. It quickly started pouring rain. Yet, I was absolutely jubilant. Before we got out of the Oslo fjord, the rainy weather escalated to a storm with heavy winds. The boat heeled at 45 degrees, rising and dropping forcefully with the waves. On the deck, we fought constantly to stay upright and on the boat. And even with our rain suits on, we got soaked to the bone. Somehow, even in the threatening situation, I laughed with delight. I never got sea sick. But after two days of retarded progress on the sea, the owner decided to make a port of call on the west coast of Sweden to find warmth and rest, and to wait out the storm. Uncertain as to how long the bad weather would persist, I had to board a train and head back to Oslo. But the forty-eight hours as a working crew member on the boat, while pummeled by an angry sea, simply intensified my craving for new and wild adventures.

Such an adventure soon presented itself when Sherri decided, for her own sanity, to leave me for several weeks and fly to the US to receive some loving support from her parents, loving support she so desperately needed. She took Heidi and flew back under the guise of making a pleasurable "grandparents" visit. I quickly planned a getaway of my own. I took a Sunday off and flew to Cyprus where I visited the Greek side of the island for five days.

Once there, I realized the island was much bigger than I had imagined. In order to explore the various towns, which I heartily intended to do, I needed transportation. I happened to notice scooters and motorcycles galore. They seemed to be everywhere. Then I noticed that motorcycle rental shops were abundant, nearly on every block. And it made sense. Cyprus was a major holiday destination for Europeans. And motorbikes apparently were their preferred choice of transportation. I had ridden a minibike when I was a teen. I had ridden a Vespa Scooter once, with Sherri as my passenger. So, why not rent a motorcycle for my exploration purposes?

I went into a rental shop in the small resort town where I was staying and, after thirty minutes, to my nervous surprise, I signed a two-day contract for a Kawasaki 500 LTD. This would be my first time to ride a "real" motorcycle.

I killed the engine four or five times trying to leave the property. That was embarrassing enough. But then, when I pulled out into the street I aimed automatically for the righthand lane, forgetting that Cypriots drive on the left side, and was instantly confronted with an oncoming car. I instinctively moved farther to the right, only to scrape a concrete wall, and almost dropped the bike before I managed to stop. The driver of the oncoming vehicle—most likely accustomed to tourists attempting to drive on the wrong side of the street—honked his horn, slowed down, and gave me a look of complete displeasure.

I frantically and promptly found an empty parking lot

where I taught myself to shift through the gears smoothly, make capable turns, and stop quickly without losing control. After twenty minutes or so, I felt confident enough to tackle the streets, this time on the correct side of the yellow line.

The next few hours introduced me to a therapeutic thrill that still plays a prominent role in my life—the thrill of motorcycling. Riding the bike placed me out in the open at automobile speeds where all my senses were activated to the max—feeling the wind, smelling the island, tasting the air, hearing the surrounding sounds, and seeing details of the road—all of it changing by the millisecond. It was analogous to reading a thriller with new surprises on every page. It was absolutely tantalizing, so much so that after riding half a day in one single area of the island I could barely wait to venture long distances to other towns and sites. But, I didn't want to experience the adventure alone. So that evening I stopped dozens of people on motorcycles in and around the town where I was staying, and told them, "I'm recruiting motorcyclists for an all-day tour of the island tomorrow." I told them we would rendezvous at 8:00 AM sharp. I gave them the name and address of my hotel where we would gather. And I encouraged them to invite friends.

How many of those individuals, if any, would accept my overly enthusiastic invitation? I, of course, had no earthly idea.

The next morning I was more than excited when twelve motorcycles showed up. In the round of introductions there were twenty-two people, twelve guys and ten gals—mostly strangers to one another—representing twelve countries. I was pleased to find out that three of those individuals were from Norway. I automatically felt a bond with them.

Everyone in the group, it seemed, was ready for an epic

adventure. It was visible in their attitudes and energy. And my anticipation was probably greater than anyone's in the group. I had mapped out a route in my head that would take us on a 250-mile circuit. So, I took the lead and posed as if I had been adventuring on motorcycles for years.

Leading the group was exhilarating. Even though we were basically strangers to one another, riding in a pack imposed an immediate sense of community.

That evening—at the thirteen-hour mark of our trip when we were utterly fatigued—we finally reentered the outskirts of Larnaca, a necessary gateway back to our hotels thirty miles away. It was Friday night, party night, and the big city was alive with traffic and partygoers. Nightfall was coming fast, so I asked the only Cypriot in the group, who happened to be familiar with the streets of Larnaca, if he would lead us through the city.

"Absolutely," he assured me with a smile.

Up to that moment, the day had already engendered one adrenalin rush after another. But the hit of adrenalin was about to go hyper. The Cypriot held his arm high until he had the attention of everyone in the group, then shouted, "Follow me!" With no further pause, he twisted the throttle forcefully and was gone.

There was a moment of group assimilation.

And then...everyone commenced the chase. It was a mad dash through the city that could have easily led to injury or incarceration. Yet, oddly, the whole event produced an intoxicating high that one seldom experiences in life. If it's possible to get physically drunk or inebriated from an infusion of fun, then that's what happened collectively to our pack.

When we pulled into the town where we were lodging, I

realized it was a miracle no one in our group had been maimed or arrested. I breathed a sigh of relief. And almost immediately, I decided *I've got to do this again at some point in my life.*

Chapter 26

Back in Oslo, I was reminded of just how much I had lost my heart for being responsible. The next Sunday I stood before my congregation and, holding back tears, shared my aimless spirit. "As you know, Sherri will be in the states for another four weeks. I can stand here during those weeks and lead the Sunday worship services, but to be honest—and many of you are aware of the struggle going on in my life—my heart just wouldn't be in it. I would just be an empty machine." I paused. "What I really need to do is just step aside a while longer. So...I ask you as friends, will you give me permission to...to just run away for a few more weeks? I think I just need to run."

Some of the people who were aware of my inner turmoil had already reached out and offered a listening ear and a promised confidentiality. But I had turned down their offers. Since they had never experienced my journey as a disillusioned and confused pastor, I concluded it was impossible for them to understand my crisis. What I needed, and secretly looked for, was an older pastor who had walked my path, and survived; a pastor who could put his arm around me and graciously and wisely reassure me that I wasn't a complete anomaly. But I had not found such a person. Therefore, to my detriment, I fought my battle alone.

"All right," one of the church leaders expressed dejectedly, speaking on behalf of the leadership team, "we'll give you permission to run, but if you make stupid decisions, we'll not be able to change the consequences. So, if you need to run…go ahead and run. You're free, my friend. Go."

Thanking the heavens for a congregation of friends who would dare grant me such bold freedom, I immediately started planning my next escape.

Due to the low cost of a last-minute package deal, I fled to the Greek island of Kos, five miles across the water from the mainland of Turkey. On my second day on the island, I took a one-day side excursion to the Greek isle of Patmos where the apostle John had been imprisoned. To breathe in the air of such an iconic place left me feeling a part of history's fabric, and richer for it.

And somehow freer.

Was now the time, I wondered, to make the ultimate break from everything I knew and start chasing endless dreams with total abandonment? The surging temptation was totally mind consuming. I simply couldn't shake it. Yet, I was too hesitant and too afraid to take the final step over the edge, the final step of no return.

God, where are you? I begged. *I'm slipping here.*

There was still one lingering truth that I was certain was an absolute and eternal truth and not a manmade fabrication. It was that one truth that stood as my last connection to hope. It was the same truth King David clung to during his losing battles with his wayward heart. It was the supreme truth that God is the consummation of all knowledge, all life, all power, all authority, all love, all grace, all justice, and all truth. And once that truth is known and embraced, where can one run – other than to God? There was simply no other place to go. So, as I had drummed into my head over and over, I decided I would never—not out of shame, guilt, fear, or defiance—run FROM God. Rather, I would run TO him, even when my heart had gone numb for everything else that was good. In running to him, I would spill the secrets of my heart. I would confess my prodigal longings. I would express my anger toward him. I would praise him. I would love him. I would beseech him. Like King David, I was determined to be a man who chased after God's heart – both in the valley of dark failure, and on the mountain top of bright victory. And that's what I did.

So, where are you? I pleaded again.

In spite of my yearning, God—as far as I could tell—appeared to be distant and silent.

Appeared to be.

And then, back on the island of Kos, I went to dinner.

I selected an outdoor establishment for my evening meal. I had just begun to partake of the great-looking dish I had ordered when a late-evening shadow fell across my table. I looked up. There, looking down at me, stood a tall, handsome blonde male. With his striking features and thick hair, he could have been a model or movie star.

"Excuse me," he said in English, "Do you mind if I join you?"

At the moment I honestly wasn't in the mood for conversation, not even with a movie-star-looking individual. I looked around and noticed several empty tables and wondered why the man had chosen to bypass them. I was hoping my head gesture would send an unspoken message. But the man didn't move.

"Is it okay?" he reasserted.

I didn't speak. I simply shrugged.

The man took a seat on the opposite side of the table. He never asked if I could speak or understand English. And I had not issued a single word in his presence. I could have easily passed as a European from a number of countries, especially east European countries like Latvia, Lithuania, Estonia, and Poland where English was not readily spoken. Yet, the man spoke to me in English, even after introducing himself as a doctor from Sweden.

I just rolled my eyes at his introduction. But he didn't stop talking. "You know, I've only been on the island for two days and I'm already so bored I can hardly stand it." He paused until I looked at him. When we made eye contact, he continued, "I've been chasing happiness all my life and just can't seem to find it. As a single guy with six weeks paid vacation every year, I've literally traveled two times around the world, visiting every exotic and adventurous destination I can think of. But traveling has lost its lure. Yeah, places are different, cultures are different, but people are the same, with the same basic needs and desires, no matter where I go. And toys! I've owned every expensive toy a man can dream of – sports cars, motorcycles, boats, watches, hifi systems, fitness equipment, mountain cabins, penthouse apartments. And none of it has ever brought me long-term happiness or fulfillment."

I still had not spoken a single syllable, yet the man was obviously resolute about unloading the inner conflict of his soul, and doing so in a language that was not his mother tongue. I knew the Scandinavian temperament. Scandinavians would hardly share their personal struggles with friends, much less strangers. The whole nordic group—the Swedes, Norwegians, Danes, Finns, and Icelanders—was known for being stubbornly reserved. Except when they were under the influence of alcohol. Only then were their inhibitions lowered, or vanquished.

But the man sitting across from me was not drunk. So, why was he confiding in me? Whatever the reason, the man's subject matter had definitely seized my attention, even if I refused to hold eye contact.

"And then there's the women," he added. "I've been with so many, I've lost count. European women. American women. Asian women. Hispanic women. African women. Most of the encounters were one-night stands. A few budded into more than that. But those physical relationships, as fun as they might seem, have left me empty." He paused again, and waited for me to look him in the eye, which I did. "But there's one thing that's eluded me. And I'm sure that's the one thing that would give me ultimate peace of mind and contentment. I know this might sound crazy. But if I could find one good woman and love her and only her. And if that woman would reciprocate and love me and only me. And if we could have children and teach them important things in life. What I'm saying is, if I could just have an old fashioned family, I would give up every toy, every exotic trip, every one-night stand. And I would be the happiest man on the planet."

At that point, I was looking into the man's eyes. I still hadn't uttered a word. The man didn't know my name, my nationality, my career, or where I was in life's journey. Yet, he had selected a place at my table, and in English told me seriously one-on-one that everything I was planning to spend years chasing would ultimately lead me to a stark and unexpected dead end. And that everything I had back home was indeed the real treasure.

When I finished my meal I left the table. With the sun now below the horizon I aimlessly wandered the darkened streets of Kos. I wept. I had beseeched God to hear the anguished cry of my heart and help me. Either he had sent an angel posing as a Swedish doctor, or he had manipulated the real Swedish doctor's evening plans and placed him at my table and unlocked the man's heart, contrary to the man's probable tendency. If the man had been American, English, Greek, or any other nationality, I would have most likely dismissed his outpouring of the soul as worthless babble. But he was precisely from the region of the world that had captured my heart. And from the exact people group I had grown to envy. The Swedish doctor, of all people—and against all odds—had successfully pinged the nearly-stopped-up ears of my wandering spirit. I continued to weep. I couldn't stop.

But, would the encounter, as extraordinary or as "supernatural" as it might be, make a difference? I honestly didn't know. And that scared me.

Chapter 27

I returned to Oslo a few days before Sherri.

The congregation at my international church had been more than gracious to let me run. But instead of satiating my wanderlust, the unforgettable adventures on the Greek islands had provided me with a real-life taste of freedom, and I now wanted more. But the Swedish doctor's words wouldn't leave me, no matter how roughly I tried to dismiss them. Now more confused than ever, I felt like I was suspended in a no-man's land. In my heart I wasn't functioning as a husband, father, or pastor. But neither was I operating as a totally free prodigal who had cut the umbilical cord of all responsibilities. And I was miserable. There were days when I truly wanted to stop breathing just to get relief. Plus, an early demise on my part would graciously release Sherri from the heart-wrenching misery I had created for her. I oftentimes begged God to kill me and then angrily wondered why He didn't or wouldn't. I was certain I deserved it. And I was pretty certain at that point that Sherri would have welcomed it.

Yet, when Sherri flew back into Oslo with Heidi, Sherri was the one who made the urgent and repeated attempts to close the emotional chasm between us. But my heart didn't have the will to participate. Consequently, Sherri went to bed night after night unable to hold back a torrent of tears. Our Independent Baptist culture—with its influence and pressure—dissuaded her from considering divorce as an easy or acceptable option. So, with growing despair and confusion, she pleaded with me to "emotionally come home."

But selfishly, before I could even try to "emotionally come home," I was compelled to find out if the Swedish doctor's assessment on life was true all around, or just true for him. Would chasing dreams around the world with no commitments to anyone really lead to a heartbreaking dead end? I had to know. So I immediately set out to talk to Norwegians who, like the Swedish doctor, had placed both hands on the rainbow. Would they confirm the doctor's conclusion, or would they debunk it? In such a small population as Norway's, the rich and powerful who reveled in extraordinary freedoms were easily accessible. So over a three or four month period I ferreted out and "interviewed" several such men and women—men and women who happened to be physically beautiful, socially famous, politically powerful, and boundlessly rich. And what I discovered shocked me to the core. Every one of those people, without exception—regardless of how free, attractive, or powerful—admitted in their own words that they believed the "grass was greener on the other side of the fence." Not a single one was totally fulfilled. The element of the interviews that demanded my attention was the fact that each of the individuals was speaking from personal experience, not from philosophical conjecture. I was truly stunned. The doctor's analysis of life had not been hyperbole after all. It had not been just one man's truth.

So now what? Yes, my heart had grown undeniably cold,

but my mind wasn't yet completely stupid. Because of all the confessions of being-free-but-not-fulfilled I was now afraid to turn my back on my moral and official roles and walk away. So, was I doomed to live in an emotional and psychological wasteland? Had I created a hell for myself?

In my listlessness, God continued to lovingly pull back the curtain on his majesty to show me that He, His mission, and His values were all undeniably worthy of my devotion. Around that time, for example, a young Christian lady from Thailand became a part of our international church family. She had left Thailand seven years earlier as a Buddhist and converted to Christianity while living for a while in the US. In sharing her testimony with our church, she revealed her desire to one day return to Thailand to take the Christian message to her family. The people in our congregation were so moved by the lady's manifest burden that they voted to purchase a roundtrip ticket to Bangkok for her.

Humbled to the point of tears, the young lady flew to Thailand for the first time in seven years and passionately presented the message of Jesus, along with her conversion story, to her relatives and childhood friends. Gloriously, she was able to lead her younger sister out of Buddhism to a saving faith in Christ. She actually watched as her newly converted sister burned all her household idols of Buddha.

A few weeks after returning to Norway, the young lady received a lengthy handwritten letter from her sister that, when shared with our congregation, spoke dramatically to everyone's heart - especially mine. In the letter, the younger sister explained that she had recently traveled a day's journey on foot, with her six-month-old baby, to once again share her new faith with their brother. A short distance from the house she detected that her baby wasn't feeling well.

When she finally knocked on the front door, the brother

shouted from the other side, "Are you back to try to convert me to your foreign god?"

"Please," she pleaded, "I just want to tell you all the ways this new God has helped me. I've never experienced this much peace before. And I want you to experience it with me."

"As long as you forsake Buddha, you are not welcome in my house. And I will never change my mind."

"I'm your sister. I love you. Please, just listen to what I have to tell you." There was silence from the other side of the door. "Can I at least have shelter for the night, then? It's going to start raining soon, and my baby is not feeling well."

And then came the brother's unforgettable words. "You're not my sister anymore! As long as you cling to this Christian god, I want nothing to do with you. Go away!"

The sister then heard the lock on the door being engaged. At that point, the brother stopped responding. With no money for lodging, there was no option but to turn around and head for home into the approaching rain and into the night. She had only proceeded a mile or two when she saw the dark ominous storm approaching. The darkness covered the entire horizon. She feared for her baby. For the infant to be soaked and then spend the night wet and chilled would most likely be fatal. She remembered, as she had been told, that the Christian God—unlike Buddha—had eyes that could see, ears that could hear, and hands that could help. So, she cried out to her new Heavenly Father. "I have no money for shelter. And I'm a stranger to everyone in this region. So I don't know how I can protect my baby from the coming storm. I don't know what to do but keep walking. Is there any way you can possibly keep my baby safe? Please!"

And then the miraculous happened.

When the storm reached her, the wind was so significant

that it was bending trees, cascading trash, and blowing a deluge of rain at uncommon angles. Yet, the wind and rain never touched her or her baby. Inexplicably, as she continued to walk into the storm, heading homeward, she found herself cocooned in a pocket of dryness and warmth. With amazement, she witnessed the wind and rain raging within feet all around her. In the early morning hours when the storm had passed and the sun started to show its rays, the infant was completely dry and sleeping soundly. The mother, in awe, made it back to her home unable to hold back her tears of wonder and gratitude. She promptly wrote the letter now being read to our congregation. She couldn't thank her older sister enough for introducing her to the one and only living God. She was now going to tell everyone in her village about the God who could actually see, hear, help, and—most of all—grant genuine forgiveness and peace to those who opened their arms and cried out to him.

For me, the letter shouted at my heart once again that no matter how much I yearned to be my own master, I would be an absolute fool to deny God's sovereignty over all.

I avowed anew to never run FROM him, only TO him, even in my resentment, and especially during my insolent wanderings.

Chapter 28

One afternoon, shortly thereafter, I was sitting alone outdoors at a downtown restaurant in Oslo. Over a steak lunch I was daydreaming about wild and unbridled adventures when I spotted activity in a major plaza that ignited my curiosity. Two young ladies and two young men, nicely dressed and wielding pens and clipboards, were stopping people and engaging them in some type of interview. After answering a few questions, some of the people shook their head and walked away. Others nodded and were escorted around the corner and out of my sight. My intuition told me the interviewers probably belonged to a cult of some kind. I was in a reckless mood, so after paying for my meal I got up and intentionally walked into the path of one of the young ladies.

"Pardon me," the lady said in Norwegian, making eye contact with me. "My name is Bente. My friends and I are on the streets today offering a free personality test. Can I have about five minutes of your time? You'll find the test to be extremely valuable."

I asked the lady if she could speak English. Without hesitation, she repeated her introduction in nearly a flawless American accent.

"Sure," I told her. "I have time."

At her request, I gave her my name and then listened carefully to ten questions, one at a time, as the lady "X"ed out the boxes of my multiple-choice answers.

After going through all the questions, the lady looked over the checked boxes and declared, "Congratulations, Randy, your answers show you're a natural leader with the capacity to be a great influencer. Some additional good news is we have professionals nearby who can help you understand your personality traits better and even help you develop your leadership skills. And they would love to do exactly that at no cost to you. They would just need an hour of your time. The insights you'll receive can improve your social standing for the rest of your life. So, what do you think? Would you like that kind of input and support?"

I played along. "Sure. Why not?"

"All right! Well, follow me then."

I was led around the corner, down half a block, and into an office building up to a second-floor office equipped with a couch, table, and movie screen. There the lady introduced me to a slightly older male who shook my hand and welcomed me. The guy explained that he would administer the personality test that would dig deeper into my self perception and reveal my strong suits as well as my weak ones. The test would consist of two-hundred questions. I would check my multiple-choice answer to each one. An "auditor," a person high up in the organization, would then analyze my answers. While that was being done I would watch a fifteen-minute film that would introduce me to the organization sponsoring the test. The "auditor" would then discuss with me the findings that my answers revealed.

When I agreed to the process, the guy handed me a

clipboard that held the sheets of printed questions, along with a pen, and said, "So, have a seat on the couch. The questions are self explanatory. Just answer them as honestly as possible. It'll take about thirty minutes to go through them all."

When I glanced over the first ten of those questions—questions such as: "Do your past failures still worry you?" and "Do you make thoughtless remarks or accusations which later you regret?"—I was more persuaded than ever that I was now approaching a mind-trap set by a cult. The questions were designed, it seemed, to focus on one's weaknesses. And I was quite sure that this particular group—whoever they were—would claim to be the sole entity that would be able to "save me" from myself.

So I answered every question, not admitting to a single character flaw or subpar practice. I then submitted my answers.

While my test was being scrutinized by an "auditor," I watched the fifteen-minute film. In the narration, I was told that the group administering my test was a community called Scientology, and that Scientology could help me develop such an extreme mental acuteness regarding human behavior that if I let them, they could teach me how to achieve a mental mastery over all negative and destructive feelings and subsequently live a richer, more productive life.

Following the film, I was led to a back office and introduced to my auditor, a thirty-something Norwegian woman sitting behind a wooden desk.

"Have a seat," she instructed in English, pointing to a chair directly in front of her desk.

I sat down and promptly propped my feet on the desktop. The lady gave me a look that was incredulous. I didn't even blink.

"Okay," she said with the tone of an overly-stern school teacher. "Your answers to the test questions show some kind of anomaly."

I simply lifted my eyebrows as if to say, So?

"According to your answers, it seems that in your thirty-one years of living you've never been sidetracked by anyone, any pain, or any experience – and that you've never experienced fear of any kind."

"That's true," I bluffed. "I've never been afraid of anything." I was so calm, it felt surreal.

"And you've never had a regret...not a single one...ever?" she asked with blatant sarcasm.

"Never...none that I can remember."

"And no significant failures in life? With family, friends, employers?"

"No failures. No setbacks. No crises."

"And no feelings of insecurity? Ever?"

"None that I'm aware of."

"So, am I sitting in the presence of the most perfect human being on the planet?"

"I don't know. Maybe not THE most."

The lady shook her head with unmasked cynicism.

I figured, since she was a high-ranking achiever in the organization, that she was assumedly well on her way to mastering all her negative emotions. But within five minutes or so, the lady became so perturbed with my cocky attitude that she eventually stood up, literally slapped the desk, and yelled at me in disgust, "You can leave now! You're not ready for Scientology! Get out! Now!"

I promptly left the building, gleeful that I had demonstrated, at least to myself and hopefully to the female auditor as well, that Scientology—a "religion" created by a science fiction writer—was NOT the cure for the volatile human psyche.

Reflecting on my own psyche over the next few days I finally admitted that in my current state of mind my presence in the ministry was no less a joke than that of the Scientology auditor. I had already hung on to my pastorship for too long. Even I could now see that my church was hemorrhaging both people and morale. And it was all due to my ghostly leadership. I needed to start looking at career options outside the ministry. But after fifteen years of serving the church in sundry capacities what would I do?

Chapter 29

Within a few weeks Sherri and I were required by IBWO to attend a four-day field conference for all the IBWO missionaries living and working in Europe. The only redemptive element about the gathering was it would take place at an old Bible college campus on the mountainside of Beatenberg, Switzerland, overlooking the extraordinarily scenic valley of Interlaken. Otherwise, I felt mentally nauseated about the prospect of walking back into a highly legalistic environment where everyone would pretend to be pure, holy, and super spiritual. The piety and judgmental attitudes would be unbearable.

And I was not wrong.

The president of IBWO, who flew in from Tennessee for the occasion, gave the salutatory presentation. With Sherri at my side, I sat near the back of the small auditorium with a cleanly shaven face for the first time in months. My stomach was tied in knots as the president, in his opening words, expressed his appreciation for IBWO and its distinctive and high-caliber missionaries who were more rooted, more loyal, more trustworthy, and definitely more effective, than all those missionaries out there serving with "liberal" and "neo-evangelical" mission agencies.

"Let me give you an example of what I'm talking about," he lambasted with a sanctimonious spirit. "There was a missionary husband serving in Africa with a well-known mission board that talks all the time about love, love, love. But they have no godly standards. The man one day just disappeared. His wife and kids had no idea what happened to him. They didn't know if he had been kidnapped, murdered, or laid up in a hospital somewhere because of an accident. All their efforts to find him came up empty-handed. Now, listen to me carefully folks. The man's liberal theology gave him no anchor, no conscience. To make a long story short, the man was found two years later on the streets of Los Angeles as a homeless alcoholic." The president carried on with the story, highlighting all the failures of the so-called Christian denominations and agencies with no standards, implying that IBWO missionaries—with their black-and-white, hard-and-fast rules for everything under the sun—were beyond such waywardness.

Squeezing my eyes shut and wanting to vomit, it dawned on me that in all my years with Tennessee Temple and IBWO, I had never, NOT once, heard a professor, a pastor, a missionary, or an evangelist admit in public that they struggled in life with anything – their faith, their marriage, their kids, their ministry, their team, their self-image, their discipline. I had been absolutely left to believe as a young impressionable preacher boy that there was a certain level of spiritual maturity that, when reached, would allow the saint to take off his spiritual armor and for the remainder of his days gloriously bask in his spiritual strength. I now realized that all such pretense up and down the Independent Baptist ranks was nothing more than putrid bile. Here I was, dying on the inside, and I'm sure I wasn't alone. Yet, there wasn't a person in the room I would trust to be my spiritual confidant. It was more than sad. It was utterly maddening.

The moment not only infuriated me, it rekindled in full force my desire to one day finish my novel *Wisdom Hunter*. It had been months since I had worked on the project. But I still felt compelled to shout at my peers in story form that legalism was repugnant from head to toe, that it contaminated and destroyed nearly everything it touched, even if its devotees refused to admit it. Throughout that night and the next day I was obsessed with the thought that I somehow had to find a way to complete the manuscript. Going into that evening, though, I had to face the grim reality that I was such a dysfunctional mess that I would probably never finish the project. Thus, by dinner time I was berating myself.

Reaching the dining hall, Sherri and I sat alone at a table for four. I was in no mood for hobnobbing with any of the other IBWO personnel while pretending that all was okay. As the other tables filled with people and conversation, Sherri and I were silently isolated in our own worlds of pain, wondering what in the world we were even doing on the grounds.

We were five minutes into the meal when the surreal happened. The main doors to the dining hall suddenly opened. Two strange men—one middle-aged looking, the other much younger—stepped inside, paused, and looked around. Everybody but me and Sherri were clustered at one end of the big room and seemed to be oblivious to the entrance of the two men. I started to dismiss their presence myself, assuming they worked at the Bible college, when the older of the two led the younger one straight to Sherri's and my table and sat down as if they were the ones planning and running the conference. I was honestly a little unsettled by their forthrightness.

"You're discouraged, aren't you?" the older of the two said.

What? Who was he talking to? Out of curiosity I looked into the man's eyes for the first time. *What... Was I going crazy?* I had to intentionally inhale as I took my next breath. The man's eyes were not normal looking. They were the color of amber and looked multi-focused as if they were actively soaking up tons of data per second and could not be misled or deceived. I had never seen eyes like them—not anywhere—until I shifted my gaze to the younger man. Was I daydreaming? The younger man's eyes were identical in description, except a shade darker. Were these men some kind of biological aberration?

"We were in Norway delivering some messages when God told us to stop what we were doing and come to Switzerland to encourage you," the older man spoke again.

What? I froze. And then I broke into tears as I tried to perceive what was transpiring.

"Who are you?" I asked almost fearfully.

"We are encouragers. And the message we bring to you is that you're going to be okay. And the book you're writing will one day be completed and will be a source of help to many people."

I had never hallucinated, had never taken drugs, had never been drunk. And I had never taken medication of any kind, period. I was physically healthy. I was not imagining the sight of the men or their words. They were real. Yet, Sherri, as inexplicable as it was, appeared to be totally aloof to the presence of the men and to what they were saying. In some ways, it was as if I was the only person in the building who could see and hear the two strangers.

"God loves you dearly," the younger man spoke for the first time.

The men lingered for thirty minutes or so after dinner. They were only in my life for about an hour. During that time, they bathed me in words of reassurance, sustenance, and hope. They left the grounds at nightfall. I had no idea where they went or where they lodged. I wondered seriously if the two "men" were angelic beings of some type. How else would two complete strangers—from Norway of all places—know about my state of mind and my unfinished manuscript?

I was overwhelmed by the intimacy I felt with God that night. Even as one struggling mightily in his faith, I knew awkwardly that I was safe and secure in the arms of God. That belief never left me, even as we approached our final months in Norway, the darkest days of my life.

Chapter 30

Shanda, our second child, was born in Norway a few months later, only six weeks before we were to leave the country for good. I was there in the hospital for her birth which was an amazing event. But I wondered in the secret parts of my heart if I would be around for her infancy, her childhood, her adolescence, her adulthood. As I held the beautiful towheaded little girl in my arms, I wept over the fact that she had been born to a dad that would most likely fail her. How could I emotionally carry the extra responsibility when I was barely able to sustain my own soul?

I was truly wretched. Yet, as I reviewed my nine years of missionary labor in the Viking wonderland I was more than humbled when I remembered the many ways in which God had used even a wretch to do his bidding. One day while in a deep nostalgic mood, for example, I made a list of all the key people who throughout our church's brief history had been mobilized from a passive, periphery position to an influential leadership role.

There was Duane T. who had surrendered to full-time ministry, left the military, and had recently graduated from Bible college in the midwest to pursue a pastorate.

Dan H. had left the military and was serving as co-director of evangelism for a young international ministry based in England.

Martin J. was training for a church-leadership role in England.

Graham M. was recently ordained as a house-church leader in Scotland.

Odd V. was conducting a weekly prayer and teaching ministry in Oslo.

Claire R. was teaching a weekly Bible study for ladies in the south of England.

Ken W. was involved in Sunday school and children's church in Nevada.

Mark F. was teaching Bible classes in Maryland.

Adrian N. was leading Sunday school services for a British community.

Chuck V. was leading worship at a U.S. military chapel.

Norm O. was pastoring a church in Michigan.

Earnie F. was serving as a deacon in South Dakota.

Sam M. was teaching and preaching in various churches throughout the U.S. and Norway.

Freddie B. was preparing for an administrative role at a world renowned ministry based in Florida.

Many referred to the Free International Baptist Church as a "Christian boot camp," a camp where Christian leaders were raised up, trained, and sent out to serve all over the world. After compiling the list and being rendered nearly speechless with amazement and humility, I privately grasped that it really wasn't me God had used to cultivate such an army of Christian soldiers, but rather it was his TRUTH that I had been so careful to teach. I then read a letter that humbled my heart even further.

"My name is Jeffrey C. I've been in Norway since 1983. I serve with the U.S. Army and am stationed here at the NATO base – HQ AFNorth. My wife and I were introduced to the Free International Baptist Church in September 1983. It was shortly thereafter that I was led to trust Jesus Christ as my personal savior, and was baptized. This church has meant very much to me, not only because of its closeness to God, but because of its closeness as a family to one another. We laugh together, fellowship together, and sometimes even cry together. The church has answered many of my questions, and prayers as well. The pastor of the FIBC is the main reason we've continued to attend. He's devoted much of his time to bringing meaningful messages every Sunday, messages that scar our hearts, effect our lives, and motivate us to be better Christians. There hasn't been a time when I couldn't talk to the pastor when I've needed to ask a question or seek advice. He's devoted his time to his members. The church as a whole will certainly miss his leadership. He is unique. And the grace of our Lord is surely with him. This church has changed my life and given me new hope."

I wept profusely as I read Jeff's words. I had so much wanted to be a dynamic missionary and pastor. Maybe I had been to a certain degree. But I had been notoriously crippled—emotionally, spiritually, and mentally—because of the isolated war I had fought for nearly three years. And that war had finally worn me down. Yet, there was a part of me—the prodigal part—that wanted to stay in Norway indefinitely despite my massive failures. But Sherri was the honest one. "You're sick," she told me with bitterness. "You're killing everything we've worked hard for. You need help. I need help. You can stay if you want. But I'm leaving."

So I tearfully announced a departure date to our church. I couldn't bring myself to tell them I might never return. I was still fighting the inevitable. So I convinced three men in the church to temporarily serve as a team of co-pastors for three to six months. "By then I'll know with certainty if I'm coming back," I told them. One of the men was Norwegian. One was Indian. And one was American. God had used Sherri and me—in spite of our weaknesses, failures, and fears—to raise up a unique, intelligent, and strong church. Over thirty nationalities had been part of its DNA. I now did my best to help stabilize the congregation for when I walked away.

In my last weeks in Norway, Sherri and I hosted a yard sale and sold all our household furniture, along with our car. At the same time, I revisited parks, restaurants, forests, stores, and waterfronts—along with multiple friends—to say a broken-hearted "good-bye." I felt like my soul was literally being ripped out of my chest. I cried so much that I thought several times I would throw up.

On my final Sunday as pastor, I reminded the congregation that they were my favorite church in the whole world, then apologized for failing to give them a hundred percent of my passion and energy. I choked up. I told them I still wasn't certain about my future role at the church. At the same time, I told them to pray for my family and to not be surprised if they received news one day that God had taken me to heaven early. I was feeling more and more unworthy of life. And if I sensed anything from God, it was that I had perhaps used up all the grace allotted me.

And then it was over – the farewell parties, the last words, the final hugs. I bawled even when I told our landlord—a World War II sniper for the Norwegian resistance during Germany's occupation of Norway—our final good-byes.

Heidi, seven at the time, was sad as well. Norway, with its backyard snow tunnels, its child-conscious culture, its wonderful outdoor kindergartens, was the only home she had ever known.

Sherri, on the other hand, was numb. I had all but killed her emotionally. She could hardly wait to be "off duty" as a pastor's wife and be back in the loving embrace of her immediate family.

Shanda, of course, was only six weeks old and would never taste all the great pleasures of the Nordic wonderland, one of the most special places on earth.

Chapter 31

Back in Georgia for only a few weeks, I felt completely hopeless and full of shame for the way I had emotionally crashed as a husband, father, and missionary. I aborted a planned trip to California to commence training for commercial diving. I had momentarily given up the idea of an alternative career. I was absolutely convinced God was going to take me home at any moment anyway. After grim contemplation, I painstakingly composed a letter of resignation to give to IBWO. I was now walking in darkness.

Sherri, at the same time, demanded we go somewhere alone for a couple of days and talk about the fate of our marriage. My life was in shambles. I listlessly planned a three-day trip to the north Georgia mountains.

The day we left Atlanta I drove out of our way to Chattanooga, to first stop at IBWO's international headquarters. I hand carried my letter of resignation directly to the European director. Sherri and I sat silently in the man's office as he read my three-page announcement. It was the moment that Sherri, for over three years, had begged for. The words on the paper conveyed in detail my loss of heart for ministry, my struggle with legalism, my utter fatigue of spirit, and my unbalanced state of mind regarding life.

It was a no-holes-barred letter. My disclosure couldn't have been more honest or more clear.

When the man finished reading, he stood and somberly whispered, "Follow me." He led us to the office of IBWO's president. "Can you spare a moment?" he enjoined through the doorway. "We have an urgent situation here."

The president, caught off guard, said, "Sure. Come in and sit down."

We all sat. The European director handed my letter to the man at the helm of the agency. The man read quietly and slowly.

Sherri and I had served with the mission board for ten years. Sitting there in the headquarter's most powerful office, I was sure our faces and posture shouted volumes about our mental uncertainties. We couldn't hide it or deny it. We probably even looked suicidal.

"All right," the president spoke when he lowered the pages, "my advice is that you hold the letter for two weeks and not make a final decision today. Who knows? Maybe you'll change your mind in the next week or two."

Ten minutes later, Sherri and I were back in our car. We couldn't have been more confused. Neither man had asked us a single question. Neither man had stopped to pray for us. Neither man had offered us the slightest smidgen of help. And, in everybody's eyes, we were still IBWO missionaries.

And then...when we checked into a rental cabin in north Georgia, Sherri declared, "I'm filing for divorce!" We were unpacking our duffel bags in the bedroom when Sherri blurted her intentions. We had just passed the ten-year mark in our marriage. "I'm taking the girls and leaving. I can't take it anymore. So, you're free. Chase your dreams. Move back to Norway. Do whatever you want. It's over. As soon as we get back to Atlanta I'm starting the paper work."

Words from my mother, my most ardent defender in life, echoed from a week earlier when she had planted her flag with Sherri and declared, "If I was you, I'd divorce him. Not a negative word from our family will ever be said about you."

For three years I had dreamed of being single and free, and—to the detriment of my marriage—had emotionally functioned that way. But during those years, God had never permitted me to sail through life without a constant reprimand. Even the words of the Swedish doctor that "the greatest treasure in life is the family above all else" had persistently flared inside my head.

I hung my head in silence. I had married the girl I loved. She had believed in me. Trusted me. Traveled to a foreign land with me. Labored tirelessly as a teammate in ministry with me. Bore my children. And what had I given in return? I had completely crushed her—her heart, soul, and spirit. And all along, I had selfishly focused on me and my feelings. The weight of her insufferable pain surfaced in those four courageous words, "I'm filing for divorce."

Those words, and the intensity behind them, instantly awakened me to my atrocity. It was one of those rare moments in life when the brain flips a switch and leaves one stunned.

What had I done?

And there in the bedroom I did something most women in the world would consider pathetic, and rightly so. With tears washing down my face I closed my eyes and begged, "Don't do it." I spent the next forty-eight hours on my knees, face, and belly asking Sherri to give me one more chance, even if it was only for a few weeks—if I lived that long. I promised I would change. I would stop defending myself and stop offering excuses for my behavior. I would humble myself, admit my sin, and start focusing on her and her needs.

Sherri burst into tears. "It's too late!" she sobbed. "I've held out my arms to you for three years! I think you're totally oblivious to the damage you've done!"

I didn't argue. I just continued to beg for one more chance, and promised through the heaviest of tears that I would change.

Sherri in the following two-hour window, a millisecond in the overall scheme of things, made an equally unexpected declaration. Trying to hide the resentment in her heart, she looked at me and—quite inexplicably—spewed, "Six months! Not a day more! That's all I'll give."

To say that 'my decision and her decision were both baffling to everyone around us' would be an understatement. The remainder of the trip, as might be expected, was spent in relative silence, each of us marinating in the tense feelings coursing through our souls. I stepped back and, with extreme difficulty, tried to refocus. I would now make every effort to restore to Sherri the needed attention, love, and support I had so blatantly smothered. That was my new pledge, but secretly, It scared me. Was I even able to make a comeback?

To prevent additional and unnecessary upheavals, I abandoned any notion to leave the ministry. IBWO knew my condition. I had laid it all out for them. Yet, they had discouraged my resignation.

So now, I would simply fight through the situation and do the best I could.

With those decisions made, it was incumbent upon me to "check back in" at the IBWO headquarters in Chattanooga, announce my change of mind, and start planning an itinerary to visit our supporting churches and give a ministry report.

But before I made a return trip to the IBWO home office, I bought a motorcycle, a new 1985 Yamaha 700 Maxim X. Ever since my motorcycle bonanza on the island of Cyprus I had longed for a bike of my own. The Maxim X was my first adult-sized bike. Plus, I thought it would be a great tool to bring me and Sherri together for local outings and long-distance trips?

When I returned to Chattanooga a few weeks later, I rode the motorcycle. Plus, I was sporting a closely cropped beard. Nothing had been said earlier about the beard during Sherri's and my "resignation" stop at the home office. So perhaps IBWO was relaxing a little bit regarding some of their hardline regulations. With a beard, long hair, and leather motorcycle jacket, I walked into the front office to announce my decision to carry on as a IBWO missionary. The receptionist welcomed me with a stammer and quickly escorted me to the office of the European director.

Later that evening, when I was back in Atlanta, I received a follow-up call from the director. "Randy, you need to make some changes before you hit the road. The receptionist at the home office was completely unnerved when you lingered in the lobby this morning with your beard, long hair, and leather jacket. She told several of the staff that you're the most unprofessional-looking missionary she's ever seen, and that you're a bad testimony for the organization. So before you start visiting your supporting churches, you need to shave off the beard, get a haircut, and start dressing like a professional. Is that understood?"

My head dropped. But I consented. With plans to remain in the ministry, I should have once and for all severed my relationship with the Independent Baptist denomination and transitioned to a different mission agency. But now, while trying desperately to salvage my marriage, I felt the urgency to invest my time and energy in that effort, not in building a totally new network of supporters with an alternative denomination. So, for the time being, as awkward as it was, I would stay with IBWO and comply with the rules.

As I made plans to visit our supporting churches, I also took the initiative to honor Sherri's long-ago request to read self-help books focusing on marriage. I was determined to reconstitute myself as a half-decent husband. And I seriously needed help. So, contrary to my norm, I read bestselling volumes such as *Love Must Be Tough* by Dr. James Dobson, and *The Act Of Marriage* by Tim and Beverly LaHaye. And for the first time in years, I found the unction to think constructively and optimistically about my and Sherri's relationship. I actually tried to put into practice the principles heralded in the books. I even found the will to assist more with our kids, especially with Shanda who was only three months old.

I didn't know if my efforts were reaching Sherri's heart or not. She was difficult to read, and I wasn't going to push for her to give me a grade. To do so seemed premature and possibly counterproductive. So I just held my breath and endeavored every day to be a more focused husband and father. Work-wise, though, I couldn't just sit around and do nothing while waiting to see if Sherri was going to stay in the marriage. So, I started visiting our supporting churches, especially the ones closest to home.

One day I stepped out on a limb and asked Sherri if she would entertain the notion of returning to Norway. With fury-filled eyes, she instantly snapped at me. "Are you serious?

I'll never move back to Norway with you!" She let me know quickly that in her mind Norway was my 'mistress,' that Norway was the one that had stolen my heart and sabotaged our family. My spirit went completely flat.

A few days later I received a phone call from one of the co-pastors of the Oslo international church. "Randy," he said, "We need to know if you're coming back. If you are, we'll carry on as is until you get here. But if you're not, we'll go ahead and invite *Robert to step into the role of senior pastor."

Robert, his wife, and three daughters had moved to Norway a year earlier. They were serving as missionaries with a different Independent Baptist mission agency. Robert had settled in Oslo with the specific goal of planting an Independent Baptist church for Norwegians. While he and his wife attended Norwegian language classes, he and his family attended the international church on Sundays, both for the English-speaking fellowship and nourishment. Before I left Norway I had asked Robert to preach on a few occasions. The three co-pastors now leading the church were inviting him to speak semi-regularly. They felt he would gladly serve as the senior pastor if I wasn't coming back.

At that point I literally made one of the hardest decisions I've ever made in life.

Chapter 32

"I can't believe I'm saying this," I choked up, "but it looks like our days in Norway are over." It nearly killed me to say the words and to know they were true. "Yeah...so...go ahead and ask Robert if he'll step up to be the senior pastor."

With the hope of returning to Norway no longer an official part of my life, I really just wanted to crawl into a corner somewhere and die. I couldn't have felt emptier. Yes, Norway had been the merchant of my near-disintegration. It had seduced me and shown me the depth of my heartlessness. But more so it had been my most treasured experience in life. It had taught me, matured me, and shown me my potential for spiritual passion and leadership. It had stretched me in a way that was irreversible. And, inexplicably, I wanted more.

But it was over.

And in secret I wept uncontrollably. Now that Norway with all of its wonders had slipped indelibly from my life, could I even find the energy to move on? I honestly didn't know.

The ensuing days, weeks, and months passed numbly. I tried to be a more attentive husband and father. And I spoke in our supporting churches. But beneath the surface, I carried a sadness that colored everything I did.

When Sherri's sixth-month deadline finally arrived, I held my breath. I didn't know if I had done enough to redeem myself or not. She didn't mention the time line. So, I figured, in spite of my melancholy spirit over not returning to Norway, I had somehow managed to recapture a smidgen of her heart, or at least a bit of her hope. Or maybe it was my willingness to sacrifice Norway for the sake of our marriage that made her feel slightly forgiving. So, I continued to forge ahead and report to our supporting churches.

If we were going to keep our family intact, we had to decide soon if we were permanently staying in the States or returning as missionaries to another foreign country. I was missing Europe so badly that I grew nauseated by the very thought of remaining stateside. So, one day I sheepishly broached the subject. "Do you think you'd be willing to try again in another country?" I muttered to Sherri.

She didn't immediately answer.

After some time, though, she sketchily hinted that neither our marriage nor our ministry was a lost cause. Perhaps it was her calling at the age of fifteen to be a missionary; perhaps it was her yearning to do what was right regardless of her feelings; perhaps it was just her womanly strength; perhaps it was a fusion of all three, but one day she agreed to give it one more try, but not in Norway.

Where would we go then? That became the big question. It would definitely be somewhere in western Europe. That's where we felt the greatest needs were. That's where we felt God would give us another chance. But where exactly?

It was eventually decided—with what we perceived as God's approval—that West Germany would be the land where we would write the next chapter of our marriage and ministry. The country of the Saxons and Prussians would present a clean slate for us. We had only set foot in that part of Europe on two occasions; once while passing through—by train—on our way to Italy; and once while briefly visiting a IBWO missionary family. Otherwise, our knowledge of the country, the culture, the people, and the cuisine was the tiny amount we had picked up from television.

I promptly commenced talking to every German I met, every American from German descent, and everyone who had travelled to Germany for business or vacation. I took mental notes.

Our goal in ministry would be to plant another international church. This alone dictated that our next place of residence would be one of the huge metropolitan areas that claimed numerous international cooperations and schools—Hamburg, Frankfurt, or Munich. Nearly everyone I spoke to with any firsthand knowledge of the country said, "Of those three, Munich is where you want to be."

So, in the absence of any audible instructions from God, I decided once again, by faith—with Sherri's consent—to select a direction and head that way, trusting God to slam the door if I was choosing wrongly. So, based on the cumulative voices and insights of others, I selected Munich as our next home. Munich, the birthplace of the world renowned Octoberfest and the home of six major breweries, was the state capital of Bavaria. The population was 1,270,000. The city was only thirty-five miles from the foot of the baby Alps. The location, with a mountainous terrain like Norway, would be a minor consolation.

With a measure of certainty restored to my life I felt a tinge of excitement for the first time in months. I immediately sent out a newsletter informing our supporters of our new direction.

> Dear Friends,
> We are pioneers again. And that means we need your prayers and support as much as ever. After turning the international church in Oslo over to new leadership and seeking God's face for new guidance, we feel he is opening the door for us to start a new international church in Munich, West Germany. We're both excited and hopeful. But we don't underestimate the challenge. Our goal will be to duplicate in Munich the ministry we had in Oslo. As we gave additional emphasis to reaching the Norwegians while in Oslo we will give the same additional emphasis to reaching Germans while in Munich.

I justified my decision to stick with IBWO by iterating to myself that others in the organization, both at executive and field levels, skimped on the rules and policies when not around hardliners in the group. If others could do it, so could I. So, right or wrong, I kept us under IBWO's umbrella simply because it was less disruptive to the process of returning overseas. Plus, we were being supported—above all else—for the purpose of establishing a Bible-believing church, an ongoing presence of light and truth for the international community. And I was confident we could achieve that goal. We would certainly give it our all.

Committed to our new direction, I started announcing our plans in-person to our supporting congregations. And, soon, extra financial support started streaming in.

Nine months before our set departure date, however, the world was shocked by the news of an explosion at the Chernobyl Nuclear Power Plant in Ukraine. The plume of radioactive fallout was blown hundreds of miles northwardly and westerly, dangerously contaminating grain and dairy products. Munich, the "dairy farm" of Germany was 860 miles due west of Chernobyl.

"Surely you're not moving there now!" friends and relatives exclaimed. "It's too dangerous!"

Feeling that there were now just too many things in motion to reverse course, we decided to stubbornly move forward and trust God with our lives.

But when we were only a few months away from departure, an incident did happen that made me regret my decision to proceed with IBWO.

Chapter 33

I had just finished giving an on-site report and missionary challenge to a supporting church in Indiana. I sensed that I had established rapport with the people and that my message had reached their hearts. A sweet spirit held the crowd gently in its grip. Not wanting to just coldly and abruptly kill the moment, I asked everyone to join hands in a circle around the periphery of the auditorium. I then asked two or three people to pray out loud, one-at-a-time, for whatever was on their heart. Several people prayed. There were even a few tears.

Too soon, it seemed, the meeting was over.

The pastor immediately pulled me aside. "What did you just do?" Before I could even understand the meaning of the question or attempt to respond, he launched into a tirade. "You never do anything like that without talking to me first! I'm really angry right now! That whole thing smacked of pure pentecostalism! Standing in a circle! Holding hands! Have you gone completely charismatic?"

I was speechless.

"Well!"

"No, I'm not...uh...pentecostal or charismatic."

"Well, you've just left me with a lot of doubt! As a matter of fact, our church really needs to reevaluate whether we should keep supporting you or not!"

In the car, driving back to Atlanta through the night, I was so distraught over the pastor's over-the-edge legalism that I couldn't wait to pick up my *Wisdom Hunter* manuscript again and once and for all illustrate in a true-to-life drama the irrationality of such legalistic behavior. I suddenly remembered the words of the visiting stranger in Switzerland, "the book you're writing will one day be completed and will be a source of help to many people." I determined that night that I would pick up where I had left off in the story and do my best to finish the manuscript. Besides, my source material for the storyline was now greater than ever. First, though, I needed to know if the 260 pages I had completed years earlier were even readable.

So in the next day or two I unboxed the partially written story, bound in a three-ring notebook, and carefully selected four individuals outside IBWO's circle to be my test readers. With eagerness, the individuals took copies I'd printed. Their enthusiasm increased when I explained the premise of the story. They indicated they would give me feedback within a week or two.

I hoped, of course, that their response would be semi-positive. When two weeks passed, though, all four of the test readers, one by one, returned their copy, confessing they had managed to read only a few pages. The typical response was, "I wanted to read the whole thing. But time just got away from me." And "I know you're under a deadline. So I'm going to go ahead and give it back." I was pretty certain what they really meant was, *What you wrote just isn't interesting. Nothing about the style of writing, the story, or the characters held my interest or pulled me through.* All four individuals were southerners by birth and were just too polite to be forthright. They didn't want to hurt my feelings.

I was deflated and wasn't sure exactly what I should do. Had my dream of shouting at my peers in 'story form' died a quick death? Had the Swiss encouragers been wrong? Perhaps I should just throw the pages in the garbage and forget the whole idea. But my anger toward legalistic, authoritarian pastors was just too deep. So I made a last-ditch decision. I approached a published writer in my community, a Christian lady who was a successful educator, and said, "I'll pay you if you'll read all two-hundred and sixty pages and give me an honest critique." She agreed. And we settled on a price.

Less than two weeks later, the lady contacted me. "I read every page you gave me. But I did so, only because you paid me. All I can say is, it's obvious you know nothing about writing a novel."

"No," I stammered in embarrassment, "I've never taken any writing courses. I was just guessing at it and trying to do my best."

The lady raised her eyebrows. "When you present the storyline orally, I believe it has potential. But the story as you've written it here is honestly...worthless." She reached for a pen and paper. "Here, let me give you a list of ingredients that are required for the making of a good novel." She made a list of about six items:

- Develop all the primary characters, with full emotions and thoughts
- Establish a hook that will keep the reader wondering
- Keep every action plausible and true-to-life

- Balance the pace
- Balance the descriptive details
- And don't forget the usage of colors, smells, sights, and sounds

"If you really want this story to be published," she stressed, "you'll have to trash what you've given me and start over at page one. And please, if you start over, take the story out of first person and put it into third person. That alone will make it easier for you."

The lady's words, which I reluctantly embraced, took the last bit of air out of me as a hopeful creator of a significant novel. Instead of trashing the 260 pages, though, I packed them away for posterity, never again to be the starting point for a book. Over the following week I sighed with genuine sadness. Maybe...just maybe...I'd give it another try one day and start over at page one. I kept the lady's "list of ingredients."

A couple of weeks later, when I had recouped from the emotional hit and was focusing on other things, I went to Sherri and said, "What would you like for us to do for our upcoming anniversary?" Considering the delicate state of our relationship, I wanted to be attentive. With as much energy as I could muster, I wanted to make our eleventh anniversary a special occasion.

"I don't really care," she rejoined with a low dose of enthusiasm. "I'll do whatever. You plan it."

Her lack of interest made me nervous. What could I do to make the occasion memorable? I decided it was time to create a husband-and-wife memory using the motorcycle. "What about a motorcycle trip?" I quizzed. "We could ride to Asheville, North Carolina and tour the Biltmore House." The Biltmore House, the largest privately owned house in

America, had been attracting tourists for a hundred years. Sherri didn't look overly excited. I quickly added, "I know this would be your first lengthy ride. So, I would make it easy. We would stop and take a break every thirty minutes or so. We would take two days to get there and two days to get back." At that time in 1986 there were no major expressways linking Atlanta to Asheville. It took seven hours to make the one-way trip on country highways.

"If that's what you want," she responded flatly.

I wasn't sure how to read her. But personally I felt enlivened. Here was a great opportunity to be alone—just husband and wife—without the kids. I truly hoped it would be a great adventure for us. It would be something we had never done before and would possibly help renew our bond.

The morning we loaded the bike to leave Atlanta, though, an ominous storm darkened the entire horizon to the southwest and was moving our direction. To stay dry I sped northward to outrun the rain, wind, and lightening. In our flight, I failed to keep my word to stop every thirty minutes. To keep us dry, I ran for an hour and a half before I pulled into a convenience store parking lot for our first break. By that time, we were just south of Gainesville, Georgia.

When we got off the bike, Sherri was unusually quiet. All she said was that her head and back were aching. She appeared seriously tense. I tried to lighten the mood. "We outran the bad weather!" I exclaimed in celebration. "Here, let's get a snack and something to drink. And we'll rest awhile."

And then I innocently made one of the biggest mistakes I could make at that point in our delicate egg-shell marriage.

Chapter 34

Standing outside the convenience store, Sherri and I were eating a pack of peanut-butter crackers and enjoying a coke when four motorcycles, with a couple on each, pulled in at the store. The motorcycle community is interwoven with an incontestable camaraderie. After the lead biker helped his wife off their bike and removed his helmet, he approached me on his way into the store. "How are you doing, man?"

"Doing great. And you?"

"Just heading north to eat dinner at the Dillard House this evening. How about you guys?"

"We're celebrating our anniversary. We're working our way to the Biltmore House in Asheville."

"Well...you're going in our direction. If you don't have any hard and fast plans for the next few hours, why don't you join us? The Dillard House is one of the best restaurants in the state. Have you eaten there before?"

"No," I confessed, shaking my head.

"Oh man...you and your wife would absolutely love it! We're going to be here at the store for a few minutes, so think about it and let me know."

As the couples disappeared inside, memories of the group

ride in Cyprus commandeered my thoughts. Suddenly, here was a rare opportunity to reenact a group adventure and introduce Sherri to the excitement of such a unique experience.

The Dillard House, located in Dillard, Georgia, was thirty miles farther north than I had planned to go for the day. But I so badly wanted us to have the fun experience that I convinced myself the extra time and miles would fly by because of the group synergy. Instead of overnighting where I had planned in Clarksville, we could simply overnight in Dillard. I had not made hotel reservations anyway. Besides, wasn't flexibility a key part of a great adventure?

Minimizing the fact that Sherri had already told me her head and back were aching, and that, by all appearances, she was not in a jovial mood, I selfishly asked, "What do you say? Shall we ride with them?"

"Whatever you want," she responded brusquely.

So I told the leader of the group we'd join them for their jaunt to the Dillard House.

"Before we pull out, though," the leader informed me, "one of my buddies has to repair his helmet-to-helmet communication set. Once he's ready, we'll leave."

I simply nodded. The delay would give Sherri a few more minutes to stretch and relax.

What we were not expecting, though, is that the "repair" would take forty-five minutes. By the time we left the parking lot and pointed our bikes northward, the storm that Sherri and I had earlier outrun was within sight and bearing down on us. It soon overtook us. The team leader found a canopy at a liquor store where we took shelter for a few minutes. But, by that time, everyone in the groups was already wet. For thirty minutes, we watched the rain pound the earth around us. The moment the heaviest of the clouds moved off in a north-easterly direction, leaving a light sprinkle, the other four couples removed rain suits from their panniers, put them on, and said, "Let's hit the road."

Sherri and I didn't have rain suits.

By the time we reached the Dillard House, we had long since left the rain. But our soaked attire had chilled us to the bone. And our extra sets of clothes— stuffed inside a duffel bag strapped to the sissy bar—were now soaked as well. The sun was too low in the sky to provide any substantial warmth. And the wait to be seated for dinner was an hour and fifteen minutes.

At that point, I was feeling like scum. I had not stopped every thirty minutes to take a break. And I had already taken us thirty miles farther than I told her we would go the first day. She was acutely aware of my violations. The ache in her back and head had spread to her neck, shoulders, and buttocks. She was wet, cold, and utterly miserable. Understandably, she was also consumed with a low-boiling anger. But she was also hungry. All we had eaten throughout the day was a pack of crackers. So, we waited in line with the four couples.

I asked a few people around us about hotels in the area.

"There's only one here in town," I was informed. "It's up the street on the lefthand side."

I told Sherri we would go over to the hotel immediately following the meal, check in, and take a hot shower. This was the best news she had heard all day. Her eyes revealed a glimmer of exasperated relief.

When we finished dinner, we left the four couples and went straightaway to the hotel. It was 8:30 PM. But, there was no room available.

Neither was there a room available in Franklin, North Carolina—the next nearest town, twenty miles further up the road on our northernly route. "I'm sorry," a hotel clerk explained, "We're having a big gem cutter's convention. All the hotels in town have been booked for weeks."

No! No!

We faced the same situation in the town of Dillsboro, another twenty miles northward, over a portion of the Nantahala Mountain range.

This is an outright nightmare, I told myself as I slapped my helmet. *This can't be happening!*

I could now hear Sherri weeping.

Thirty miles further, in the dead of night, we arrived in Maggie Valley, a resort town with numerous hotels. But, as I rode up and down the strip, all I saw was "No Vacancy" signs flashing in the night.

At 2:00 in the morning, I stopped at the first hotel I saw near Asheville, the town that was our ultimate destination. I shuffled to the front desk. My hips and legs were so stiff I could barely walk. I'm sure I looked like a patient who had just prematurely left the emergency room of a hospital. Before I could open my mouth, the middled-aged woman at the desk said, "If you're looking for a room, we're fully booked."

I stood there for a few seconds in disbelief, then mumbled a plea. "Can you call another hotel and find a room for me and my wife. We've been on a motorcycle all day. We just can't go any farther."

"I'm sorry. I've already called around for a few other people who've stopped by. And I haven't been able to locate a room anywhere. It's probably because of the big music festival that's going on."

I shook my head. I was utterly stunned. Why, oh why, hadn't I made hotel reservations for this special occasion in our life? As I returned to the motorcycle where Sherri was standing with our duffel bag, I tried to brace myself as the bearer of the worst possible news. But before I could say a word, Sherri could see in my face and demeanor the bleakness of the situation. She simply dropped her helmet on the asphalt with a thud, walked across the parking lot with the duffel bag in her arms, and disappeared into the woods on the back side of the property.

"Sherri!" I wheezed.

She totally ignored me. I quickly moved the motorcycle so it wasn't blocking the hotel's doorway and went in search of my wife. I found her lying on the ground beneath the hotel's giant satellite dish. I laid down and made an attempt to snuggle up behind her.

"Don't touch me!" she articulated with the intensity of an emboldened kidnap victim.

I backed away. There, on our eleventh anniversary, we squirmed to get comfortable on the hard ground, with a stray dog sniffing us, and eventually fell asleep.

Around 5:00 AM, I felt an elbow jab me in the chest. "Huh…what?" I muttered.

"Get up and find a room where someone's checking out early. We can use the room till check out time." The words were not a suggestion; they were a command.

Groggily I made my way to a grassy knoll overlooking the whole row of first and second floor rooms. I sat down. I was so sleepy, my head was nodding and jerking. Finally around 5:30 I saw a door open. A man carrying a small suitcase stepped out and walked to a car two slots from his door. I stood up and staggered in his direction.

"Excuse me, sir," I said, trying to sound alert. "Can I speak to you for a moment?" I gave him a rambling overview of Sherri's and my plight. And then leveled the request. "Can we possibly use your room until check-out time?"

The man seemed on the verge of dismissing me as a kook. And then Sherri stumbled around the corner. The man took one look at her, turned to me with a look of shock, and said, "Sure. Here's the key. Just please be out by eleven."

In less than a minute, Sherri and I stepped into the room and locked the door behind us. We had five blessed hours before check-out time. The room was set up with two double beds and two sets of towels and washcloths. Only one bed had been used, and only one set of towels. The clean bed, clean set of bath linen, toilet facilities, and hot water were a taste of heaven. We could not have been more appreciative. We hurriedly showered, spread out our clothes to dry, jumped in the bed and fell asleep.

We didn't want to budge when the alarm clock sounded. But we had no choice. Right before we exited the room at eleven, Sherri gave me another no-nonsense order. "Call the Charm House in Clarksville and make reservations for tonight." The Charm House was a beautiful antebellum home utilized as a Bed and Breakfast. We had gawked at the classy lodge when we shot through town the day before, the town where I had promised to stay our first night.

I called and secured a reservation.

Knowing we had a place to sleep for the night, we stuck to our original plan, loaded the bike, and rode six miles to the Biltmore House for a tour of the world-famous property. What we saw of the mansion, in between incurable nods of fatigue, was more than impressive. But half sleeping through the presentations, we registered only a small portion of everything the guide told us. At the end of the tour, we explored the prestigious grounds a bit, and then crawled back on the motorcycle for a half-day ride back to Clarksville.

The afternoon ride was relatively quiet.

We finally arrived at the Charm House around 5:00 PM. We checked into our room and promptly fell asleep. We awoke around 7:30 and asked the hostess to recommend a restaurant for our evening meal.

"Well, it's Sunday evening. There's only one place in town that's still open. It's right across the street. But they close at 8:00. So you'll need to hurry."

We dressed and rushed over.

Sherri and I were the only customers at that hour. The only available food was a leftover assortment of meats and vegetables that had been sitting on the steamer all day. We dined on the wilted, tasteless grub while the only server on duty stacked chairs and mopped the floor around us.

"Happy eleventh anniversary," I mumbled to Sherri.

She barely looked at me.

Heidi, seven at the time, listened to Sherri's description of the trip when we returned home and thought the whole story was hilarious. "Tell about your eleventh anniversary," she would forever beg when we were with a new group of people. Sherri, though, never thought the adventure was worth laughing about. And together we never went anywhere again without a confirmed booking or reservation.

Except to Munich.

And that would be another huge blunder, on my part, that would nearly push our whole family over the precipice.

Chapter 35

As we prepped for our family's move to Munich, I raised additional money to buy used furniture and a used car once inside Germany. I decided I would ship the motorcycle over, along with a few other household goods. The Yamaha would serve as a second vehicle.

A couple of months before our departure, Sherri and I received a long distance phone call from Heidelberg, Germany. On the other end was a young American husband and father we knew well. He and his wife had been among the first members of our international church in Norway. The couple had surrendered to full-time ministry while at the church and had ended up in Heidelberg serving as missionaries with a nondenominational mission agency.

"You guys are welcomed to stay with us in our apartment while you scout out Munich and search for a house," came the generous offer. Heidelberg was three and a half hours by autobahn from Munich. Distance-wise it wouldn't be convenient. But it would save us a bunch of hotel money while I tried to find a house to rent. And it would give us friends to talk to.

"I don't know how long it'll take to find a house and sign a contract," I confessed. "It might take a week or two."

"We have room," our friend assured us.

"Alright then. Let's plan on it."

Sherri, Heidi, Shanda, and I flew into Frankfurt on December 28, 1986. The motorcycle was flown into Munich and would be stored there till later. Our host family greeted us at the Frankfurt airport with enthusiastic smiles and hugs. We all piled into their van and made our way to their apartment in Heidelberg. It was the second time Sherri and I had uprooted our household and moved to a country that was foreign to us. We didn't know a single soul in the country except for the husband and wife hosting us, and their children. We didn't know the language. We didn't know the culture. Yet, because of our previous experience in Norway, we assumed we were better prepared for the inevitable culture shock. But, we learned that moving internationally is analogous to taking a cold shower. Once a person takes a cold shower, he knows the shock the body undergoes when hit with freezing water. He can tell his body not to flinch the next time. But it doesn't help. His body will still jerk, and will still fight with every nerve and muscle to flee the biting discomfort.

So, again we wept the first few nights in Heidelberg wondering what in the world we were doing. Had we made a big mistake? Consequently, we were not in the mood for celebrating New Year's Eve. But we put on happy faces and watched the sky-filled fireworks from atop the apartment's parking deck.

Two days later, I went to work. My initial objective was to purchase a reliable, pre-owned automobile. The shopping and test driving went unusually quick. Within forty-eight hours we were the glad owners of a two-year-old, red and black Opel Kadett.

A couple of days later, I awakened early and drove to Munich on my inaugural scouting trip. My goal for the one-day venture was to locate the section of city where the greatest concentration of expats lived – teachers from the international schools; engineers and reps from the big international firms; officers and staff from the consulates; etc. That's where I would seek to find a house or apartment.

When I entered the Bavarian capital for the first time I was nearly overcome by the scope of the place. I felt like a minnow in the middle of the Pacific Ocean. I didn't know a single soul among the 1.2 million people who inhabited the metropolis."

Within thirty minutes I was standing inside an Immobilien office (real estate office) speaking to a sales agent. My Heidelberg host had helped me with this bit of information. The middle-aged lady in the office informed me that "Starnberg is the suburb where a lot of expats choose to live."

I promptly drove to the southwestern suburb, thirty minutes away, and surveyed the area. The town was beautiful, sitting on the northern shore of Lake Starnberg. The district, I quickly learned, was one of the most coveted places to live in the Munich area.

"I'm looking for a furnished single-family home for around twelve-hundred dollars a month," I explained to a local real estate agent.

The agent, an older man, laughed at me. "Number one; it's not possible to find a furnished house or apartment in Germany. Number two; ninety-five percent of the people in Munich live in attached housing. A single-family home is almost impossible to find. Number three; if you do find a single-family home, it's going to cost you a lot more than twelve-hundred dollars a month. And number four; I don't know if anyone has informed you, but there is a real shortage of inventory right now. So, I think you're out of luck."

To my dismay, this same message was repeated by three other real estate agencies.

Over the next two weeks I made several three-and-a-half hour trips from Heidelberg, convinced I would find a place to live in spite of the stated odds. Yet, only one house even became available to look at. And I was shocked to find the kitchen devoid of cabinets, sinks, counters, and appliances. Cold and hot water pipes protruded from bare, naked walls. "This is standard in Germany," the real estate agent explained. "The renter has to buy and install all his own kitchen hardware. He also has to provide his own wardrobes since our houses do not come with built-in closets."

What! I had indeed raised money for furniture – a bed or two, a kitchen table, and a sofa. But there was definitely not sufficient funds in the account to outfit an entire kitchen, along with everything else. This was demoralizing.

I decided shortly thereafter that the one-day excursions here and there were not an efficient use of time or gasoline. So, as a family, we thanked our host and hostess for their immense kindness and moved down to Starnberg where I secured a hotel room for a few days. I then spent all day, everyday, searching for a place of residency.

But quickly, we were tapping into our "furniture fund" to cover the cost of an extended hotel stay. And there was no end in sight.

Sherri was weary all over again, and rightly so. Prior to our move to Germany, I had spent 99% of my time and energy preparing for our departure, and only a miserly 1% preparing for our arrival. Before leaving the States I should have learned about Germany's housing shortage. I should have learned about the necessity to purchase all the kitchen hardware for rental properties. I should have learned that we would need free-standing wardrobes. I should have been better prepared. And I wasn't. Of course, it didn't help that IBWO, who had commissioned missionary families for years to minister across Germany, had not offered us a single iota of information about transitioning to the central European country.

In order to salvage some of our furniture money, I moved us out of the hotel and into a vacation efficiency that had been closed for the winter. The one-bedroom apartment with a small kitchenette and sitting area was located on a dairy farm isolated on the eastern shore of Lake Starnberg. The owners graciously re-opened the apartment and allowed us to stay there for as long as we needed during the winter months. The cost per night was about one-fifth the cost of the hotel. So, we settled in and intensified our search for a place to call home. Every morning Sherri and I scoured regional papers for listings of available rental properties. We quickly learned the German words for "house," "apartment," "rooms," "bedrooms," "square feet," "bathrooms," and "utilities." We became proficient at reading rental ads.

While I chased leads, Sherri home-schooled Heidi in her second-grade studies and tried at the same time to entertain Shanda who was now an active one-and-a-half year old. Workwise the days were long and tiring. Daylight-wise, they were short and frigid. The cold, the snow, and the extended darkness simply piled on the dreariness we felt.

Two weeks into the isolation on the farm, with still no prospective home, Sherri snapped. We had just perused the morning papers. There wasn't a single listing, either a house or an apartment, that we could afford. Without warning, Sherri stood up, grabbed her coat, and walked out of the apartment. She slammed the door behind her. Heidi, Shanda, and I all just looked at each other.

I ran to the window.

Sherri, in jeans, was trudging across a field covered knee-deep in snow. I watched her disappear over a hill, a hundred yards away. I started to throw on my coat and run after her. But Shanda started crying uncontrollably. I had to let Sherri go. She probably wanted to be left alone anyway. If she didn't return in an hour's time I would follow her trail and find her.

Almost exactly an hour later, right as I was getting ready to look for her, Sherri—with swollen and tear-stained eyes—walked back into the apartment. A mile away, she had found a small Catholic chapel where, alone in the building, she had angrily emptied her heart and soul before God. "I was at least willing to come to this God forsaken place!" she'd blasted the heavens. "Why can't you at least give me a place to live!"

There, alone in the presence of the Almighty, she'd found the smallest bit of strength, strength enough to at least face another sunrise and to keep breathing.

Chapter 36

One morning, after five weeks at the vacation efficiency, we saw an ad in a small rural newspaper that was hardly believable. A house had come to the market place, a house that was fully furnished and at our $1200-a-month price point. The downside was the location. The house was in the countryside thirty-eight miles from Munich and thirty miles from Starnberg. It was nowhere near our targeted audience. But we were so desperate for a place of our own, having burned through most of the money in our furniture account, that we immediately called the listed number. A secretary answered. She explained that the owner was a single man in his forties who was a journalist in the pop music industry. The owner's name was Wolfgang Heilemann.

We made an appointment to meet with Heilemann that afternoon at the rental house.

As we drove southward into the country for the rendezvous, I kept thinking that the distance from Munich to wherever we were going was just too great. Planting an international church in downtown Munich from so far away just would not be practical. As excited as we were about looking at the house and hopefully having first options to rent, I was convinced we were wasting our time.

And then we saw the house.

Throughout the dairy region of Bavaria, the architectural norm was for the farm house and barn to be linked together by a large utilitarian mudroom. The farmer, during the winter months, could access the cows and farm equipment from his house without having to venture outside for lengthy periods of time. Many of these structures were "L" shaped, the house comprising one wing, the barn the other. Such was the house we were now ogling. Heilemann the owner, though, had paid to have the barn section rebuilt as part of the house. The property was absolutely gorgeous, looking like an iconic home in a magazine ad. The large "L" shaped house was a three-story white stucco structure with ceramic red-tile roofing. Painted flowers adorned the brown shutters. The property was surrounded by a well-built wooden fence. There was even a two-car garage attached to the house. Everything, at least from the outside, looked to be top-quality craftsmanship.

And I liked Wolfgang the moment I met him. He was slightly cross-eyed and looked older than he was. But he smiled a lot and was refreshingly forthright. Because of his work in the pop music industry he spoke fluent English

"Welcome to Reindlschmiede," he said, highlighting the name of the surrounding village. With a natural air of authority, he promptly ushered us inside the house, explaining that only one wing of the big "L" shaped house was for rent. The other wing was his weekend getaway retreat. "So, what brings you guys here from the States?" he asked as we stepped into the entryway.

"We've come to start a church for Munich's international community," I replied. I had learned in Europe, from firsthand experience, that I should always avoid saying *I'm here as a missionary to your country*. That particular combination of words was just too offensive and off putting. However, it was completely benign to say *I'm here to plant a church for the expat community*. Most Europeans, even though unchurched, received this purpose statement with no resistance at all. It was as if they thought *Good, the international community needs it; thanks for your service*.

"So you're a priest?" Heilemann probed.

"More a pastor than a priest," I offered, attempting to distinguish myself from Bavaria's state Catholic church.

Strangely, Heilemann asked no further questions about my pastoral role. Most importantly, he didn't seem to be put off in the least. Rather, he carried through with the tour as if Sherri and I were the only potential renters in the country. The wing he showed us was a three-story, four-bedroom, one-and-a-half bath Bavarian marvel. The house had a fully functional kitchen – a full range of built-in cabinets that were painted decoratively in Bavarian bauernmalerei, a built-in sink and counter, an oven, a stove, and a refrigerator. The dining room was equipped with a heavy wooden table and chairs that could seat six. The living room, though tiny, was furnished with sofas and a TV. Sherri and I could hardly believe our eyes. The windows throughout the house were even dressed with custom-made curtains and curtain rods. The master bedroom was furnished with a king-size canopy bed, along with built-in closets highlighted in bauernmalerei. The remaining bedrooms were furnished as well.

"And, of course, half the garage would be available to you" Heilemann added.

Sherri and I were nearly speechless.

"If you're interested," Heilemann stressed, "I'm ready to

move fast. All I need is two months rent up front as a deposit and a letter from your employer guaranteeing you are gainfully employed and have an adequate monthly income for living in Bavaria. And then we can sign a contract."

Sherri and I didn't need to even confer with one another or have a discussion. This felt like a bona fide gift from God; a magnanimous gift from His generous heart. "We'll take it," we both voiced our consensus.

Three days later, when all the conditions had been met, Sherri and I sat with Heilemann at the Reindlschmiede house and signed the contract. The only part of the contract that didn't thrill me, but was standard in Germany I was told, was the paragraph that said when we eventually moved out of the house we would be obligated to leave the interior walls newly painted from top to bottom.

A day later we took possession of the keys and moved in.

Two days afterward, the crate that had been held in storage, containing the motorcycle and a few household goods, was delivered to the house. As Sherri and I unloaded the goods and put them in their place, we were once again amazed beyond words at God's provision. How could it be – a playboy in the pop music industry gladly renting his house, one of the only furnished homes in Bavaria, to a U.S. pastor and his family! To us, this had God's fingerprints all over it.

Still, we were too far out in the country, it seemed, to have any kind of effective ministry. Perhaps we could continue to look for a house in downtown Munich while we used our time in Reindlschmiede to learn the German language.

As we settled into the village, a cluster of thirteen homes, our life for the first time in months quickly fell into a rhythm of blissful normalcy. I busied myself acquiring resident permits, bank accounts, health insurance policies, German driver's licenses, and such. Sherri melded into the routine of homeschooling Heidi for the final half of the second grade. Everybody in the village knew from community gossip that an American family had moved into the neighborhood. Only one person, though, could greet us in English. That individual was a thirteen-year-old girl. Her name was Kerstin. She was a confident, delightful teen who lived with her mother and grandmother on the other side of a major two-lane highway bordering the village.

Drawn to our intact family, Kerstin was at our house nearly everyday after school, often for meals. Heidi and Shanda loved her. Kerstin quickly became an integral part of our household. As a plus, she assisted in translating for us while we shopped for groceries or tried to understand German documents.

Life was good.

As spring approached, Sherri enrolled in a German-language course offered once a week for ninety minutes in a nearby town. The class was far from intense, but was the only available option in the area. Plus, Bayerisch—the dialect spoken in Bavaria—was not actually taught in the program. Rather, High German was the curriculum used. I stayed with the girls when Sherri attended the class. I decided I would try to pick up the language later.

My focus and priority shifted to ministry. In all my running around to legally register our family in the country I became familiar with several of the small towns on the south side of Munich—Penzberg, Bad Heilbrunn, Bad Tolz, Konigsdorf, Benedikbeuern—and at the same time discovered there were two U.S. military bases not far from our new address. One of the bases was located in Bad Tolz. The other was in Bad Aibling. The presence of the American communities so close by intrigued me. So, why not take the initiative and attempt to start a weekly Bible study with a few Americans? Those Americans might possibly adopt our vision and help us plant an international church. The idea sounded both plausible and exciting. So I joined a "special forces" softball team at the Bad Tolz military base and started making friends.

But before I could launch an official Bible study, our family was struck with an unimaginable tragedy that completely sidelined us.

Chapter 37

I was on the softball field at Bad Tolz, playing left field, when a soldier ran up to the foul line at third base. "Is there a Randy Dodd here?" he shouted breathlessly.

"Uh...yeah...I'm Randy Dodd," I yelled, waving my arm. *Had I done something wrong?* After all, I was a naive civilian on a highly secure "special forces" military base.

"Sir, you need to report home immediately!" the soldier blurted. "We've received word your daughter's been hit by a car!"

"What!" No...no...! This can't be! It's got to be a mistake! The entirety of my insides instantly constricted to the max. "Which daughter?" I screamed. "Is she okay? Is she dead? Is she alive?" I was breathless as I shot past the solider bearing the news.

"I don't have details, sir!" the solider's words followed me as I ran to my car.

I broke all traffic rules trying to get to the house as quickly as possible. Halfway home, an ambulance—with lights and sirens a blazing—passed my car in the opposite direction, heading back toward Bad Tolz. *Was Heidi the occupant? Was Shanda?* I felt like my head was going to explode with all the nightmarish scenarios that were assaulting me. I kept gasping for breath. *Oh, God! No...No...No!*

My heart rate, if possible, accelerated even more when I approached our house and saw Kerstin and a few neighbors on the side of the road engaged in a group discussion, looking panic-stricken.

When Kerstin spotted me, she ran to the car. Her eyes were swollen from intense crying. "She didn't listen to me!" she screamed. "I told her not to cross the street alone! I told her! But she didn't listen!"

"Who, Kerstin? Who?"

"Heidi! It was Heidi!"

"Is she okay? Is she alive?"

Kerstin shook her head and burst into tears again. "She was when the ambulance took her! But I don't know!"

"Was she taken to Bad Tolz?"

Unable to speak at that point, Kerstin just nodded as she gasped to breathe.

I sprayed gravel turning the car around on the shoulder of the road.

When I reached the hospital I ran inside and, like a man possessed, demanded to know where to find my wife and daughter. The nurses, looking perturbed, pointed me to a room in the emergency ward. Without seeking permission, I bolted into the room where Heidi was writhing on a table, screaming, "My stomach! My stomach!" I was terrified. I couldn't have imagined a more horrifying scene for a dad. Doctors and nurses surrounded the table in various modes of action. Sherri was standing at the end of the table, holding Heidi's head. When I approached, the doctors and nurses ignored me. Sherri, in a mystifying show of strength, looked at me with the most ghostly-looking eyes I'd ever seen and decried, "I'm doing everything I can to help! They've just taken x-rays! They're getting ready to sew up her head!" There was an open wound from Heidi's forehead, down through the eyebrow, into the eyelid. The skull was visible.

While Sherri stayed with Heidi, I fell apart. I darted out of the room to find the radiologist. I needed to know the extent of my daughter's injuries. What were the x-rays uncovering! Was my eight-year-old going to survive! Or was she facing a losing battle with too many grotesque injuries! I was on the verge of hyperventilating.

When I found the radiologists, they were scrutinizing the x-ray images taken minutes earlier. The images consisted of about twelve hard copies lined up across two wall-mounted tracks. The two male radiologists were looking back and forth from the images to one another and exchanging words. I gave them only ten seconds, then verbally hijacked their discussion. "Is she going to be okay!" I shrieked in English. "I'm her father! I need to know!"

My presence took the men by surprise. They looked silently at each other and then at me. The look in their eyes was one of uncertainty, even confusion. "Is it true your daughter was hit by an automobile, thrown thirty meters, and landed on pavement?" the older of the two men wanted to know, now looking even more confused.

My brain instantly calculated that thirty meters was one-hundred feet. *ONE-HUNDRED FEET!* How was that even possible! Every bone in her body must be broken! The panic that I felt jumped to a new level. "I just got here!" I cried. "The only thing I've been told is that she was hit by a car! That's all I know!" I held my breath, waiting for the men to tell me what the x-rays were showing.

"There's something not right," the younger doctor

pitched in. "We're going to have to take another set of images." With a new mission, they left me standing there and hurried back to Heidi's room.

With no one around to give me instructions or additional information, I quickly followed.

One of the surgeons had just stitched the cut across Heidi's forehead. He explained that it was whipstitched and was ugly. But he had needed to close the wound quickly in order for the other medics to attend to the other injuries. If Heidi lived, the stitch job could be redone at a later date by a cosmetic surgeon.

The x-ray technicians hurriedly transitioned Heidi, still screaming, to the x-ray room again. Sherri stayed at her side.

I paced the hallway like a caged tiger and frantically begged God to please spare the life of my little girl.

When the radiologists started examining the second set of images, I was right there in the room trying to subliminally rush them to tell me what they were viewing. The younger doctor finally broke the silence. "I don't understand it," he declared. "This doesn't make sense."

What? What? I tried to convey with my expression. *What in God's name are you seeing?*

"We can't explain it," the doctor added. "We've x-rayed your daughter twice from head to toe, from every angle. The head. The neck. The spine. The shoulders. The arms. The abdomen. The hips. The legs. Other than the head wound that the surgeons have just dealt with, we don't see any injuries. Nothing. No broken bones. No splintered bones. No internal hemorrhaging. Nothing. Absolutely nothing out of the ordinary. This is truly amazing. All I can say is, an angel must have been at your daughter's side."

I followed as the radiologists marched back to Heidi's room and gave their report to the head doctor.

Sherri and I stood perplexed as the doctors in the room carried out a hurried conversation in German.

"All right," the lead doctor announced to everyone. "First we need to get the pain under control. Secondly, there are no displaced or non-displaced fractures. But the patient HAS received a severe brain concussion. So we will administer drugs to try to halt any swelling. The next three days will be crucial. If the medications work, we will keep her here in Bad Tolz and monitor her around the clock. If the drugs prove to be ineffective and swelling starts to occur, we will have her flown to Munich. The hospital there will drill holes in the skull to release the pressure. So, let's do our best here."

The doctors and nurses jumped into action.

The head doctor turned to me and Sherri and pulled us aside. "As you've heard, the radiology report is a welcomed surprise for everyone. Nevertheless, don't be too optimistic. If her brain swells...well, I'll be honest with you...she can become paralyzed. She can go blind. She can become mentally impaired. Or even die. There can be an untold number of adverse effects, short term and long term. It's just impossible right now to predict the outcome. We're going to help her sleep in a few minutes. So, you're welcome to stay. You're welcome to go home and get some rest. Either way, the next three days are going to be pivotal. If you decide to go home, we'll call you the moment anything changes."

Sherri insisted on staying. She made the decision instantly. She asked me, on the other hand, to go home to take care of two important matters. My head was reeling with fright. I couldn't thank God enough that Heidi had been spared broken bones. *But possible paralysis! Blindness! Or a host*

219

of other disabilities! Even death! I squeezed the bridge of my nose until it hurt and took a deep breath. "All right, what two matters do I need to deal with?"

Sherri asked me to pick up Shanda at Kerstin's and try to comfort her, and to call our families and our home church in America and try to mobilize hundreds, if not thousands, of saints to intercede for Heidi. Sherri was, and had been, in the thick of the crisis, yet she was thinking more clearly than I was.

"Okay!" I nodded, wiping my eyes and taking another deep breath. "But first, what in the world happened? I mean...I'm a total wreck. And I don't even know anything."

Sherri hastened through the narrative of what she knew. Kerstin had been keeping Heidi and Shanda at her house for a couple of hours while she, Sherri, spent time alone baking. She had been in the middle of a recipe when Kerstin burst through the door screaming, "I told her not to cross the road by herself! I told her! I told her! But she didn't listen!" Learning within seconds that Heidi had been hit by an automobile, but not knowing if she was dead or alive, Sherri dashed out of the house barefooted and ran down to the highway. A crowd of people had already gathered around Heidi who was screaming from the middle of the road. When Sherri shoved her way through the crowd, she saw an older man kneeling over Heidi. He was gripping one of Heidi's hands that was extended from beneath a big, thick blanket covering Heidi's complete body from the neck down. The blanket was moving as Heidi writhed and screamed. The moment Sherri approached, the kneeling man turned and looked Sherri directly in the eye. And in a village full of Germans, where no one but a thirteen-year-old girl could speak English, the man declared in perfect English, "I'm a doctor. I'm taking care of your daughter. Do whatever you can to console her. I've called the paramedics. They're on their way." Sherri immediately laid down beside Heidi on the asphalt, grabbed Heidi's other hand from under the blanket, and began singing worship songs. As Heidi started to calm down, Sherri couldn't help but cry. The only part of Heidi's body that was visible was her head. And it was split open. Sherri could only imagine the myriad injuries lurking beneath the fabric. Her mother's heart sank. But she fought valiantly to remain strong and clear-headed for what was to come. And in that fight, her mind throbbed with an explosion of questions. Who was this doctor? Had he been driving the car involved in the accident? How did he know she was the mother? How did he know to speak English? How had he called the local paramedics? There was no pay phone in the area. When the ambulance arrived and the medics went into action, a young man ran up to Sherri. "I'm so sorry!" he wailed in anguish. "I didn't see her until it was too late! She ran out in the road from behind the bushes! I didn't have time to put on the brakes until after I hit her!" He explained that he was a soldier on his way home for the weekend. When he hit Heidi, she went up in the air, came down head-first on the hood, and was thrown thirty meters (one-hundred feet) up the road. Sherri saw his car, a VW Beetle. It had made contact only with Heidi, yet the hood was bashed in, the headlight was broken, the fender was dented, and the windshield was cracked. At that point, Sherri feared for Heidi's life. How could the fragile frame of an eight-year-old sustain such a traumatic impact and survive? The police arrived at the very moment Sherri climbed into the back of the ambulance with Heidi and was whisked away. Kerstin, a nervous basket case, was keeping Shanda.

Hearing the details of Sherri's account, I was left speechless. Mentally processing what I had just been told was going to take more than a few minutes. The emotional twisting and turning had barely begun and I already felt like I had surpassed my limits for stable-mindedness. Contrary to everything in me, I willed myself to comply with Sherri's urging to go home, pick up Shanda, and notify our loved ones in the States of what was happening.

Just as I was getting ready to head to the car, one of the medics walked up to us. "We've just put your daughter in a hospital gown. I saw that her skirt and blouse were torn and ripped. But...she has no asphalt burns. Or abrasions. Not one. Anywhere. She just has one thumb-size bruise on her left buttocks. How is that possible?"

Chapter 38

On day two of Heidi's stay at the hospital, I became such a disruptive figure for the doctors and nurses with my nonstop questions that I was literally banned from the property until notified otherwise.

That afternoon, at our Reindlschmiede house, Kerstin showed me where the doctor had knelt with Heidi on the asphalt. I measured the distance from there to Kerstin's driveway. The distance was indeed one hundred feet! One hundred unbelievable feet! Earlier that morning Kerstin found one of the shoes Heidi had been wearing the day of the accident. The shoe was lying about twenty yards off the pavement in a roadside field.

"The police said the driver was traveling at 90 kilometers an hour when he hit Heidi," Kerstin informed me. 90 KPH! That equated to 55 MPH!

The speed. The distance. The bashed car. The shoe. It was truly a miracle Heidi had not been killed on impact. And now there were thousands of people all over America and Europe praying she would survive the imminent threat of a brain-swell. And my mother and sister-in-law would arrive the next day to help with Shanda and assist in any other needful way that might arise.

The next morning, after picking up my mom and Sherri's sister at the airport and taking them to the house, I was invited to return to the Bad Tolz hospital to hear the lead doctor's updated report. My mom and Sherri's sister were not allowed to join me and Sherri for the appointment. So, Sherri and I met alone with the doctor.

"Gratefully," he reported with an earnest sigh of relief, "the medication has been successful. We've passed the critical three-day mark. Her brain hasn't swollen. And the odds now are that it won't."

Sherri and I embraced each other with utter joy. The moment felt surreal.

"It's still likely, though," the doctor emphasized, "that in the short-term she will suffer some loss of physical or mental coordination. It's common with concussions. So we'll keep her here for a few more days just for observation."

Sherri and I thanked the doctor profusely for the hospital's care.

Almost immediately following the greater-than-expected report, Jorgen—the young soldier who had been driving the VW Beetle—stopped by the hospital unannounced. He was overjoyed to hear that Heidi was still alive and was doing so well. He brought a stuffed animal, a pink Platypus, as a gift. He apologized over and over for the accident. We assured him that we didn't blame him. He choked up when he realized we had accepted the accident as a total twist of fate. He then answered a few questions for us.

"Regarding the doctor at the scene of the accident," Jorgen replied in thoughtful English, "he told me he was headed home to Frankfurt, eight hours away, from a holiday getaway. He didn't say why he was on back roads. But apparently he was right behind me and saw what happened. He actually stopped me from picking Heidi up and moving her off the road. He told me he was a doctor and would take care of her. He covered her with a thick blanket that he was carrying in his car. He called for the paramedics from some kind of new mobile phone inside his vehicle. When the ambulance arrived, the man mysteriously disappeared. No one got his name. Not unless you did," he said, nodding at Sherri.

Sherri gestured that she didn't.

When Jorgen finished telling us all he knew, Sherri and I stood transfixed in our thoughts. We wanted to thank the unnamed doctor. But how could we learn his identity? Was it even possible at this point to track him down? Or was the man even human? If the man indeed was a doctor from Frankfurt, his arrival in Reindlschmiede, coinciding with the accident, wasn't by chance, even if he didn't know it. Sherri and I were convinced God had orchestrated the timing. On the other hand, maybe the man was not human at all. Maybe he was some kind of celestial being, an angel. Maybe that explained the absence of broken bones and skin abrasions on Heidi's part. Maybe the "angelic doctor" had actually provided protection, or administered healing, on site. Sherri and I—emotionally spent at that point—wept just at the wonderment of the possibility.

Before Jorgen left the hospital, I garnered permission for him to meet Heidi and present the stuffed animal to her. Heidi, with her head fully bandaged, welcomed him with a smile, joyfully embraced the Platypus, and promptly named it Jorgie.

Over the next three days the doctor permitted a free

flowing rotation of visitors—me, Sherri, Shanda, Kerstin, my mom, Sherri's sister, and even Wolfgang Heilemann, our landlord. Heidi exhibited no loss of physical or mental coordination. To the contrary, she was constantly sneaking out of bed during the brief moments she was alone and was visiting kids in other hospital rooms who were immobilized with broken legs or crippling diseases. Finally, around day ten, the doctor announced, "We can't explain it, but your daughter is a walking miracle. There's really no reason for us to keep her any longer. So, we'll fill out the necessary discharge papers and she will be free to go. Do keep an eye on her, though. If she loses any physical or mental agility, notify us as soon as possible."

Two evenings later, I shouted upstairs for Heidi to come to the dinner table. She didn't respond. So I went to find her. To my surprise, she was no where in the house. We finally found her in the back yard. She was two stories high in a tree. She never lost any physical coordination.

Regarding the whole affair, someone suggested the enemy was perhaps saying, "Welcome to Germany. I'll make it really difficult for you!" But God intervened and said, "No, not this time; that's a little too much right now."

Within the framework of a few weeks, life for our family returned to a normal pace and focus. Sherri finished homeschooling Heidi who easily completed her second grade requirements. I continued to plot our new church plant, making new friends and continually searching for an available locale for a public Bible study on the southern outskirts of the capital. As we entered the beautiful months of summer, life was good. But in early August we received a phone call that slammed us with yet another round of disruption.

"Hello, is this Mister Randy Dodd?" the German female voice asked in English.

"Yes, this is Randy Dodd."

"Mister Dodd, I'm calling from the district's department of education."

"Okay."

"We see, according to official records, that you are a new resident in our area."

"For a few months now; that's correct."

"And the records show you have an eight-year-old daughter who is school age."

"Uh yea, that's correct as well."

"Well, we're not finding any documentation showing that your daughter is attending school anywhere."

"Yeah, that's true as well. My wife is teaching her here in our home."

"You mean homeschooling?"

"Exactly," I confirmed, believing the call had come to a satisfactory conclusion.

"Well, I guess you're not aware, Mister Dodd, that homeschooling is not lawful here in Germany."

Not lawful? "I'm sorry. But my wife and I both have college degrees. We're completely qualified to teach our daughter at her age level."

"I don't think you understand, Mister Dodd. You can have a doctorate, and even be a university professor, but you're still not permitted, according to German law, to homeschool your child here in our country."

I felt my pulse accelerate. "Yes, but we're not German."

"The law applies to every resident, regardless of nationality."

"And what will happen if we continue to homeschool?"

"Then it will be our obligation to report you to the

authorities. At that point, they will give you a warning. If you ignore the warning, they will revoke your resident permit and have you expelled from the country."

"Expelled from the country?"

"You're not in America anymore, Mister Dodd. You're in Germany. We have our own laws, and if you want to live here, you have to respect and obey those laws."

"Is this law just a state law in Bavaria? Or is it a national law for the whole country?"

"It's a national law. And there are NO exceptions. So, you have two weeks to register your daughter at the Bad Heilbrunn elementary school for her third grade studies." I was given the address where we had to report in person and file the registration. And the call ended.

I quickly made a few calls to other sources to confirm there was truly such a law. I learned to my shock and disappointment that the law was in place and well known.

Sherri was equally unsettled.

This was an unexpected twist that would alter the next three years of Heidi's education. How had we missed this "well-known law" in our preparations to move to Germany? Not one person or office that we talked to in advance of the move had ever mentioned this law. Not one. Not even IBWO. And IBWO had been sending missionaries to Germany for more than twenty years. What an oversight on IBWO's part to not provide us with this bit of information. It felt inexcusable.

Should we leave the country and stand by our conviction about our daughter's education? Or should we reluctantly roll with the punches, like missionaries usually did, in order to fulfill our ministerial calling?

After earnest prayers and heavy discussions, we enrolled Heidi in the Bad Heilbrunn school. We would reevaluate our decision during the school's winter break.

In late August, Sherri and I drove Heidi to her first day of classes at the German school. It was a grade-one-through-six country school with an enrollment of a hundred-and-fifty students. Heidi would be the only non-German in attendance. The headmaster said he would give her until Christmas to learn Bayerisch. At the beginning of the second semester, at the turn of the year, the teachers would grade her classwork as if she were a natural-born German.

Since the situation was unsettling for us, Sherri and I were allowed that opening day to observe the first ten minutes of class just for reassurance. It was heartbreaking as a father and mother to watch our daughter, so innocent and vulnerable, sit bug-eyed on the front row and not understand a single word spoken or written. Would she be able to handle this – day after day? Would we?

I teared up as we left the school grounds. *Oh, Father,* I prayed, *you knew this would be our reality all along. I just remind you that we're here at your commission to help advance your Kingdom. So please grant us wisdom and strength to deal with this setup. You've already performed one miracle for Heidi. Is it too much to ask for another? Please! Please help her mentally grasp the language! Somehow turn this into a blessing and an asset. Please! In Jesus' name* I pleaded.

In the ensuing weeks, the routine of our life became a highly-welcomed normal again. Heidi, with a gritty resilience, gradually rode out the mental strain that was placed on her. Even though she fell behind her American counterparts academically, she picked up more and more of the Bayerisch language. Sherri invested her heart and soul into the daily job of helping Heidi with her homework and encouraging her to be optimistic. In addition, she—of course—mothered Shanda every waking hour and walked her daily through a regiment of potty training. I picked up the pace of visiting the military bases and trying to find believers interested in attending a Bible study and helping start an international church.

And then in early November, something wonderful and unexpected happened that lifted our spirits high above the norm and touched our hearts anew.

Chapter 39

Our landlord, Wolfgang Heilemann, asked if my family would spend Christmas Eve with him and his girlfriend, Ingrid, at the Reindlschmiede house. He particularly wanted me—his "private priest" as he had started calling me—to conduct a fireplace service and explain the birth of Christ as told in the Bible. He would even be willing to listen to an actual Bible reading, something he normally wouldn't welcome.

"Absolutely! We'd love to!" I affirmed. Here was a man, we'd learned, who was a senior photographer for one of Europe's leading pop-and-rock music magazines and hung out with the Beatles, the Rolling Stones, the Bay City Rollers, the Bee Gees, ABBA, Elton John, Bob Marley, Jimi Hendrix, and a pantheon of other movers and shakers across the industry. And, yet, he was choosing to spend Christmas Eve with me and my family. I accepted Wolfgang's invitation as a gift from God, and probably a once-in-a-lifetime opportunity.

A week or so into December, Wolfgang asked if there was another couple we might want to invite to the Christmas Eve gathering. It so happened there was. Sherri and I had met a German couple who had recently returned to Germany after living in the States for more than a decade. They were in the throes of reverse culture shock, big time. The couple—Manfred and Renate—gravitated to us because of the fact that we were from the U.S. They simply loved Americans and wanted to be around them. Living and working in Munich where they had no family, they joyously welcomed our invitation.

On Christmas Eve, the atmosphere at the Reindlschmiede house was electric. The aroma of homemade soup, freshly baked bread, homespun cookies, and cinnamon tea filled the air. Burning candles in every nook and cranny enhanced the magical feeling. A smoldering fire in Wolfgang's fireplace highlighted the decorative Christmas tree and added just enough warmth to make the setting cozy to the max. Everyone was in a cheerful mood.

When we were all seated for the evening meal, Wolfgang—not a believer—asked me to say a prayer of thanks. Not only did I pray aloud and thank God for the bounty before us, but I capitalized on the moment and thanked God for his unconditional love for Wolfgang, Ingrid, Manfred, and Renate. At the conclusion of the prayer, both Ingrid and Renate had tears in their eyes. *Oh, Father, touch their hearts and open their minds,* I implored inside my head.

The mealtime was filled with great conversation and laughter. At the end of the fabulous feast, all the adults watched as Heidi and Shanda tore into their Christmas gifts with dramatic hoopla. Nostalgic smiles dominated the background. When the wrapping paper was eventually collected from around the room and put into a trash bag, Heidi and Shanda disappeared with their new toys to our side of the house.

The adults then gathered in an intimate circle around the living room coffee table. It was time to hear the Christmas story as told by Scripture. To everyone's surprise I produced four German-language Bibles. I gave one to Wolfgang, one to Ingrid, one to Manfred, and one to Renate. I had bookmarked the pages in the Gospel of Luke that I was planning to read out loud. I later learned it was the first time the four Germans had held a Bible in their hands since childhood.

Not only did I give them Bibles with which to follow along verse by verse, I also assigned each of them a few verses to read aloud themselves. They were caught off guard by the request. But no one resisted. The whole thing turned out to be quite amazing. Collectively, with six voices—one after the other, including Sherri's—we read (Sherri and I in English; Wolfgang and the others in German) until the entirety of chapters one and two of Luke's Gospel had been recited. I watched with fascination as each of the Germans vocalized God's proclamation concerning his Son, the Savior of the world, and did so with total reverence. Luke's narrative provoked so many heartfelt questions and discussions that after the reading we talked for a full hour or more, with requests to discuss the issues even further. It was a glorious evening of watching God touch hearts. It was one of the most meaningful Christmas celebrations Sherri and I ever experienced.

And for Ingrid, Wolfgang's girlfriend, the occasion was life changing. She had been living with Wolfgang for ten years—since she was eighteen—and was deeply unsatisfied. Going forward, whenever she was in Reindlschmiede, she started asking us faith-related questions in private. Can a person really have a living relationship with Christ? If so, what does that kind of relationship look like? In a dramatic moment a few weeks later, Ingrid humbly chose to embrace God's gift of redemption and enter into a life-altering relationship with her Creator. Shortly thereafter, she confided, "I can't live with Wolfgang like this any longer. I'm just not at peace. How do I go about breaking up with him?" She soon moved out on her own and commenced a brand new season of life.

Wolfgang carried on with other companions.

Three months later, when we started the international church, Ingrid started attending our gatherings.

And once again I was pastoring.

One of my goals when we finally started the Munich church was to create a forum where people did not feel the need to pretend to be better than they were and end up playing religious charades. I had played politics in the legalistic camp of Tennessee Temple and IBWO until I was completely nauseated. And I didn't intend, not for a second, to superimpose that oppressive culture onto my Munich church. I desired for the church to be a haven for authenticity.

So, at one of our first gatherings as an infant congregation—in a hotel bar-room that we rented—I looked at the small group of seventeen people that Sherri and I had befriended from the military bases and the international civilian community, and underscored, "We're beginning a journey together that I hope will be an adventure of a lifetime. I will do my best to make it so. And if together we succeed in achieving something out of the ordinary, whatever you do, do not put me on a pedestal. Like everybody else on planet earth I'm the owner of a Jeremiah 17:9 heart, a heart that is sick and difficult to understand. With Christ as my helper and teacher, I'm, of course, capable of rising above the sickness. But I'm also capable of being defeated by the sickness just like anyone else. So, again, don't put me on a pedestal. We're all on equal ground. As we go forward, let's spur one another on toward spiritual health and good deeds. And let's lift one another up whenever someone in the group succumbs to the sickness and falls. Together, let's build a brotherhood of love, grace, and support, not a brotherhood of piety and judgment."

To help generate this type of authenticity, I started a monthly couple's night where I led the way in gradually peeling back the customary mask of "everything's good; everything's fine."

Finally, after being in the country for a little over a year, Sherri and I felt like we were settling in. The foundation stones of our new church had been laid—with a meeting place, a budding congregation, a doctrinal statement, a commitment to God's Word, and a vision going forward.

With our primary objective of planting an international church well underway, I was drawn once again to revisit the *Wisdom Hunter* project that had gone untouched for nearly two years. Was now the time to start over, beginning at chapter one?

Yes, I decided.

Yes, it was.

I had now learned too much to remain silent.

Chapter 40

The premise of the *Wisdom Hunter* story was quite simple:

My main character, Jason Faircloth, would be a high-profile pastor who—in his role as husband, father, pastor, and friend—mirrored the destructive legalistic mindset of most of the Independent Baptist pastors I knew. The character's absurdly long list of extra-Biblical rules, along with his judgmental and *I'm-never-wrong* attitude, would destroy the lives of his wife and daughter. He would at that point leave the ministry and for the first time in his life question the integrity of his beliefs. He would simultaneously discover he had a granddaughter whose identity and location were being kept a secret from him. But when he hears that the little girl is being abused, he doggedly sets out to find and rescue her. As he searches for her, he—as a broken and disillusioned man—angrily lets go of everything he's ever believed about Christianity and starts over at square one. (I would use my grueling journey out of legalism to accurately describe his pain, disillusionment, and eventual recovery.) Trying not to completely lose his heart for God, he becomes a self-avowed wisdom hunter. He desperately wants to know what is true. He creates a journal in which he records his new realizations.

The entire novel would be built around his "wisdom book" entries, insights that I and the main character learned from our abject failures as blind legalists: (1) student attitude verses authoritarian attitude (2) honest questioning versus blind believing (3) Bible teachings versus believers' traditions, and (4) Spirit pressure versus peer pressure. Adopting these insights as core practices, the main character would eventually redeem himself when he finds his granddaughter and makes a life-saving difference in her life. The beginning of the story would show the destructive nature of legalism. The middle of the story would show the arduous journey from legalism to grace. The latter part of the story would illustrate the power and beauty of grace and kindness.

Of course, to tell this story and make it intriguing for an audience, I would have to add the complexity of character development, realistic dialogue, a plausible plot line, and enough suspense to keep the reader engaged. It was a daunting dream, but it was a dream that wouldn't die or go away. So on a beautiful summer afternoon, I took a pen and sheet of paper and started over at chapter one. I shifted the story to third-person according to the published writer's recommendation from two years earlier, and once again looked at her list of ingredients for a worthwhile novel. I wrote, rewrote, edited, and reedited for four days before I was satisfied with chapter one.

This time, however, I wasn't going to write hundreds of pages before I asked a few people to proofread my work. So, a couple of days later I presented copies of the first pages to three individuals. "Will you read this chapter," I asked, "and tell me if it would pull you into a second chapter? And, please. Be brutally honest."

When the three readers returned their copies, they each gave their honest feedback. "No," they all said, "As is, this chapter would never entice me to keep reading."

I sucked up the negative critique and inquired, "Why? Why wouldn't it pull you through to a second chapter?"

One of the readers pointed to the fact that I had not established a literary "hook" of any kind, a hook that would provoke the reader to ask *How is this going to be resolved,* or *What's behind this malicious behavior,* or *Who is this mysterious character?* So I scrapped the first rewrite of chapter one and started over again. This time I attempted to create a "hook."

A week or so later, when a thoroughly revamped version of chapter one was lying on my desk, I procured three new test readers. Again I asked, "Will you read these few pages and tell me honestly if they would make you want a second chapter?"

After reading the few pieces of paper, their answers—like the first group's—were a unanimous "No."

"Can you articulate the reasons," I pushed. "I really want to get this right. And I need your help."

"Well," one of the three underscored, "there are no descriptive colors or smells. There's just no background texture. It just feels...what can I say...sterile."

I ended up rewriting the first chapter eight times. I learned a significant lesson with each new effort and each new round of constructive criticism. And I made applicable changes with every rewrite. And finally...finally...a group of test readers asked, "Where's chapter two?"

"Yes!" I celebrated inside my head. "Finally, finally!"

But my optimism was premature. I assumed, based on

all I had learned, that chapter two would come together quickly and solidly. So, I was somewhat deflated when the proof readers for the next chapter—a completely new group—considered my initial copy of chapter two a dismal failure. Again, at my request, they outlined the reasons the best they could. So, I went back to a clean sheet of paper.

Like chapter one, chapter two required seven or eight rewrites before people were wanting additional pages. Chapters three, four, five, six, and seven all required the same amount of labor.

By the time I sat down to compose chapter eight, I had written and rewritten so much over the weeks that I felt like I had completed a college course in "Creative Writing." At that point I had developed a style of writing that was uniquely mine, a style that readers seemed to enjoy. So to maintain consistency in my writing I went on a reading fast. I pledged I wouldn't read another book of any kind, except for the Bible, until I finished my entire manuscript. I simply didn't want to be tempted—consciously or subconsciously—to mimic another style of writing that I found inspiring, and thus mess up my own.

I slowly and steadily, in my spare time, managed to add one chapter after another, determined to one day finish the story that had burned in my heart and mind for more than four years.

One of the individuals in my Munich church was so enthralled by the project, that they—without consulting me—purchased me a six-month subscription to "Writer's Digest" magazine, a periodical aimed to teach and encourage professional and amateur writers. When my first copy arrived at our Reindlschmiede address, I took one look at the cover and tossed the magazine in the trash. The cover highlighted the issue's main article, *The Difficulty of Being Published As An Amateur.* I never opened another copy.

Even though I was joyously making headway with my novel, my pastoral ministry was my primary focus. And I gave it my all. Our congregation quickly outgrew the hotel barroom we were renting. So the owner of the hotel, at my request, relocated our meetings to two adjoining hotel rooms. When our numbers filled those rooms, the hotel owner moved us to the ballroom. When we started having thirty to forty regular attendees every week, the hotel owner declared, "This is too much. You need to find another location for your meetings." So I scoured the surrounding areas for a new venue. Through tireless searching, I eventually procured a permanent and spacious place for our gatherings. It was the fellowship hall of the Lutheran church in the small centralized village of Holzkirchen. It was a wonderful locale that provided a great atmosphere for additional growth. And grow we did. Fifty to sixty people—from Germany, America, England, New Zealand, and Scotland—were soon attending the services. And Sherri and I tried to give our heart and energy to each one. Not only did the door of our Reindlschmiede home become a revolving entryway with church members regularly coming for dinner and fellowship, but we were constantly discipling and encouraging individuals in their homes as well.

We even won the friendship of our liaison at the Holzkirchen Lutheran Church, a single man in his twenties. He initially checked out our group by attending a couple of our Sunday services. He was so moved by the spontaneous songs, testimonies, prayers, and questions—in stark contrast to the rigid liturgy of his own church—that he started coming around more and more. He, at one point, even invited me into his home to lead a weekly Bible study for German singles, a meeting I gladly inserted into my schedule. The impact of the casual, interactive sessions was quick and noticeable, demonstrated by the singles' increased involvement in our international church.

Our ministry was quite honestly developing beyond our expectations. This included the monthly couple's night. At our seventh gathering, fourteen couples met in a home in Bad Aibling. We commenced the meeting around 6:30 PM. Fourteen men and fourteen women sat in a leisureley circle in the living room.

"All right," I announced, "In recent months we've stepped out of our comfort zone more and more as we've acknowledged that a hundred percent of the human race struggles in life. Some struggle more frequently than others; some more intensely. But every one struggles, including believers. That includes me. That includes you. So this evening I'm going to challenge us to step even further out of our comfort zone. I'm going to ask a question that, if answered, will help us be more authentic. And, if possible, I'd like for each person in the room to at least try to answer it. I'll begin. And we'll work our way around the room counter clockwise. If you feel you're not ready to answer the question, then when it's your turn, simply tap the person to your right to let them know you are passing."

People nodded. Some looked a little nervous.

"Okay. So here's the question. Ready? Here we go. What is the greatest pain you've ever experienced in life? And, as a bit of instruction, your answer cannot refer to any type of physical pain. Again, what is the greatest pain you've ever experienced in life?" I waited for every one to digest the challenge. "Okay. I'll answer first." I paused and inhaled slowly and deeply. I then told them about my loss of heart years earlier for being a husband, father, and pastor. I told them about running away from home, about emotionally abusing Sherri, about living on the brink of divorce, about drowning in so much guilt, confusion, and pain that I literally wanted to give up and die – all while trying to serve as a decent pastor. When I finished talking I could tell by the facial expressions that some of the people had never heard a pastor or ministry leader admit such things. I was exhausted. I had poured out my heart for a full thirty minutes.

Figuratively speaking, I then gave the baton to the lady sitting next to me. I knew instinctively that the outcome of the meeting would be determined by the next two people. Would they continue the truthful sharing? Or would they choose to pass? Or simply share something benign?

When the lady sitting to my right understood it was her turn, she silently buried her face in her hands. Ten seconds passed. Twenty seconds. Thirty seconds. Forty seconds. "Okay," she ultimately whispered through a strained voice as she raised her head. "My greatest pain!" She went silent again for another twenty seconds. She then blew a puff of air as she wiped her eyes. "What I'm about to share is something only my husband and two adult children know about. Nobody else in the world has ever found out." She went silent again as her knee started bouncing nervously up and down.

Every face in the room, I noticed, looked taut. Had I pushed too far? Had this been a bad idea?

"For seven years," the lady continued, "I was hopelessly addicted to prescription drugs. During those years I created a hell inside my home. My kids still hate me to this very day because of the way I abused them. My husband is here tonight only by God's grace. He threatened multiple times, and rightly so, to divorce me. And what makes this story so tragic is that at the time, my husband and I were a leadership couple in our church. And nobody outside the family knew about my addiction." She paused and inhaled strongly. "I grew to hate the church. I wanted so many times to pull off the mask and say *Somebody help the girl.* But I didn't trust anyone. I knew I would be quickly judged, condemned, and rejected. And nobody wants to be treated that way." The lady, like me, took thirty minutes to unpack her journey through hell. Her pain was palpable. Nearly all twenty-eight people in the room were wiping tears from their eyes.

The lady next in line could hardly breathe when she was given the floor. There was another round of heavy silence. The battle inside the lady's head of should-I or shouldn't-I was written clearly in her eyes.

Oh, God, don't let this go wrong. Please! I begged.

"A few years ago," the lady enunciated slowly, "I underwent gastric bypass surgery. Until then—because of other physical issues—I had struggled all my life with being overweight. As a child I was bullied, made fun of, and left out of my school's social networks, all because of my size. It was worse during my teenage years." She elaborated with enough detail that everyone in the room could feel the edges of her pain. Even after becoming a believer she had felt neglected by the Christian community. She had felt lonely and rejected all her life...until the gastric bypass surgery. Once she had become thinner, those who had previously scorned her suddenly welcomed her into their social settings. "Why does excess weight make a difference?" the lady questioned all of us in the room. "I still find that I'm bitter sometime over just how insensitive Christians can be."

Again, there were tears of empathy from all around the circle.

We had begun at 6:30 PM. The last person in line finished sharing at 3:30 AM. All fourteen men and all fourteen women were depleted of tears. All the pain that had been shared was absolutely mind-boggling, nearly incomprehensible – rape, abuse, infidelity, abortion, divorce, jail time. I had never imagined that so much pain could be represented in such few lives. One lady had even seen her two-year-old son kidnapped out of her front yard. She had recently learned of his whereabouts. The boy was now twenty-one.

Understandably, a special bond of grace and trust developed among the fourteen couples that night. Since these men and women were the core members of our congregation, the church quickly became a place of openness. And it was an absolute beautiful thing to behold. For example, it wasn't out of the ordinary, thereafter, for a mother to stand up during a Sunday gathering and say, "Pray for me as a mom. I'm literally hating my thirteen-year-old right now. I need for those of you who are parents to teach me, advise me, and encourage me. I'm just exhausted. And I need help." Or...for a husband to stand up in humility and say, "For the first time in our marriage, my wife and I are talking about divorce. We know that some of you have been in that place and have fought back and won. Please, we need for you to rush into our lives, kick us in the pants, challenge us, help restore our perspective."

I couldn't have been more pleased with the way our young church was evolving.

Chapter 41

Unbeknownst to me, though, a monumental safety net was about to be yanked from beneath us. And it would be done by none other than IBWO, in the form of a declarative letter to all the missionaries serving with the agency.

In the letter that arrived at our Reindlschmiede address, IBWO's business manager announced that due to investment strategies that didn't meet expectations, the IBWO board had found it necessary to restructure its pension plan. Unfortunately, it was explained, every missionary under the age of forty—for the sustainability of the newly revised program—would have to sacrifice all vested rights that had been accumulated up to that point and start over at "zero."

What? Was this an awful joke of some kind?

I was thirty-six. And after serving with IBWO for thirteen years, I was already a hundred percent vested in the retirement program. IBWO had deducted a significant amount of dollars from our support literally every month for THIRTEEN YEARS and invested it for our retirement. And now, because of poor investment decisions on their part, were they going to pretend it was okay to just "steal" this money from us?

Was this even legal?

So much for trusting the 'experts' who were responsible for caring for us. They had literally wasted thirteen year's worth of pension deposits. I was stunned. And they took no further measures to apologize. How many other IBWO missionary families, I wondered, were being ransacked like this? I suspected hundreds.

I wrote a letter to the business manager, expressing my disbelief and frustration. His response was as follows:

> "We take exception to the fact that we lost a lot of money through poor investment in a 'bunch of old houses' as you put it. We bought a few houses and rented them out mostly to missionaries and Temple students. When we found out what was involved in the renting and maintenance end of the real estate market, we sold them. The feeling was that it was too time consuming for the staff to keep up with and until the property was paid for did not generate enough income to justify the time. The real reason the plan had to be changed was to protect the younger missionaries. So many older missionaries were retiring and so many younger missionaries were quitting and taking their vested rights that no plan closely approximating ours could survive. Both actuarially and practically, we had to do something just to protect either group."

Yeah, well, what about my group?

There was nothing consensual on my part in the entirety of IBWO's aggressive action. My innocence regarding a sense of financial safety was taken from me. I brooded for weeks.

During the days of adjusting to this painful setback, I received a long-distance call from Georgia that sent my mind spinning in a completely different direction.

"Randy," a longtime friend declared over the phone, "your dad recently made a profession of faith."

I was stunned into a moment of silence. "Oh, sure!" I eventually replied in disbelief.

"No, seriously. His decision seems to be genuine."

Yeah, right, I told myself. My dad was 69. There was no way I could accept the call as having any validity. Growing up as a kid, I heard my mom literally every Sunday invite my dad to join us for church. My dad had always refused. Some hurt that he never divulged had long ago destroyed his respect for organized religion. He despised church.

Yet in many ways my dad was a good man. He was hardworking. He was honest. He was loyal. He was disciplined.

But on the dark side he was verbally abusive, and stridently so, to my mom. My mother, it seemed, could never do anything right in my father's eyes. She would, for example, put a banquet of food on the table. And my father would taste one bite and snap, "You've been cooking this meal for over twenty years! How come you can't get it right? What did you do; empty a whole bag of salt on it?" This type of verbal abuse persisted day after day, year after year. My mother was emotionally beaten to mush. Yet, from the time I became a believer until I moved overseas, I regularly overheard my mom in the living room at night praying for my dad's salvation and change of heart. I had often joined her. At some point, though, I had shamefully given up praying for my dad. He simply had a hard heart. And I had come to the conclusion that he would never humble himself in repentance.

"So then, tell me about this conversion that you believe is so legitimate," I hesitantly implored my friend.

What I heard over the phone was that my mother a few weeks prior had invited my dad, as usual, to go with her to church on a Sunday morning. My mother told him that a guest speaker—an evangelist named Sonny Holland—would be starting a week-long series of revival services. To my mother's utter shock, my dad said, "Yeah, I think I'll go with you." And he did. It was the first time in thirty years my dad attended church with her. It still wasn't known why he decided to join her. That Sunday afternoon my mom asked if he would like to go back that evening for the next service. "Sure, I'll go," he told her. And he did. He also went Monday night, Tuesday night, Wednesday night, Thursday night, and Friday night. It was during the Friday night gathering when the miraculous happened. My dad walked the aisle during a public call to salvation and "ran into the arms of the Savior." And he was shamelessly telling people about the encounter everywhere he went.

When the call ended, I had to ask if I was locked subconsciously in a dream of some kind and would momentarily wake up to the truth that my dad was still the same old church-spurning individual? I wasn't sure I could even imagine my dad as a devoted Christian. The words "dad" and "Christian" combined in the same sentence sounded like an oxymoron. But now the story was irrevocably planted in my head.

"God, let it be true," I petitioned.

Over the next few weeks—amidst the routine of pastoring, preparing sermons, working on the *Wisdom Hunter* manuscript, and coming to grips with the loss of our retirement fund—the prayer for my dad continued to be a staple.

And then it was confirmed. My dad, according to my mom's personal declaration to me, had become a changed man. He was even attending church every Sunday. I was floored. I had to ask God to forgive me for my doubting heart. I had always believed my dad was outside God's reach. Now I understood that no one was beyond God's wooing grace.

A new thought suddenly mesmerized me: Would my dad now understand and accept me? He had always held it against me that I moved out of the United States—'forsaking me and your mother' as he worded it—to be a "foreign missionary."

When I picked up my pen the next time to compose another chapter for *Wisdom Hunter*, I wondered if the fact that I was writing a novel, a faith-based novel at that, would make my dad proud. I had never in the entirety of my life heard him say, *I'm proud of you*. Not one time. Not for anything. Purportedly his conversion had changed him as a man and as a husband. But would it transform him as a father as well? I could only dream.

On and off as I continued to produce paragraphs and chapters for the *Wisdom Hunter* manuscript, my mind would sporadically drift to my newly converted father. His parents had pulled him permanently out of school at the end of the third grade to work on the family farm. He had always been cognizant of his robbed education and had done his best to hide the disadvantage. But again, would the fact that I—his son, a college graduate—was writing a novel bring a gleam to his eye? Or would it simply add to his easily-felt humiliation and self-deprecation?

Perhaps I would know the answer sometime soon, as I was bearing down on the *Wisdom Hunter* epilogue and would be able to show him a completed manuscript.

Life was moving along beautifully. Heidi was back in school, speaking Bayerisch like a local, and was putting up decent grades. Shanda was potty trained and thriving. I was preaching regularly and discipling several individuals on the side. The church was growing numerically with a host of fascinating people. And we were seeing lives changed.

And then one day, in the natural scheme of things, I typed the last three pages of the *Wisdom Hunter* manuscript. To say it was a moment of absolute jubilation would be an understatement. I had written a novel! A blessed novel for heaven's sake! And not just a trivial novel. But a novel I hoped would one day help set people free from the stranglehold of legalism. I had been able to corral all my angry and abstract thoughts regarding legalism, analyze them, and then describe them in words and formulas that drew the ugly beast from its abusive shadows and spotlighted its outright destructiveness. I didn't know if I should be proud or humble. I did know, though, that it wasn't all serendipity. If the work was ever going to be published, it would have to undergo a major edit from front to back; I was certain of that.

Before I turned the pages over to a professional editor, though, I first wanted to place the manuscript into the hands of a dozen or more people who represented the general reading market, people from diverse backgrounds – Christian, non-Christian, old, young, European, American, educated, uneducated, married, single, conservative, liberal, male, and female. I was convinced that a solitary editor, representing just one set of eyes, would never be able to pinpoint all the weak spots and correct them in a way that would maximize the story to its full potential. I was sure an assortment of eyes would have a better chance of ferreting out all the obvious and not-so-obvious mistakes. Plus, the overall feedback of a plethora of readers would tell me quickly if I had created a story with promise. Or if I needed to do a major rewrite.

But just as I was preparing to dispatch copies of the manuscript to the first group of readers, I received a long distance call from Georgia informing me that my dad had been diagnosed with stage-four cancer. The monstrous cells had already metastasized from his kidney to his brain. He only had a few months to live.

I arranged for a few men in our church, along with a nearby Wesleyan missionary, to cover for me at the church for three months. And the Dodd family headed back to Georgia.

I wanted to be with my dad in his last days.

I, of course, took a single copy of the *Wisdom Hunter* manuscript with me. I wanted my dad, before he died, to at least see the manuscript and touch it. I wanted him to know that his son had achieved something noteworthy.

Chapter 42

We arrived back in Georgia on a Monday. A Christian family in the Stockbridge area provided a basement apartment for us, rent free, for the duration of our stay. Another Atlanta couple loaned us a van to use. And it was arranged for Heidi to attend classes at the private Christian school founded and operated by our home church, Mt. Vernon Baptist.

On Wednesday afternoon, my dad—who bore all the signs of imminent death—mumbled with almost zero energy, "I'm sure you're tired from your flight, but would you like to attend the midweek church service with me and your mom this evening?"

I was astounded. I had never once seen my dad willfully sit in a church auditorium to sing worship songs or listen to a sermon. Now here he was, barely able to walk, and he was inviting me to join him for both. And at Mt. Vernon Baptist none the less.

"Of course, I'll join you," I stammered.

As was typical, approximately three-hundred people gathered for the Wednesday evening service. Because of dad's debilitating condition and limited endurance, we sat near the back of the sanctuary, right near the entrance where it was the easiest for him to get in and out.

Once the service began it was more than strange to witness my church-rebuffing-father of the past trying shamelessly to mumble his way through praise-filled hymns, and to listen with genuine interest to a Bible message. Despite his sickness, he remained engaged throughout the duration of the hour-and-twenty-minute program. My musings and emotions, nevertheless, couldn't find a comfortable resting spot. I just didn't have the capacity, it seemed, to process what I was seeing. It was like wanting to taste a gourmet-prepped morsel, but unable to handle it because of the weird texture.

When the pastor finally got ready to end the service with a prayer, he suddenly paused and looked silently over the crowd. "Before we dismiss," he stated, "I wonder if anyone has anything on their heart they would like to share. If so, feel free to raise your hand."

Fifteen to twenty seconds of silence ensued as people mulled over the opportunity.

"Anyone?" the pastor iterated.

It looked as if no one was going to volunteer when suddenly out of my peripheral vision I saw a hand go up.

It was my dad's. I stopped breathing.

"Yes, Toy," the pastor said.

Dad slowly lifted himself to a standing position. "Is it okay if I come to the microphone?" he asked the pastor.

"Absolutely! Come on up."

While other men assisted my dad up the aisle and onto the platform, I sat motionless. I was too shellshocked to even help. My dad was an introvert. What was he doing?

Once he was stabilized behind the podium, he purposely leaned in toward the microphone. "Most of you already know," he announced with an anemic wheeze, "that I'm dying with cancer. But I'm ready." He broke into tears. "I am ready because of that woman back there." He pointed to my mom. "She loved me, prayed for me, and forgave me during all the years I despised her religion." He paused. "I now have only one regret. And that is that I didn't accept God's grace as a little boy. I've wasted my life." He wept again. "If you are here tonight and have refused to bow your heart to God, I beg you...don't waste your life like I did. Surrender to Jesus now."

Over the following days and weeks, I realized I no longer recognized this man named Toy Arthur Dodd. He was gentle. He was kind. He would say things to my mom like, "that was one of the best meals I've ever had." He even said repeatedly to her, "I love you." He had truly become a new creature. He had been...born anew.

As expected, he didn't have the energy or focus to read even a portion of the 560-page *Wisdom Hunter* manuscript. But he did hold it in his lap. "And you wrote all this...uh...?" he muttered in the weakest of voices. I acknowledged that I did. I tried to explain the content. But his spiritual journey—so new, so brief, and so untouched by legalism—made it difficult for him to grasp the reality of the story. But he did smile. And he did give me a pat on the hand. And perhaps that was enough.

As he physically withered from day to day, he persisted in his gentleness. And he displayed no fear of dying whatsoever. I was touched more than anyone would ever know..

As Sherri and I bided our time and tried to help my mom and dad as much as possible, I decided—against my initial intentions—to put the *Wisdom Hunter* pages into the hands of one of our supporting pastors. The pastor I selected was the only supporting pastor we had in Atlanta at the time who was not a hardline legalist. It was still a risk. But I decided to take it. To my surprise, the pastor read the entire book in a little over a week. He understood the content and was well aware of the fundamentalist pastors I'd stereotyped in the story. "I love what you've done here," he confided in me with genuine candor. "If it's ever published, the book will help a lot of people. But...you will be crucified. You know that, don't you? So...is it really worth it to you?" The question was rhetorical. And then he added, "I hope you know what you're doing."

It was the book's first review.

I focused primarily on the 'helpful' part and tried to set aside the 'ominous' warning. But, yes, I knew all along in my gut that if the book ever went to press I would suffer ecclesiastical consequences. But, that was...IF...the book went to press. And if that ever happened, then like Martin Luther of old I would simply be publicly nailing my ninety-five theses to the door of a denomination that taught things in the name of God that I totally objected to. And I would have to hold my head high and bear the fallout, whatever it might be. Anyway, I cherished the pastor's feedback and told him so. His critique actually fueled my optimism regarding the book's potential. I was secretly elated.

Because of the better-than-expected review, I actually ignored my cautionary U.S. plan and asked two more people—a middle-aged husband and wife team—if they would read the 560 pages. "Please," I told them, "I don't want it to be widespread knowledge right now that I've written a book. So don't tell anyone." They promised. They were members of the same church as the pastor who had given the encouraging assessment.

My hopes for the book soared when both the husband

and wife, independently of one another, finished the book in record time and raved about its content. "There are so many people who need this message," they declared. They became some of my most avid cheerleaders for the book's publication. All of this, of course, gave me an emotional high. And I treasured it.

But the exuberance was quickly overlaid with sadness. We had been back in the States for ten weeks and dad—to the amazement of all his physicians—was still hanging on. But the Munich church was asking us to please return as originally planned in the next fourteen days. The church was struggling without us. Sherri and I discussed our options. If we extended our stay a few extra weeks, it still might not be long enough. For the church's sake, could we really afford to stay away any longer? In the end we decided—as melancholy as it was—to once again willingly leave my parents behind and say a final "farewell" to my dad.

Six weeks after our return to Munich, Dad passed. Because of Mt. Vernon's generous financial assistance, we were able to return for the funeral. At the chapel and graveside services I experienced a bit of heavyheartedness, but was never moved to tears. It bothered me for a few months afterward that I was unable to cry at my own father's passing. I came to understand after much soul searching, though, that a person doesn't grieve over something he doesn't lose. And, in essence, I never had a father to lose. As I was growing up, Toy Dodd—as I explained in the opening chapter of this book—provided shelter, food, and clothing for me for which I'm eternally grateful. But he never invested in me mentally, socially, or spiritually. He never threw a ball with me. Never helped me with homework. Never had a man-to-man conversation with me. Never told me stories about his childhood or youth. Never affirmed me with words of love or assurance. Of course, this was during his unregenerate years. And then, once I moved away to college at age eighteen, I took up the permanent responsibility for my own physical needs and comforts. So, sadly, from my perspective I never "lost" a "father."

Near the end, though, he had run into the arms of the Savior. And for that, I couldn't thank God enough.

Chapter 43

Back in Munich for the long haul, I quickly reassured the church and helped them settle down. Sherri once again began cooking meals and inviting families and singles over for food, fellowship, and ministry. Heidi reentered the Bad Heilbrunn elementary school.

Once life was reset and showing signs of normalcy, I felt comfortable enough to solicit a few new test readers for the *Wisdom Hunter* manuscript. I asked them to be brutally honest in their critique. I could barely contain my anticipation as I awaited their response. I soon discovered the efficacy of asking a diverse group of people to scour the book's pages. Some people, I learned, naturally looked primarily for spelling errors. Others looked for grammatical mistakes. Others for misstated facts. Others for plot weaknesses. Others for inconsistencies in character development. Others for the pacing of the storyline. And, of course, all these areas must be given attention if a novel is going to be genuinely good.

My test readers—ultimately fourteen unique individuals—one at a time submitted their lists of notes, comments, along with recommended changes or modifications. Their collective evaluation was hugely transformative for the book. And eye-opening for me as a writer. Yet, regardless of the needed edits, the story in its raw form pulled ten of the fourteen readers excitedly all the way through to the last page. Many didn't want the book to end. Their enthusiastic feedback bolstered my hopes for the book even further. After I made the corrections and changes that had been suggested, I felt like I was holding a strong, solid, substantial manuscript that could withstand the scrutiny of any publishing house. For the first time I truly felt like a genuine writer. But the biggest prize of all was the therapeutic healing I had experienced in the overall process of creating, telling, and editing the story. I was no longer disillusioned or confused by my denominational leaders. After years of step-by-step analysis, I now understood their extremism. And I couldn't thank God enough that I was no longer an authoritative know-it-all that blindly suffocated the hearts, lives, and minds of His people. I was far from being a giant in the faith, but at least I was endeavoring to be a gracious, kind, and sympathetic leader. For me, that was monumental. Feeling that I was finally recovering from a spiritual disease—Oh happy day!— I ironically put the *Wisdom Hunter* pages in a closet and became so pleasantly engaged in my pastorate that I ceased to focus on the book's publication. I was just happy living life.

Several of the test readers, however, began gently scolding me for not actively pursuing a publishing deal. Trusting their assessment of the story's value, I eventually said, "Okay, okay! I'll try."

At that time, though in 1990, Christian fiction was not a common commodity. Charles Sheldon's *In His Steps* was available. A few faith-based romance novels by Grace Livingston Hill and Janette Oke were on bookstore shelves. And then there was *This Present Darkness* by Frank Peretti. It had been on the market for three and half years but was just becoming a good seller and was gaining momentum in the marketplace. The publisher for Peretti's book was a group called Crossway. Since the novel was obtaining notoriety, I decided to send a copy of *Wisdom Hunter* to Crossway. So I pulled the bound pages from my closet, secured them in a box with a cover letter, and sent them on their way to the Crossway headquarters in Wheaton, Illinois.

So much was happening in our ministry at the time—working with seventy-five people from twelve different countries—that I barely had time to wonder about Crossway and their response.

Several weeks later, the *Wisdom Hunter* manuscript was returned. Someone at Crossway had simply deemed the book of no interest. There was not even a note of explanation, just the returned book along with my cover letter.

Now what?

It appeared to me that the most prolific bestselling fiction writer in the Christian market at the time was Janette Oke. Her novels were all published by Bethany House. So I retyped my cover letter and mailed my manuscript to Bethany House in Grand Rapids, Michigan.

Again, the manuscript was returned. But this time it was accompanied by a letter from Bethany House's senior editor. "I personally loved the book—the storyline, the message, and the characters—but the book is a little too risqué for Bethany House's conservative reputation. I highly encourage you, though, to pursue publication with a different house." It was a rejection letter, but one that excited me. Since ending my 'reading fast' a few months earlier, I had been gorging on books. I had just read the secular novel *The Clowns of God* written by Australian novelist Morris West. His story was centered around the papacy with an overt religious theme. The book, a bestseller, was published by Bantam. If Bantam was willing to stamp their label on West's novel that was so unashamedly religious in nature, maybe they would take a look at *Wisdom Hunter*. The *Wisdom Hunter* story certainly wasn't too risqué for a secular publishing house. So for a third time I packaged the ream of 560 pages. The destination this time was New York, New York. The manuscript, though, was quickly returned to our Munich address. A letter was enclosed that said, "Bantam Publishers does not review unsolicited manuscripts. A manuscript must be recommended to us by a literary agent before we give it time or consideration. Sincerely yours." I assumed all literary agents worked for hire. And I certainly didn't have sufficient capital to pay for that type of service. So I felt I had no option but to try at least one more Christian publishing house. For whatever reason the faith-based companies had not required the mediation of a literary agent.

So next, I submitted the manuscript to InterVarsity Press. They returned it, saying, "Sorry, fiction is not part of our mission."

At that point, I shelved the manuscript and gave up. A few weeks later, Sherri and I were visiting a man who had recently started attending our church. As an artist he showed us multiple pictures he had painted. The paintings were of Christ in modern-day settings. Knowing he had a unique, impressive style that mesmerized people, the artist had tenaciously pursued publication of his work. But like me, he had encountered closed door after closed door. As a resource for finding a variety of potential publishers, the artist had subscribed to a Christian publishers' magazine used by numerous companies to promote their latest products. The artist gave me a back issue to peruse. So I took it home. About three-quarters of the way through the periodical I spotted a small ad for a soon-to-be-released Christian novel called *Sunset Grill*. The ad noted that the publisher was Questar Publishers out of Sisters, Oregon. I had never heard of Questar Publishers, but obviously it was a Christian publishing house that incorporated fiction in its lineup of books.

A week or so later, I sent the *Wisdom Hunter* manuscript once more across the Atlantic, this time to Oregon. By now my expectations were less than high. Two weeks later, though, I received a phone call late in the evening that caught me totally off guard.

"Hello, is this missionary Randy Dodd in Munich?"

"Yeah, that's me."

"Randy, my name is Allen Dust. I'm the senior editor at Questar Publishers in Oregon. I'm calling in regard to the *Wisdom Hunter* manuscript you sent to us."

(If needed, read Prologue again.)

Chapter 44

Thankfully Allen called back the next day after I hesitated to accept Questar's initial offer. Speaking on behalf of the entire Questar staff, he wanted to know if I would reconsider.

"If I sign a contract with Questar," I wheezed, "could the contract specify that the book would be released in September of next year instead of April? That way, we would already be back in the states. If you would do that for me, I might consider accepting your offer."

Seconds of quietude ensued.

"Let me talk to our president, *Dallas Jackson, and I'll find out if that's a point he's willing to negotiate. And I'll call you back as soon as I have an answer."

"All right. Sounds good." I thanked Allen again for the offer and hung up.

Two days later, Allen called again.

"Randy, I've talked to our president. He says he doesn't want to change the release date. But he wants to put forth a suggestion that might help you. He wants to know if you'll consider having the book published under an alias. Publishing the book under a name your mission board doesn't recognize would keep you safe, so to speak, from April till August. This would allow you to finish out your time in Munich with all the necessary closures. Once you're back in the States you can tell the mission board about your book whenever it suits you."

I realized, as a non-published writer who had never earned a single dollar from a book sale, that I had no further leverage for negotiating. I seriously wondered, though, why the book's release date couldn't be delayed until September. But not being familiar with the idiosyncrasies of the publishing world and their understanding of the market, I simply didn't know if I was being bluffed or not. And I certainly didn't want to cause offense or burn a bridge by arguing the point. At the same time, the proposal to utilize a pen name was not something I was expecting. I definitely wasn't ready to give a quick answer. I needed to ponder all the possible angles.

"I'll need at least a couple of days to think about it, Allen," I asserted. "I just can't make a decision like that right here on the spot."

"All right, but don't take long. Our offer is not without an expiration date."

"Okay, thanks."

After breaking away from the phone call, I realized I needed objective feedback about going with an alias. So I called four of the fourteen individuals who had been my test readers and who were now pushing me toward publication. I told them about Questar's offer, my dilemma, and Questar's proposal.

They were all elated for me.

"Would using a pseudonym be wrong for me as a Christian?" I implored.

The four individuals fielding the question were Christian friends who possessed years of Bible knowledge and Bible-related ethics. I don't know if their excitement for me skewed their thinking, but they all, independently of one another, gave me the answer I secretly wanted to hear.

"Writers use aliases all the time," the most seasoned believer in the group responded. "There's absolutely nothing morally wrong with it."

Another added, "Why, as far as we know, the writer of Hebrews didn't even attach his name to his all-important document. And it's part of Scripture."

Their words assuaged my conscience. So, after wrestling over the matter, I finally elected to go with Questar's proposal. But deciding on a pen name wasn't easy. The part of my conscience that was feeling a tinge of guilt surrounding the matter didn't want the alias to stray too far from my legal name, Randy Arthur Dodd. After trudging through a lot of mental backwaters, it dawned on me that I had never used my middle name in public. There might have been six or seven people, at most, who could recite my middle name upon request. Thus, I began toying with the idea of somehow incorporating my middle name into the alias. Could it be used as a first name? A last name? And what about a name to accompany it? I finally settled on Randall Arthur. My birth name was Randy. But Randall was nearly identical, yet different. I liked it. Randall Arthur. That would be it then. No one in my world of Independent Baptist constituents would connect me to that particular name. Even if the sales of the book were disappointing, I surmised that someone in the Independent Baptist circle was still bound to hear about it just because of the subject matter. So I would definitely feel much better using the pen name, knowing our season in Munich could finish well without being cut short.

The life-changing call came as expected a couple of days later.

"Well, time is running out," Allen reminded me. "So, have you made a decision?"

"Let's do it!" I blurted. "I'll use the name Randall Arthur." I explained the reason for that particular selection.

"Good, good! Everyone here will be glad to hear it. We'll start working on a contract immediately. We'll overnight it to you through FedEx in the next week or two."

Indeed, the Questar contract arrived by FedEx a few weeks later. On the first page was the letterhead, displaying the Questar logo, and then the fabulous words:

> Randy Arthur Dodd,
> named here "the Author"
> and
> Questar Publishers, Inc,
> named here "the Publisher"
>
> This Agreement concerns the Author's written work tentatively titled *Wisdom Hunter* named here "the Work"
>
> The Publisher desires to publish the Work, and the Author desires to have the Publisher publish the Work on the terms and conditions set forth in the publishing Agreement.

The contract, six pages long, covered all the basics in an author/publisher agreement.

<u>The Grant of Rights</u>

<u>The Royalties</u>

<u>The Publication and Marketing</u>

<u>The Copyright</u>

<u>The Options on Author's Next Work</u>

<u>Signed</u>

For the Publisher: _____
Date: _____
Witness: _____

For the Author: _____
Date: _____
Witness: _____

As I carefully read every point and sub-point of the six-page Agreement I was nearly overcome by feelings of both excitement and trepidation. On one hand, I realized I was the rare recipient of a coveted document that could perhaps change my life. On the other hand, I wondered if this was a good contract. Was it fair and generous? Or was it primarily one-sided in favor of the publishing house? I honestly didn't know. The only way to find out, as far as I knew, was to call other publishing houses and other authors and ask them outright if there was such a thing as a standard contract and if so, did the one in my hand fit that category.

So that's what I did.

Coincidentally, during the few days when I was making the long-distance calls, I received a notice from Questar informing me that if I signed the contract, Questar would cut me an advance royalty check for $30,000.00.

Chapter 45

Thirty-thousand dollars! I could scarcely register the number in my head. Thirty-thousand dollars was a sum nearly equal to a year's salary for us. The number was genuinely staggering. But before I signed the contract or accepted the advance I sat down and made some serious calculations.

If I signed the contract-in-hand I figured I would earn somewhere around sixty cents per book sold, based on Questar's wholesale price. I squeezed my chin. At that rate, fifty thousand copies of *Wisdom Hunter* would have to be sold to cover the $30,000.00 advance. I had already been told by several people in the publishing industry that the average book on bookstore shelves sells no more than six-thousand copies in its lifetime. If that number was accurate, then I truly doubted that *Wisdom Hunter* would exceed that number. And I surely didn't want to be in debt to Questar. If they presented me with a check for $30,000.00 and I only earned $4,000.00 or $5,000.00 in actual royalties, I would have to repay them $25,000.00. The very thought frightened me.

So, with a sickened heart I declined the $30,000.00 advance.

It would be six years later before I learned that an advance from a publishing house was the author's to keep—in full—regardless of the book-sale numbers. There was absolutely no risk on the author's part in accepting an advance. All the risk was on the publishing house. Yet, no one at Questar questioned my level of understanding, or lack thereof, regarding 'advances.'

Maybe in the end, though, my refusal to take the advance was better for me. Since I didn't take the $30,000.00 up front I was able to negotiate a slightly better royalty deal. I had learned in previous phone calls to a couple of publishing houses and an author that a twelve and a half percent royalty rate—per my contract— was on the low end of the average spectrum. Thus, I was able to negotiate a basic royalty rate of fourteen percent, and a better graduating royalty rate as well. If the book sold more than twenty-five thousand copies, the royalty rate would increase from thirteen-and-a-half to fifteen percent. If sales surpassed seventy-five thousand copies, the royalty rate would top out at sixteen percent.

I eventually signed the contract and returned it by mail to the Questar office in Sisters, Oregon.

Upon receiving the contract, Allen Dust, the senior editor at Questar, called me. "All right; let's get started. I'll be your editor. What I'll do is edit five or six chapters at a time and overnight the edited pages to you by FedEx. You'll review the edits and mark the ones you don't like. You'll return the pages to me via overnight express, at Questar's expense, and we'll talk through the edits you marked. The process should be pretty simple. Do you have any questions?"

"Yeah...how much editing do you think will be required?" I expected to hear that the edits would be minimal. After all, tons of editing had already been done. Based on the input of all my test readers, I felt the manuscript had reached a point where it was already clean and precise.

"The editing will be quite extensive," Allen announced emphatically. "So I suspect it will take four to six weeks to complete the project."

Extensive! My mind immediately tried to deny the assessment. Extensive? How could the manuscript I had sent him require anything near an 'extensive' edit? Was he talking about my *Wisdom Hunter* manuscript? Really?

"Allen," I heard my voice quiver, "When you say 'extensive,' I'm not sure I understand. I thought the manuscript was pretty tight and nearly ready to go."

"Unfortunately, that's not the case at all. There's a lot of wasted words in the manuscript that slow the pace of the story. I'll help by streamlining the text and making it a much smoother and faster read. Plus, we need to eliminate all the profanity."

Wait; what? Wasted words. A pace that's too slow. Make it smoother and faster. Eliminate all profanity. I was being hit by multiple arrows and I didn't know quite how to respond. I felt like I had handed Questar a beautiful baby, a baby that multiple people had claimed was absolutely gorgeous, a baby about which Allen was saying, *Actually, it's not a beautiful creature at all. It needs several major cosmetic surgeries to make it attractive. But that can be done.* I felt like I had taken a powerful punch to the gut. Regarding the profanity, yes, there were ten or twelve scenes in the book where I had incorporated the use of curse words. But the profanity hadn't been used for gratuitous purposes. The swearing had been included only where emotions had been explosive and where nothing approaching kindness or civility would have ever been said in real life. I had attempted to maintain plausibility in those scenes.

But had I become so subjective in my judgment regarding the manuscript that I was now totally blind as to what could be done to make it better? After all, I had been blind before. That was the very purpose of *Wisdom Hunter*; to help the blind to see. Was I blind again, but in a different way?

"Okay," I reluctantly and painfully whispered, "but please approach your decisions carefully. This is not going to be easy for me."

So the editing process began.

When I received the first three edited chapters, my heart sank. The edits were indeed extensive. And I groaned and labored over every single change.

The following six weeks were some of the most taxing days of my life, both emotionally and mentally. I spent sleepless nights fretting. A part of me was convinced Allen was ruining the integrity of my story. Yet, oddly enough, another part of me couldn't help but see on occasions that many of his edits were magical. At some point during the project, though, I learned that Allen, somewhat to my dismay, was a successful author of children's literature and that, therefore, his propensity as a writer/editor was to cull a body of work to its barest elementary state without losing its overall substance. But was he achieving that balance with *Wisdom Hunter*, or was he trimming too much from the text? By the time we made it to the epilogue, a full twenty-five percent of my original pages had been eliminated as "non-essential." And I wasn't sure how to process that fact. The whole editing process, with two strong-willed people constantly butting heads, had been a battle of sorts, not something I expected. When it was all over, I was left with a slightly unpleasant taste in my soul concerning

Questar's 'extensive' editing approach. Questar, to my minimal pleasure, though, did agree to leave three or four of the "profanity" scenes in place.

"Our publishing house has never released a book that included profanity," the president of Questar informed me. "This will be a first. And I just hope it doesn't come back to bite us." He did tell me up front that he would write a letter forewarning the bookstore owners and book buyers of the profanity, and include a copy of the letter in every case of *Wisdom Hunter* that was placed into the distribution chain.

I understood and didn't argue.

As was typical in the publishing industry, before *Wisdom Hunter* was released to the marketplace, multiple copies—without any cover art—were sent to key people for review. One of the first reviews that came back was astounding. It was written by Paul Griffin, Senior Vice President of Multnomah Bible College in Portland, Oregon. Mr. Griffin proclaimed, "I read about 250 books each year, and *Wisdom Hunter* is the best I've read in ages. Not only does it tell a gripping story I could hardly put down, but along the way it blows the doors off 'packaged' Christianity. If you only read two books this year, make one the Bible—and the other *Wisdom Hunter*."

I could hardly believe it. And for a debut novel. Was this an industry fluke? Or was my faith just too fragile to believe that God had actually blessed the book with His favor?

To my utter amazement, the accolades continued to pour in—even before the book was released to the public—along with invitations for me to give radio and TV interviews. Living in Munich and still intending to live below the industry radar, at least until we returned to the States in August, I turned down every invitation, to the chagrin of the

Questar president and marketing team. Nevertheless, the novel quickly became a bestseller.

Maybe Allen's editorial judgment hadn't been so haphazard after all. I pondered that point deeply. Just as the international congregation in Norway had edited my perception of Christianity—which proved to be a life-altering lesson for the good—Allen likewise had edited my work as a neophyte novelist. And that too had obviously been a good thing. I started to see a theme, a life lesson. This thing called 'editing'—the positive and helpful correction provided by outsiders—was actually a necessity for one's spiritual, social, psychological, intellectual, and technical growth. It was something, however, that one's pride did not easily receive. But once experienced, one's soul registered its immeasurable value. I wanted to remember this for the rest of my life. Nearly everything in life, I surmised, could possibly be edited for the better—one's behavior, one's beliefs, one's work, one's life. I remembered that even King Solomon, the wisest of all men, had declared in Proverbs 12:1 and 15:32, that "whoever loves discipline (loves being edited) loves knowledge, but he who hates reproof (hates being edited) is stupid;" "the one who heeds correction (heeds editing) gains wisdom."

I was trying to learn. I really was.

I was trying to be a good student.

I was trying to be a genuine wisdom hunter.

Oh God, open my heart; open my mind.

And then, as *Wisdom Hunter*'s official publication date was only a few days away, I again started to feel guilty that IBWO knew nothing about the book. So I changed my plan and wrote a twelve-page letter to IBWO's president and to the European director. In the letter I carefully explained my burning desire to challenge those who still catered senselessly to a legalistic mindset, and told about my new book that illustrated the destructiveness of that behavior.

Before I mailed the letter, I asked six men in my church to proof it. They all read it and earnestly counseled me to rip it up and throw it in the garbage.

Whether right or wrong, I did what they suggested.

Chapter 46

My input was never solicited when Questar designed the cover art for *Wisdom Hunter*. But I was absolutely thrilled with the composition. The red-foil title, along with the distinct black silhouettes of a motorcycle, plane, boat, and collection of people spread across the bottom of the book, on front and back, was spectacularly beautiful. It was unique and memorable.

When I held my first printed copy in early April, I couldn't help but flip through the pages and admire the cover. I sighed with thankfulness. I, an adventurous young boy from Georgia who had hated school when growing up, was now a bonafide novelist. I was now a member of a small group of men and women in history whose written stories provided the world with a specialized source of entertainment and education.

Yes, I raved over and over inside my head. I was physically exhilarated.

The book was soon thereafter released to the market, backed by a strong advertising campaign.

While everything with Questar was moving along as scheduled, everything at our international church was progressing equally so. One of the men in our congregation, to the excitement of the entire church family, had just proclaimed God's call on his life to pursue seminary training and become a full-time minister. I ordained another man as the assistant pastor of our assembly. I continued to baptize new converts as we witnessed a regular influx of new congregants.

In late April I led the church in a weekend retreat at the historic Mittersill castle in Austria. About forty people participated. Our guest speaker, for four sessions, was a Dallas Theological Seminary graduate. In his opening presentation he shared a personal story to illustrate a particular Bible truth. His story stuck in my head, but for a different reason than he perhaps intended.

"In the first day of my Romans class," he told us, "the teacher at the end of the period said, 'Your homework tonight is to read verse sixteen of chapter one and write down five observations.' When I was ready to turn in the completed assignment the next day, the professor announced, 'Hold your paper; take it back home and record five more observations from the same verse.' I had to stretch my brain, but I finally managed to list five additional insights that I felt were plausible. When I was ready a second time to turn in the paper the professor said, 'One more time; keep the paper and make five more observations.'"

As I listened to the speaker tell his story, I felt a renewed flicker of genuine irritation toward my old Tennessee Temple professors. In the first day of my Romans class, the teacher—when he reached verse sixteen of chapter one—said, "Here's a sheet of paper outlining all the truths from this famous verse. Take the list home and memorize it. Be ready to repeat it back to me on a pop quiz."

Dallas Theological Seminary had taught the guest

speaker HOW to think. Tennessee Temple had taught me WHAT to think. As my emotions sizzled with the reminder, I vowed again that I would try to be a thinker for the rest of my life, at least for me if for no one else.

Regardless of the pitiful flashback, I was thankful that our congregation's three days together was a time of deep and blissful interaction. Even the new families in our group felt the exceptional warmth and closeness.

Soon after the retreat, Sherri and I commenced our step-by-step preparations to leave Bavaria and move our family back to the States. Our tentative plan was to spend a year, maybe a year and a half, in Georgia and then return to a new destination in Europe to plant a third international church. I was fully aware, though, that the fallout from *Wisdom Hunter* could possibly alter, or even annihilate, those plans.

A few weeks later, in the midst of our piecemeal packing, Sherri answered a phone call.

"Randy, it's for you," she announced, "It's Michael W."

I squinted. I only knew of one Michael W., and that was Michael W. Smith, the internationally famous singer. I mouthed silently to Sherri, "THE Michael W.?"

Sherri nodded affirmatively.

Surely, it couldn't be.

I cleared my throat and took the phone. "Hello, this is Randy speaking."

"Randy? Is this Randall Arthur, the writer of *Wisdom Hunter*?"

"Yes...that's me."

"Randall, this is Michael W. Smith, singer/songwriter, calling from Nashville, Tennessee. I just finished reading your book. And I'm blown away. I'm so moved I have to reach out to you and say thanks." For thirty minutes, Michael and I talked. He was truly excited that a book underscoring the destructiveness of legalism had hit the market, and had hit with a bang. "Man, the church needs a book like this right now," he exclaimed. "It's going to minister to a lot of people." It was a call I'll always remember.

A week or so later I received a call from Steven Curtis Chapman. Steven expressed a sentiment similar to Michael's. Additionally, he emphasized his appreciation for the craft of formulating a tight, fluid story. "Great job!" he told me.

I tried not to let the accolades from such famous voices enlarge my ego.

And then another call came—along with an invitation from California—that left me even more dumbfounded. The voice on the other end of the phone introduced himself as a representative of Dr. Tim LaHaye, a famous pastor, political activist, and author of internationally known books such as *Spirit-Controlled Temperament*, *The Act of Marriage*, and *How To Win Over Depression*. "As you perhaps know," the man stated, "Dr. LaHaye has authored numerous bestselling publications. But he's never written a work of fiction. And that's why I'm calling. Dr. LaHaye has filled a small notebook with ideas, characters, and plot lines for a fictitious story about the end times. He's read your novel *Wisdom Hunter*. And he loves your style. He wants to know if you'll consider using his notes and ghost writing the story for him. The working title is *Left Behind*."

Once I caught my breath, I said, "Tell Dr. LaHaye I'm truly honored by the extraordinary invitation. However, I'm not sure I'm the one he really wants to ghost write his book."

"I'm not certain I understand," the male voice expressed with a tone of disappointment.

"Well, you need to know first of all that I'm not a full-time writer. I'm a missionary pastor who writes sporadically on the side whenever I have some free moments. Secondly, I'm a slow writer, a very slow writer. Thirdly, I've started planning a second novel of my own, a follow up to *Wisdom Hunter*. And fourthly, my family and I are approaching an international move back to the States. Over the next two months I'll be focused on a whole list of things that have to be done in order to bring closure to our life here. And when we're back in America, it'll take at least three or four months to completely set up house there. For all these reasons, there's just no way I could work under a deadline during the next two years and churn out a quality book for someone as important as Dr. LaHaye. Besides, *Wisdom Hunter* was born out of personal experience and pain. It was easy for me to transfer my emotions to my main character. It was easy for me to be passionate about what I was writing. I'm not so sure I could convey such passion in someone else's story. So to be fair to Dr. LaHaye, I think I'll have to decline. Please tell him, though, I'm more than grateful that he's honored me with such a privileged invitation."

I learned that Dr. LaHaye eventually found a novelist who agreed to ghost write the *Left Behind* story for him. That author was Jerry Jenkins.

Under Jerry, the book morphed into a twelve-volume series that sold more than seventy million copies.

Chapter 47

During our last two months in Bavaria, the remarkable reviews for *Wisdom Hunter* continued to pour in, in spite of the small number of expletives scattered throughout the book.

Reviews such as:

"Dear Dallas (Questar President),
As of Friday, I finished reading *Wisdom Hunter*. I think it is fair to say this story is unlike anything I've ever read. Talk about gripping! I'd promised myself I would only read the novel at home—with no real distractions. The first night alone, I read until 1:30 AM. Unfortunately, I had to get up at 5:30 AM. I didn't care; it was worth it! This author knows how to write. I want to thank you for publishing such an incredible volume."
- Mary Risley, Christian Herald Book Club.

And:

"Many publishers send complimentary copies of

books suitable for pastors. If I had the dough, I'd put a copy of *Wisdom Hunter* in each of their hands...although me thinks a few of the pastors might be more than a little offended. I continue to recommend that book everywhere I go. Fantastic book!" - Jack Hager, Public Relations, Family Life Network.

And:

"Dear Randall, I cannot send this letter without letting you know how much I thought of *Wisdom Hunter*. I began reading it the day it arrived, and read it every spare moment until it was finished. I had finished Frank Peretti's *Prophet* the week before reading your book. Although I enjoyed both tremendously, *Wisdom Hunter* definitely gave me more food for thought. It was convicting in the sense I felt the Lord show me areas of legalism in my life of which I was unaware. Thank you for a very wonderful and needed book." - Penny Woods, Personal assistant to Josh McDowell.

And even from TV evangelists:

"With *Wisdom Hunter*, Randall Arthur will help you see more clearly what has long grieved my heart—the painful effects of misapplied religious ideologies. Randall makes it hard to put his book down. He writes in a clear, smooth style that makes for easy reading. But I assure you, it will not be merely the author's craftsmanship that will keep you focused. It will be your compulsion to put yourself in the shoes of this troubled Christian character and walk him through his agonizing dilemma. This is the only book I've read that I could not put down until I had gone through it cover to cover." - James Robison, TV evangelist, Life Today.

I continued to be surprised with each new major endorsement.

The "praises" for *Wisdom Hunter*, originating from all corners of America, especially from ministry leaders, started to go to my head. Yet, I regularly reminded myself of the "real me, the decrepit me" and tried to stay focused on my tasks at hand.

I barely managed.

But by mid-August Sherri and I—in preparation for our return to the States—had marked off every item on our "to do" list, with the exception of one final chore. We were contractually obligated by our lease agreement with Wolfgang Heileman to leave the inside of the house, in its entirety, freshly painted. We didn't have extra money to hire a painter. So, while Sherri, Heidi, and Shanda stayed a few days with one of the families in our church, I took up brushes, ladders, and buckets of paint and did all the painting myself.

A day or so later, with tears and sadness, we worshipped with our congregation one final time. Our four and half years at the helm of the young church had come to an end. And those years had affected us all. Forever-friendships had been forged. Unbelievers had become believers. New converts had been baptized. Pew-sitters and spectators had become teachers and leaders. To show their appreciation, the church gave us—among other things—a giant, hand-carved, hand-painted decorative wooden tray to hang on the wall of all our future homes. The front side of the tray displayed a two-story Bavarian farmhouse with snow-capped Alpine mountains rising majestically in the background. The back side contained over twenty-five handwritten inscriptions of thanks—inscriptions from more than twenty-five family units. We would carry these words with us forever, words such as:

> "Dear Dodds, Thanks so much for your openness, friendliness, and realness. I have never felt so comfortable with a pastor and wife..."

> "Dear Friends, You've challenged us. You've grown us. You've been honest with us. You've raised us as a family who love each other. So, you can't leave without taking a part of our hearts with you..."

The notations of appreciation and heartfelt expressions of love went on and on. Sherri and I wept. We learned with absolute conviction that God can, and does, use broken and leaky vessels to carry drops of living water.

On the day of our departure, we had arranged to spend our final thirty minutes—before going through airport security—with the three Germans who had become our dear, dear friends. Wolfgang, our unforgettable landlord. Ingrid, Wolfgang's former lover and now a Christian and well-established friend living and working in Munich on her own. And Kerstin, the German teenage neighbor who had spent so many hours in our home over the course of five years that she had become our "adopted" daughter. They had won our hearts. We had won their hearts.

As we thanked each other for the treasured friendships, we all choked up uncontrollably. I had never been part of such a heart-wrenching goodbye. My tears flowed freely, along with the gripping hugs.

When Sherri, the girls, and I finally boarded the plane we quickly lost ourselves in our own worlds of emotional transition. It wasn't an easy place. Final farewells were never painless.

Upon landing at the Atlanta airport thirteen hours later, Sherri was greeted by her mother's first words: "Good Lord, I hope you do something with that hair before Sunday." *Welcome back to the south*, I murmured to myself, where one's outward appearance is paramount to an acceptable reputation.

Well...at least southerners were famously friendly, hospitable, and generous. One of our supporting churches—Eastside Baptist—for example, had provided a home for us to live in, rent free, for the duration of our furlough. The house had for years served as the church parsonage. But the pastor and his family had, a year earlier, moved out and purchased a house of their own. The parsonage was a one-minute walk from the church. It was a furnished three-bedroom brick home with a built-out useable basement. The house—thoroughly cleaned and stocked with groceries—was a godsend. We moved right in and started planning our upcoming year.

One of the first agendas on our "must do" list was to find the best school for our girls. Heidi needed a seventh-grade teacher who could somehow understand, and work around, her cross-cultural complexities. Shanda, who had completed nine months in a German kindergarten, needed a first-grade teacher who was good at teaching English phonics. Thankfully we found such teachers at Mt. Zion Christian Academy, a thirty-minute drive from our house. The first and seventh grade teachers at our home church's private Christian school—one of the largest in the state at the time—just didn't fit our girls' social and academic needs. We hoped the Mt. Vernon congregation and new pastor, *Terry Rogers, would graciously understand our decision.

After attending Sunday services at Mt. Vernon for two Sundays I devoted my energy to calling our supporting pastors and setting up speaking engagements for the upcoming months. None of those supporting churches had an inkling that I was the author of the up-and-coming novel *Wisdom Hunter*. Neither did IBWO. I was in the process of trying to figure out how and when to break the news to them when Questar called and invited Sherri and me to fly to Sisters, Oregon to meet the Questar staff and speak at the church where the Questar president, Dallas Jackson, held his membership.

The church announcement that was posted in the Sisters' regional newspaper read:

> "Come hear the author of *Wisdom Hunter*. Randall Arthur's exciting and powerful new novel has gripped readers across America with a clear, deep vision of what Christian faith really means in today's world. Now you can hear this author in person at Cascade Community Church…"

I started to grow nervous. It seemed as if my readers were now thinking of me as an expert in pastoral leadership and Christian living. A fan letter from a pastor in Ohio further exemplified the issue.

> "As a teaching tool, *Wisdom Hunter* is excellent, and I am encouraging most of the church members to read it. Because of this, I fully expect more questions and greater interest in changing our method of 'doing church'."

Yes, in the *Wisdom Hunter* story I incorporated many of my experiments as a young color-outside-the-lines pastor. My reason for using those stories was to show church leaders that stodgy, impersonal traditions could be challenged, even cast aside, that it was okay to be creative in church assemblies. And, yes, several of my experimental approaches as a pastor were successes, both in reality and in my fictitious narrative, but it was never my intention to imply, directly or indirectly, that I was an expert in church leadership. Yet, that was how I was now being perceived by some. They were actually seeking my advice. I tried to answer every letter that requested my counsel. But in truth, I felt inadequate in my correspondence.

But the questions and the endorsements kept coming. Singer, entertainer Paul Overstreet sent me a letter saying,

> "A friend mentioned, with great enthusiasm, a book he had read, and I thought I'd give it a try. I picked up a copy and immediately became its captive audience until the final page. That book was *Wisdom Hunter*. I recommend it as a must read (book of the year)."

As I prepared for my visit to Oregon to meet the Questar staff in person for the first time and to speak at Dallas's home church, I felt like I had been put on a pedestal, a place I didn't like. After all, I felt like one of the least of God's little ones.

My *Wisdom Hunter* story, though garnering praise, had been birthed out of pain and failure. I didn't feel like a role model at all. Not for anyone.

But off to Oregon Sherri and I went.

Chapter 48

It was our first visit to the northwest. The Questar family greeted us as one of their own. The staff was young, focused, and determined. It was truly exciting to step into their world and witness the inner workings of a successful publishing house. I thanked the key players at Questar for giving *Wisdom Hunter* a chance. I especially thanked Allen Dust for his editing skills.

After a round of introductions and a personal tour of the facilities, Sherri and I were given a schedule for the next three days. The next morning, I would be the guest speaker at Dallas Jackson's home church. On Monday, the Questar staff and I would spend a good portion of the day talking business. And on Tuesday, Sherri and I would use a rental car, graciously provided by Questar, and spend two days exploring the state of Oregon, especially the coastal region.

As I reflected on the next day's speaking engagement, I still wasn't sure what Dallas or his pastor were expecting. Since their silence had granted me some perceived freedom, I decided I would veer from the typical monologue sermon.

The next day, to a midsize Sunday-morning crowd, I

shared my honest observation that there's very little authenticity in the average church. "All across America we typically arrive at church wearing a smiling mask," I stated emphatically. "We sit isolated front to back. Many of us are dying on the inside. And nobody knows—not until they hear we've filed for divorce, given up on church, strayed in our marriage, visited a professional therapist, become an alcoholic, or attempted suicide. And yet, no Christian anywhere makes those extreme decisions overnight. So, where is the church when we're feeling so alone, when we're headed step-by-step toward a precipice? The answer is: we're all sitting behind smiling masks, thinking everybody else has it all together. But the truth is, we're ALL struggling to varying degrees. All of us. Life is a battlefield, not a bedroom. With this in mind, there are undoubtedly people sitting here this morning who are seriously discouraged. And the New Testament—in First Thessalonians chapter five, verse eleven—instructs us quite clearly to encourage one another. So instead of just teaching this verse this morning, I would like, with your permission, to lead us in an exercise where we actually put the verse into practice. Is that okay?"

With nods all across the auditorium, the people gave their consent.

"All right, here's what we'll do. There are people sitting here this morning who, to varying extents, are struggling in life. Some are mildly discouraged. Others are deeply discouraged. On the opposite hand, others are probably in a manageable season, even a refreshing season, in life. In just a moment I'm going to ask those who are at a positive place to encourage those who are at a not-so-positive place. But in order to do that, we need to know first of all who's discouraged. We don't need to know details. We don't even need to know the degree of your discouragement. There's not even a need for you to talk if you don't want to. In a moment, I'm just going to ask you to raise your hand if you're in the middle of uncertain times and could use a little encouragement. I'll then ask two or three individuals to, one at a time, offer some encouragement. They can tell you how much you mean to them and to this church. They can promise they'll go for a walk with you this week just to be a shoulder to lean on. They can give encouragement in any way they feel is helpful. So..." I paused for emphasis, "who will dare be honest this morning and raise your hand, letting us know you're somewhat discouraged?"

I paused again. I fully understood I was taking a risk that people would not respond and thus create an unforgettably awkward moment. But I had led this type of exchange in two or three other churches. And the response had been overwhelmingly positive. I suspected, knowing the desire of the human heart to be heard, that the people of Sisters, Oregon would embrace the opportunity as well.

And they did.

After ten or fifteen seconds of tense quietness, a man raised his hand. The dam was instantly breached. Five or six others followed suit.

The verbal encouragement that came next, amidst multiple tears, proceeded for a good half-hour or more. Hugs, prayers, and promises followed. People left the church service wondering aloud why that type of scriptural interaction was almost nonexistent across America's religious landscape. I've always felt saddened that the evangelical church in the west chains itself unnecessarily to a traditional format—front-to-back seating with "qualified-only" stage practitioners. This setup leaves no opening for audience interaction. Thank God for the few pastors who buck this age-old ritual.

The next morning as we commenced the business side of

the visit, Dallas thanked me for the wonderful Sunday morning service then launched into his publisher's agenda. "As you might remember," he said, "I personally wrote a letter regarding *Wisdom Hunter* that has been included with every order of books we've sent to the bookstores. The letter explains that the book includes some light profanity and some suggestive scenes. I felt obligated to let the stores know this fact before they placed the book on their shelves. Consequently, even though the book has become a bestseller, the returns of *Wisdom Hunter* have been greater than any other book we've ever published. It seems that many of the bookstores are opening the cases of *Wisdom Hunter*, reading my letter, and promptly returning the books without ever cracking the cover. They just don't want to deal with the complaints that they're sure will come from their customers. As a matter of fact, Guidepost, the famous inspirational magazine, was getting ready to promote *Wisdom Hunter* on their back cover, something they've never done for any other book before. One of the Guideposts executives was so moved by the book that he was trying to push this through. So the president of the company read the book. He immediately vetoed the idea of promoting it, simply because of the small bit of profanity included in the story. He just didn't want to taint his company's stellar reputation. So...," Dallas paused. "I think what we need to do is ask you, Randy, to go back and rewrite the sections that are causing offense. Delete the profanity, but try to maintain the same level of intensity in the scenes."

The directive—a move I figured was unprecedented for a publishing house—was not something that excited me, but I nodded my willingness to capitulate.

Dallas continued. "I can then announce to the market that a new sanitized version is on the way."

"Sure," I told him half-heartedly.

"Good, good. Then start working on it as soon as you're back in Atlanta."

Contemplating the possible changes, I promptly decided I would hold off on telling IBWO about the book until I held a "cleaned up" edition in hand. To my surprise, Dallas's decision brought a tinge of relief to my soul which I was not expecting. And it felt favorable.

One of Dallas's assistants then handed me a newly collected stack of *Wisdom Hunter* reviews that had been received at the Questar office from bookstores around the country. "Here; sit down and read a bit. As you'll see, most of the written responses have been overwhelmingly positive. So be encouraged."

With Sherri out shopping and exploring the quaint town of Sisters, I sat alone with the pile of reviews that had been handed to me and indulged in one of the great pleasures for a writer - being inundated with positive feedback from appreciative readers. I read such comments as:

> "It's rare to find a novel dealing with human spirituality and faith that holds you right on the edge from cover to cover as this book does. *Wisdom Hunter* affirms that after the Cross comes the Resurrection." - Lee Ellis, Catholic Book and Gift Shop, Tulsa OK.

> "*Wisdom Hunter* will drive you to your knees in search of unadulterated Christianity." - Carol VanDeHoef, Lemstone Book Branch, Vernon Hills, IL.

I still found it difficult to believe the profusion of

accolades was for a book I had written. After all, I had never had any literary training or experience prior to *Wisdom Hunter*. *It's got to be a fluke*, I kept telling myself.

And then Dallas broke the news to me later in the afternoon that *Wisdom Hunter* had just been nominated for Christianity Today's 'Book of the Year' award.

What? Really?

Dallas gave me a few minutes to bask in the terrific news, then told me with all urgency, "Listen, you need to capitalize on *Wisdom Hunter*'s success by churning out another novel as quickly as possible. We need to keep the momentum going." I had already told Questar that I had another story brewing in my head. But now I was being urged to put pen to paper, and to not delay.

I made a list of all the things now pressing on my time. Answer fan mail. Rewrite the "offensive" scenes in *Wisdom Hunter*. Begin my next novel. Start reporting to my seventy-five supporting churches across a fifteen state area. Help Sherri chauffeur our girls to and from school as often as possible.

There was definitely a lot to think about and plan for. But I was assured the next two days had been set aside exclusively for exploring and enjoying the northwestern parts of the great state of Oregon.

So, I cleared my head. And Sherri and I went on a road trip.

Chapter 49

A few days later when Sherri and I were settled back in Atlanta in Eastside's parsonage, we seriously missed the hardened lava fields, majestic coastal cliffs, and giant Pacific sand dunes that had greeted and thrilled us along our Oregon adventure. And we definitely missed moving around in the Questar community of high-end publishing. The perks of being a celebrity writer were definitely nice. Overall, the trip had been just too brief.

Now back in my makeshift office in Georgia and focusing on my day-to-day responsibilities, I decided one of my first tasks would be to "sanitize" the scenes in *Wisdom Hunter*. I quickly saw, though, that the modifications were not going to be easy.

As I was trying one afternoon to imagine my way through the dilemma, Sherri approached me with a completely different issue. "Every time we go to a Mt. Vernon church service these days," she stressed, "I leave the building absolutely discouraged and depressed. Pastor Rogers just screams at us all the time. I just can't handle it anymore."

She was telling the truth. The pastor, constantly brandishing an I'm-right-and-everybody-else-is-wrong attitude, was seemingly growing more and more frustrated with the congregation by the week. I had even heard him in one service yell out to the congregation, *You are the stupidest bunch of people I've ever pastored!* But since I would be traveling nearly every weekend to speak at supporting churches, I would have the pleasure of missing out on most of the man's harshly-delivered tirades.

"So," Sherri continued, "Will it be okay if the girls and I start attending the Sunday morning services next door at Eastside? Pastor James there is more of a teacher. He doesn't scream. He doesn't yell. And I don't walk away feeling verbally assaulted."

"Absolutely," I assured her. "It's more than okay. I totally support the decision."

So, the next Sunday, Sherri and the girls began attending Eastside Baptist Church. The people at Eastside were far more relaxed, not being dominated by an angry, judgmental pastor. They embraced Sherri and the kids with open arms and gracious hearts. Sherri's demeanor regarding church attendance immediately graduated to a new level of ease. Eastside even integrated Sherri's music and teaching skills into their ministry. They quickly gave her a ladies' Sunday school class, and asked her, to her delight, to serve as their interim choir director. Regarding church, she couldn't have been happier.

Our marriage, though, was beginning to show signs of slumping again. I was so immersed in my speaking and writing ventures that my emotional investment in the marriage was becoming less and less proactive. Sherri asked me, for the fourth or fifth time in our marriage, if I would seek help from a professional counselor. To my shame, I once again shunned the idea. To be on the receiving end of professional therapy in our Independent Baptist association, and for it to become public knowledge, was as damaging to one's reputation as wearing a 24/7 neon sign emitting the words 'I'M A PROFESSIONAL LOSER.' All respect from all constituents would be lost overnight. Financial support would hurriedly dry up as well.

Crushed, Sherri quietly embarked for the first time on a lone journey of self help. As I finished the rewrites for *Wisdom Hunter*, she hungrily immersed herself in a book called *Codependent No More*, a relatively new and highly-touted book claiming to educate readers about the unwholesomeness of being codependent. This was the first time Sherri and I had heard the term 'codependent.' I was oblivious to the details of the book and had no idea what research the author was utilizing. What I did know was that every time Sherri finished absorbing a new chapter, there was some kind of psychological awakening that took place in her head. I could see it in her eyes. And it actually made me a little nervous.

But I kept to my own tasks.

I soon presented the *Wisdom Hunter* alterations to Questar. Everyone at Questar validated the changes. So, I assumed the "sanitized" version of the book would show up in the market place at the next print run. I would then finally take a copy to IBWO.

Chapter 50

Immediately after submitting the *Wisdom Hunter* changes and having them approved, I set up a make-do desk in our living room and, on a new desktop computer, commenced the first chapter of my new novel, *Jordan's Crossing*. I now intended to create a story that illustrated the destructiveness of liberalism. This time I would draw from my past struggles of dangerously wanting to be my own master. My goal was to complete the entire manuscript in twelve months. The production of the novel would be intertwined with my speaking engagements that required constant travel. To finish the book in a year's time would be a herculean task, but that's what Questar was requesting.

I was only a couple of chapters into the story when I received a call one afternoon with another set of destiny-changing possibilities. The call was from TV Evangelist James Robison. He asked if I would ghost write a novel for him. Again, I was thoroughly honored by such a high-profile request. But I had no margin for another super demanding project, unless I was willing to resign as a missionary and devote all my time to writing. And I had no inclination to go that route. Plus, I didn't possess the enthusiasm that I felt I would need for writing another man's story and making it feel real and exciting.

"I'm sorry," I explained, "I'm just not at a place where I can take on the extra work load."

"I understand," the evangelist said somewhat sadly. "Maybe another time then."

The offer, had I accepted it—simply because of the evangelist's name recognition and worldwide audience—could have conceivably had a major impact on my life; how or to what extent I wasn't sure.

Regardless, I buried my mind in the creation of *Jordan's Crossing*.

Like many men who are exceptionally busy, I was content to just coast in my role as a husband, especially with so many responsibilities calling my name. I tended to forget about the accumulation of offenses over the years that had not been properly dealt with. And Sherri, like many wives, allowed numerous affronts to slide by until the buildup of hurt was just too much to handle. And that's when she would erupt in a spillage of emotional distress.

"I don't feel like a priority in your life," she declared one afternoon. "I feel used and unappreciated. I wonder if you even love me. Why don't you just leave me and set yourself free!"

Those words—words I had heard before—always jerked my thoughts to a standstill. At that moment, I did something that surprised even me. "All right," I responded, "I'll get help! But you have to as well!" Sherri froze in silence. "If you can find a qualified counselor that you trust, make us an appointment." I then turned and walked out of the room, hoping I hadn't just jeopardized our reputation of being a stellar couple.

Like most couples, Sherri and I were opposites in many ways. I was a goer. She was more of a homebody. I was a risk taker. She was more cautious. I was a night owl. She was an early bird. I withdrew in anger and became mute. She ignited in anger and felt compelled to talk through her feelings. Offenses—from people, movies, and songs—rolled quickly off my mind. Sherri was a sponge that was negatively effected for days by the sights, sounds, and actions that offended her. I heard the rules all around me and looked for loopholes. She adhered obediently to the rules. I liked cities. She didn't. The only adhesives that held our marriage together were our love for God and ministry, and our stubborn commitment to one another. But to carry on in a manner that would be emotionally healthy and satisfying, we both needed help. And I, and I alone—because of my enduring pride and naivety—had refused professional help for way too long. So, when a reputable counselor was found on the north side of Atlanta, I kept my promise. I agreed to go, but was still apprehensive.

When Sherri and I drove to our first counseling appointment, my mom babysat our girls. We simply told her that we were going out for some adult time. We didn't dare tell *anyone* our true destination.

Halfway through that first therapy session, I began to relax. The counselor, a man in his late thirties, had promised up front he would not show favoritism toward Sherri. Or me. Rather, he would take sides with the marriage. And that's what he so brilliantly did. He was not shocked by any of the "dirty laundry" Sherri and I pulled from the past or the present. With extraordinary grace, he accepted us as we were and seemed to genuinely care about our union. Granted, I paid high dollars for the man's grace. But at least he blessed us with grace, a healing approach that was totally absent in our Independent Baptist network. Plus, he was bound by confidentiality. At the end of the session, I thanked the man with genuine tears.

During the first three or four sessions—meeting once a week—I was able to unload my husbandly failures, along with my complaints. And Sherri was able to share her side of the marital story. The sessions were intense and sometimes uncomfortable. But the counselor continued to be observant, gentle, fair, and wise. It was as if we had handed him a knotted ball of twine and he instinctively knew which strings to pull first, and in which direction, to untangle the mess.

The results, of course, were not always pleasant. As we headed home following the fourth or fifth meeting, Sherri and I found ourselves embroiled in a heated argument over something that surfaced through an honest admission. The ugly exchange quickly intensified until I was tempted to physically shake her to make her understand my point-of-view. At that point, I pulled the car over into the I-75 emergency lane in downtown Atlanta, near Georgia Tech, and jumped out of the vehicle. Standing outside the car, as traffic brushed by at 75 miles-per-hour, I yelled at my wife of seventeen years, "I do not want to talk to you right now! I can't handle it! So just take the car and go!"

With no further words, Sherri huffed her way into the driver's seat and squealed the car tires as she accelerated back into traffic.

I stood alone. I had a seventeen mile walk ahead of me. In the dark. Along a dangerous stretch of interstate. And I was glad.

Far more perilous at night, the solo trek, nevertheless,

proved to be therapeutic from the start. With each step toward home, my thoughts and emotions slowly found blessed release. One reason is that God heard more than an ear full as I vented, begged, and complained—knowing He was patiently listening.

In the meantime, Sherri—I would learn later—immediately upon her arrival at the house called the counselor. "What am I supposed to do?" she pled. "Randy got out of the car in a dangerous section of Atlanta and is walking home in the dark.! Should I go back and find him? Should I call the police and get them to help?"

"Relax. Breathe," the counselor told her when hearing all the details. "He's a big boy. He'll be fine. Go pop some popcorn. Get yourself a Pepsi. Sit down and watch a movie. And then go to bed. That's the best thing you can do for yourself. And for him."

And that's what she did.

I slipped into the house six hours later. My body was exhausted, but my soul was purged. The therapist had been right. I had badly needed the long walk—just me and God, with no outside interferences.

During our next session with the therapist a week later, the trained counselor, in an effort to help Sherri overcome her codependency, looked her in the eye and declared, "You've been an enabler, young lady. Your marriage would have been a lot healthier had you learned years ago to look Randy in the eye and say, 'Hell no.'"

In Sherri's defense, she grew up in a home led by a strong father who didn't play around when it came to discipline. Sherri, with a natural propensity to yield and to obey, never crossed her dad. When she married me, only three weeks after turning eighteen, she found it natural to behave in the same submissive manner toward me, her husband, who was also a strong-willed leader. It never occurred to me that she was hurting herself by shying away from setting up firm boundaries in our relationship. Only when the counselor verbalized the unwholesomeness of that type of negligence did I grasp the truth of it. So much for a counselor not being able to tell me anything I didn't already know.

From that day forward, Sherri started setting up boundaries. I can't say her change of behavior was fun, but it did produce a healthier relationship. I witnessed both her inner strength and social strength grow exponentially from that month onward. For the first time in our marriage, she became an equal. She learned to look me in the eye and say, "Hell no."

Life started to calm down a bit as we moved through the Christmas and New Year holidays.

As 1992 commenced and school started up again, Sherri and I gravitated back to our routines. I started traveling again, giving in-person updates at our supporting churches, and continued to churn out chapter after chapter of *Jordan's Crossing*. Sherri resumed chauffeuring Heidi and Shanda to and from school every day and became even more involved at Eastside Baptist, next door.

I learned that *Wisdom Hunter* did not win Christianity Today's book of the year award for 1991. But the novel continued to surprise everyone in the industry with its robust sales. And, as a neophyte author, I was pleased with at least that much. I was more than a little worried, though, that Questar had not yet released the sanitized version of *Wisdom Hunter*. I couldn't understand why they kept delaying the agenda. The book had now been in publication for nine months, and I was feeling more and more guilty that my mission agency and supporting pastors still didn't know I was the author.

By the time late March came around—and the cleaned-up edition of *Wisdom Hunter* still wasn't in print—I decided I could not wait any longer. I simply had to inform IBWO. They would just have to see the original version that included the graphic scenes and the profanity. The book had now been in bookstores for a full year. So I psyched myself up one morning and called the IBWO home office in Chattanooga, Tennessee to make an appointment with the President.

"IBWO; how can I help you?" the receptionist answered.

I took a deep breath. "Yes, this is missionary Randy Dodd calling from Atlanta."

"Good morning, Randy. I hope you and your family are doing well. How can I help you today?"

"I need to make an appointment as soon as possible to sit down with Dr. *Sykes and discuss something that's rather important."

After waiting on-hold for a few minutes, I was told, "Dr. Sykes can see you next Tuesday morning, March 31st, at ten, if that'll work for you."

"That will be great. Thank you. I'll mark my calendar."

The few days leading up to the appointment were understandably peppered with anxiety for me. Even though I had long suspected I would be fired, I hadn't spent a lot of time developing an exit plan. And I wasn't sure why.

On the morning of the scheduled meeting, I drove the two hours from Atlanta to Chattanooga alone. Going unaccompanied was my sadistic choice. In my possession that morning was a copy of *Wisdom Hunter*. I had gone through its pages and marked in red all the words of profanity and all the scenes that some felt were too graphic. I now wanted everything out in the open. I wanted total disclosure.

When I entered the IBWO brick building, with its notable clout in the Independent Baptist world, I noticed—of all things—that everything and everyone appeared quite normal. There were comings and goings and pockets of serious conversations. Would my revelation, I suddenly wondered, in any way upset the system? Or would the thing I was about to reveal even create a ripple? I was about to find out.

"I'm here for my ten o'clock appointment with Dr. Sykes," I informed the receptionist.

"I'll let him know you're here," she affirmed with an earnest work face.

Dr. Sykes stood a few minutes later and greeted me with a smile when I entered his office. He was in his fifties, but was already grey headed. His build and posture were utilitarian. He and his wife had years earlier served as missionaries in Asia. As the IBWO President and General Director he now shouldered the responsibility for a thousand missionaries and their collective relationship with five-thousand Independent Baptist churches that supported those missionaries financially. Consequently, there were always "fires" that had to be dealt with. And I, it seemed, was about to start another one.

Dr. Sykes and I exchanged pleasantries. I thanked him for meeting with me, and then quickly segued to the purpose for my visit. "Dr. Sykes, the reason I'm here this morning," I tried to spout assertively, but heard my voice crack, "is to let you know I've written a novel that to my shock and surprise has become a bestseller."

Dr. Sykes's expression conveyed a bit of neutral confusion. He waited in silence for me to continue.

"And I need to let you know that the theme of the book is the ugliness of legalism. So, you'll probably want to read the book and let me know if all this is going to be okay."

Still caught off guard and somewhat confused, Dr. Sykes naturally unleashed a few questions. My no-holds-barred answers fueled additional questions. "When did you write this book?" "What do you mean by the ugliness of legalism?" "Do any of your supporters know about the book?" "Why are you just now letting me know about this?" "How many copies have sold?" "Why the pseudonym; were you trying to conceal your identity?" "Did your publisher know there might be a conflict of interest here?"

For thirty minutes or more I answered the inquiries in full, holding nothing back. Dr. Sykes's eyes widened with each of my responses.

And then I showed Dr. Sykes all the pages where I had earmarked words and paragraphs. "The book has become quite controversial," I confessed. "Not only because of its theme, but also because of these sections that I've singled out."

Dr. Sykes flipped slowly through the pages, now giving serious attention to the pinpointed elements. After scouring the last of those pages, he looked at me with an avalanche of anger in his eyes. "I can't believe this, Randy!" He sighed. "You've just placed a bomb in my lap! And I don't like it!" He huffed with rising disgust. "We sent you to Europe to change the culture, but you...you disgracefully let the culture change you!" He again shook his head in disbelief. "So, what did you do; just sit in the Alps for the last five years and write this book to get something off your chest while your supporters unwittingly financed your secret project?"

I reacted immediately. "Oh! No! No! No! My supporting churches sent me to Munich to plant another international church. And that's exactly what I did! I can give you the names of nearly a hundred people who can testify to the number of hours I spent in the discipleship of their lives! I did not; I repeat, I did not just sit and write a book. I wrote in my spare time. And the writing did not distract me in any way from planting and pastoring a church. A very fruitful church, by the way. That's a fact that cannot be contested!"

Dr. Sykes's entire body tensed up. "Missionaries have no business writing books!" he snapped.

I didn't throw out the name of the Apostle Paul at that moment, though I was tempted. Plus, I wanted to ask why it was perfectly alright for pastors and evangelists to write books, but not missionaries. But I refrained.

Dr. Sykes sighed again, this time forcefully. "I'll work this into my reading schedule over the next two weeks. And then I'll let you know my decision. But this doesn't look good at all. Not at all! In the meantime, just stay quiet about it!"

I nodded, shaking uncontrollably on the inside. I left Chattanooga before noon and headed back to Atlanta.

That evening around nine-thirty Sherri answered a phone call that came to our house. "Randy, it's for you," she said, "It's Dr. Sykes."

Chapter 51

"Randy!" Dr. Sykes half growled, "I want your letter of resignation on my desk tomorrow morning! I've spent the afternoon and evening reading your story. I'll read the rest of it tomorrow. But this is a disgrace! You're finished, my friend! Fax the letter of resignation! Again, I want it on my desk by tomorrow morning! Is that clear?"

I inhaled deeply and gulped. "Yes, sir," I mumbled. I had tried for a full year to prepare myself mentally for this very moment, but all the supportive truths I had embedded in my mind were instantly forgotten.

"And...," Dr. Sykes proceeded, "we'll expect you to come back to the office one final time to sign some papers and to answer some more questions! We need to understand what has happened here!"

A date and time the following week was set for my last trip to the IBWO home office...after seventeen years of faithful service.

When the call ended and Sherri learned what had happened, she paused, then promptly shot her hands into the air and shouted, "Yes! Yes! Yes!" I was shaking my head, astounded by my wife's reaction. To the contrary, my mind was running to all the worse-case scenarios. Crazily, I saw Sherri continue celebrating as she literally broke into a dance and song, bellowing, "Thank God I am free! Free! Free! Thank God I am free! Free! Free!"

It was Sherri's bombastic and jubilant reaction that kept me from sinking head-deep into despair.

My next course of action, I decided when my mind was able to think a little clearer, would be to contact all seventy-five of our supporting pastors and let them know about *Wisdom Hunter*. I wondered bleakly if they would react like Dr. Sykes. I was sure most of them probably would. After the full fallout, Sherri and I would need to find a new mission board, a task that would be arduous, and probably have to raise a substantial amount of new support as well which would be even more difficult. But before I took any of those steps, I wanted to go back to Chattanooga and put the final meeting with Dr. Sykes behind me.

The next week I chose to return to IBWO, once again unaccompanied. I, and I alone, had written *Wisdom Hunter*—expressing my disdain for legalism and the church leaders that embraced and promulgated the legalistic paradigm—and I, and I alone, would now offer up my defense. I assumed the final meeting would include only three people - me, Dr. Sykes, and Dr. *Rob the European Director. When I walked into the gathering, however, I was surprised to find five IBWO officials seated around a conference table. All the men wore suits and ties, as was standard, and sported close-cropped haircuts. Without exception, each of the men displayed a stern expression. I was given a chair at the end of the table. I uncomfortably took my seat. Some of the men had just finished reading *Wisdom Hunter*. So the inquisition promptly began, basing the interrogation on the contents of my novel.

"Do you believe drinking alcoholic beverages is okay?" "Are you and your wife social drinkers?" "Is profanity a part of your everyday vocabulary?" "Do you believe profanity is okay?" "Do you honestly believe your main character, Jason Faircloth, at the beginning of the book represents most Independent Baptist pastors?" "Is that how you view the pastors that support you financially?" "We sent you to Europe to help change the post-Christian culture, but you let the culture change you; isn't that what happened?"

I held my ground and answered all the questions truthfully. "I believe drunkenness is clearly a violation of God's will. But, no, I don't believe the simple consumption of alcohol is a sin." "Yes, I've tasted wine and beer on a few occasions but never acquired a taste for any of it. So, no, neither I nor my wife are social drinkers." "No, profanity is not part of my daily life. But I would be lying if I told you I've never cursed." "Yes, I believe the main character in my book does indeed mirror the authoritarian and destructive attitude of many Independent Baptist pastors. It's a serious problem that needs to be acknowledged and addressed." "Yes, the European culture has changed me, especially the European Christians. They've helped me see that a lot of the dos and don'ts the Independent Baptists preach in the name of God are nothing more than the feeble traditions of men."

The men shook their heads in disbelief. "People are going to die and go to hell because of this book," one of the men angrily surmised. "And their blood is going to be on your hands. How can you live with that?" Another pronounced, "It'll definitely steer people away from Bible believing churches. I just can't believe this is happening."

Following more exchanges and more questions that only heightened the agitation in the room, Dr. Sykes finally reclaimed the floor and proclaimed, "You've obviously lost your way, Randy. So we, the IBWO directors, have decided to send a letter to all your supporting churches, rejecting you and your book. We want to clear our name from this whole mess as quickly as possible. And since the book is selling so well, we expect you to use your royalties to repay all your supporting churches the money they've given you over the past five years."

The men were still convinced I had deceptively squandered five years of support dollars sitting and writing the novel instead of ministering. And to my knowledge, they never contacted anyone in our Munich church to investigate the truth of the matter.

"What I will do," I retorted, "is offer to repay my supporting churches the dollars they've given us during the seven months we've been back in the States. That would be fair! But that's all!"

My final departure from the IBWO organization, family, and facility—after seventeen years of employment—was a cold, pitiful, tension-filled event. IBWO felt cheated. I felt cheated. I should have listened to Sherri and changed mission boards years earlier. As I drove home, my feelings ran the gamut from bereavement to anger to relief to elation - and back again.

Sherri greeted me at the house, feeling terrible when I described what I had faced alone, but persistent in her joyous certainty that breaking ties with IBWO was a magnificent plus.

IBWO wasted no time composing and releasing their public letter. The document was sent straightaway to our seventy-five supporting churches and, I believe, to the thousands of other churches that partnered with all the other IBWO missionaries. The letter, printed on IBWO's colored stationery, was written by the European Director.

> Dear Supporters of Randy and Sherri Dodd,
> At the request of the Board of Independent Baptist World Outreach, Randy Dodd has submitted his resignation to be effective immediately. The Mission will not be processing funds for Randy Dodd's account past the date of this letter. Anyone wishing to continue to support Randy Dodd must work that out with him personally as to where monies should be sent.
>
> IBWO's request for Randy Dodd's resignation came about as a result of a book which Randy has published and IBWO feels to be very much out of character for the Christian's standards and values of the Mission. Randy will also be sending out a letter of explanation to his supporters.
>
> A further consideration was the fact, as Randy stated in his letter, that the book was written, published, and circulated without the mission's knowledge or consent while he was still a missionary. IBWO feels that supporting churches and IBWO were unknowingly financing Randy Dodd's project during a two year period of time and particularly during the year since the book has been published.

Thank you for all that you are doing for missions. We cherish your friendship and prayers. I am

Yours sincerely for Christ,
R. R. - For the Personnel Committee
Independent Baptist World Outreach
Psalm 27:1

The words *'while he was still a missionary'* leapt off the page at me. *What?* Did IBWO intend to say *while he was still a IBWO missionary*. If not, did they really believe my severance from the Independent Baptist world of missions—simply because I had embraced a position that was 'out of character for the values of the Mission'—meant that God had suspended my missionary calling? I never had a chance to ask. To my shock, though, they actually cut me a check for $6,000 as a 'pension' payment.

My letter to our supporting pastors was postmarked shortly after IBWO's.

Chapter 52

ATTENTION!
CHANGING MISSION BOARDS!
EVERY PASTOR PLEASE READ!

Dear Supporting Pastors and Individuals,

The majority of you have now been standing behind our ministry for fifteen years. During this time I have regularly shared my heart with you through newsletters, through personal letters, from your pulpits, and especially through one-on-one conversations. You have followed our lives from the early days of our arrival in Norway until now. You have been made aware of our struggles, our discouragements, our victories, and our fruit. You have helped us establish two international churches that have proven to be a life-changing influence on the lives of hundreds of people from over 65 different nations. You have maintained your confidence in us.

By no stretch of the imagination, however, have we been model missionaries. But our three terms of fruitful missionary service in Europe have validated the fact that we have tried hard to be efficient, productive, and true to the Scriptures. Anyway, because of the publication of a controversial novel I wrote, the IBWO personnel committee has demanded my resignation from IBWO, effective today.

The title of the novel that has forced this resignation is WISDOM HUNTER. It was published last spring by Questar Publishers, Inc. under the name Randall Arthur. (Arthur is my middle name.) The story is about a high profile Atlanta pastor who, because of his narrow-mindedness and know-it-all attitude, loses his teenage daughter, loses his wife, and then, because of disillusionment, almost loses his faith. In the middle of his crisis, he discovers he has a granddaughter whose identity and location are being kept a secret from him. He discovers she is being abused. He sets out to find her. The trail that he picks up leads him out of the ministry, through four years of wandering throughout the United States, to England, to Cyprus, and finally to Norway where his life is salvaged by a wise old mentor.

It is a fictitious, but true-to-life drama that attempts to show that when we add to the Bible (and in the name of God enforce on people) the extra-Biblical convictions of men, the personal teachings of idolized men from former generations, and the teachings of our American culture that have become intertwined with our Christianity, we tend to become destructive.

It is a novel that was born out of much pain, many tears, and a therapeutic need to put into writing the things I was feeling, thinking, and learning.

Does writing such a book mean I have now become a liberal? The answer is a resounding NO! A liberal is one who takes away, subtracts, and deletes from God's Word. I have never done that, and hope I never will. But on the other hand, I do not want to add to God's Word either. Subtracting from and adding to His Word are both destructive. God warns us in Deuteronomy, Proverbs, and Revelation that we should not be found guilty of doing either one. I am a literalist. I accept the Bible literally as it is, fully and completely. My goal is to teach and preach those things which are clearly written. I am a fundamentalist who believes in the Biblical fundamentals of the FAITH. I am not a neo-evangelical who compromises the fundamentals of the faith for associational reasons.

Anyway, my request is this: Will every pastor and individual who presently supports us please get a copy of the book and read it. You can find it in nearly all the major Christian bookstores. If you cannot find it at your local Christian store, then call Questar at 1-800-933-7526. You can obtain a copy through their office. Several of my supporting pastors and individuals have already testified how refreshing the book has been to them. I am sure that many of you will also find the book to be an enjoyable and refreshing read. But, because of the controversial nature of the book, it is inevitable, I suppose, that others of you will choose, for personal reasons, to terminate our support.

And if we are going to lose some of our support, then we need to know now—before our family returns to Europe—so that we can schedule meetings with new contacts and rebuild that lost support.

Therefore, after you read the book, will you please fill out the enclosed postcard and return it to us as soon as possible so that we might know whether you will or will not continue to support our ministry.

For the next month or two, until we establish a working relationship with another mission board, all donations should be sent (effective now) to:

Missionary Randy Dodd
P.O. Box 360758
Decatur, Georgia 30036

Please understand that IBWO should not be held accountable for the publication of WISDOM HUNTER. I, and I alone, am responsible. IBWO knew nothing about the book until I brought it to their attention. Wrongfully, I didn't make sure they knew about it sooner.

Since I waited so late to report the book to IBWO, the personnel committee feels that, as a token of my apology, I need to make an offer to pay back, as much as I can, the support you've given to us during the months we've been home on furlough.

Therefore, in an effort to demonstrate that I want my heart to be right, I have volunteered to use the pension money coming to us next week as 'repayment' money.

I've been told that after my one remaining financial debt to IBWO is deducted from my pension fund that I will have approximately $6,000 left. If you are offended by the book, and feel that I owe you a refund on the support you've given to us during the time we've been back in the States, then please let me know before the middle of May. At that time I will total up the amount I am asked to repay and will distribute the available $6,000 proportionately.

Please understand also that the writing of the novel did not in any way distract from our church planting work in Munich. This fact is evidenced by the visible fruit of our missionary efforts. The people who were part of our church can, and will, gladly testify to the amount of time we gave in the discipleship of their lives. This is a point that simply cannot be contested.

Our goal in the next five or six weeks is to decide—through prayer, inquiries, and God's leading—which other mission board to serve under.

As soon as I can, I will send out another newsletter that tells how much support we have lost (and will have to rebuild) and with which new mission board we have joined ranks.

I apologize for any awkwardness I've created because of the publication of the book, but I felt that some things needed to be said. Some of you, I know, will understand.

Sincerely,
Randy Dodd

PS-Please read the book in its entirety before you make a judgment call. Things quoted out of context through the grapevine can give wrong impressions and appear to be something they're really not.

Along with each letter, I inserted a pre-addressed, pre-stamped postcard that gave the following instructions:

Please check appropriate box:
____ We will continue our support
____ We will terminate our support
    ____ Immediately
    ____ At the end of May
    ____ At the end of June
    ____ At the end of July

Pastor: _____
Church: _____

Within a day or so of mailing the copied letter around the country, I received a handwritten letter from Allen, the senior editor at Questar publishers.

Chapter 53

Allen's handwritten letter, scribbled in blue ink—along with a printed contract for the publication of *Jordan's Crossing*—read,

Dear Randy,

I was just walking into Dallas's office to let him see this draft copy of the *Jordan's Crossing* contract when Dallas told me your big news. Somehow I find myself feeling elated for you, which I guess is not the appropriate response when someone loses a job, but I sure hope this frees you up to some new and exciting things in the future.

Regarding the contract, Dallas asked me to ask you about an advance. Dallas wants to know if you feel it could be beneficial at this point.

We have upped the higher-bracket royalty rates

to 16 and 18 percent, from 15 and 16 for *Wisdom Hunter*. We have also returned the motion picture rights share to 50% for you. Dallas feels he really does want to treat all our authors the same on those kind of issues.

Look this over and let us know what you think. We can send a final draft once it's worded in a way we all want.

Best wishes and God's peace to you in this new chapter of life.

Allen

I was more than grateful that Questar offered the advance, but I was still uneducated regarding the fine points of a publisher's advance. I still assumed I would have to pay back any of the advance monies that the sales of the book did not recoup. And I didn't like debt. So, again, in my ignorance I forfeited the offer because I did not want to risk becoming a debtor to the publishing house.

But I did sign the contract.

That same week I started contacting mission agencies whose beliefs, visions, and policies I thought Sherri and I could readily welcome, and co-exist with. As a missionary, I never again wanted to dance around the irrational demands and expectations of any mission board.

Two well-known mission organizations that I called actually invited us with open arms to join their ranks. One of them asked if we would consider leading a team of three families to Paris with the goal of planting an international church. One asked if we would work for them in Latvia. As wonderful as the invitations were from these mission leaders, I just didn't feel in my gut—after further research—that I was ready to form a long-term alliance with either of them. I was still wary of an institution's polity, especially when old-traditions and religiosity were prominent.

And then unexpectedly I heard about a young mission agency based in California. The agency's all-consuming goal, I learned, was to plant high-impact international churches across Europe.

Really?

The group was Christian Associates International. I reached out to them immediately. The founder and CEO of the group was *Larry Michaels. I learned he would be in Atlanta shortly and would gladly set aside time to sit and talk with Sherri and me.

A few days later, Sherri and I met Larry for lunch at a restaurant on the north side of Atlanta. When we finished sharing the meal together, we jumped right into the business portion of the conversation. I told Larry up front, "I'm tired of pretending, tired of trying to cast the image of being a professional missionary who has it all together. I want to serve with an organization that recognizes the fact that all missionaries struggle in life, to varying degrees. I want to belong to an organization that extends grace and support to its missionaries when they need help—when they are fighting depression, when they're seeing their kids go astray, when they're floundering in their marriage. As a matter of fact, Sherri and I are seeing a marriage counselor right now. I don't want to hide things like that any more."

Larry squinted and looked at me as if I had just stepped off a plane from an antiquated culture. "Why? Was authenticity such a scarce thing with your Baptist mission board? I mean...did they never encourage transparency?"

"Encourage? Are you kidding?" I expressed bluntly. "In seventeen years of missionary service and four years of Bible college, I've never heard one pastor, one evangelist, one professor, or one missionary in my denomination ever admit publicly that they struggle in life with anything - fear, anxiety, addiction, marriage, ministry. They all project the image of always being the conqueror, the victor, the bulwark. The truth is: the denomination's dos and don'ts are so unrealistic, and the pronounced judgments on those who violate those dos and don'ts are so severe, that no leader dares peel back their mask, not even a little. Consequently, the pretension that's fostered at the top trickles down to everyone. And I mean everyone. So, everybody tiptoes around on eggshells. Because if it's discovered you're a lawbreaker of any of the dos and don'ts, there's no grace for you, only merciless judgment. It's absolutely Pharisaical and destructive!"

Larry raised his eyebrows and shook his head. "I can't relate. But I'll tell you openly; my wife and I have struggled in our marriage like everybody else. That's only normal."

I actually started weeping. It was the first time I'd heard an evangelical leader confess publicly that he was human. Larry won my heart right there on the spot.

"We'd be glad to have you on our team," he accentuated after hearing more of our story and asking an array of questions. I had revealed to Larry that Sherri and I were considering the German capital of Berlin as our next destination for planting another international church. So, he drove home his invitation by saying, "Berlin is one of the next major cities on our vision list. Considering your achievements in Oslo and Munich, we would be honored if you would lead a church-planting team into Germany's number-one city for us."

That simple validation of our overseas work was more uplifting than Larry would ever know. I automatically gave him my respect. I even liked him. And I deeply appreciated everything I was learning about the dynamics, vision, and ministry profile of Christian Associates International. Suits and ties were discouraged. The NIV translation of the Bible was the translation of choice. A man's hairstyle was not an issue. Missionary wives could wear slacks. CAI missionaries lived in an interdenominational world. Baptists were just one of many denominations represented. I was certainly drawn to the organization. I actually longed to be part of such an authentic, grace-filled community. But...it was the word "team" that caused me hesitation. A big part of me wanted to initiate the application process that very day, but another part persuaded me to pause in my tracks. The concept of leading a team of missionaries didn't bother me. What did bother me was the idea of CAI recruiting and building the team around Sherri and me. What if Sherri and I lost so much financial support because of *Wisdom Hunter* that replacing the funds proved to be so slow and so exhausting that we gave up? What if our marriage started to unravel again? What if we changed our mind about Berlin as a destination? It was simply too early, I decided, for us to make such a consequential commitment if it had to involve three or four other families—their marriages, their kids, their futures.

And teams, I learned, were CAI's mode of operation, a non-negotiable.

"I'm honored by the invitation, Larry. More than you know. But Sherri and I will need time to think about all this. And, of course, we'll make a list of questions. Then we'll get back to you."

Larry nodded his agreement. "Absolutely. Take all the time you need. It's a big decision."

Returning home that afternoon, Sherri and I excitedly discussed the pluses of Christian Associates International. We were still talking about the proposition of joining CAI when we arrived home and checked our mailbox. Included in the pieces of mail we collected was an envelope from Questar Publishers. Someone at Questar had sent a copy of a marketing letter they had written and mailed to hundreds of book buyers around the country. It read:

> Controversial Book Gets Author Fired
> From Large Missionary Organization
>
> From his own tough experiences in seventeen years as a missionary for a large, Tennessee-based fundamentalist group, Randy Dodd wrote a gripping novel of a man whose family and career were destroyed by the enslaving hypocrisy of legalistic Christianity.
>
> Writing under the name Randall Arthur, Dodd kept his connection to the novel a secret from his organization's leaders for almost a year after it was published, for fear of losing his job. His fears were well-founded. On March 31, he met with the mission group's general director and finally revealed his involvement with the book, entitled *Wisdom Hunter*. Overnight the general director read half of *Wisdom Hunter*, which was all it took for him to ask for Dodd's resignation the following day.

A copy of *Wisdom Hunter* has been provided to you with this news release, along with a letter from the author. For further details, you may contact the author in suburban Atlanta at 404-987-8797. You may also call the publicity department of Questar Publishers at 1-800-933-7526.

WISDOM HUNTER by Randall Arthur
Nominated for Christianity Today's 'Book of the Year Award in fiction

Being a shrewd businessman, Dallas Jackson, the President of Questar, wasn't going to pass up a great marketing opportunity. He knew the controversy surrounding *Wisdom Hunter* would generate a greater interest in the book. Thus, the marketing letter.

At that juncture I had no objection whatsoever. I figured I had nothing else to lose. Or at least that's what I surmised until I received a phone call a couple of days later from Dr. Sykes at IBWO.

"Randy," he declared with a determined tone, "IBWO has decided to file a law suit against you and your publisher!" He couldn't accept the fact, it seemed, that I had successfully planted and pastored a church while writing *Wisdom Hunter*. He convinced himself that my writing had taken preeminence during our season in Munich and that I had wasted supporters' money. After informing me of the forthcoming litigation, he contacted Dallas Jackson at Questar with the news.

Mentally quick and highly intelligent, Dallas responded without hesitation, "Awesome! Please go ahead and do it! As a matter of fact, please do it today! This will blow the sales of the book right out of the water! Again, please do it, I beg you!"

I don't know what else Dallas told him, but I nervously held my breath for a few days until I heard that IBWO had finally withdrawn their threat to sue. I was thankful, for sure, to be spared the legal entanglement. But I had by no means skirted further consequences for writing the book. Letters from angry supporting pastors quickly started arriving at our mailbox.

Chapter 54

"As I see it, you no longer study the Bible objectively but subjectively, allowing your experiences to mold the Word. I certainly don't believe that your 'Jason Faircloth' reflects the vast majority of separationists. "
- Georgia pastor

"Your book has sown much discord among the ranks. Plus, I don't think the spirit of the book is one that would honor the Lord Jesus. These factors have resulted in a decision of our church by a unanimous vote to cease your support."
- Indiana pastor

"I am appalled that you would write a book that you knew would not be approved by your mission board. We will be dropping our monthly support of your ministry. We also believe it would be appropriate for you to refund

a proportionate amount of our support to you during the term of your furlough."
- Virginia pastor

"I was saddened by the statements in your letter about what is 'added to' the Bible - 'the extra-Biblical convictions of men.' I do not know to whom you have listened, but as I have shared many times with others, my standards and convictions are God-given from the Word of God. Our church has voted to discontinue your support effective immediately. The deacons and I agree that we should ask you to return the money we sent you in support during the last two to three years while you were writing the book. I ask this and write this letter with a saddened heart. I pray that you will allow God to work in your heart in the future."
- Tennessee pastor

And then there were letters like this one. The original was sent to IBWO. A copy was sent to me.

"Dear IBWO Directors,
As one of Randy and Sherri's supporters, it is my opinion that Randy and Sherri are as good a character as any missionaries on the mission field. We intend and have already continued to support them. And we would never consider taking back any of the money we have given them in the past. When I picked up Randy's book and started reading, I didn't want to put it down. It is a true picture of a good many of our

churches today. I think Randy has learned perhaps the most important lesson Jesus taught and that is one of love and not to be like the Pharisees. I do not believe that God objects to us authoring a book, and I feel that the book was in good taste, with down-to-earth facts. Legalism is a turn-off to those who need love. I am living proof, as love won me over to Jesus."

- Georgia supporter

For me and Sherri both, our thoughts and emotions as veteran missionaries were stretched and twisted in so many directions that it was confusing. Had I made a grave mistake by submitting *Wisdom Hunter* for publication? I stood by its message a hundred percent. But was the novel doing more harm than good, driving more wedges than buttresses? I seriously wondered.

Thankfully, Eastside Baptist—the church next door that was providing a house for us—never flinched in their support of our ministry. And humanly speaking, their decision to not castigate us became the crucial linchpin that ultimately held our family together throughout our tumultuous transition. Because of Eastside's great act of kindness we didn't have to relocate, didn't have to assume the expense of a rental property elsewhere, and didn't have to pull Heidi and Shanda from the school they were attending and enjoying. The Eastside pastor and congregation literally kept our family from stalling and crashing.

And then one afternoon while I was writing refund checks to the five churches that requested the return of seven months of support, I was unexpectedly blessed with another glorious godsend.

"Randy, this is Scott," I heard the familiar voice come through the phone. "It's my understanding that you're currently in a state of flux. If that's true and you need a place to officially hang your hat to give your ministry some stability, know you're welcomed to come up under the umbrella of European Partnership Ministries. It can be for just three or four months, or for the long haul, whatever is best for you and your family."

Scott was a graduate of Dallas Theological Seminary and had previously served as a senior pastor in an Atlanta suburb. A year or so earlier he had stepped down from that position and founded European Partnership Ministries where he functioned as the full-time president and lead missionary. EPM was a small mission board with only three missionaries, but it focused on Europe and was a legally registered entity. Scott and the other two missionaries regularly recruited, trained, and led short-term mission teams to work alongside European churches. I had known Scott for six or seven years. Wasting no time I arranged to meet him and discuss his proposition. The churches that were continuing to partner with us were at the moment rerouting their support dollars, at my request, to a P.O. Box near our home. The setup, though, was not professionally satisfying for me or the churches. I needed to connect with a recognized mission organization as quickly as possible.

After brainstorming with Scott—and with Sherri—and after seeking out all possible pros and cons and finding virtually no cons, Sherri and I proudly joined forces with Scott and the EPM team. If we successfully rebuilt our support network and made it to Berlin, without the burden of carrying a team, we would be EPM's first full-time church planters.

We promptly announced our decision to all the churches still supporting us.

We could finally breathe a little.

Not wanting to leave Larry Michaels wondering about our possible involvement with Christian Associates International, I called him in California and outlined the sudden opportunity that had been proffered by EPM, a small mission board in our own backyard.

"I do have a suggestion, though," I told Larry. "If Sherri and I, as newly appointed EPM missionaries, make it to Berlin before CAI and are able to organize a new international church, let's entertain the idea of eventually transferring the church leadership to the CAI team, when they arrive. This could be a win-win for both of us."

"I like it," Larry assured me. "Let's plan on it."

So the verbal agreement was endorsed and placed on the table.

As Sherri and I settled in with EPM and its board of directors and staff, the public controversy surrounding *Wisdom Hunter* continued to fume all around us. And it was kindled even more so when Sherri and I accepted an invitation to appear on a Christian TV talk show called 'Action Sixties' hosted by Herman and Sharron Bailey in Largo, Florida.

Chapter 55

The TV appearance was arranged by an influential lady in the Largo vicinity, a lady who owned and managed a thriving Christian bookstore. It was reported that the lady and her staff had sold more copies of *Wisdom Hunter* than any other retailer in the nation. And the lady wanted all the *Wisdom Hunter* fans in her community to see and hear the man behind the story. I felt indebted to her for her tireless marketing of the novel, so I agreed to be a guest on the show.

It was my first TV interview. And I procured a place for Sherri at my side. Even though Sherri was not the author of *Wisdom Hunter*, she had experienced the same topsy turvy journey out of legalism, with all the guilt, confusion, anger, and regret. And she knew the ideological language fluently. I knew she would be an asset to the program.

Once the cameras starting broadcasting, Sherri and I relaxed and moved easily with the flow of the interview. It actually felt good to tell our story to a large audience.

At some unrehearsed moment in the middle of the show, Herman Bailey, the infectiously energetic host—middle-aged with stylish blonde tresses and a big smile—posed the question to Sherri, "As Randall's wife, were you surprised when the mission board fired you?"

Sherri assertively shook her head. "No, I wasn't surprised. And I wasn't sad either. I felt we had outgrown the mission board a long time ago."

'I felt we had outgrown the mission board a long time ago' was impromptu verbiage that came from her heart. Those in the listening audience who had been the harangued prisoners of legalism, and were now free, rightly understood Sherri's words to mean *'we no longer fit inside legalism's straitjacket; we no longer fit inside that mindset.'* The legalistic pastors, churches, and organizations, however, interpreted the word "outgrown" to mean *'we were better than them.'* We learned this fact when a fourteen-page letter—typed on church stationery, single-spaced, stapled, numbered, and never-folded—arrived in our mailbox in a large brown envelope a week or so later. The epistle, on custom letterhead, was from one of our supporting pastors who happened to see the TV show. The pastor, from Florida, was recognized by the Independent Baptists as one of their premiere pastors in the sunshine state.

Here are some excerpts from the pastor's typed pages.

> "...You shared your opinions and observations of Fundamental Baptists. Now I want to reply to your public portrayal of us!
>
> ...You should have found your therapeutic release by coming home a year or two ago and stating your change of attitude toward IBWO, and resigning. IBWO wouldn't have been blamed, and the nation

would not have an angry missionary's portrayal of Fundamental Christianity.

...The lost world reads, and they will read your book and relish it. If I was a lost man and read your book, I would never darken the door of a fundamental church or have any confidence in a fundamental pastor. I wonder how many lost people will be turned off to fundamentalists' efforts to reach them and will die lost forever because they read your book.

...I think you have done a great injustice to churches and pastors who have taken care of you through all these years. You charge us of preaching extra-Biblical convictions of men. That equates us with the scribes and Pharisees and their traditions (Matt. 15:1-9). I have never preached anything that I didn't feel was the Word of God and could give chapter and verse for it.

...Our church should have dropped you years ago. We are dropping you now. My heart cries out for mercy for you, but I think correcting your ethics is more needful than mercy. Please refund the support given you by our church during your time in the States.

...I rejoice that I am the pastor of an Independent Pre-Millenial, Fundamental Baptist Church. I don't care for our quarreling sometime, but I prefer that to the 'love everybody syrup' of liberalism.

...I saw you on Channel 22 in St. Petersburg, Florida Saturday afternoon. I received a video and showed it to my church Sunday night. Your wife stated that you folks had 'outgrown' the mission board a long time ago.' Boards don't support missionaries; churches do. The Board represents the churches. This church heard that you had 'outgrown' us. That's pride! If you have outgrown the churches and you are now mature and adult believers, it's only logical that you not ask for support from immature and legalistic believers.

Our church is praying for you."

In most of the fourteen pages, the pastor—from his point of view—defended his position regarding a multiplicity of issues that I challenged in my novel. I was simply a wayward missionary, he declared, who despised discipline, authority, and God's Word. To make his position known nationwide, he sent a copy of the fourteen-page memorandum to twenty-four nationally-known pastors, evangelists, Bible college executives, and mission leaders in the Independent Baptist community.

That night, after Sherri and the girls had gone to bed, I laid prostrate on the living room floor in the dark and wept. Did I really despise discipline? Was that truly the underlying reason I had penned *Wisdom Hunter*—because I wasn't fond of short haircuts, a clean-shaven face, hymn music, and the King James Version of the Bible? Wasn't the issue, instead, that these standards were taught wrongfully in the name of God as the only right way and then forced on people as proof of true spirituality?

Shellshocked by the scope and intensity of the letter, my mind suddenly felt muddied and unclear. Again I wondered if writing the story of *Wisdom Hunter* had been a mistake, a miscalculation. In my heart I had only wanted the story to open people's eyes to an extremist branch of religion, not drive people away from the life-saving truths of their Creator.

Oh, God, I groaned. *I need to hear from you right now! I'm begging you on my face in all humility to talk to me! Ever since I was a teenager I've only wanted your will in my life. You know that!* I clinched my fist and beat the carpet. *If* Wisdom Hunter *is sending a wrong message, then kill the sales of the book right now! And if I'm blind, then open my eyes and help me see! Otherwise, tell me everything's going to be okay! Please! Please talk to me! I'm begging you!*

I continued to cry, pray, and pound the floor. But there was only silence. Confusing and maddening silence. I finally collapsed into a state of exhaustion with the accusatory words of the fourteen-page letter dragging me into a psychological nightmare.

And then, the next day, God's answer to my frantic plea was handed to me in a large white envelope. It was a gift beyond my imagination. It was another fourteen-page letter.

Chapter 56

When I opened our mailbox the next morning and spotted the large white envelope, my heart sank. *Again? Are you kidding me?* I didn't recognize the name on the return address, from Arizona. I went into the house, braced myself, and slowly removed the thick stack of pages. I couldn't believe it. Was I daydreaming? I squinted and pinched the bridge of my nose to make sure I wasn't in the twilight zone.

Another epistle-size letter. Fourteen pages—typed on church stationery, single-spaced, stapled, numbered, and never-folded.

Was this some kind of cosmic joke? I nervously began to read.

Dear Mr. Arthur,

I rarely read any genre of fiction, but your book, *Wisdom Hunter*, was so mesmerizing that once into it I couldn't put it down. I'm afraid I read it straight through in one sitting. After finishing the book, I recommended it to my brother who also pastors a church here in Phoenix. He too read it in one day, and has recommended it to four or five former pastors who are now attending his church. My wife also recently read it, finishing it in one day.

I'm a pastor myself, so I can of course identify with Jason. What is most interesting, however, is that the underlying premise of your riveting story is similar to some events in my own life.

...My spiritual odyssey began the day after Christmas in 1986. My wife and our two children had been visiting my mother at her cabin in Payson, Arizona. Christmas day had been filled with the warmth of family fellowship, but it would be even more memorable for the children if we could take them further up the mountain to the popular Cinch Hook sled run.

Arriving at the play area, we parked our cars and the children tumbled out into the parking area. Armed with our new sleds, we began marching up the sledding hill.

Finally, my son and I were standing at the head of the line. I sat down in the back of the thin plastic sled, positioning my son's six-year-old frame in front of me, folding him securely between my legs. Excitedly I pushed the sled forward from the crest of the hill. Gaining momentum rapidly, our descent was exhilarating. But suddenly, my exhilaration turned to apprehension. I noticed a dangerous looking rocky area next to some trees at the base of the hill. Desperately I extended my legs over the sled's sides. I dug my heels in as I struggled to slow our downward plunge. Adrenalin surged through my body as I realized I couldn't control the sled's speed or direction. An erosion ditch suddenly coiled directly in front of us. Flinging us across the small chasm at tremendous speed, the sled slammed into the rocky far side of the ditch. Instantly my back exploded. My son and I tumbled airborne through yards of empty space. Landing face down in the snow I began vomiting uncontrollably. Through the shock I sensed the limp impotency of my rag doll body lying motionless. My son, uninjured, was sobbing uncontrollably, standing to the left with people I didn't recognize. Suddenly I noticed I couldn't feel my legs. In the ambulance ride I was consumed by the disbelief that something so terrible could happen to a Christian pastor like me. I had always believed that quoting and believing Bible promises would somehow exempt me from the suffering I was now experiencing.

Like Jason, my life began to unravel. There was the seven hour orthopedic and neurological surgery. The internal installation of two fourteen inch stainless-steel rods wired to my spinal column. The six inch spinal fusion using bone removed from my left hip. The month and a half rehabilitation in a spinal injury rehab center.

More months of tedious rehabilitation laced with constant pain. The loss of a sizable majority of my small church's membership. The loss of all but one of my board members. The evaporation of two thirds of my pastoral support. The second surgery for a different but related medical problem. The exhausting trauma of a third surgery for an emergency appendectomy. The forced declaration of bankruptcy. The Federal Tax Levy against our bank accounts. The Federal Tax Lien filed against our home and personal property. The high levels of stress, tension, and hostility these events produced in our family. The unanswered prayers for physical healing. The vicious backlash of depression.

These mysterious trials, like the trials of Jason, helped strip me of my self righteousness.

But it is your story of Jason in *Wisdom Hunter* that helped me put my tragedy in perspective. *Wisdom Hunter* helped crystalize and clarify a truth the Lord has been sharing with me. After reading your book, I noticed that something began to change inside me. I felt a greater sense of liberty to share my personal ordeals with others.

The Sunday morning after I read your book, I walked laboriously, leaning heavily on my crutches as I shuffled up the ramp leading to the front doors of my church. For five long years I had catheterized three times a day. I had to artificially induce bowel movements because of the paralysis affecting my lower intestines. The morning worship service preceding the sermon was lively and joyous. I offered the pastoral prayer before the sermon. Then I looked out over the familiar faces and began my message.

"Most of you have never seen me walk without crutches," I began. "You've seen me trying to stand behind the pulpit, holding onto it for balance. You've seen me sitting in my wheelchair, doing my best to teach God's Word. But today, I have a confession to make, and I must ask you to forgive me for not telling you the whole truth before now. I have failed you my brothers and sisters by failing to share my inner life with you. The epistle of James tells us to confess our faults one to another, and to pray one for another, that we might be healed. I've been guilty of not personally applying this truth, of not being an example of living that kind of confessional life. I've been guilty of allowing you to think I've been doing okay, that my family has been doing okay. But the real facts of our lives are otherwise."

Tears were flowing from my eyes. As my voice crackled with emotion, I told the congregation how our family had been crushed and devastated by the physical, emotional, and financial pressures that had engulfed us. I shared how your book had convinced me that I should share my own personal life with the people, and not worry about what others might think. Several in the congregation were now crying. They began sharing personal difficulties they were struggling with, and asking for prayer for God's strength. And then standing hand in hand in a circle, we ended the service by praying for one another.

Like Jason Faircloth in your book, the pressures in my life have finally broken me. God's work in me is not complete yet, but I'm happy to report that my performance oriented legalism is slowly being replaced with a more authentic—a more gracious—experience of his love. Your *Wisdom Hunter* has enabled me to take a look, through Jason's eyes, at my own life, and to interpret my own fear, shock, sorrow, and disappointment in the light of God's working in my life. I know that God's work of transformation in me is not finished, but I am learning that God is more concerned with my state of 'being' than he is with the technical excellence of my performance. I can praise the Lord because I know that God's power to heal my inner man cannot be limited by any mere physical disability, even a tragic permanent disability like paraplegic paralysis. Thank you for expanding my understanding of Romans 8:28. Thanks again for your wonderful book.

Sincerely
D.L., pastor

By the time I reached the word 'sincerely,' I was shedding tears on the page. I had to take a break and consciously breathe.

For me, the moment was far bigger than the scope of the letter. The letter, I was convinced, had to be God's heartfelt and merciful response to my uplifted hands, begging earnestly for his divine feedback. The odds of receiving two fourteen-page pastoral letters on custom letterhead—typed, single-spaced, stapled, and never folded—back to back in large envelopes were as unlikely as being struck by lightening twice-in-a-row during a drought. I had never received a 14-page letter previously. And I've never received one since. To me, the letter from the Arizona pastor had God's fingerprints all over it. To me, God had answered the cry of my heart.

Never again would I wonder how God felt about *Wisdom Hunter*. Never again would I doubt the validity of the book.

Yes, as many claimed—including the high-profile pastor from Florida—I had been wrong to stay with IBWO when I stopped believing and endorsing IBWO's legalism. Yes, I had been wrong to carry on covertly, ministering with the financial backing of IBWO-supporting churches. And, yes, IBWO's anger with me, and their decision to fire me, had been absolutely justified. I admit; I terribly bungled the prolonged way I detached from the Independent Baptist ideology. My journey had indeed been two-faced and messy.

But…writing *Wisdom Hunter* had not been wrong. Or bad.

Chapter 57

Yet, the book continued to cause dissension. One morning while preparing a sermon for an upcoming meeting, I was surprised when I received from Questar a fresh-off-the-press August issue of *Christianity Today*, the premiere monthly magazine for Christian evangelicals all around the world. There was a note telling me to look at page 49. I flipped quickly to the noted page. Staring back at me was a Randall Arthur headshot, a color photo of *Wisdom Hunter*'s front cover, and an article with a headline that read 'Baptist Author Fired for Book.'

Really? I sighed. The article was printed beneath a headline banner that read "CONTROVERSY." The write-up said:

> Author and missionary Randy Dodd was asked to resign last April from Independent Baptist World Outreach, (IBWO), an independent Baptist mission board, after revealing he wrote the controversial novel *Wisdom Hunter*.

Published under the pseudonym Randall Arthur, the novel attacks "legalistic Christianity" via the story of a high-profile fundamentalist pastor who eventually questions his faith and convictions. *Wisdom Hunter* was released in April 1991 by the Oregon based Questar Publishers, which recently purchased Multnomah Press.

A letter sent by IBWO to Dodd's supporters said, "IBWO feels (*Wisdom Hunter*) to be very much out of character for the Christian standards and values of the mission...A further consideration was...that the book was written, published, and circulated without the missions knowledge or consent while (Dodd) was still a missionary."

In a promotional letter to church pastors across the country, Dodd defended the importance of his book's message to struggling pastors and lay leaders, saying "Legalism...is doing much to destroy churches, homes, and individuals all across America, but especially in the Bible belt." Dodd and his wife, Sherri, worked for IBWO for 17 years.

The editors of *The Sword Of The Lord*—an appropriately named national newspaper for the Independent Baptists—hurriedly prepared a response for their hardline audience. A senior editor wrote an introduction about the controversy, then allotted Dr. Sykes, the IBWO president, the bulk of the copy. Dr. Sykes wrote:

Christianity Today stated in the article that a Baptist author was fired for a book he wrote. This is rather strange language. We do not fire missionaries, nor do we hire them. Independent Baptist World Outreach accepts missionaries from local fundamental Baptist churches as missionaries affiliated with IBWO. This means, in essence, that we recommend these missionaries to the churches to which they are going. This gives the missionary the credibility of a well-known fundamental Baptist mission organization. Of course, when a missionary departs from the fundamental position, that missionary is asked to resign. This was the case of Randy Dodd (pseudonym, Randall Arthur). Mr. Dodd was a missionary with Independent Baptist World Outreach. He wrote a very controversial book. The book was very derogatory toward any preacher who would take any stand on any issue whatsoever. I feel it was a very unfair treatment of the subject. In addition to this, there were many places in the book that used profane 'gutter' language that we feel would not be acceptable reading for Christians. Perhaps the most disgraceful thing which came out of the whole situation was Mr. Dodd's method of publishing the book. He knew IBWO would not approve of the book, thus, he published it under a pseudonym. He did not tell anyone in the mission organization that the book had been published. He stayed in America for nearly one year and unfairly took the support of Bible-believing, fundamental churches, knowing that if churches knew that such a book had been

> published his support would have been dropped. He received support for nearly one year from Bible-believing fundamental Baptist churches who believed that he planned to go back to the mission field to do the work of a missionary.
>
> My regret is that the book has found such wide acceptance among so many people. The president of Questar, the publisher of the book, did not seem to have any regrets that he had aided a missionary in taking money from churches deceitfully.
>
> It is a sad day when a preacher who has any standards and convictions is called a 'legalist'. Thank God there are thousands of fundamental Baptist preachers who guide their family and their flock in the right way.

Dallas Jackson, the president of Questar, actually liked the article. He knew it would drive a lot of readers to purchase copies of the book. And he was right.

I, on the other hand, was simply reminded once again that I was marked with "guilt" for not notifying IBWO about the book immediately upon my arrival back in the States. Whether a valid defense or a flimsy excuse, I had simply wanted to wait until the sanitized version was available, and then take a "clean" copy to Dr. Sykes. The sanitized edition, however, was still lingering in the pipeline. I was glad, though, that I had at least refunded seven months worth of support dollars to the churches that requested it. And for that, I felt good.

PART II

JORDAN'S CROSSING

Chapter 58

Within three months of being excommunicated from IBWO we lost the support of fifty-six congregations. The returned postcards from our supporting pastors across the eastern part of the United States told the story: "We will terminate our support—immediately."

As we entered into August, the supporters who were still actively helping us were still weighing us in the balance.

As I continued to work diligently on *Jordan's Crossing*, I shifted my fundraising focus from churches to individuals. I especially reached out to those men and women who knew and understood our theological bent. Thankfully, new support started showing up in our account at European Partnership Ministries.

And Berlin indeed seemed to be our next field of service. But before I announced this as an official decision, I wanted to take a scouting trip to the German capital to collect real-time information regarding the spiritual climate of the city, the prominent location of the expat community, the number of churches—if any—reaching the expat community, and the international school situation. I marked a date on my calendar and planned the trip a couple of months out.

One afternoon, when Heidi and Shanda were back in school for the fall term, I was making final arrangements for the Berlin trip when I received a phone call out of the blue from the secretary at Mt. Vernon Baptist, our home church.

"Randy, this is Mrs. *Moore calling from the church. Pastor Rogers told me to give you a call. He says you and Sherri need to meet him in his office tomorrow morning at ten sharp."

The edict, quite nervous-sounding, came so starkly that it caused me to pause. "Uh...okay...let me check my calendar," I finally responded. "Give me a moment." I checked my to-do list for the following morning and saw that I had no appointments. "All right; we're free at that time. So...yeah...tell the pastor we'll meet him at ten."

The phone call was over in less than sixty seconds.

When I returned the phone to its cradle, I paused and looked across the room. I had never heard Mrs. Moore speak so brusquely. It wasn't her style. So, why now? Had she simply been rushing to take care of another impending task that had been demanded of her? Or was there something more uncomfortable going on? Something about the phone call just didn't feel right.

Pastor Rogers's expression, when Sherri and I entered his office the next morning, didn't persuade me otherwise. He didn't welcome us with a smile or a handshake. From behind his desk he said, "Have a seat." The words were more of a command than a gesture of politeness.

Sherri and I sat in the chairs arranged for us on the opposite side of Rogers's desk.

"How many years now has Mt. Vernon been your home church?" he began.

"About twenty-four," I told him. "We both became believers here, were baptized here, were married here, were commissioned here. Plus, I was ordained here. We were part of Mike Bove's youth group. We served as bus captains for the outreach ministry. We served as Sunday School teachers." I intentionally gave him more information than he asked for. Since he had functioned as Mt. Vernon's senior pastor for only five years, and since we had lived overseas for four of those years, I wanted him to understand our long and significant history with the church.

"Then why," he blurted out, looking straight at me, "are your wife and kids attending Eastside Baptist Church every Sunday?" Before I could offer up a response, he plowed ahead. "I know you're traveling almost every weekend, meeting with your supporting churches and attempting to find new supporters. But for some reason I had just assumed all along that Sherri and the girls were traveling with you. But, no! I find out they're attending Eastside. Not only that, I've also learned that your girls are enrolled at Mt. Zion Christian Academy. So, Randy, I ask you again. Why are they attending Eastside Church and Mt. Zion Christian Academy instead of our church and our school?" The question rolled off his tongue like spit.

I felt energy sucked out of me. "First of all," I said, trying to breathe normally, "I assumed everyone here knew that our girls were at Mt. Zion. It's not something we've tried to hide. I mean, several of the teachers here have known about this all along. And, of course, Sherri and I had very clear reasons for choosing Mt. Zion. When we moved back to the States last year, our oldest daughter Heidi needed a teacher who had lived or travelled overseas and could understand Heidi's reverse culture shock and how that state of mind could possibly affect her focus in school. Mt. Zion's seventh grade teacher fit that bill. Mt. Vernon's teacher didn't. Our youngest daughter

Shanda needed a first grade teacher who taught phonics in her reading class. Again, Mt. Zion's first-grade teacher was known for that very thing. Mt. Vernon's first-grade teacher at the time only taught sight reading. Those are the reasons we chose Mt. Zion." At that juncture in my explanation, I paused. Pastor Rogers didn't offer a response. He just stared at us like we were quislings. So I cleared my throat and added, "We don't have anything against Mt. Vernon. But since the girls made so many friends last year at Mt. Zion, they naturally wanted to go back this year. And we wanted to give them some consistency. So, that's why they are there."

Rogers leaned forward in his chair. "And you don't see a loyalty issue here?" I closed my eyes and tried to wish the fog away. Was I missing something? Maybe I had lived in Europe way too long. Were American pastors typically so exclusive and territorial? I started to tell the pastor that, no, I really didn't see a loyalty issue, but before I could speak he lambasted me again. "And what about Eastside? Why are they attending the church there?" He directed the question at me as if Sherri wasn't in the room.

I blew a puff of air. "As you know, Eastside has allowed us to live rent free in their parsonage that had been sitting empty. When we moved in, we attended one of Eastside's Sunday services to tell the people thank you. The people welcomed us like we were family. Sherri and the girls attended a few more times; it was just so convenient. At some point, Pastor James at Eastside asked Sherri if she would consider teaching a Sunday school class and serving as the interim choir director. Sherri felt really at ease there, so she accepted both roles."

"Felt really at ease?" Rogers interrupted, his face tightening.

"What; do you not feel at ease here at your own home church?" Rogers was now looking at Sherri.

Sherri spoke in the meeting for the first time. "To be honest; no, I don't. I'm accustomed to Randy's style of teaching which is very relaxed. The few times I've attended here since being back in the States, I've left feeling depressed and discouraged, because I felt like I was being screamed at the whole time. I felt beaten down. I felt worthless."

Oh boy, I thought, *here we go.*

Rogers hesitated, caught off guard perhaps by Sherri's candor. He then stood up and leaned over his desk. "I'm not sure what's going on here. But maybe, young lady, you're at a point in your life where you need to be screamed at!" For an instant Sherri and I were both struck speechless by the pastor's raised voice and pitiless words. Before we could gather our wits and respond, he kept going. "So, Randy, here's the deal! You either move your girls to our school and tell your wife to start attending the church here where she and the kids belong, or you simply need to move your membership from our church! Is that clear?"

When I had been a naive teenager I had honestly admired Independent Baptist leaders like Rogers who exerted their authority and proudly ran roughshod over anyone and everyone who disagreed with them. But now such behavior was repulsive to me. I had seen over and over again the trail of broken lives it left in its wake. Having been severed from IBWO I was beholden to only one other such authoritative, legalistic figure. And that was Pastor Rogers. It wouldn't be easy to walk away from our home church where we had such a lengthy and meaningful history with so many people. But perhaps it was time to cut the last tether of legalism that was attached to our lives.

I looked at Rogers and shook my head. "I cannot, and

will not, pull my kids out of Mt. Zion right now. That wouldn't be fair to them. And I'm certainly not going to tell Sherri she has to walk away from Eastside where she's teaching a class and directing the choir. So I guess that leaves me with no other choice but to transfer our membership to Eastside." Rogers's countenance contorted, displaying an expression of disbelief as if his authority was seldom, if ever, challenged. "But...if this is what you insist on," I amended, "I'm not just going to walk away in silence and disappear into the night. Through the years, that has happened too often with too many people around here. If we leave I want to stand before the congregation and tell them in my own words that we're leaving. And I want to tell them the reason."

Rogers didn't like the idea and told me so.

But I held my ground. "If you don't let me stand before the people and tell them what's going on, I'll simply call the core families one by one and explain to them what's happening."

Rogers clinched his jaw. "All right! But you'll only be hurting yourself! And just know when you walk out that door today, refusing to be accountable to the authority in your life, your ministry will start going down hill; I can assure you of that!"

I shrugged my shoulders.

The meeting was over. So Sherri and I 'walked out that door.'

I was informed shortly, thereafter, that a day and time had been noted on the church calendar for 'Randy Dodd's Update' to be shared with the congregation. The gathering—'for anyone interested'—was set for a couple of weeks out on a Sunday afternoon at 4:00.

I marked my calendar and started thoughtfully preparing my presentation.

Chapter 59

Understandably, I was nervous about my tenuous relationship with my home church, the church that had been my ministry bedrock for nearly a quarter of a century. Had the relationship really run its course? Was it really coming to an end?

As the days quickly passed, I was soon standing behind a portable lectern at floor level on Sunday afternoon staring out at a hundred or more Mt. Vernonites who Sherri and I had known for more than two decades, people who had watched us grow up, people who had cheered us on and supported us throughout all our Bible college and overseas years. Yet, because of our sporadic visits over the previous fifteen years, they were not fully aware of just how much Sherri and I had changed. Of course, not being consistently on site in Atlanta through all the shifting seasons of the congregation's life, I was ignorant of their recent story as well. I wasn't sure if the individuals who made up the congregation were still blindly loyal to Pastor Rogers and his authoritarianism, or if they were secretly wishing he would quickly and permanently disappear from their lives. But I was about to find out.

With all eyes on me, I began by reading an eight-page

opening statement that I had prayerfully and painstakingly crafted. Here is a portion of that letter.

> Dear Pastor, Executive Missions Committee, and Board of Deacons,
>
> I can't speak for the other missionaries who have their membership here at Mt. Vernon, but this is the first time since I was ordained and sent out by this church seventeen years ago that the board of deacons, the missions committee, the leaders of the church and I have met together as a group for any kind of official meeting or debriefing. A pattern of little, or no, face-to-face communication between me and the group of church leaders has been the norm throughout my missionary career. This is understandably neither good nor healthy. Therefore, I'm thankful for the opportunity to meet with you, along with the congregation, this afternoon. The outcome of this meeting, however, will reveal whether or not this effort to communicate has been postponed for too long.
>
> Mt. Vernon has now been my home church and home base for twenty-five years. It has been Sherri's home church and home base for twenty-three years. It has been our sending church for nearly eighteen years. And I want to say emphatically that throughout all of these years, Mt. Vernon as a home church has stood faithfully behind us. In addition to monthly financial support, the church in 1989 purchased

roundtrip tickets for our family to fly back to the United States during the time period when my father was dying with cancer. The church purchased roundtrip tickets for us again so that we could attend my father's funeral when he died two and a half years ago. For all of this help—financially, socially, and prayerfully—we are eternally grateful. The assistance we have received from this church means more to us than anybody will ever realize.

But...we have given to Mt. Vernon also. We gave Mt. Vernon the best years of our youth. Only God would be able to accurately tell how many hours of zealous labor we gave to this church in visiting, witnessing, leading, and teaching during those years. And for the last fifteen years now, we have worked sacrificially as an arm of this church as we have served Christ on foreign soil.

So, why are we here this afternoon? Well, several people have been asking why Heidi and Shanda are at Mt. Zion Christian Academy this year, and not at Mt. Vernon, and why Sherri and the girls are attending Eastside Baptist instead of Mt. Vernon. So, I want to take time to publicly answer those questions.

When Sherri and I arrived back in the States last year, Sherri's main priority was to enroll the girls in school. Now please understand that our girls get one shot at the American school system every five years. Because of the extra hard uprooting they have to go through—from one country to another, one culture to another, and one language to another—it is very important that their one year in the American school system be as positive, as secure, and as solid as possible. Upon our arrival in Georgia, Sherri immediately within the first day or two inquired here at the school offices about the upcoming school year, only three weeks away. She learned that the school had no principal, had been declining in attendance and morale for several years, and was financially in trouble. She learned that the first grade teacher for Shanda's class was going to be a stranger who was unknown at Mt. Vernon, and thus had no track record with the people here. Sherri asked one of the school officials a few questions that the official couldn't answer. The official told Sherri they would contact her by phone and give her the information as soon as possible. The school official never contacted her. From Sherri's perspective, the school simply did not appear to be stable. It was not a school that we felt would be the best choice for our girls. After making inquiries at approximately seven or eight other schools, Sherri finally opted, after much prayer I might add, to enroll the girls at Mt. Zion. That particular school appeared to be unquestionably solid, with its enrollment having increased every year for the last five or six years. The teachers who Sherri spoke with extolled the school as being exceptional in its academic standards, its overall organization, its morale, and its financial stability.

Plus, one of the seventh grade teachers for Heidi's age group was a former missionary kid. Another one had lived in Germany for several years. And another one had an extraordinary reputation, based on a proven track record, for being loved and respected by almost every sixth and seventh grader who had ever sat in his class. As you can understand, this appeared to be an ideal school situation for Heidi, a youngster who had just spent four years in the German school system and was needing a teacher or teachers who could experientially understand her special needs as a missionary kid in the midst of a major cultural adjustment.

The first grade teacher for Shanda's age group had a well established reputation for being an above average phonics teacher. This was excellent for Shanda. Since Shanda had just spent a year in the German kindergarten system learning German, her groundwork for learning to read English was poor. She needed a good English phonics teacher who could help her build a solid foundation for learning to read and write English, her mother tongue. These are the reasons we enrolled the girls at Mt. Zion. When we arrived back in the states, I hit the ground running. I had supporting churches scattered throughout a fifteen state area that I had to visit.

Sherri and the girls, once the school situation had been ironed out, automatically started attending the church services here at Mt. Vernon. But Sherri found it difficult, because of certain emotional strains she was bearing, to benefit from Pastor Rogers's style of delivery. In her words, she felt 'screamed at' during a time when she needed to be encouraged. Let me make it very clear at this point that Sherri and I are not saying Pastor Rogers's style of preaching is wrong. It is just a matter of personally feeling 'screamed at' when we felt a need to be uplifted and refreshed.

Since we were, and still are, living in the parsonage next door to Eastside Baptist, Sherri asked if she and the girls could just slip down to the services there whenever I was going to be out of town. The Eastside pastor is more of a relaxed teacher. Whether I was right or wrong, I told her it was okay with me. Those visits became more frequent, and before we knew it, Sherri had been given a Sunday school class to teach, and the girls had gotten involved in the youth group. And recently, Sherri accepted Eastside's invitation to be their interim choir director. Some of you, I have been told, find this somewhat disturbing, especially since Mt. Vernon is presently supporting our ministry with $450 a month.

But, with all of the emotional turmoil that has engulfed our lives during this last year—being fired from IBWO, and losing over half our monthly income—it would be heartless of me at this point to uproot Sherri and the girls from the place where they have found a temporary source of emotional security. It just wouldn't be healthy.

Obviously I have put myself in a dilemma with you, my home church family. But please understand that in twenty-five years of being a member here, and in fifteen years of serving overseas as an arm of your ministry, this is the first time I have ever brought offense to the church. Therefore, I need to hear from the body of church leaders. What advice or counsel would you recommend? I am trying to see our behavior through your eyes. I do need to hear what you are thinking and feeling. In just a moment I will give you the opportunity to share with me any advice or counsel you feel I need to hear, and to ask any question that's on your heart. I will answer every question as honestly as I possibly can.

When I finished reading my opening statement, I took a deep, deep breath. Before I extended an opportunity to the people to offer questions, feedback, or advice, I opened my mouth one more time and spoke impromptu from the heart.

Chapter 60

"We've aligned ourselves with a new mission board," I told them. "It's called European Partnership Ministries. It's a small non-denominational mission agency headquartered in Atlanta. And we're rebuilding our support to return to Europe to plant a third international church, this time in Berlin, the German capital. And for those of you who've read *Wisdom Hunter*, please understand that the last half of the book mirrors our philosophy of ministry. We no longer believe that Baptists have a monopoly on truth. We no longer believe that America has a monopoly on truth. God is not," I stressed, "a white American Baptist! We still believe, embrace, and teach the fundamentals of the faith—the depravity of the human heart and its need for redemption; the deity of Christ along with His death, burial and resurrection; the exclusivity of Christ as the one-and-only Savior of the world; the gift of salvation by grace alone; and the infallibility of Scripture. But we're no longer going to pretend that the extra-Biblical standards preached by the Independent Baptists are God's measuring stick for determining a person's spirituality. Rather, we're going to use God's measuring stick, and that would be the fruit of the Spirit outlined in the book of Galatians—love, joy, peace, patience, goodness, kindness, faithfulness, gentleness, and self-control. So, if all of this sounds too extreme and you're not comfortable with it, then tell us now and we'll withdraw our membership. We're simply not going to play politics anymore with this church, with any of our supporting churches, or with any mission board."

I also told them I was writing a new novel.

The meeting went on for an hour and a half. Questions were asked. Comments were made. In the end, the congregation expressed their unhappiness with our "new" mindset. Sensing that we would hold fast to our "new" points-of-view and not reverse directions, a majority of the people—people we had known nearly all our lives—concluded we were "too far gone" to salvage. So they unceremoniously prompted us to slip out of their lives.

Though disheartened, we honored their preference and placed our membership at Eastside, the church that knew our philosophy of ministry and still welcomed us with open arms and a loving spirit.

In spite of losing lifelong friends and an enduring home church, I—Randy Arthur Dodd, to my surprise—recovered quickly from the sadness and soon felt thrilled to finally be able to soar with no legalistic tether in sight. None. *Thank you, God! Thank you! Thank you!*

With the Eastside congregation as our new stateside family I announced officially—both to our few remaining supporters and our newly acquired partners—that our next field of service would be the German capital of Berlin. Our life focus immediately shifted toward achieving that move.

One of the first steps I took in that direction was to take

a hurried trip to Berlin to gather information about the best possible schools in the city for Heidi and Shanda and where those schools were located in relationship to the expat communities.

Once on the ground in Berlin, I learned about the John F. Kennedy international school. The school had been founded as an undertaking to help integrate the American and German communities. To achieve that goal, the founders created an educational structure that required fifty percent of the student body to be German and fifty percent American; fifty percent of the teaching staff to be German, fifty percent American; and fifty percent of all classes to be taught in the German language, and fifty percent in English. Every student would become proficiently bilingual. The school offered grades one through high school. Each grade level was restricted to exactly one-hundred students divided into four homerooms. It was a prestigious school. The great news was the tuition was free and the spectacular campus was located in a part of the city crowded with expats. The bad news was there was a long line of applicants for every grade level. Many families had waited for years to get their kids into the school.

I became quickly convinced this would be the best school for our girls…if we could get them enrolled. I was even more convinced after conversing with the head of the school's music department. He eagerly gave me forty minutes out of his busy schedule to answer every question I could think to ask.

Before I left Berlin I managed to venture to the edges of the city to see small sections of the Berlin Wall that had yet to be demolished. Over the previous year and a half, most of the wall had been pounded into pieces and piled in landfills. Yet, the reunited city, along with the reunited country, was still in the throes of acute social and economical adjustments, so much so, that many Berliners were saying they wished the city and the country were still divided. For me, the city— as it wrestled in its turmoil—was simply ripe for a new crop of missionaries who could bring Good News to a troubled populace. And I was glad that Sherri and I would be among the first of those missionaries to minister in the newly restored capital.

When I returned to Atlanta, I felt equipped with a lot of good and needed information. And I was especially praying that Heidi and Shanda would be given a place at the JFK school.

With a bolstered sense of purpose I picked up the pace of my fundraising.

Having learned that we could ship an automobile to Germany duty free if we owned the vehicle six months prior to our move, I went out and bought a new 1992 three-cylinder Daihatsu Charade, a tiny economical car with a manual transmission that I figured would be ideal for commuting throughout the city limits of Berlin. It was only the second new car I had ever owned. And even though it was a subcompact I couldn't have been more thrilled. So I parked my big old Ford LTD—that I had been driving—up near the street with a "For Sale" sign taped to the windshield.

That same afternoon I noticed a man and a teenage girl circling the Ford, inspecting it with keen interest. I walked up and met them. It was a father and his seventeen-year-old daughter. The girl had dropped out of high school due to a sporadic, life-altering, illness. But she had recently landed a part-time job and needed a means of transportation. Since the LTD was her favorite type car, they wanted to know if my asking price was negotiable. Sensing they were a poor, hard-working family, my heart went out to them. So I dropped the price a few hundred dollars.

"Can we take it for a test drive?" the father asked.

"Absolutely," I said.

Returning from a fifteen-minute spin, the girl—along with her dad—beamed with genuine satisfaction.

"I love it!" the teenager grinned sheepishly.

"Is there any more wiggle room?" the dad asked nearly in a whisper, truly wanting to provide for his daughter.

"Let me talk to my wife," I told him. I consulted with Sherri about something I was contemplating. She listened to my thoughts and within minutes gave me a vote of approval. I walked back to the father and daughter. "All right," I explained, "I've made a final decision. Here's my deal."

The dad's expression instantly faded into one of doubtful hope. "Okay," he puffed slowly, waiting to hear the bottom line price.

"So, here's my deal. If you and your daughter can promise me that she will do whatever is needed and not give up on school, but will keep studying until she earns her GED, then...I'll give her the car for free."

After recovering from the unexpected offer, the dad and daughter looked at each other. And then promised. With tears. And more tears.

I handed the keys to the daughter, then signed over the title.

The girl threw herself into my arms like I was a long-lost brother. She couldn't thank me enough.

Sherri and I had been blessed far beyond what was rightly ours. It felt good to help someone else who needed an unexpected blessing.

Chapter 61

With a new mission board, a new home church, a new group of supporters, a new freedom, a new overseas destination, and a new—nearly completed novel—I, along with Sherri, felt we had found a long-overdue rhythm in life that was pleasant, a rhythm that allowed us to breathe joyously again.

With great delight, I soon finished the *Jordan's Crossing* manuscript and submitted it to Questar. Questar, knowing that the completion of the manuscript was imminent, had already designed the cover art for the book.

But when I received a sample copy, I felt my heart deflate. *Really? Was this a prank?* The cover art was literally the most amateurish I had ever seen. It was so cartoonish that it looked like a last-minute rush job from a non-talented middle-schooler. I couldn't believe it. Questar had pushed me to finish the book in a timely manner so that it would hit the market quickly as a grand follow-up to *Wisdom Hunter*.

And this was the cover they were planning to use?

I had invested my precious time and labor to tell a story that was now going to be bound in cover art that would receive a thumbs-down across the world. What was Questar thinking? How could they honestly give their approval to this embarrassing book cover?

But this was only the first red flag regarding my "highly marketed and anticipated" second novel. When the first edits were returned to my Atlanta address, the revisions seemed like those of a non-talented novice as well. And that seemed confusing. I had secured Questar's agreement that Allen Dust, the editor of *Wisdom Hunter*, would also edit *Jordan's Crossing*. But the editorial changes didn't look like Allen's work. To give Questar the benefit of the doubt, though, I tabled my suspicions. Maybe Allen's craftsmanship was momentarily suffering due to his being pushed too hard and not obtaining sufficient sleep. But after trudging through five chapters of poor editing, I knew with certainty that Allen wasn't the one behind the pages. So, I called Questar and asked to speak directly with Dallas Jackson, the president.

"I'm panicking, Dallas. I know there's a deadline for editing *Jordan's Crossing*. But I feel like we've wasted three days here. Whoever is editing the book doesn't seem like a professional. I mean, the first five chapters are...just terrible. We need to start over. And Allen needs to be the one doing the editing, like you promised."

It took three days of holding my ground before Dallas admitted that an editor outside Questar had been hired to do the editing. Agitated by my insistence that all the ongoing edits be canned, Dallas finally capitulated and assigned Allen to the project. He agreed to fly me out to Oregon to work with Allen on site. He would give us four days to edit the book from front to back. And then the volume would be prepped for printing, period.

It wasn't until I was in the Sisters, Oregon office that I discovered it had been Allen all along who had not wanted to edit any more of my work. The *Wisdom Hunter* project over two years earlier had been too much of an emotional rollercoaster for him. Not wanting a repeat performance, Allen had asked Dallas to find a different editor for *Jordan's Crossing*.

Still not wanting to work on *Jordan's Crossing*, but having now been sequestered by Dallas to do so, Allen commenced the editing endeavor with a not-so-happy attitude. It was a bad start for both of us. By the middle of the fourth day Allen and I had reached an impasse regarding four or five sections of the book. Dallas was away on a business trip and simply wasn't there to intervene. So I marched into the office of one of his high-ranking assistants, explained the situation, and beseeched him to offer his objective, third-party feedback about the highly contested areas.

"I'm sorry; I can't get involved," the man announced blandly.

"I'm just asking for another person to look at the pages and give a fresh opinion!" I begged, lifting up the sheets in question. "I'm not asking you to make a ruling of any kind!"

To my utter dismay, he refused. Not a single individual in the office would help. It didn't make professional sense. Not in the least.

Jordan's Crossing was my baby. I wanted it to be delivered to the marketplace as a solid, excellent piece of artistry. I assumed the publishing house, since their name would be on the label, shared the same desire. But Allen appeared to be hellbent against making any compromises that would typically be normal between an author and editor. It was absolutely mind-boggling. So the novel was announced as officially ready for publication. And only two sets of eyes had even looked at it.

When the galley proofs came off the office printer I was there collecting and scrutinizing every page that slid onto the tray. My heart was pierced when I spotted six typos on the first four pages. I immediately ushered them into Allen's office. I freaked out. "We've got to correct these, Allen!"

"Forget it, Randy! We're finished!"

"What do you mean, finished? We can't let the book go to press like this!"

But it did. The highly promoted followup to *Wisdom Hunter* was published with over three dozen typos and a major chronological mistake. I was so embarrassed by the finished product—the book cover and the shoddy editing—that I wanted to erase my name from the book. I promised right then and there that if I ever wrote another novel, I would pursue another publishing house.

So I was taken by complete surprise when the reviews of *Jordan's Crossing* started trickling in.

> "*Jordan's Crossing* is an absolute must read. Randall Arthur writes obviously from experience, even to the story's locations. This is a captivating, no put-down book. You'll want to buy as many as you can to give away."
> - A.C.

> "I have read few authors that gripped me the way Randall Arthur has in his two stories. Thank you for being honest about the good and the bad in the church and our lives, and about God's grace and His presence through both. I truly thank God for you, brother. I really do."
> - M.M.

Jordan's Crossing within a few months climbed to #20 on

the ECPA (Evangelical Christian Publishers Association) bestsellers list. I was thoroughly puzzled. Where were the critics lambasting all the typos, not to mention the rudimentary cover art? The successes and failures in the publishing industry, as often pointed out to me, were a true mystery. And I was now staring at one of those mysteries pointblank. Still, I resolved to find another publisher for any future book I might write.

With the *Jordan's Crossing* project behind me, but with an unpleasant taste still in my mouth regarding the experience, I could now try to focus entirely on our preparation for moving to Berlin.

Sherri let me know quickly, though, that she would not move to Berlin—like we did to Munich—without a home address secured ahead of time. And I respected that. But that meant I'd have to make another trip to Berlin several weeks before our moving date to find a rental property and sign a contract.

So, in early April, 1994—two and a half months before our scheduled move—I sent the following newsletter to our supporters.

> Dear Friends and Supporters,
>
> I am now making plans to fly to Berlin around the fifteenth of this month. The sole purpose for this trip will be to find and secure a house for our upcoming move in the latter part of June.
>
> Please pray for a housing miracle! It takes on average two to three months for an outsider moving into a major German city to find a place

to live. Pray that God will allow me to find a sufficient house within two to three weeks. The average rent for a small, one-thousand square foot, three bedroom apartment in Berlin is $2,000 a month. Pray that God will provide us with a furnished four bedroom house for far less.

Thanks for praying with us to this end. Hopefully, when you hear from us again, we will be packing our household goods and our suitcases and will be only days away from settling in Berlin.

Because of His resurrection,
Randy Dodd

A week or so later, I flew into the German capital determined to procure adequate living quarters for my family. Thankfully, a Presbyterian missionary couple—introduced to me by a United States bookstore owner—provided lodging for me during my house search. They resided in East Berlin, a metropolitan expanse that was still dark, grungy, and sooty from the Soviet-occupied years. It was a depressing environment. Everyday, I hurriedly rose early and took a train into West Berlin, to the south side of the city where the John F. Kennedy International School was located. And there I carried out my house search.

The ensuing three weeks in the infamous city, though, plunged me into the deepest pit of fear and depression I had ever faced. I honestly felt like I had walked into Satan's lair.

Chapter 62

On my return flight to Atlanta, I poured out my heart in a newsletter that I intended to send to our financial partners. But I never printed it, never mailed it out. The contents seemed too raw at the time for public consumption.

> Dear Friends,
> Since departing from the Berlin airport two hours ago I have not been able to stop crying. During the last three weeks that I've spent here searching for a house I've experienced a severe crisis of faith, asking fearfully with tears if moving back to Germany is a right decision.
>
> During the last two years of furlough in the States I've been approached by dozens and dozens of *Wisdom Hunter* readers, along with several acquaintances in the publishing industry, who have asked me to remain stateside and write Christian fiction full time. I've also been asked by relatives to consider staying in the States so

we can be close by. In addition, I've received invitations to pastor a couple of churches. These suggestions and requests have presented temptations. But for some reason beyond me, I have deflected these promptings and have insisted on returning to Europe to try to duplicate in Berlin the international ministries we had in Oslo and Munich.

Berlin—a dark and gloomy metropolis with nearly 4 million people. As the situation now stands, my family and I will be moving there around the 20th of June.

But the heavy and all-consuming cloud of depression that hangs over that city—a cloud that many attribute to Satan's stronghold on that region—has in the last three weeks left me longing to escape and never return. I have never in my twenty-eight years of being a Christian personally experienced spiritual oppression of this kind and magnitude.

I reached a point during the course of the last three weeks where I was secretly hoping God would close the door and keep us out of Berlin by not allowing me to find a house. For two and a half weeks I searched tirelessly—with the help of eight real-estate agents—for an apartment or row-house, and found nothing that my family and I could afford or fit into. I was starting to feel relieved.

And then with only two days left, a four bedroom single-family house became available, one of only 20,000 to 30,000 single-family dwellings in a city with over 1 million duplexes, row-houses, and apartments. The house is a sixty-year-old structure that has never been renovated. It is dim and dull, with individual hot water heaters hanging on the kitchen and bathroom walls. But the place does have size and potential for ministry purposes. The monthly rent is $1,700, slightly less than the average rent of $2,000 for a three to four bedroom apartment.

Hesitantly and nervously I proceeded to walk through the open door, while at the same time begging God to slam the door in my face by persuading the landlord to reject me as a possible tenant.

The door didn't close.

A contract was signed last night just before midnight.

And now I'm on the plane weeping my eyes out. Why? Because I'm afraid to go back. I'm afraid to face the darkness, the dullness, and the depression again. And with the dollar now suddenly dropping in value against the German mark I'm wondering if our slim financial support will be sufficient enough to keep us from facing major financial problems along with all the other emotional, cultural, and spiritual adjustments we will face.

Like a frightened child I have begged God here on the plane to somehow speak to me and just let me know that I'm in His will and that everything is going to be okay. But for the moment, all I hear is HIS silence.

I've cried so hard that the lady sitting next to me just got up and moved.

Never in my eighteen years of missionary service have I experienced this type of loneliness. And never, until now, have I ever felt the urgent need to share my heart so openly in this fashion. What I'm saying is: I can't take my family to Berlin and move into that house and attempt a church planting ministry in that city unless I know you are standing at our side with intense prayer support, and heart-to-heart friendship.

Please assure me of that support before I go into battle.

An experienced soldier, suddenly filled with doubt and fear,
Randy Dodd

Three nights before my flight back to Atlanta and before I penned the aforementioned letter, I had sought relief from my mental distress by going to the one and only Berlin theater at the time that showed American movies in their original language. I had simply needed to escape, at least in my mind. When I walked into the lobby of the theater—the Kurbel—there was a long line of people waiting to purchase tickets. I took a place in the queue. In less than a minute or two, I felt someone tap me on the shoulder.

"I know you, don't I?" a man's voice said. There, standing at my side, was the John F. Kennedy music teacher I'd met months earlier when scouting out the school. Before I could respond, the man said, "Yes, yes, you're the one coming to Berlin as a missionary; right?

I nodded.

"Have you already made the move?" came the earnest follow up.

"Actually," I barely managed a response, "I've been here for three weeks looking for a house, but with no success."

"Are you okay?" the teacher probed with a hesitant tone. "You look absolutely exhausted."

I told him about my search. "Only two places have even become available to look at. One was a tiny two-bedroom apartment that was just too small. The other was the second floor of a two-story private house. The owner there said we wouldn't even be allowed to use the yard if we lived there. Not to mention the fact that the man and his wife would hear every step we took on the creaky, wooden floor right above their heads." I explained that I had turned down both offers. "So, I'm now back at square one," I sighed. "And I'm leaving in two days."

"Here, let me write down a name and phone number for you." He gave me the contact info for a lady working in the administrative office at the JFK school. "She's responsible for finding houses for our teachers. Housing information comes across her desk constantly from a variety of sources. So, give her a call. You can tell her I recommended that you reach out to her."

I called the lady the first thing the following morning.

"I'm sorry," the lady told me after I introduced myself and explained my search, "but my folder containing housing leads is completely empty at the moment. But that's not to say I won't receive a housing notice later today or tomorrow. Multiple calls, letters, and notifications come to my desk throughout the year, so call me back later today or tomorrow morning. I never know what information I'll receive."

With no further help that day from the real-estate agents that were trying to assist me, and convinced now that all the doors to Berlin had closed, I—simply for obligatory and committal reasons—contacted the JFK administrator again before she left her office for the day.

"Mister Dodd, are you sitting down?" the lady blurted. "I can hardly believe this, but less than an hour ago I received a phone call from a German landlord who lives in a neighborhood adjacent to the school. He has a large three-bedroom, two-and-a-half bath single-family house he wants to rent. And it falls within your budget."

Standing dumbfounded in a public phone booth I learned that, being near the end of the school year, all the JFK teachers were sufficiently housed at the moment, and that the German landlord would not hold the rental property until the fall semester when three or four new teachers would be arriving. So, the lady had told him about me and my family. "Let me give you the man's name and address, and he'll show you the house this evening."

No! No! It's too late now! I've already given up! I'm going home the day after tomorrow, and I never want to step foot in this city again!

But...if I didn't visit the house and talk to the German owner, how could I with a clear conscience look my supporters in the eye and tell them I had truthfully exhausted every possible lead? Squeezing the pay phone with a death grip I tried to suppress my angst. "All right," I told the lady, "give me the man's phone number and address."

A few hours later I was walking up the driveway of the rental property at Buelow Strasse 13A in a neighborhood called Mexikoplatz, a major stop on one of the S-bahn train lines. The house was no more than a fifteen-minute commute—by bicycle, bus, or train—to the JFK campus. At the top of the driveway was a dedicated parking pad for the residents, unlike the majority of dwellings in the city where residents had to fight for a parking space on the streets.

I knocked on the front door. When the door opened, I thought for a moment I was staring into the face of Sean Connery. The movie star lookalike spoke first. "Hello, are you the American who's interested in renting the house?" the man questioned. His voice carried a deep, no nonsense tone. So did his demeanor.

"Yeah, that's me," I announced, sounding half-hearted I was sure.

"I'm Heinz Frotchner."

"My name is Randy."

We shook hands. The man's grip was formidable.

Wasting no time, Heinz walked me through the house room by room. On the ground floor was a fully functioning kitchen with all the appliances, a formal dining room, a living room, a spacious sunlit room that could be utilized as a home office, and a large outdoor concrete porch. There was a finished basement with three good-sized rooms and a full bath. The second floor of the property housed the master bedroom, a small bedroom with a fun-looking loft, and a full bath. The house, the yard, the tree-covered neighborhood, and the location in proximity to the JFK school matched literally everything on our wish list. If one wanted to live in Berlin, one couldn't find a more idyllic setup.

But I no longer wanted to live in Berlin. Yet...how again could I be true to my calling as a missionary if I refused to listen to the terms of the rental agreement? Contrary to every feeling stampeding through my soul, I told Heinz in my limited German that I would like to know more about the place, along with the rental terms.

At that juncture, Heinz and I quickly reached a stalling point. His English was not proficient enough to vet me with his long list of questions. And my rudimentary abilities in the German language were not sufficient enough to comprehend the legalese of a rental contract. So...I asked him if I could return the next day and bring an interpreter.

"Of course," he replied.

The next evening—after Heinz had completed his work day as a contractor—he met with me again at the rental property. This time I was accompanied by the Presbyterian missionary who had provided lodging for me during my three-week search. The missionary's German was more than adequate to interpret the business dialogue for both Heinz and me.

While there was still sufficient sunlight, I first walked through the house and took photos of every room, along with multiple pictures of the outside yard. When I was ready to sit down, Heinz commenced the business at hand by asking about my family.

He then explained that the house was his and his sister's inheritance. The arrangement was for his sister, when she retired in five years time, to permanently move into the house. Thus, they didn't want to take the risk of renting to a German family. A German family, at the end of five years, might put up a fight to stay in the house indefinitely. And German laws would be on their side. "That's the reason we want to rent to a transitory family such as yours," Heinz clarified. "Plus, the previous tenants were American. And they were fantastic tenants." He paused. "So again, you are planning to stay in Berlin for only four or five years; correct?"

That was our plan. I was still in contact with Larry Michaels at Christian Associates International in California. Our intention, if we were successful in planting a church, was to hand over the leadership roles of the church to the CAI team. And we heard that CAI had already recruited four couples and two singles to be part of their Berlin team.

"That's correct," I assured Heinz.

"And explain to me again what kind of work you do," Heinz forged onward.

I refrained from using the word 'missionary' which could sound condescending. "I'm here to start a church for the international expat community. I'm a pastor."

"A Lutheran?" His question was understandable. The State church of Brandenburg was Lutheran. For nearly five-hundred years, ever since the reformation instigated by Martin Luther, Lutheranism had been the paramount expression of Christianity in the region. It was the religion the Berliners were familiar with.

"No...no. No denomination at all, actually."

For the first time during the exchange, Heinz appeared to step back. For twenty minutes or more, he drilled the interpreter strictly in German. He wanted to know with certainty that I was not a member of some right-wing fanatical cult. The interpreter, step by step, assured him that I wasn't.

Heinz then wanted to know if my income was sufficient to cover the rent each month. I produced a letter from my mission board, European Partnership Ministries, stating that I was duly employed and would receive monthly finances that would cover my family's cost of living.

I then asked Heinz my array of questions.

At ten minutes before midnight—before I was scheduled to leave the country early the next morning—Heinz slid a copy of the rental contract and a pen across the table where I was sitting. I stared at the paper. If I signed my name, I was promising to return with my family in exactly seven weeks. On the day of our return, I would be obligated to pay Heinz for the first month of rent, along with a deposit that was equal to two months rent. I didn't want to sign the document. The darkness of the city had already laid waste my missionary innocence. I felt like a bloodied victim. And I didn't want to knowingly subject Sherri and the girls to such a nightmare. How could I? I wanted to stand up and shout *NO!! I cannot, and will not, sign it. I'm out of here!* I wanted to fly out early the next morning and never return.

I stared intently at the contract on the table and choked up. I'm sure Heinz and my Presbyterian host wondered awkwardly what was happening inside my soul. But I simply couldn't hold back the tears. And then it seemed as if God, against my will, picked up my hand, stretched open my fingers, and clutched the pen. I watched in agony as my hand, almost beyond my control, signed my name on the signature line of the contract. My head drooped.

So...it was to be.

The next morning, on my return flight to Atlanta, I wrote the aforementioned letter to my supporters, a letter that I eventually put away and never mailed.

Chapter 63

Sherri greeted me at the Atlanta airport upon my return. It was her observation when she first spotted me that I looked like a prisoner of war—emotionally emaciated and strengthless. She genuinely empathized with me over the following days as I explained the unexpected darkness that had descended upon me while in Berlin.

Yet...from her perspective, she decided, "God has answered our prayers! He's given us the exact type of house we've asked for! It's got a fully furnished kitchen. It's got a private yard. It's got plenty of bedrooms. And look," she pointed to the tiles in the photo of the master bathroom, "the tiles even match the towels I recently purchased. To me, it feels like a God-wink."

She was so enthusiastic about the place that I asked her to write the next outgoing newsletter. And she did.

IT'S A MIRACLE! GOD DID IT!

Kitchen Calendar Verse for April:
"He brought me into a spacious place; he rescued me because he delighted in me."
Psalm 18:19

Kitchen Calendar Verse for May:
"Blessed are those whose strength is in you, who have set their hearts on pilgrimage."
Psalm 84:5

God, in His love, has once again provided abundantly above all we could ask or think. Randy was able to secure God's housing miracle for us on his last day in Berlin. The landlord of a four bedroom, two bath, house came down on the monthly rent by $200 a month. How we praise God for this! The house is 60 years old, but in good condition. We will have the space we need to live and minister. The landlord is re-painting the inside walls before we arrive, and the color of the bathroom tiles match the towels I already own! Isn't God great?

Normally it takes two to three months to find housing in Berlin. God gave us this house in less than three weeks for a price several hundred dollars below the going rate. Normally, three months rent is required up front as a deposit. We only have to pay two months rent as a deposit. We didn't have to pay a realtor's fee which is normally an additional two months rent. Often houses come with no kitchen cabinets or appliances or light fixtures. This miracle house on Buelow Strasse has a complete kitchen with fixtures. It has a 6300-hundred square foot yard and the landlord is providing the lawn-mower.

The previous renters are even leaving us all their curtains! God is an awesome God!

"The Lord is my shepherd, I shall lack nothing." Psalm 23:1.

Please keep us in your prayers as we sort and pack our belongings. Saying "good-bye" again will not be easy. We send a special "thanks" to all of our new supporters. We appreciate your partnership with us. To God be the glory, great things He has done,
Sherri

Within a week or so I managed to calm down a bit and accept the fact that there was no longer any margin for changing course. My family and I were moving to Berlin. Sweet and simple.

To help generate some needed excitement, I took Sherri, Heidi, and Shanda shopping one afternoon for mountain bikes. I knew there were no mountains in or around Berlin, but there were hundreds, if not thousands, of miles of bike trails all throughout the city and its outlying parks. The region was supposedly a bicyclists paradise. Mountain bikes were in vogue at the time, so I splurged. I bought us each an expensive Trek bike. Each one was handpicked, both for color and size. We carted them home and packed them with our household goods that would be airfreighted on a pallet directly into Berlin.

As the days and weeks ticked off we once again brought closure to our life in the U.S. We shipped our Daihatsu to Bremerhaven, Germany from Charleston, South Carolina.

We said our gradual goodbyes to family, friends, teachers, and supporters.

Two days before our departure we donated Sherri's car—a Dodge Shadow—to Mike Bove our old youth pastor who had returned to the U.S. with his family after serving in Indonesia as missionaries for many years.

Several people from Eastside Baptist Church threw a farewell send-off for us. Sherri and I thanked the pastor and congregation profusely for supplying us with a great house, rent free, for the duration of our extended furlough, and for not withdrawing their friendship and financial support because of the embroiling controversy surrounding *Wisdom Hunter*. We assured them we couldn't have survived the *Wisdom Hunter* fallout without their encouragement and assistance.

When we finally boarded the transatlantic flight to Berlin as a family, we were all once again lost in our private worlds of mental and emotional maelstrom.

But we at least had a clean and empty house waiting for us on the other side of the ocean. That alone was worth something.

The day after our arrival in Berlin, five single adults from the church we started in Munich—four young men and one young lady—made the seven-hour drive to help us collect our household goods from the airport and place the assorted items throughout the house. They also cleaned windows, made runs to the grocery store to help stock the kitchen pantry and refrigerator, and assisted us in setting up our phone service. One of the young men was an elder in the Lutheran church that rented out their fellowship hall to the international church Sherri and I had planted in Munich. The young man continued to be so inspired by the international congregation that he had become a regular attendee at the services and somehow felt beholden to us, the founders. He was just excited that we were planning to start a similar church in Berlin. We were deeply touched by his belief in us.

Since Shanda, who was nine at the time, wasn't able to intuitively help set up house, she asked if she could ride her bike while everybody else worked. She was emotionally distraught over the move and vocalized her sadness multiple times a day. Feeling her plight, I wanted to create some healthy distractions for her, so I took a long pause and walked with her around our giant residential block. A cobblestone sidewalk circled the entire perimeter. Together we scouted the half-mile-long walkway as a potential route for bicycling. Seeing firsthand that the cobblestone path was safe for a bicyclist and that the neighborhood was safe for a nine-year-old girl, I gave her permission to ride around the block alone.

Back at the house we readied her bike. "Just report to me in person when you've completed the circuit," I instructed. "Go ahead. Take your time and enjoy the ride." As I watched her pedal away down the driveway I begged God with a lump in my throat to bring consolation to her young heart.

Throughout the next hour or two she notified me each time she made it safely around the block. For her, it was a day of somber exploration, and a day that initiated her lifelong use of new wings. For us as a family, it was a day of accepting our fate. We were in Berlin under a rental contract and, despite any adjustments involving the city or the culture, we were not going to be leaving anytime soon. We simply had to grit our teeth and wake up each morning determined to be intentional, creative, and productive.

So that's what we did.

When our friends from Munich returned to their home in Bavaria we started scouring the local newspapers for used furniture sales. At the same time we learned, to our mild surprise, that all the mighty military bases in West Berlin—American, British, and French—were in the process of permanently shutting down after forty-nine years of providing a deterrent against Russian expansion westward. The Russian bases were closing down in East Berlin as well. We learned that every military family, thousands of them, would be gone from the city within six weeks. Going forward, only the embassies would utilize a minimum number of armed-forces staff, typically guards and attachés.

So, as we were moving into the city, the majority of Americans were moving out. The exodus was somewhat sad, and something we had not foreseen. Yet, the pull-out did provide one giant nicety: the JFK international school would have immediate openings for American students. We promptly enrolled Heidi and Shanda for the fall semester.

With so many Americans hustling to and fro to bring closure to their stay in Berlin, reliable babysitters were suddenly needed just about everywhere. So Heidi as a fifteen-year-old posted her babysitting services, along with our new phone number, on a bulletin board at the Clay Konserne during its final days. In less than twenty-four hours she received a call. Ironically, a new family moving into the city to work at the American embassy needed someone to watch their two adopted children several hours a day for a full week.

Heidi was hired.

When the husband and wife learned from Heidi that I was planning to start an evangelical church for the international community, they wanted to talk with me. Following a lengthy meeting with the couple I was shocked when, as devoted Christians, they announced they would like to help us start the church—to just let them know when we were ready. It seemed to be another God-wink.

Chapter 64

As a family, we moved forward with the house setup, along with regular outings to explore the city and its extensive century-old public transportation system that incorporated subways, trains, buses, and trams. On July 4, the kids and I, at Sherri's insistence, attended a gigantic blow-out fest for the American military community. Highlighting the event were the Pointer sisters and a fireworks show that must have exhausted a decade's worth of accumulated pyrotechnics. It was the largest and lengthiest display of fireworks we had ever seen. It was a farewell hoopla fitting for a nation that had pretty much rebuilt Germany and protected it from further devastation following World War II. It was the passing of the baton to a reunited and strong German nation, now a major western ally.

As Heidi and Shanda made new friends throughout our part of town that summer, I met a few more times with the embassy couple that wanted to become charter members of our envisioned new church. I cultivated a relationship with them and cast my plans and hopes for the new ministry. Sherri began engaging them as well.

Around the same time, we started finding and purchasing

used, high quality furniture that we transported to the house with rental trucks. I even purchased carpet that I installed in the living room and home office.

When I was alerted that our Daihatsu had finally arrived in Bremerhaven, I bought a one-way train ticket for the four-hour journey to the coastal town. By nightfall the next evening, I was back in Berlin with our family's automobile.

With the work of setting up house mostly behind us, I decided it was time to start integrating into the international community and establishing contacts. So I began at the John F. Kennedy school. A couple of weeks before the fall semester I went to the campus and asked at the admin department if there was any type of volunteer work I could help with.

"Absolutely," was the reply from one of the offices. "Our librarian needs help as we speak. She's moving the school's entire library to a new area across campus. And there are only a couple of people working with her. She can definitely use an extra pair of hands."

For the next three days I helped haul, categorize, and shelve hundreds of books. When the librarian heard my reason for moving to Berlin she pulled me aside and said, "I don't know if you have an interest, but there's an on-campus Bible study group that just lost their leader. Perhaps you could offer your assistance. Let me give you the name and phone number of one of the seniors in the group."

It felt like another "God" moment. Of course I was interested.

But before I had a chance to call the high school student that evening, Sherri received word from the States that her grandmother had died. Annie Price was a woman who had, perhaps more than any other adult, inspired Sherri as a young girl to seek after her Creator. Sherri, even into adulthood, constantly quoted her family's matriarch: *'Have a good time in a good way.' 'Live good, pray lots, and remember me.' 'I'll meet you here, there, or in the air.'*

Sherri wanted badly to attend the funeral back in Georgia. But the burial date coincided with Heidi and Shanda's first days of school at JFK. Because of her overpowering drive as a mother to prioritize the care for her young, Sherri opted to remain in Berlin and give support to the girls. It was a tearful sacrifice, but one that was made with a mother's love.

When I eventually made contact with the JFK senior who assisted with the on-campus Bible study, and offered my help, I was enthusiastically welcomed to attend the first gathering of the school year, meet everyone, and see if there was a mutual fit. I was told a time and date for that first meeting.

When I showed up on the designated afternoon, I was pleasantly surprised to meet a half dozen confident, mature, and intelligent young people who had a genuine desire to study the Scriptures. After a round of introductions and a time of briefly sharing my story, purpose, and ministry, I was invited to be the group leader for the school year. I accepted the responsibility without hesitation.

To integrate further into the international community I participated in serious volleyball games every Saturday morning with military guards from a variety of embassies. And Sherri joined a couple of international ladies' clubs in the city.

Soon, Sherri and I had generated enough budding friendships to invite people to our home for a Sunday afternoon Bible study. The adoptive couple that had hired Heidi to babysit remained true to their original declaration. They, from the first gathering in our home, became a bedrock family that attended every meeting, served in every way they could, and invited others regularly to join us.

The Sunday group quickly grew numerically to a point that we were hosting more people than we could seat. A few of those were the high school students who were part of our JFK Bible study.

Shortly thereafter, I searched for, and found, a rental facility that could accommodate a hundred or more people. It was the fellowship hall of an old German-speaking Lutheran church. They would rent the space to us on Sunday afternoons, following their Sunday morning service. I signed a contract. We named our fellowship Gateway International Church and scheduled a charter date.

The ministry flourished from the start.

At home, though, Shanda was withering—in every facet of the human experience. She cried herself to sleep every night, begging me, "Daddy, please! Can't we move back to America? I hate it here! Can't you be a pastor in Georgia somewhere?" Sherri's and my heart bled a little self-assurance every time Shanda declared her depression. But what could we do? We had made the move. We had signed a rental contract. We had birthed a promising ministry. We were now committed. After a lot of contemplation, we determined there was at least one initiative we could take to add a little relief to her life. Her primary teacher at the JFK school was a German man who was overly demanding, along with an inability to clearly explain the difficult math and science in his curriculum. He was also cold and impersonal. His personality and teaching style only weighted down Shanda's misery. One of the other sixth-grade teachers was an American lady named Mrs. Parker. Her care for, and engagement with, her students were noted throughout the community. When that particular information came my way I promptly made a trip to the elementary school office. I sat down with the principal, explained Shanda's mental and emotional despair as a newcomer to the city, and requested that she be reassigned to Mrs. Parker's classroom. "I'm convinced," I told him, "that the better classroom environment will help reduce the stress level in her life."

"I'm sorry," the principal replied, "but our school policy doesn't afford your daughter that option. I'm afraid she will have to stay where she's been assigned. Just give the situation a little more time. I'm sure she will adjust and do just fine."

But I was sure she wouldn't. And I told him. "Look, you're an educator. Plus, you know the stresses that come with living in a foreign culture. I know my daughter. And I know that in her current state of mind she will never thrive in her present homeroom situation. You've got to help us out here!"

"I'm sorry, Mr. Dodd. But there's nothing I can do."

I waited another week, then showed up at his office again. "Shanda is still not adjusting," I stressed assertively. "If anything, she's becoming more despondent. It's my judgment and my wife's judgment that she needs to be transferred to Mrs. Parker's homeroom class as soon as possible. Please, think about the student here!"

The principal refused to bend.

A day or so later, one of the ladies in our budding church, after hearing about our school dilemma, asked to speak with me in private. The lady worked full time as an administrator at the JFK school. "I happen to know," she divulged when I stepped aside with her, "that the principal you've been talking to moved his son from a homeroom class simply because the young boy didn't like the teacher. I just thought you'd like to have that bit of information." She smiled as she passed along the scoop.

The next day, I visited the principal's office again. For the third time, the man's secretary ushered me into the director's sanctum. When the principal saw me, he sighed. "You're wasting your time, Mister Dodd," he spouted.

"Maybe not," I retorted. "You told me when I first approached you that the school policy prohibits students from being reassigned to a different homeroom, and that there are no exceptions. Yet, I understand that at least one exception has been made." I stared at the principal and raised my eyebrows. And just in case he had doubts about what I knew, I added, "Please, as a father of a JFK student, you of all people understand my father's heart. You intervened for your kid. Let me intervene for mine."

The man wasn't pleased. He turned and gazed out the window for a good thirty seconds. "Meet me here in the office tomorrow at the same time," he finally snapped as he twisted to face me.

The following day Shanda was reassigned to Mrs. Parker's homeroom class with the understanding that I would not broadcast the decision to anyone in the community. And within the week, Shanda was smiling for the first time since leaving Georgia. Mrs. Parker quickly became our youngest daughter's cultural salvation. Sherri's and my heart sighed with relief. Some things were definitely worth fighting for. With Shanda's improving spirits, she—with our permission and encouragement—ventured out more and more, both on foot and on bike. It seemed that nearly every other day she was seeking permission to extend her parameters of exploration. And more often than not, we granted the requests. After all, the city was kid safe. And we wanted to bolster her independence. She began to culturally take flight.

In the meantime, Heidi—fearless by nature—was having the time of her life. She loved Berlin. Compared to the suburbs of Atlanta, Berlin with its endless array of subways, trains, buses, and trams afforded new adventures every day. For Heidi, a 15-year-old extrovert, the city was paradise.

For me personally, I was feeling the darkness of Berlin less and less as the community of believers at Gateway International significantly multiplied. My sense of belonging strengthened even more so on the day Gateway officially organized. The following day I contacted Larry Michaels, the president of Christian Associates International in California. "Well, we did it!" I exclaimed. "We've planted the church. So, let your Berlin team know we're up and running. As the couples complete their fundraising go ahead and send them this way and we'll phase them into leadership roles."

PART III

BROTHERHOOD OF BETRAYAL

Chapter 65

As the founder of Gateway International Church, I decided not to unilaterally initiate programs, committees, or officers. I wanted the people, when they were ready and hungry for such elements, to initiate a request for them. But my decision to be silent upfront regarding those issues nearly backfired.

A concerned church member informed me one afternoon that there were three or four key families in the church poised to leave our group.

"Why?" I asked with an accelerated heartbeat.

The informer didn't know.

I immediately reached out by phone to one of the families that was reputedly ready to 'cut-and-run.' They didn't want to talk about their disgruntlement over the phone. "Can we meet in person, then?" I pleaded. "I really need to understand what's going on inside your head."

They reluctantly agreed to host a meeting in their home if I would allow the other families who shared their sentiment to attend.

"Absolutely; please!" I consented.

At the appointed meeting, the four families in attendance verbally unloaded on me. "You're not involving others," one denounced. "No one has a sense of belonging. It's just you and Sherri up front all the time," another piled on. "There's no sense of family. It just doesn't feel like we're building a church."

The initial minutes of the emergency council were as tense as can be imagined. But I heard the complaints loud and clear. I hastily diffused the angst by humbly acknowledging that every expressed disappointment was valid, that I had indeed moved too slowly as a responsible leader. "Give me one more chance," I petitioned. "I promise I'll do better."

The men and women convened in a huddle to make their decision. After a few minutes they tiredly opted to grant me one more chance.

I quickly honored their decision. The next Sunday I announced, with the support of the people, that I would promptly launch a weekly interactive men's Bible study in our home. The purpose of the gathering would be to go through the New Testament book of Titus verse by verse, examine the qualifications for church leaders, and at the end of the series nominate some qualified men in our church to serve as the first leadership team at Gateway International. The leadership team, as representatives of the church, would then cast vision for the future programs, offices, and outreach ministries of the church.

Six men faithfully attended the weekly study. The cumulative conversations, questions, insights, and conclusions were life-changing for the group. Afterward, four men were elected to the leadership team. Thus began the real legacy of Gateway International.

And just as the young burgeoning church started to

make a name for itself within Berlin's Christian community, another significant event occurred.

Sherri whispered to me with a huge smile. "I'm pregnant!"

It had been 9 years since Shanda's birth. Sherri was now 37. Thrilled to the max, she decided straightaway that the child would be delivered in Berlin. Heidi and Shanda had been born in Oslo with outstanding medical expertise and care. And Sherri was convinced that the German maternity wards were as progressive and efficient as the Norwegian and American counterparts. So we would not plan a special trip back to the States for the child's birth. Being delivered "overseas" would be a badge of prestige that this progeny could also carry.

As we celebrated the anticipated birth of our third child, we planned a surprise party for Heidi's sixteenth birthday.

On the day of the big event I took Heidi on a father-daughter shopping spree downtown. Three hours later, when we returned home, the last thing on Heidi's mind—I was sure—was the fact that she was about to be greeted by a house full of friends shouting Happy Birthday!

And stupefied she was.

The party turned out to be a welcomed success. Not only was Heidi surprised to the max, but Sherri and Shanda were going to knowingly embarrass me in front of the birthday crowd. They wanted to give everyone an unforgettable laugh at my expense. The source of the lampoon was my poor skills with the German language. Heidi had told me weeks earlier that a coveted birthday gift would be a paper cutter. She wanted to be able to cut photos in myriad shapes and sizes for her creative photo albums. Wanting to be a supportive dad I had gone one day to the stationery section of a large department store. A dignified male clerk dressed in a suit and tie welcomed me and asked, "Kann ich Ihnen helfen?" (Can I help you?)

For days I had rehearsed my answer - *Ja, können sie mir sagen, haben sie ein Papierschneidemaschine?* (Yes, can you tell me if you have a paper cutting machine?)

But when I asked the question out loud in the man's presence—even pumping my arm up and down to illustrate the cutting motion—I saw the guy abruptly stop in his tracks, throw his hands in the air, roll his eyes, and shake his head in droll distaste. Without another word, he turned and walked away, leaving me alone and disconcerted.

I stood momentarily in a daze. What had I said?

As I turned and slowly sauntered away, I went over my question word by word, syllable by syllable. It took a minute or so, but I finally realized I had omitted the letter "n" in "schneide." I had asked the man if the store sold a paper "scheide" machine. When I returned home, I pulled Sherri to the side, explained my mistake, and asked if she could figure out why the salesman had reacted the way he did.

"You actually asked him that?" she quizzed with a look of humorous unbelief in her eyes.

"Uh...yeah. So what did I say to the man?"

"You..." she laughed with a knee-slapping holler, "you...asked him if he had a paper vagina machine." She was laughing so hard that Shanda came running into the room wanting to know what was so funny. When Sherri divulged the story—barely able to talk, she was cackling so hard—Shanda joined the course of nonstop hilarity.

Great, I thought. *I'm a bumbling idiot.*

And now at the birthday party, when Heidi opened my gift—I had finally found the paper cutter at another store—Sherri brought the house down in a hail of laughter by telling the story.

Well at least I was a pastor who was real, approachable, and relatable. And those characteristics, I continued to believe, were important elements that contributed to our congregation's sense of brotherhood. And it was that growing brotherhood that infused our congregation with a unique strength.

Sherri and I needed that strength about six weeks later when she experienced the heartbreaking mishap of a miscarriage - the miscarriage of a daughter that Sherri named November Joy. The support of the congregation during those days was vital for us. The ladies of the church especially rallied around Sherri with a chorus of sympathy, support, and encouragement.

The strength of our congregation soon began to manifest itself in other ways. And they were quite dynamic. The church, for example, early on gave birth to an annual "missionary conference." The day-long symposium was for all the missionaries—regardless of denominational affiliation—living and ministering throughout the greater metropolitan area of Berlin. The first of those conferences, attended by forty people or more, was so uplifting that a lady in our church who helped serve throughout the day dared to envision an even greater affair. "I'm pretty sure," she said, "that there are a lot of Christian ladies—stay-at-home wives, career women, and students—in the city who feel terribly isolated and lonely. We know the number of Bible-teaching churches here is minimal. And the ones that exist are small and probably have no support group for ladies. So...as Gateway has reached out to support and encourage the missionary families, let's reach out to encourage the Christian women."

My mind was hit by the unexpected. But I was instantly and genuinely curious. "Go ahead; I'm listening."

"Let's send a notice to the women—married and single—of every evangelical church we can find and invite them to come under one roof for a half day of fellowship and exhortation—including a lunch. If it proves to be a success, we can possibly make it a quarterly event." As the lady talked, her passion poured from her eyes and her voice.

My mind momentarily froze with all the positive what ifs.

"If Gateway will support it, I'll coordinate it and lead it," she enthused. "I just need your blessing." The lady was a former TV broadcaster. She was outgoing, articulate, smart, and a natural leader. Plus, she had a heart for God, and for ministry. She was more than qualified.

"Okay..." I conceded. "Sure...let's take it to the leadership team and see what they say."

Shortly thereafter—when listening to the lady's pitch—the decision makers of our church voted unanimously for Gateway to back the lady as she pioneered what everyone hoped would become the inaugural meeting of the Christian Women of Berlin. Several leaders in the church, including Sherri, and even a few men answered the lady's call to help out as co-laborers.

Countless hours over a three-month period were invested in the big event. And big it was, at least for Berlin standards. Around fifty women from all four corners of the city attended. The spiritual thirst was so evident among the attendees, that it was decided then and there that the event should be a quarterly affair. And become a quarterly event, it did, eventually drawing as many as three-hundred women in a single gathering.

In a town so spiritually drought-stricken, Gateway International became a significant oasis. Youth, adults, singles, and families were all being nurtured, discipled and mobilized. The overall morale was absolutely refreshing.

Chapter 66

Always trying to think beyond the barriers of tradition, I asked eight people one day to each take an upcoming Sunday and publicly share their stories of faith in one of our church services. Several of those individuals had never spoken publicly to an audience before. But after being gently nudged a few times they finally said, "Okay."

I instructed each of the eight to take no more than ten minutes when up front. I asked them to write out their presentation or memorize it, but not to speak extemporaneously. I didn't want them to mentally wander and lose track of time.

A few Sundays into this series of testimonies, we were a few minutes away from commencing a church service when a lady of the congregation walked up and introduced me to a drop-in visitor. "This is *Ricky," she told me. "He's asked to speak personally with the pastor."

"Ricky," I repeated the name as I extended my hand. "I'm the pastor. My name is Randy."

Ricky shook my hand and looked me in the eye with an all-serious demeanor. "Thanks for giving me a moment," he said in a midwestern American accent. "As the lady said, my name is Ricky. I'm an American working here as an architect with a German firm. I've been here for about a year working on a project that has kept me totally immersed in the German language and German culture. And at the moment I just need to come up for air and hang out a bit with some English speakers. So that's why I'm here." I started to welcome him when he added, "But know up front, I'm not a church goer. If anything I'm an atheist, at least an agnostic. I'm only here to reconnect with Americans and make friends; that's all. I have absolutely no interest in religion. Zero. Nada. Zilch."

"All right then," I told him as I quickly regrouped. Registering the undertones of his loneliness, I said, "You've come to the right place. Every one here speaks English. And no one is going to pressure you to change your mind about anything. So, mingle and make yourself at home."

And he did. He sat through the entire service that day, hearing the story-of-faith shared by one of the assigned eight people, along with a message I shared from the Scripture. When I learned at the end of the service that he was single and didn't own a vehicle, I offered to drive him home. He gladly accepted the offer. Not much was said about the church service during the jaunt across town. I primarily focused the conversation around him and his work.

He showed up at Gateway again the next week. And the next. As I chauffeured him back to his apartment on that third Sunday, he—to my surprise—interjected into the conversation an observation about the church gatherings. "These personal stories that the people are sharing every Sunday are quite interesting," he admitted.

"Yeah? How so?"

"Well, to be honest, I always figured Christians were somehow less educated, less experienced, less aware. A little less in everything I guess. But the people who've shared have surprised me. They're articulate, well-positioned, actually intelligent." There was a significant pause. "They're not delusional, are they?"

"No, they're not delusional."

Ricky stared at me. His eyes were filled with curiosity. "Do you have a story like theirs?"

"I do." As Ricky listened, I described my personal journey to a life-changing faith in Christ. When I finished sharing, Ricky simply absorbed my words in a reflective silence. Eventually breaking the silence, I made an off-the-cuff proposal. "Why don't you share your story one Sunday?"

"What do you mean? Uh...I'm a little confused. I'm not sure what you're aiming for here."

"It's simple. Stand up, tell the people where you're from, what you do, that you're attending the church, not because you're interested in Christianity, but because you need English-speaking friends."

"Are you serious?"

"Absolutely."

"And that's okay in a Christian church?"

"Of course it is."

Ricky contemplated the offer. "All right. Yeah...I'll do it."

A few weeks later Ricky indeed shared his story during a Sunday service. He explained that he was an agnostic, not interested in religion, but just needed friends.

A family invited him home for dinner that day. Over the next week or two, others invited him into their lives as well. The stories of faith he was hearing, substantiated by lives displaying a viable relationship with Christ, progressively opened his mind to the existence of the living Savior.

Here are a few of Ricky's exact words.

"Attending college, I studied architecture and was taught to think critically. The result was a questioning of everything that had previously happened in my life, from the heroic portrayals of history that I was taught in school to the existence of God. My overall naiveté was replaced with cynicism. When I received my diploma I moved to Berlin as an architect. My first year in the city was full of excitement, adventure, and challenges. But I felt 'lost' more than ever. I visited a few of the German state churches in my search for truth and identity. But all I found was social clubs. They were not places where people with real problems could find comfort in fellowship. That brings me to where I am now, Gateway International Church. I cannot say my doubts have been erased overnight since coming to this church. But the close-knit family has encouraged my questions, provided as many direct answers as possible, and most of all welcomed me with an unconditional love. I still struggle with life's questions, but thanks to my new-found friends I feel I'm much better equipped to deal with these struggles. I feel for the first time in life that I'm headed in the right direction."

After a couple of more weeks, and dozens and dozens of additional questions, Ricky became a believer. It was a majestic moment when he ran into the arms of the Redeemer who he had for so many years rebuffed and denied. His life instantly changed. Dramatically.

Our church, though, didn't have a singles ministry. I gladly told Ricky about a good church that did have a notable singles group. He visited there and was quickly absorbed into the group. There he was enthusiastically discipled by two or three key men who won his respect. A while later, he announced to the Christian community that he was walking away from his successful career as an architect and planning to attend Bible college. He felt "called to serve in full-time ministry." He ended up at Columbia Bible College in South Carolina where he received his theological and missional training.

Ironically, one of the professors at Columbia had read my novel *Wisdom Hunter* and had introduced it to his students as required reading as a treatise on spiritual growth.

That particular revelation was more than satisfying. The truths of God, I was starkly reminded, not only had an impact when delivered in person, such as with Ricky, but equally so when presented in print. That fact built a new fire in my soul to write another novel. The incident at the IBWO European conference years earlier in Switzerland had given birth to a storyline that I had mulled over for years. When the IBWO president had stood up and reported that a non-Baptist missionary had disappeared from his field in Africa and was found years later as a homeless alcoholic on the streets of Los Angeles, he had done so with what I perceived as a pious, holier-than-thou attitude. And it made me seethe. *The missionary deserved what came to him* had been the president's final and graceless indictment.

It was my conviction that men like the wayward missionary should be helped instead of shunned. So I wanted to spotlight the sheer ugliness of abandoning one of our wounded. I had almost been there myself. I knew and understood the cries of the heart beneath the prodigal exploits. But the church, instead of being a brotherhood of solidarity, reaching out in love and grace to its fallen soldiers, demonstrated more often than not that it was a brotherhood of betrayal. Typically, church leaders who "fell" and betrayed their people were instantly disavowed by the church as "worthless." Those "fallen" ministers then turned on the church and regularly voiced their perpetual anger. It was truly, truly ugly. And I wanted to bring the topic to the table.

So I brought out my pen and paper and created an outline. And in my spare time, I started writing *Brotherhood of Betrayal*.

Around the same time, Sherri and I received some exciting and welcomed news that we had anticipated for quite awhile.

Chapter 67

Sherri and I had known for weeks that the first of the four CAI families, slated to succeed us as pastoral leaders at Gateway, would be flying into Berlin at any time. We learned that this first couple would be *George and Rachel Dixon along with their three children.

When George and Rachel and their kids arrived at the Tegel airport, Sherri and I shuttled them to the townhouse for which they had signed a rental contract via fax.

This was the Dixons first time as Americans to move abroad, but from all appearances, they settled quickly into an energetic and productive rhythm of life. Of course, the Gateway congregation immediately provided a home away from home, and a family away from family. That all-important provision enabled them to make a rapid and stable adjustment to the spiritual desert that was Berlin.

Miraculously, within four or five days, George and Rachel announced they were eager and ready to jump into the church's itinerary and offer help wherever they were needed. They became an instant asset to Gateway's ministry. They were always excited and never resorted to excuses. I liked them immediately. The thought that there were three more CAI couples and two singles still raising funds to join us simply stirred my imagination as to how Gateway International could, over time, become the premiere evangelical church in Berlin.

And just when we thought life was already so rich and promising Sherri made an announcement that brought an added smile to everyone's face. "I'm pregnant again," she beamed.

Because of Sherri's age, at 38, the doctors catalogued her pregnancy in a *high risk* category. Consequently, she received special monitoring. As a result, we learned within a few months that the life inside her was a baby boy. We were thrilled. Sherri had especially wanted a boy. So did I.

We naturally started discussing names. I've always been keen on unusual ones. For example, I had really wanted to name Heidi, Diamond. I had met ladies named Pearl, Ruby, Sapphire. But I had never heard of a lady named Diamond. Sherri's response was, "Diamond Dodd? I don't think so. She might turn out to be a stripper, but we're not giving her the name of one." Regarding Shanda, I had pushed to name her Shandy. It was a combination of Sherri and Randy. "It sounds too much like shanty," Sherri declared. "The answer is No!" And now I proposed that we give our son the name Swade. It was virtually an unheard of name for a man. But, it was tough sounding. At least to my ears. "And if he has a twin sister," Sherri quipped, "are we going to name her Polly...Polly Esther?" Again my initial suggestion was vetoed.

Nevertheless, Sherri had been willing to compromise a little with each of the girl's names. Gratefully she compromised again. After hours of filtering through traditional names, unusual names, and made-up names, we finally agreed on a name that we honestly thought was our original creation— Cayden. The name would be a combination of the Welsh name Cei, meaning 'fiery rejoicer,' and the Norwegian definite article 'en' which is placed as the suffix of a noun. Thus, the meaning of the fabricated moniker would be 'fiery rejoicer, the' or 'the fiery rejoicer.' Our son, the fiery rejoicer. His middle name would be Jeremiah - Cayden Jeremiah Dodd. Even Heidi and Shanda liked it.

Yes, it was a good season in life. And for a while, pleasant surprises continued to come our way. For example, our landlord and his wife—unbelievers, and initially skeptical of our beliefs and purposes—showed up for a few of Gateway's church services. Their feedback as straight-talking Germans was an outpouring of genuine smiles and sincere words of admiration. Seeds of God's Truths were planted in their hearts. This was obvious, judging from their words, eyes, and demeanor. Only God could have orchestrated such a positive reception on their part. This was an answer to prayer. And we have continued to pray for this couple through the years.

On top of this significant event, one of my childhood dreams unexpectedly came to fruition. Prior to surrendering as a teenager to being a preacher and missionary I had dreamt of becoming a professional baseball player. I was so devoted, however, to my new ministerial calling that I forsook baseball both in my high school and college years. I, of course, enjoyed playing softball on a church team in Norway, but had never satiated my longing to play on a baseball team. But that suddenly changed.

One afternoon while running errands I drove by an old baseball field that had been built years earlier by, and for, the American military troops. When the US military base closed, the field had been turned over to the German public. I was puzzled, though, when I saw a baseball team, in uniform, playing on the field. Just out of abject curiosity I stopped. I got out of the car, leaned against a perimeter fence, and watched. I quickly deciphered, by spotting a coach in action, that the players were simply in the middle of field practice.

It was just one team.

When the coach, who was quite animated, strode nearby where I was standing, I lifted my voice, "Excuse me, is there an actual baseball league here in Berlin?"

In English, the man issued an order to the pitcher, then swung to face me. Taking my measure, he said, "Yeah, there's a very active league. Why do you want to know?"

The guy was an American.

"Do any of the teams need a new player?"

The man squinted at me. I was 42 years old. "Why? Are you wanting to try out?"

I really wasn't expecting such a positive reaction. "Uh...sure. Yeah...yeah I guess I am."

"Have you ever played?"

"Only sandlot games." I heard the man chuckle. So I quickly added, "I did play in a NATO softball league a few years ago, and was a key player."

"What's your strength?"

"In softball I always played in the outfield. I have great eye-hand coordination. I'm fast. I've got a good arm."

"All right, let's see what you got. Grab a glove lying there on the ground and run out to center field."

I grabbed a mitt and hustled to the back side of the field.

The coach instructed the batter to hit some fly balls to me. In my mind I was suddenly back on the sandlot fields of my youth. Adrenalin engorged my muscles. As the baseballs flew my way I focused, pivoted, and tracked down every ball. The coach then directed the batter to hit ground balls. I scooped them up with equal agility and fired them to the infield. Line drives were next. I rushed them and snatched them out of the air or off the bounce. After fifteen minutes the coach pulled me aside.

"All right, let's see what you can do at the plate."

Nervously, I made my way to the batter's box. I had never attempted to hit a baseball thrown by an adult at 70 to 80 mph. I promptly explained that fact to the coach, the pitcher, and the catcher. I then asked them, "Is it okay if I just stand here for three or four pitches and let my eyes get oriented to the speed of the ball?"

The coach nodded to the pitcher.

I placed the bat over my shoulder for a pretend-swing. Almost before I could visually calculate what was happening I heard the baseball smack the catcher's mitt with a hard pop. *Dang! Really?*

For the next pitch I focused with greater intensity.

And for the next.

And the next.

Finally, when I was able to optically isolate the ball as it approached the plate, I informed the coach that I would like to simply extend the bat, without swinging, just to see if I could make contact with the ball.

Again, the coach nodded his okay.

I failed during the next two pitches to put the bat in line with the ball's trajectory.

Swish! Pop!

Swish! Pop!

Come on, I chided myself. *Thousands of people do this all the time!*

Swish! Pop!

I huffed.

And then, with maximized concentration, I mentally pretended to receive the next ball in slow motion. As I stood there, staring, I was convinced I could see the red stitching this time as the ball hurled my way.

Clunk!

The ball dropped a few feet in front of me. I smiled.

I made contact with the next seven or eight balls. "All right, I think I'm ready to swing," I announced.

Within minutes, to my delight, I was slamming balls—thrown at 50 to 60 mph—back out into the infield. And in very little time I was hitting quite a number of the ones hurled at 70 to 80 mph. I was invited on the spot to join the team roster, with the understanding that there were only thirteen games remaining in the season.

Within the week I was issued a uniform and batting helmet with the number #60. I started, and played, in ten of the thirteen final games. I even played in the playoffs. It was my teenage fantasy come true. I quickly developed a reputation throughout the league. "He's fast, and he can hit," were the words that spread. I was definitely not a slugger or home-run hitter, but it seemed I was hitting a ton of singles and doubles. In the end, our team failed to win the playoffs, but only slightly.

During the postseason award ceremony, I was shocked when the coach called my name as the recipient of the Joe DiMaggio, Most-Valuable-Player award. My batting average for my short time on the team was .620. I smiled like a high schooler when I received the trophy. The brief season of play was a once-in-a-lifetime gift, and one I'll always treasure. I actually thought about signing up for the following season, but with a growing church, a growing family, an upcoming novel, and a business trip to the US tentatively planned for the next summer, I simply didn't have the margin in my schedule.

The business trip to the US, alone—if it occurred—superseded any further baseball aspirations. It would be a visit to Nashville, to the headquarters of Word Publishing, the premiere name in Christian publishing at the time. Word wanted to negotiate a contract for my next novel *Brotherhood of Betrayal*. With Word I would perhaps join an elite family of authors that included Charles Swindoll, James Dobson, John McArthur, and Max Lucado. I was more than humbled by the prospect.

Chapter 68

As I continued to make progress with my new novel, Sherri approached her due date buoyed psychologically by all the positive reports from her doctors.

When she finally went into labor, it was late one evening when everyone in our family was at home. The moment she felt the first contraction, she notified us and said, "I'm going to go take a hot shower and freshen up. In a few minutes, be ready to take me to the hospital." The birth of Heidi and Shanda had been relatively quick. Sherri knew her body. And she knew the statistical data. She was adamant that Cayden would not linger.

By the time she showered and dressed, the contractions were coming at ten minute intervals. I helped her to the car and drove her to the well respected Waldfriede Krankenhaus, the hospital designated for her delivery, literally just a mile from our driveway. Heidi and Shanda followed us on their bicycles.

At the hospital, nurses confirmed that Sherri's and the fetus's vital signs were satisfactory, then encouraged Sherri to soak in a hot tub of water laced with special aromatic oils. In the care of a great medical staff, Sherri relaxed as much as her mind and body would permit. She soaked, and breathed rhythmically through her contractions, for an hour.

And then, at a moment when she and I happened to be alone, she announced, "I'm ready!"

"Ready to get out?"

"Ready to give birth to this baby!" she declared.

"Like ready, ready!" I gulped.

"Yes! That's what I said!" she asserted.

I summoned a midwife who helped Sherri out of the tub and onto an examination table. Checking Sherri's dilation, the nurse said, "It's still going to be a while."

"Nope!" Sherri corrected her. "I'm ready now!" The nurse started to dismiss the optimistic wish when Sherri blurted, "I'm ready to push! NOW!"

To the surprise of the midwife, she and her team delivered Cayden in the next twenty minutes, a little before one in the morning. Sherri had been in labor for less than two and a half hours.

"It's a healthy little boy!" was the whisper that quickly circulated throughout the otherwise quiet ward.

Heidi and Shanda, who had been in the waiting room the whole time, were allowed to come up and see their new baby brother lying in Sherri's protective caress. The girls were elated. They hung around and lovingly enjoyed the event for an hour or so. Heidi left first. Shanda, who was eleven, left by herself a bit later. We learned afterward that a policeman on night duty stopped her at 2:00 AM on a side street and wanted to know why she, as a preteen, was alone on her bike in the middle of the night. Shanda offered her off-the-wall explanation. Satisfied with her answer, but concerned for her safety, the policeman escorted her the rest of the way to our house.

I followed about an hour later, leaving Sherri and Cayden to rest in the exceptional care of the hospital's night staff.

Cayden's baby laughter that surfaced a few months later filled the house to overflowing with irresistible smiles. Sherri was glowing with maternal pride. She thrived in the role of motherhood. The role definitely stretched her, though, as she dealt with a teen, a pre-teen, and now a newborn all at the same time - a teen who 'knew it all,' a pre-teen who was on the edge of hormonal swings, and an infant who required twenty-four hour care.

Heidi, as a 'know it all' teen, was learning the dance steps of life. She was learning that many so-called friends, naively trusted, were ill-behaved dance partners, and that others, though extremely rare by comparison, were beautifully considerate and supportive. It was a life lesson she was learning in the midst of much confusion, pain, and disillusionment, but a lesson that everyone, in some way, has to eventually face.

Shanda, as a pre-teen, was finally adjusting to Berlin and was even encountering favorable feelings for the city. The freedom she possessed to move throughout the city on her own—something she cherished—simply was not a feature of life that was experienced by young girls living in Atlanta. And as a natural risk taker, like me, she was slowly discovering that 'adventurism' and 'wanderlust' were an integral part of her DNA.

Settling into a revamped rhythm of life with the added cares and needs of a third child, I—as the household leader—was actually at a good place, all things considered. Everybody in the family was functioning at an accelerated pace. The plans of transitioning the leadership of the church to the CAI team and eventually moving our family back to America or a different location was still the hard-and-fast agenda. But according to official CAI updates, it would be at least two more years before all the Berlin team members were on site.

So, as the Dodd clan, we dug in for the long haul.

Chapter 69

Even though George Dixon was not the individual appointed to be the upfront teacher for the CAI team—he was more of an accountant type—I nevertheless mobilized him into a teaching role. The other CAI personnel were not in place to implement their CAI vision and polity, so I went ahead and asked George to deliver the Sunday morning message once every five weeks or so.

And he did.

And he improved each time at the podium. I was glad to give him the opportunities. But I was, of course, anxious to see the skill sets of the other CAI team members. Berlin, after all, was a place where Christian laborers were few. The more voices of truth we could amass, the better for every pocket of the region.

Therefore, I especially rejoiced when I heard that our young friend Ricky, who was studying hard at Columbia Bible College, was also making plans to one day return as a missionary to the very city where he had found his own life-changing redemption. He, more than most, understood the need of the region firsthand. I also heard that he had fallen in love with, and become engaged to, a female classmate who years earlier had surrendered to be a missionary...to Germany...of all places! Consequently, he and his bride-to-be had decided they would one day move to the northeast sector of East Berlin—where communism and atheism had ruled for fifty years—and attempt to plant a church for the younger generation. What a story! Every detail, it seemed, had God's providential marks all over it.

Without a doubt, Berlin was proving to be an unforgettable place for us. This was true, not only because of the spiritual fruit we were seeing, but also because of the sheer power and historical significance of the city itself. The spiritual darkness was ever pervasive, and probably always would be, but the metropolis with its endless points of interest was steadily capturing our fascination.

For example, it was surreal when I stood for the first time at the site of Hitler's bunker, on the very plot of earth where Hitler's incinerated corpse was found by the advancing Russian army. It was nearly unfathomable to believe that one human being—confined to one skeleton, one set of lungs, and one sheath of skin—could push the whole world into an unrestrained war that claimed the lives of 60 million people, shattering families, dreams, and fortunes on literally every continent. One solitary man!

And then there was the Wannsee Conference House—located on Wannsee Lake, just a few miles south of our address—where the 'final solution' was discussed among the supreme Nazi leaders, and made official. It was determined inside this lakeside mansion that the eleven million Jews scattered across Europe would be proactively 'exterminated' - gassed or machine gunned, then burned.

There was the breathtakingly beautiful stadium used for

the 1936 summer Olympics. It was the oval arena that could seat 110,000 spectators where the black American superstar, Jesse Owens, caused Hitler outright humiliation and anger by competing side by side with the best of the 'master race' and outrunning and out jumping them. To meander throughout the stadium complex and know that Adolph Hitler, Rudolf Hess, Joseph Göbbels, and Hermann Göring had actually stood there was like traveling in a time machine back to that moment. I could almost sense the odious presence of these sociopaths still lingering in the air.

There was Checkpoint Charlie which during the cold war years had been the heavily guarded and heavily barricaded border crossing between West and East Berlin. It was the very heart of the cold war divide. It's where American tanks and Soviet tanks faced off with each other in a sixteen-hour drama in 1961. Those bullish weapons of war were pointed at each other just one-hundred yards apart. A third world war could have been easily ignited because of the heightened tensions and heightened rhetoric that flared that day.

There was the Pergamum museum that housed a gigantic portion of the pagan altar built in ancient Greece for the worship of Zeus. German archeologists had uncovered the altar during one of their digs in 1879, disassembled the front portion piece by piece with official permission, and reconstructed it in Berlin where it was displayed in the museum. The Bible even hints at this altar in Revelation 2:12,13. It's a fascinating piece of ancient history. Another piece of mind-boggling antiquity that's housed in the same museum is the 38-foot-tall blue-brick Ishtar Gate. This gate to the inner city of historic Babylon was commissioned by King Nebuchadnezzar around 575 BC as a monument to the goddess Ishtar, the goddess of fertility, love, and war. It was the very gate that Daniel, Shadrach, Meshach, and Abednego of Biblical fame would have been paraded through as captives of the Babylonian army. The gate was reconstructed inside the Pergamum museum in 1930. The museum is located in East Berlin and was thus inaccessible to the western populace during the 28-year duration of the Berlin Wall. But my eyes were seeing it, and my hands were touching it.

The list of the city's fascinations continued with the Brandenburg Gate, the Opera House, the Rubble Mount, the TV tower, the Flak towers, the Charlottenburg Palace, the city-block that had been the Statsi-Headquarters, the Gestapo museum, the Dietrich Bonhoeffer House, the Berliner Dome, the Reichstag Building, the Berlin Zoo, and the Spandau Prison.

The prison, all by itself, heaped on a new layer of city-interest for me. The Spandau facility is where Rudolf Hess, Albert Speer, Admiral Karl Donitz, and four other high-ranking Nazi officials were incarcerated following the Nuremberg trials at the end of World War II. The penal institution had space for six-hundred inmates, but was utilized at the end of the war to house just these seven war criminals. The property was leveled in 1987 when the last of the seven inmates, Rudolf Hess, died. The buildings were destroyed to prevent the property from becoming a neo-Nazi shrine. The structure was no longer standing when we resided in Berlin, but I happened to meet a man who had been personally familiar with the prison, and its seven captives. His name was Lt. Colonel Eugene Bird, a retired American Army officer. I met him one evening at a special town-hall event where he introduced the key speaker, Charlie Duke, one of the twelve American astronauts who walked on the moon. In the introduction, Eugene Bird alluded to his and Charlie Duke's Christian faith. At the conclusion of the program, I shook hands with Charlie Duke, but hearing that Bird was a permanent resident in Berlin and had spent years working at the Spandau prison, he was the one I bombarded with questions. I introduced myself as the pastor of Gateway International Church. He had heard of our congregation. It so happened that he lived less than a mile from our Buelow Strasse address. As Christian brothers, we met a few days later at a neighborhood bakery for a lengthy chat.

I became quickly enthralled by his story. He had been the American commandant at the Spandau prison for seven years, from 1964 to 1971. The commandant, or director, was responsible for the entire prison operation during his country's watch. That responsibility was rotated every quarter between the Americans, French, British, and Russians. So, for one three-month stretch every year—for seven consecutive years—Eugene Bird oversaw the daily needs of the prison and its inmates. Consequently, he talked face to face on multiple occasions with Albert Speer and Rudolf Hess.

For several years, Bird had secretly interviewed Rudolf Hess on a regular basis, in a joint collaboration, to write Hess' version of his World War II actions. When Bird's notes and manuscript pages were made public in 1971, Bird was placed under house arrest and interrogated extensively. As punishment for his "crime" he lost his post at Spandau and was exited from the military. Bird claimed that his interviews with Hess were condoned all along by his superiors, and even encouraged, but that military discipline was levied against him only when the manuscript pages became known publicly and generated controversy. Bird's book, *Prisoner #7: Rudolf Hess*, was published in 1974 in the U.S. by Viking Press. In Europe, under the Secker and Warburg label, the book was titled *The Loneliest Man in the World*. The volume quickly became a bestseller. And Bird became a much-in-demand interviewee for journalists and TV hosts, both in the U.S. and Europe.

Our newfound friendship was peppered with unexpected and interesting similitudes. We were both authors. We had both been "fired" because of the controversy surrounding our books. And we were both still telling our stories.

Bird continued, though, to stir controversy in his post-military years. To the chagrin of many who believed Rudolf Hess should suffer in hell because of his role in the Third Reich, Bird claimed he had led Hess to a saving faith in Christ inside Hess' prison cell and that the war criminal died a forgiven man. He also claimed that Hess did not commit suicide in 1987 at the age of 93 as officially stated, but that the Russians had hanged him during their watch, right before Hess was to be finally released.

Every time I was with Eugene Bird thereafter, I never forgot, in a bone-chilling and disturbing kind of way, that I was only one connection away from Albert Speer and Rudolf Hess, and just two connections away from Adolf Hitler, Reinhard Heydrich, Heinrich Himmler, Josef Mengele, Adolf Eichmann, Josef Goebbels, and a host of other Nazi leaders who heartlessly wreaked havoc across the planet.

I was also reminded, with a debt of undying gratitude, that my father, an infantryman in the U.S. army, had helped liberate Europe from the tyranny of the Nazi war machine by fighting in the third wave of the D-Day invasion and the Battle of the Bulge.

I learned that the weight of human history, with all its detailed intricacies and variables, was absolutely mesmerizing. Sometimes distressingly so. At other times spectacularly so.

But, of course, the dramas of life that accentuated historical moments—either on a broad scale or compact scale—were never far away. And they didn't handpick only those with authority, wealth, and fame. Those emotional-stretching insertions were completely non-prejudiced, showing up in everyone's life whether coveted or not.

And unexpectedly, it knocked on our door again.

A few months before Heidi's graduation from the John F. Kennedy High School, Heidi made the announcement, "Trisha and I have selected our college."

"And?" Sherri and I replied.

"Western Carolina University in Sylva, North Carolina!" came the energized response.

"What! Where? Sylva! We've never heard of Sylva! Where exactly in North Carolina is this place?"

"In the foothills of the Smoky Mountains," Heidi crooned as if she were a native of the region excitedly setting up a guided tour.

"In the foothills of the Smoky Mountains," I echoed rhetorically.

Heidi nodded.

"So why this particular university, in this particular location?"

"It's the only university Trisha and I have been able to find on the east coast that offers both our majors—interior design and pre-med studies."

"How did you learn about the school? Was it recommended by a school counselor?"

"No, no! We found out about it through a brochure"

"A brochure," I again echoed.

Trying to be sensitive to our daughter's abiding friendship with Trisha, an all-time favorite schoolmate, Sherri and I willingly listened to Heidi's expressed idea, and openly explored the pros and cons of such a potential move. But quickly, with the full support of Trisha's parents, the verbal dream morphed into action steps. Sherri and I reluctantly yielded to the momentum. Applications were submitted. Applications were accepted. Dates and deadlines became major directives. Monies were transferred. Airline tickets were purchased. And all too soon, it felt, Sherri and I were watching our oldest child leave the nest.

Sherri, out of parental concern, joined Heidi on the trip to Sylva to assist her in the major transition—a move from one of the world's premiere cities to a tiny, in the middle-of-nowhere, town nestled in a backwoods valley of North Carolina where a Walmart store was the big attraction. Trisha would make her trip about ten days later. Sherri helped Heidi find a cheap automobile—it was all we could afford. And she helped buy a few accessories for Heidi's dorm room. The night before Sherri was scheduled to return to Berlin, Heidi—in a motel room with Sherri—fell apart emotionally. The reality of the move suddenly trumped the fantasy. Sherri spent several hours trying to console our eighteen-year-old as Heidi bawled uncontrollably until she nearly vomited. Sherri became so distraught that she called me in Berlin to elicit emotional reinforcement. It just was not practical at that juncture to abort the progress-in-action and bring Heidi back home. So, Sherri returned to Germany two days later, leaving Heidi to navigate the tumultuous adjustment on her own. The unsettling ordeal was truly heartbreaking for both me and Sherri as parents. But there was no magic wand to wave, either for Heidi or for us. It was simply one of those uncomfortable and life-impacting chapters in life that one had to face head-on.

But then...eight weeks later...

"Is this Randy Dodd, Heidi Dodd's father?" the female voice resounded in our house phone.

Oh no! My pulse instantly accelerated. "Yes, this is Heidi's dad."

"Good, good. Upfront I'll let you know this is not an emergency call. But it is necessary and urgent." I took a deep breath. I had no idea what to expect. "I'm calling from Western Carolina University. I need to let you know that Heidi has been sick for a few weeks. She's currently in the school infirmary where she's been diagnosed with mononucleosis. She's already missed a week or more of classes. Unfortunately, these absences have placed her in a difficult spot academically. If she makes a miraculous comeback and is able to attend classes again soon, she can—with a lot of intense work—salvage the school year." The lady paused as if I were taking notes. "Another reason I'm giving you this information is to let you know that the deadline for a monetary refund for the semester is just twenty-four hours away. So I encourage you to talk to your wife, talk to Heidi, talk to Heidi's academic advisor, and talk to the school's finance department. Decide quickly if Heidi should withdraw from the school today or tomorrow with a medical release, or if you guys want her to stay put and tough it out."

Chapter 70

Following a conversation with Heidi and with the school's finance department, Sherri and I—with Heidi's concession—decided to let Heidi immediately withdraw from the semester with a medical release. We learned to our chagrin that our daughter's academic grades were already on the low end due to her teenage decision to party more than study, and that those grades would be nearly impossible to raise to a passing level because of all the sick days she had taken.

Thus, the months of planning and executing Heidi's move to the US—with all the invested time, energy, and setup money—were now a wash.

Our inclination was to believe Heidi's sickness was caused by her excessive partying and sleep deprivation. *How could she be so irresponsible?* But after further questioning, we discovered there was likely another reason for her illness, and that the reason was partially our fault. Heidi had called us weeks earlier and asked if we could fax her immunization records to the school. The immunizations requirements at the school had just been made known to her. Only two vaccines were mentioned. Heidi had received those vaccinations as a child, but surprisingly—considering our proclivity for organization—Sherri and I were unable to locate the documents.

"Either I've got to show the school I've already had the shots," Heidi declared one day over the phone, "Or, in order to stay enrolled, I'll have to get the vaccines here at the infirmary."

"Well," I told her, "it's finally dawned on us that all your immunization records are somewhere in storage back in Georgia. And it would be a nightmare to try to find them. So I guess you'll have to take the shots all over again." That call was the last communication we had with Heidi until the school informed us of her ongoing illness.

The day after Heidi officially annulled her enrollment at the university, it came to our attention that she had been given not two but seven vaccinations at the school's infirmary, all within a ten-minute time span—vaccinations for the mumps, measles, rubella, meningitis, HPV, influenza, and whooping cough.

To say that Sherri and I were flummoxed by the medical staff's decision to give so many inoculations at one time to a young girl already so exhausted and fatigued would be an understatement. The individual who administered the shots had possibly derailed Heidi's entire school year, maybe even the trajectory of her life. But the university, of course, accepted no responsibility for contributing in any way to Heidi's sickness.

Upon our instructions, Heidi sold her car—with the help of Sherri's parents—and returned to Berlin, back into our home. Laden with mono, she was totally listless. She could barely manage to get out of bed each day. Seeing no end in sight to her sickness, Sherri and I gave her few responsibilities. We simply allowed her to lounge around in a protective environment until her body could heal itself.

In the meantime, everybody else in the family carried on with their lives. Sherri, as a source of needed distraction and fun, continued to venture out, as she had been doing for months now, to the famous Berlin flea markets to collect antique china sets—matching tea cups, saucers, and desert plates. The acquisition of the three-piece settings from Germany, Poland, Denmark, Holland, Austria, France, and the Czech Republic had become somewhat of an obsession for her. The exquisite pieces—considered highly valuable in the U.S. at the time—were simply out-of-date junkets in Berlin and could be purchased for pennies. Yet all of it had survived the bombardments and atrocities of World War II and had endured the Cold War years. Some of it had reputedly been buried in backyards during the end of the World War for protection against bombs and thieves. Sherri often wondered aloud how all the settings, made in sundry countries, had ended up in Berlin? *If each set could only tell their stories!* Understanding the historical significance of the pieces, Sherri had decided the collection should serve a greater purpose than just adorning our dining room. So she had put the tea-cup sets to use as part of her everyday ministry as a pastor's wife. The settings, conveying hot tea to the lips of myriad women, had become a topic of conversation during luncheons, light snacks, and ladies' Bible studies. The pieces had even inspired spiritual lessons. For example, one can be cracked, scarred, or tainted, but can still fulfill the purpose for which it was crafted. Or each set is sought out, handpicked, then purchased by the collector and is therefore precious in his sight. Or the uniqueness of each setting actually highlights its beauty.

While Sherri was consumed by motherhood, ministry,

and her china-collection I stayed busy studying, mentoring, and teaching—and in my spare time completing *Brotherhood of Betrayal.* It was a glorious and triumphant afternoon when I finally typed the closing words of the novel—"More and more, Clay McCain became a faded memory."— and brought the heartbreaking story to a close. It had taken me longer than anticipated to finish the manuscript. And since we were less than a year away from moving back to America, it was decided that my business trip to Word Publishing in Nashville would be postponed until we moved back to Georgia and settled in for our year-long furlough.

During our final months in Berlin, Sherri and I, amidst all our other activities, eagerly welcomed the arrival of two more of the CAI families and one of the singles. I had been utilizing George Dixon more and more in preparation for the leadership handover to the CAI team. The plan that had originated four years earlier was now seriously coming together. And my vision for Gateway International soared. Our congregation had already accomplished more in three years than anyone would have imagined. But now! I grew more and more excited as I witnessed with my own eyes the formation of the CAI crew on Berlin soil. Considering all the arriving energy and talent—four couples and two singles when everyone would finally settle in—it looked as if Gateway had the chance to now become one of the prominent evangelical churches in the entire city, a church with the manpower to be a real mover and shaker. There would be ten full-time laborers that would replace Sherri and me. And their collective skill sets when it came to teaching, pastoring, counseling, administrating, working with youth, and leading worship would be extraordinarily expansive.

As the new couples maneuvered through all the necessary steps of becoming legal residents and setting up house, our family began the step-by-step process of closing down our lives in the country. Selling furniture. Crating items—including Sherri's china—that would be airfreighted back to America. Unenrolling Shanda from the German school system. Selling the tiny four-person Daihatsu Charade that had served our family so well and that had generated the laughable memory of hauling six of us—me, Sherri, Heidi, Shanda, Heidi's best friend, Shanda's best friend, and all our luggage—on a three-day trip to an indoor waterpark on the Baltic coast. Cancelling the car insurance. Paying the final bills. Deregistering our family as German residents.

All too quickly, we were attending farewell gatherings in homes and at the church, saying our final goodbyes to the people who had become our dearest friends in the world.

When we entered Berlin four years earlier, Shanda had absolutely abhorred the place and had barely survived the initial pounding of relentless depression. My feelings for the metropolis had not been much better. Sherri, a people-oriented person, had found contentment quickly when we started to build a network of friends. And, of course, Heidi had loved both the town and the culture the very moment we had set foot on the region's black soil. But since then, all our hearts had been completely seduced, romanced, and captured by the mysterious power of the city. And not one of us wanted to leave, not even Heidi who had made a full recovery and was now convinced that Germany afforded a better lifestyle. But the execution of our agreed-upon-plan with CAI was now too far down the track and, for all practical purposes, irreversible. So, for the third time in our twenty-two years of ministry, our hearts and souls were being ripped apart by the agony of walking away from everything and everyone we now loved while having no clue where we would serve next. After our furlough, would we prayerfully choose to move into Copenhagen, Barcelona, or maybe London, with the goal of establishing another international church? We were definitely inclined toward that notion. But we just weren't sure.

Fortunately, a supporting couple from Eastside Baptist, our home church at the time, had arranged for us, if we desired, to utilize one of their properties during our upcoming furlough. It would be a tentative place to lodge while we visited supporters and made a decision about our next overseas move. It was a house that belonged to the man's mother. The elderly lady had recently been moved into a nursing home, so the house was standing unoccupied and was still partially filled with the lady's furnishings. But we were welcomed to live there and help take care of the property if we wanted. Our only overhead would be the cost of the gas, water, and electricity we used. The property was in a high-crime area, but with no other place to live, we gratefully accepted the offer. The house would be accessible immediately upon our return to Atlanta.

During our family's final week in Berlin, we tried to wrap up our lives as completely and efficiently as we could.

And then, as if the minutes on the clock accelerated…it was time.

On July 15, one day before Cayden's second birthday, Sherri, Heidi, Shanda, and Cayden—as emotionally unraveling as it was— boarded the plane for the thirteen-hour trip to the deep south of the USA. I stayed behind in the empty house and, as required by our rental contract, painted every interior wall in the house, just like I had been obligated to do in Munich years ago.

Sobbing on the plane a few days later, I followed my family to Atlanta, the last place I and my family wanted to be.

Chapter 71

Culture shock—the irrepressible jarring of one's psyche and emotions when moving to a country with a culture, climate, cuisine, and people that are foreign—is a real and universal phenomenon. Reverse culture shock—the same brutal punch to one's thoughts and emotions when one moves back to their native country following extensive time in a foreign culture—is just as real. Yet, reverse culture shock can be the cause of even greater disturbance and depression. What makes reverse culture shock so tough is that it's not really expected. After all, you're back in the land of your birth, childhood, and adolescence, a place with which you are so familiar. Yet, now you've garnered experiential knowledge of another people group and culture—along with their strong points you've grown to love and value—as an object of comparison. Consequently, you suddenly view your birth country with a more enlightened perspective. And what you see, or think you see, can sometimes leave you feeling empty, even disillusioned and bitter.

And almost immediately upon our family's return to the US, we—Sherri, Heidi, Shanda, and I—all found ourselves in the death grip of the reverse-culture-shock leviathan. My reaction was one of restlessness. I despised being back in America. The culture seemed so shallow, and based totally on consumerism. To keep from going crazy, I had to distract myself with constant busyness. Sherri was squeezed into a cocoon of habitual fatigue. Heidi fought the monster with abnormal anger. She especially found it galling that southerners would look you in the eye and fib to you in the name of politeness, just because they didn't want to offend you. And Shanda totally gave in to depression. The freedom she enjoyed in Berlin as a pre-teen had completely vanished. She now could not leave our fenced-in property without being chauffeured by an adult driver. There were no accessible sidewalks, bike paths, buses, trains, or subways. Zero. Nada. To Shanda, our house and yard felt like a prison facility. Her depression was so bad that we agreed to buy her a dog just for therapeutic purposes.

With our four collective reactions of restlessness, fatigue, anger, and depression pushed to the limit and dominating our household, the Dodd family was simply not the most pleasant group to be around.

A car, out of necessity, was our top priority. Once we purchased a vehicle—a four-year-old Infiniti G20 that would eventually be designated as Sherri's—we began shopping for a dog. We quickly brought home a beautiful black-and-silver, blue-eyed Husky, the pet of Shanda's dreams. Except that the pet didn't show any interest in bonding with anyone in the family, not even with Shanda. Adversely he tried constantly to dig his way under the perimeter fence. The animal became more of nuisance than a playful and devoted pet. Shanda, nevertheless, continued her efforts to win the canine's affection.

In the meantime, I applied my energies to finding a

second car. The fact that I would be traveling to distant cities and towns to update our supporters necessitated that we have two vehicles. And since I had driven a low-horsepower compact commuter for the four previous years I was ready for a muscle car, a car that could traverse the American Interstates with oomph and ease. While researching my options, I came across a mint-condition 1986 black Chevrolet Monte Carlo SS with t-tops. A test drive immediately won my enthusiasm. I called the leaders of our mission board—European Partnership Ministries—and sought their approval for the purchase. When the EPM executives said, "Yes," I promptly added the car to our minimal list of personal possessions. And I was readily told by car enthusiasts to vigilantly watch the car whenever I parked it in public. "It will definitely attract the attention of car thieves," they told me.

Over the next few weeks I enjoyed the car immensely as I fulfilled a few speaking engagements out of town. Yet, when I was in town I actually grew disconcerted with the inordinate number of hours I had to spend sitting behind the wheel. Every store, every friend, every restaurant, every relative, every business, it seemed, was at least twenty miles away. Twenty miles in that direction. Twenty miles in another direction. And twenty miles back home. Day after day. Week after week. I quickly grew weary of driving. I felt like I was spending most of my life in the automobile. I desperately missed the trains, buses, and subways of Berlin. Traveling by public transportation had allowed me to sleep, read, study, write, and converse face to face while commuting. Having to spend copious amounts of time in a car where total focus was mandatory became another source of my dislike for America. Living such a large chunk of my waking hours inside the four-wheel cage felt like an awful waste of hours, and so inefficient. And gradually, even the road trips—which did help pacify my restlessness to a limited degree—started pinpointing another American feature which, to me, simply emphasized the shallowness of the American culture and only deepened my reverse culture shock. That particular feature was the standard Interstate exit with its cookie-cutter hotels, restaurants, and gas stations. Ever present, like litter across an impoverished town, this collective display of conveniences seemed to be the proud presentation of American achievement and prosperity. Was this really the depth of the American culture? It seemed, sadly to me, that it was. With 90% of my traveling carried out on the Interstate system, this conclusion was only natural for me. Frankly, I just wasn't happy in my own country. But I couldn't tell anyone outside my family, lest I came across as an ungrateful turncoat.

So, I muzzled my tongue.

One morning when I was wallowing in my misery, Sherri approached me as I was getting dressed for the day and inquired, "Where did you park the Monte Carlo last night?"

I figured she was kidding with me since she had heard people warn me repeatedly about the car being a high-profile grab for thieves. Feeling downcast, I huffed, "Don't play around with me like that right now. I'm not in the mood."

"No, I'm serious," she responded. "It's not in the carport."

"What! Come on; you're joking; right?"

Together we marched through the house to the carport door.

Indeed, the car wasn't where I had parked it. It was gone. Shattered glass peppered the carport floor. The glass—I deducted—was from the driver's side window. The entryway gate to the yard, which I always locked at night, was standing wide open. The padlock had been cut. I lowered my head and almost cried. "Welcome to America," I whispered angrily as

I kicked the air. I was immediately convinced that the theft had to be the work of at least two men and that one of the men had most likely been armed. The one with the weapon had probably aimed his gun at the carport door—to stop anyone in the house who tried to intervene—while his partner broke the driver's side window and hot-wired the car. After living in Norway and Germany where street crimes were rarely an issue, I suddenly felt like I had stepped into a stinking sewage drain. I felt dirty. I shook my head in confusion. Norway was filled with atheists, but had one of the lowest crime rates in the world. Atlanta was filled with Gospel churches, but had one of the highest crime rates in the world. What had gone wrong in the city that claimed to be a Bible-belt citadel? All I knew at the moment was that I needed a gun.

In an emotional topsy-turvy I reported the theft to the police. I then took Sherri's car and went to Walmart, to the gun department. The only gun I had ever owned was a BB rifle in my youth. By the time I reached the gun counter, my head had started to slightly curb my emotions. "I need a gun for self-defense," I proclaimed to the salesman while trying to relax. "I don't want to kill anybody. But I do want to hurt them."

The man behind the counter appeared simultaneously stupefied and entertained. After listening to a few more of my nonsensical ramblings, he ended up—contrary to his own advice—selling me a multi-pump pellet air pistol. "Be careful with that thing" he smirked.

I read the man's derision. His words and gestures planted serious questions in my head. *Was I really so ignorant of my own American culture? Was I genuinely making a lame decision by purchasing a pellet pistol instead of an authentic, deadly firearm?*

Returning to the house I strode into the backyard with my newly purchased gun. I needed to become familiar with the thing, and I wanted to test my aim. So I inserted a pellet into the chamber and repeatedly pumped the pistol's forearm until it was nearly impossible to pump it another time. I then eyed a thick pine tree about thirty yards away. I raised the pistol and aimed at the center of the trunk. I slowly pulled the trigger, expecting to immediately hear the pellet slam into the bark with a powerful smack. Instead, I witnessed the small piece of lead lumber out of the barrel, arch through the air, and drop to the ground before it even reached the tree. I closed my eyes in disbelief. Suspecting I was somehow at fault, I reloaded the chamber and again pumped the forearm to the max. "Come on," I coaxed the pistol as I aimed and fired a second time. Again the pellet lumbered feebly through the air as if thrown by a five-year-old. "Come on; really!" I huffed. "What a waste!" I knew then why the gun clerk had concluded I was an idiot.

I wanted to return the pistol to the store that very moment, but because of previously scheduled commitments throughout the afternoon and evening, I would need to wait about twenty-four hours. As embarrassing as it would be, I would return the gun and seek a refund. I would then go to a dedicated gun shop, ask a lot of questions, listen to the experts, and bring home a proven firearm that would guarantee deadly force if needed.

But that very night around 11:30 when all the house lights were off, and Sherri and I were falling asleep in our bed, we were jarred awake by the sudden high-pitched scream of a security alarm. I bolted upright. I felt my pulse accelerate like a missile. The alarm was a car alarm! It was Sherri's Infiniti, wasn't it? The thieves had come back to steal our other car!

"Quick!" I shouted to Sherri as I jumped out of bed and scrambled into my pants. "Call 911! Give them our street address! Tell them there's a burglary in process! Hurry!"

I quickly grabbed and loaded the pellet pistol. Maybe it would at least scare someone away! I ran down the hall as quickly as I could in the dark. By the time I reached the carport door, with my heart racing, I was ready to hurt someone. I burst into the open carport with my gun drawn. My mind instantly stumbled. The Infiniti was still sitting there, untouched. At that moment the realization hit me that the car alarm was blasting from our next door neighbor's property. It wasn't our car after all. But still! What was going on in America! This was crazy!

Thankfully, within a few more seconds the alarm was turned off and all appeared to be okay across the way. I yelled back into the house and told Sherri to call 911 again. "Tell them everything is under control at our house, that it's the address next door where the alarm went off."

I stayed outside for another ten minutes or so just walking around taking deep breaths, trying to regain a semblance of calmness. I then joined Sherri back in bed.

We had just closed our eyes to go back to sleep when a beam of light swept across our bedroom ceiling.

Are you kidding me!

The light had been strong enough to register behind closed eyelids. My eyes sprang open again. Out of my peripheral vision I saw glimpses of light outside our bedroom window. The light seemed to be moving around erratically from a source somewhere in the backyard. In the dark I went to my knees and peered through the window. To my utter shock I saw a tall man, dressed in all black, wielding a flashlight.

He was directing the beam back and forth across the back of the house.

"Call 911 again!" I whisper shouted to Sherri. "The burglar is outside in the back!"

With another surge of adrenalin I jumped back into my jeans and snatched up the pellet pistol, pumping it to the max. For a second time I sprinted breathlessly through the dark toward the carport entrance, wanting to attack the villain from around the front side of the house. I took a gigantic breath when I reached the door. Grabbing the handle I yanked hard and rushed out into the night with my pistol drawn.

In an instant my heart nearly pushed through my chest. Standing in the carport were five men. Policemen! What the...? And I was pointing my gun directly at them. In less than a second five handguns were swept into a firing position, all aimed at me.

"Drop it! Drop it! Drop it!" a savage holler pierced the air.

Intuitively I rocketed my gun arm straight up in the air over my head in a display of surrender. I squinted—expecting to be filled with bullets—then instantly dropped to my knees.

Hearing the repeated yell to "drop it; drop it!" I quickly laid the gun to my side on the concrete.

"Don't shoot! Don't shoot!" I pressed. "I live here! I'm the man of the house! I thought you guys were burglars for heaven's sake!"

My pistol was immediately kicked away, out of my reach. Without wasting a nano-second, two of the policeman pinned me to the ground on my stomach. I didn't fight them.

There was a moment of stark speechlessness. The only sound all around was that of heavy breathing. With my heart still racing I exhaled deeply. I was just glad at the moment that I wasn't lying in a pool of blood breathing my last breaths. When I realized I was safe, I spouted angrily, "There's a man dressed in all black snooping around in my backyard. Can one of you check that out, please!"

"Get him up!" the lead officer barked, ignoring my plea.

"There was a burglar in my backyard, I'm telling you!" At that very moment the man in all black from the backyard walked around the corner. Revealed by a bit of light from the various flashlights illuminating the area, it was instantly clear to me that the man was wearing a police-issued special ops uniform. "What!" I shouted at the man, pounding a fist into my palm. "What in the heck are you doing sneaking around on my property without any forewarning, snooping around in my backyard shining a flashlight in my bedroom window. I uh....!"

"Hold it, hold it, sir!" the lead officer barked with equally as much anger. "We were notified that there was a car theft in process at this address. Don't you think it would be a little idiotic for us to approach the house blasting our sirens?"

I huffed loud enough for everybody to hear. "You almost got me killed, man!"

"Oh, you're right about that!" the officer cursed with spittle. "You don't know just how close you came to dying right now! Had just one of us pulled the trigger when you came busting out of that door with your gun pointed at us, all of us would've fired! Yes!" he snorted, "You came within a milli-second of dying right here, right now! You better be thanking your lucky stars you're still alive! And that's the God's truth!"

It took a solid minute for everyone to calm down and sort things out. For some reason, the lead officer had not been given the address of the house next door as a correction. He believed all along that he and his men were coming to our address to thwart a theft in process.

The next day—while continuing to stew over the obscene level of crime in our neighborhood—I returned the pellet pistol for a full refund and went out and bought a twelve-gauge shotgun.

Chapter 72

For several days afterward I drove through multiple apartment developments on our side of town looking for my stolen Monte Carlo.

"If it hasn't been disassembled in a chop shop already," the police had informed me regarding the car, "it's probably been sold to someone in one of the lower Dekalb County apartment complexes."

With a second ignition key in hand I fully intended to reclaim the prized automobile if I could find it. So, for three full days—armed only with my anger—I cruised up and down rows of apartment buildings while pods of young gang members stared at me in disbelief. I must of have been wearing a facial expression of absolute fearlessness, because not a single man made a move to say or do anything to stop me.

I never found the car. And now I detested my country even more.

To escape all the wild feelings that were pressing my family in so many unpleasant directions I took Sherri, Heidi, and Shanda to see a movie one evening. The movie, starring Tom Hanks was Castaway. The heart-wrenching storyline and superb acting transported us to a different world. At the end of the film, Tom Hanks stood in the middle of the empty intersection wondering desperately which way to go. Then the credits rolled, accompanied by the emotional soundtrack. I and my three girls didn't budge. We were held transfixed in our seats by the sheer emotional weight of the story. As movie goers around us stood up and left, we couldn't move. I started sobbing. I heard Sherri and the girls crying as well. After several minutes, without speaking, we finally managed to stand and exit the building.

Once in the car, it took us only a few minutes to analyze why each of us had been so emotionally hamstrung. And then we teared up again. The main character of the story survived a trans-oceanic airline crash and had washed ashore on a tiny, uninhabited tropical island. He was the only survivor. After a day and a half of sitting and hoping to be rescued he understood that in order to live he had to somehow procure water, food, and shelter, and learn how to build a fire. As a lifelong executive with no outdoor skills, and now with no proper tools, the learning curve to acquire those four basic needs was drastic and fraught with wild fits of rage. But he succeeded, just barely, while at the same time wrestling with bouts of serious depression and death-wishing. But with no rescuer in sight he, as a bonafide castaway, eventually forged a new way of living and slowly and sufficiently adapted to his environment. Four years later, as a redefined human being, he was found and rescued. Back in the U.S. among former friends and colleagues he felt obviously different. Life for his friends and colleagues had advanced without him. No one, not a single soul, understood what he had been through. And in many ways he no longer understood them. He felt painfully alone. In essence, he had become a castaway all over again.

And once again he had to figure out life in an "unfamiliar" setting.

And that mirrored our story and the story of the typical missionary who serves overseas. You disconnected from your homeland. You forged a new way of living in the "foreign" culture. You adapted. Years later, you moved back to the U.S. No one understood you. You no longer understood your home culture. You felt alone. You felt like a castaway all over again. It was heart-wrenching. That's why we were all crying. We each felt like a castaway struggling to figure out life again. The re-entry back into the States just wasn't easy.

And then, to stack weariness upon weariness and disappointment upon disappointment, Shanda's blue-eyed husky escaped the fenced-in backyard and ran away for good.

At the same time, my mother—80 years old—was rushed to the hospital because of a ruptured colon that spilled putrid bacteria all throughout her belly region. The surgeon reported that if her arrival at the ER had been delayed by as little as five minutes, she would be a dead woman. When mother awakened from surgery, she was introduced to her newly attached colostomy bag. As a people person who interacted everyday with friends, relatives, and strangers, she was horrified by the very sight of the polyolefin appendage. Her social life, she was sure, was forever ruined. She was so appalled by the situation that three months later she risked going under the knife again to reverse the operation and eliminate the bag. To her immense gratification, the second surgery was a success. But because of other non-operable issues, the doctor said she might have about three more years to live. This prognosis threw me into a flux. We had been overseas for twenty-two years. Because of the time factor, our kids had not been able to spend time with their "granny."

And since Sherri and I hadn't already settled on another overseas ministry destination, and were still in limbo, I made a promise that would unknowingly reroute the course of our lives, yet again.

"We'll stay in the States," I told my mom, "and be close by to help you during your remaining years." Or, in other words until we bury you. We were certain this would be no more than three or four years, maybe less. This wasn't a commitment that thrilled us. But as my mom's only son, I didn't feel I could abandon her at this season of her life. I felt it would be inexcusable for me to shirk the responsibility.

If there was a silver lining for our family in this arrangement, the extended stay would give us plenty of time to prayerfully and carefully plan for our next overseas venture. And it would permit me to visit all our supporters without being gone every single weekend.

Understanding now that we would be in Georgia for an additional year or more, we decided to find a new home church and, if possible, take the big step that was the nexus of the American dream - to purchase a nice house. I was 45. Sherri was 41. We had never owned real estate of any kind. And since we had never possessed a credit card, and possibly had no "credit score," we didn't even know if we would be eligible for a mortgage. Nevertheless, we commenced a house search, as well as a new-church search.

Heidi at the time enrolled in college at the Art Institute of Atlanta to make a second run at her undergraduate work, hopefully to earn a degree in interior design.

In the midst of all this, Word Publishing contacted me and said they were ready for me to come to their headquarters in Nashville. They wanted me to sign a publishing contract for *Brotherhood of Betrayal*. Even though *Wisdom Hunter* and

Jordan's Crossing were still selling moderately well and still churning out great reviews, I was ready to introduce my fans to a new Randall Arthur story. Relatively soon, I was sitting in Word's high-rise office in Nashville. I was relieved beyond measure that the negotiation unfolded smoothly and a contract was quickly signed. Since I was no longer ignorant about advances, I jubilantly accepted Word's advance of $40,000.

The editing of the manuscript would begin within the month. The release date would be approximately six or seven months out.

Regarding the publication of the novel, I presented only two requests. Number one; I knew that Word was planning to release Frank Peretti's new novel *The Visitation* during the upcoming year, and that they had invested thousands of dollars in the marketing of his highly anticipated work. "So, please," I urged, "don't release my book at the same time as Peretti's. Or else my book will be completely overshadowed, maybe even overlooked."

My second request was based on a statement I heard one of the executives make regarding the cover art for *Brotherhood of Betrayal*. He said, "Eighty percent of customers who walk into Christian bookstores and purchase products are women. So, we need to take that into consideration when we design the cover for Randall's book." Thus, my second plea, and a strong one, was that the book cover for *Brotherhood of Betrayal* have a neutral design, and not one that was effeminate.

"One reason *Wisdom Hunter* has sold so well," I underscored with the executives, "is that it's been heavily promoted from pulpits, classrooms, and offices by pastors, evangelists, worship leaders, and professors. If a romance-looking cover is used for the new book, men in the ministry will not be caught reading it or holding it in public. They just won't. They'll shy away from it all together. And that'll definitely kill the sales."

The men nodded their understanding of both requests.

Chapter 73

Right as the editing of *Brotherhood of Betrayal* began, my mom underwent another major surgery, this time on her spine. The doctors' appointments were all at Emory, a fifty-mile roundtrip. The proliferation of trips quickly became taxing for mom and me, especially psychologically.

At the same time, Heidi obtained a part-time job as a door-to-door salesperson to help cover some of her college tuition. Her bold nature enabled her to quickly become a top salesperson within the Atlanta group. She was thrilled when her boss approached her with all kind of accolades and said, "Our Savannah team is struggling. Would you go down for a week or so and see if you can inspire them with some good sales numbers?"

We encouraged Heidi to stay in Atlanta and remain focused on her studies, but she was so flattered by the boss's praise that she excitedly obliged his request. Two evenings later, while bantering after work with five men on the outskirts of Savannah, Heidi became the victim of an act so abusive and life-altering that no female on planet earth should ever have to experience. She was overpowered and gang raped. She called, hyperventilating, from a police station. Sherri answered the phone. I was on a business trip and away from home when her call came through. Sherri jumped in her car and raced toward Savannah, four hours away. Somewhere along I-16 she was pulled over for speeding by a highway patrolman. She fearlessly rebuffed the man with a mother's shrieking justification and continued to speed to our daughter's side. When she arrived in Savannah she was led to a hospital where Heidi was undergoing examinations. Two days later, Sherri returned with Heidi to Atlanta, along with a copy of the police report. The police had launched a full-fledged investigation. Heidi remained in a state of lethargic shock.

I returned home as quickly as I could.

Sherri spent time letting Heidi cry on her shoulder. I spent time pacing and wanting revenge. When I heard that the police were not making any significant headway in their search for answers, I had a father's meltdown. I immediately collected as much information from Heidi as I could and set out on my own to find the rapists. Had I found them I would most likely be in jail today. But in a travesty of justice, the men somehow eluded both the police investigators and me.

In the meantime, Heidi desperately needed therapeutic help, more help than Sherri and I were equipped to give. Some of our close American friends who years earlier had been members of our international church in Oslo heard about Heidi's tragedy. The wife, who herself had been a victim of sexual abuse in her youth, offered to take Heidi under her wing and walk her step-by-step through a renowned months-long program of spiritual, mental, and emotional healing. There would be daily work and application. If Heidi accepted the offer she would have to live with the family in Florida for a minimum of three months or longer. Such a move would, of course, derail Heidi's second run at a college education. But the invitation was too benevolent and too paramount to ignore. We all recognized it. So, with Heidi's assent, Sherri and I drove her—cocooned in her shattered psyche—to Florida where we entrusted her to the care of our cherished friend. It wasn't easy leaving her, knowing that her every-waking hour was a nightmarish recall of the heinous assault. We prayed desperately that God would meet her in the secret places of her heart and reassure her that her life was not over.

Back in Atlanta I could hardly focus on the editing phase of *Brotherhood of Betrayal* that was still forging ahead. Fortunately, the editor designated by Word for the project was far less militant than the Questar editor. So the process was less taxing emotionally and mentally. It became even less so when I learned that Heidi was embracing her therapy and beginning to encounter a bit of hope and healing. Our friend, acting as Heidi's mentor and accountability partner, had our undying gratitude. The relief we felt from this one sacrificial act alone—after being bombarded with one traumatic event after another—was nearly indescribable.

And then...I received word that $20,000 in cash that I had invested with a trusted broker—a Christian businessman trusted by bankers, attorneys, doctors, and pastors—had been pilfered. The broker had been a scam artist and had fooled everyone. In lieu of our retirement monies that had been mismanaged and taken by our previous mission board, I had placed the $20,000—a portion of the royalties earned from *Wisdom Hunter* sales—in the hands of the highly respected broker with a promise of good and solid returns. I was trying to be a good steward of our savings. And now it was gone too.

It was all too much. The international move. The reverse

culture shock. Shanda's dog. The Monte Carlo. My mom. The gang rape. The loss of $20,000.

That night I retreated to the backyard under the cover of a cloud-filled night and threw rocks at the sky. Unlike Job, I did vent my rage at the Almighty. I even begged Him to strike me dead. "I can't handle anymore! You're breaking me! Don't You understand!" I screamed. I had learned long ago that God could handle my anger, even when that anger was directed at Him...especially when I was raising my fist and running TO Him, not FROM Him. For me, taking my anger and thrusting myself into His sovereign arms was, and always would be, an act of highest trust. As I stated previously, if one acknowledges Him as the totality of all life, authority, power, truth, and justice, there is simply no other place to go.

Then, right as I was beginning to see a few rays of sunshine in my life, Word Publishing sent me a copy of the cover art for my new novel. "Really? Are you kidding me?" I bellowed alone in my garage. The editing stage had gone so smoothly. I couldn't have been more satisfied with the process. But now, all the labor seemed in vain. The book cover sported a blatant replica of a romance novel and was titled Betrayal.

I was flabbergasted even more so a few weeks later when the book was released at the same time as Frank Peretti's newest work, *The Visitation*. I didn't understand why the heads of publishing departments didn't listen to their authors. The romance-looking cover and the simultaneous release with Peretti's highly-anticipated volume was absolutely disheartening for the hopes and dreams I held for my third novel.

Betrayal was even highlighted as a dim backdrop to *The Visitation* in Word's marketing booklet called 'First Look Fiction Sampler.' *The Visitation* cover art, extremely beautiful and dramatic, dominated the front cover of the booklet. I wondered at that point if *Betrayal* would even have a chance of being significantly noticed. At least I had deposited the $40,000 of advance money which was safe in the bank. And the money was mine to keep regardless of the book's success or failure in the marketplace.

Nevertheless, I was still crestfallen.

But a few weeks later I started receiving response letters forwarded to me by Word.

> "I have never written an author before, although I have been tempted to write Frank Peretti and Tim LaHaye, but in finishing your book Betrayal in 3 days I am still in shock. Your book summed up what happened to my family 3 years ago. We are still healing. I appreciate what your book has done for my soul. For the first time last night I felt like maybe, just maybe, there might possibly be a God. And maybe, just maybe he might love me. Thank you." - Florida

> "I read until 2AM yesterday in order to complete the book in one session. When I finished the book I thought there is one person who understands and one person who has the courage and insight to tell the truth." - Canada

> "Never, in all the years of my reading, have I been touched by a story as I was in Betrayal. It was so believable!!! I felt as if I were reading a true story, which is quite an accomplishment in reading Christian fiction. I was so impressed that

I felt I had to comment on this wonderful reading experience. Thank you." - California

Reviews even started showing up in magazines and newspapers.

"*Arthur's Betrayal* is an obsessive tale of the wages of sin, the elusiveness of grace, and the difficult nature of redemption. Clay McCain, a fundamentalist missionary to Sweden, falls for a woman who is both beautiful and rich. The two journey the world doing Club Med kinds of things. By and by, Clay will awaken to his folly and die a horrid death, but of more interest may be Clay's betrayed, blameless wife, Rachel, who can find no comfort in her legalistic church back home in Atlanta. In fact, the fathers of the church regard her as an embarrassment and blame her for Clay's sins. Through them, Arthur indicts rule-bound faiths as worse than the disease. Rachel is cast to the winds and it seems almost accidental when she finds her faith again among more forgiving, less-hidebound believers. Arthur is a bit heavy-handed in his portrait of Clay's sins, but his inside view of church politics is merciless." - Missouri reviewer

And the book still was not being promoted by pastors like *Wisdom Hunter* had been. That was due to the salacious romance cover. And that was a shame. As I explained to the Word executives, pastors were not going to be caught with such a questionable-looking book in their possession. In spite of the good sales numbers, I couldn't help but ask, "How many more people could be helped and inspired if pastors all over the country were reading and recommending the book?"

But what was done, was done.

In the midst of the grave disappointment, there were some nice perks, though, that came with being a bestselling novelist of faith-based fiction.

Chapter 74

Word invited me as one of their new authors to participate in the industry's annual bookseller's convention, this time held in Orlando, Florida. My responsibility would be to promote *Betrayal* to bookstore owners and book buyers from around the nation, and to sign copies of the novel. Sherri was invited to join me. As a weary couple we welcomed the getaway with no shortage of appreciation.

On the inaugural evening of the convention, Word hosted a private dinner—as was traditional with all the publishing houses—exclusively for its participating authors. When Sherri and I boarded the shuttle that would transport us to the restaurant, we were initially unnerved, yet excited, when we saw that we would be sharing the special meal with Frank Peretti, Max Lucado, Grant Jeffrey, Angela Hunt, Barbara Johnson, and John MacArthur. We were definitely the little fish in a big pond. Not shy, though, we enjoyed every moment of every conversation.

The following afternoon I was even able to connect Joni Eareckson—taking part in the convention with a different publishing house—with a friend of mine, a quadriplegic, who lived in the area and who had joined me for a few hours. The friend had a few years earlier been riding in a jeep when it slipped off the side of a Swiss mountain and left him with a broken neck and a life filled with pain and paralysis. Death-wishing understandably was never far off. Yet, Joni's twenty minute interaction with him somehow gave him a new reservoir of energy, along with a new and more accepting perspective of his "cross." It was a beautiful case of one believer inspiring another and making a lasting difference. He later wrote: "That conversation with her was the beginning that I had to try to live life even though I was never going to be physically whole or completely healed. I had family and friends who loved me, and cheating them out of a relationship was not fair or Godly!" I would always treasure Joni's willingness to give her time, her voice, and her heart to a stranger.

Back in Atlanta, I felt refreshed and encouraged. The numerous exchanges with authors, publishers, readers, and bookstore owners had succeeded in lifting my morale. The experience was also a strong reminder of our need for community. With that in mind, we continued our search for a new church family, a more contemporary church family that we could joyously embrace for ongoing sustenance and fellowship.

I one day confided to an acquaintance, a youth evangelist, that Sherri and I were looking for a different church to join. He asked, "What are you looking for in a church?"

"It's what we are not looking for," I explained.

He lifted his eyebrows, somewhat confused.

Half jokingly and half seriously, I said, "We're longing for a church that doesn't have a Sunday night service, doesn't sing from hymnals, doesn't use the KJV, and doesn't bind its people with a lot of manmade rules."

Without blinking, the man spouted, "I know just the church. It's Spivey Community Church. And as a plus for you, the congregation has just built a new facility on Walt Stephens Road just on the outskirts of Stockbridge."

Sherri and I visited the church the next Sunday. The congregation, we learned, was in the process of securing a new pastor. We loved the atmosphere and the spirit of the place, but before we took the initiative to become members, we decided to wait until the incoming pastor was on site and functioning. Would he change the vision and direction of the church, or enhance the group's overall momentum?

In less than a month, Sherri and I were not only full-fledged members of the congregation, and pleased with the new executive pastor, we subsequently intensified our search for real estate that would give us quick and easy access to the church address. Stockbridge, Georgia was truthfully the last place on earth we wanted to live for any length of time. But I had made the promise to my mom that we would take up residence in the area in order to be nearby. And if we were going to live indefinitely in the area, even for only two or three years, we still felt it would be more prudent to become home owners instead of perpetual renters. In addition to having replaced my stolen Monte Carlo with another Monte Carlo SS—this time equipped with a LoJack tracker—I had also purchased a new motorcycle, an all-black Kawasaki ZRX1100. So I took the motorcycle out every day that I had free, and scouted the roads of Henry County for an ideal house that would fit our budget.

I particularly looked at newly-constructed tract homes since there were so many of them in our area. The prices, though, were in the $150,000 range, a little beyond our means. After examining a variety of these cookie-cutter dwellings, I saw that they were erected with cheap building materials. The same style homes that were no older than five or six years were already showing signs of the poor build quality—vinyl siding that was drooping and covered with mildew; electric garage doors that wouldn't open or close properly; roof shingles that were stained with ugly black algae; and concrete garage floors that were lined with jagged cracks. Not wanting to invest in such a cheaply made structure, we started looking at older custom-built homes. But after looking unsuccessfully at dozens of such builds, we grew a bit weary. I would occasionally find a house that suited my taste, but it wouldn't be satisfactory to Sherri in the least. Or visa versa. Or the girls would grow giddy about a particular location, but Sherri and I wouldn't find it appealing at all.

And then, in the midst of our hunt, I received a call from Scott Kirby, the president of our small mission board European Partnership Ministries. "Randy, I'd like for you to join me on a ten-day mission trip to Romania. I'm taking a team of forty people and I could use your help. I'll cover your cost if you'll go with me." Scott had been taking mission teams to Romania on a regular basis for a couple of years. He had established a network of Romanian pastors who trusted him and gladly utilized his groups. Because of my frequent trips out of Atlanta to visit supporters—churches and individuals alike—I had never entertained the thought of being part of any of Scott's overseas excursions. But, I had never been to Romania. And my schedule was flexible. So I decided to accept the invitation. I was especially comfortable with the decision knowing that we had now become members of a vibrant church family, a built-in support network for Sherri and the kids.

So I put the house hunt on hold.

And far beyond anything I had imagined, the trip to the Romanian city of Targu Mures and the surrounding villages ignited a new ministry idea in my head. The impact wasn't due to the country or the multiple ministries that our team carried out inside the country. Rather, it was the result of witnessing firsthand just how dramatically the out-of-the-box cross-cultural adventure—albeit only 10-days long—opened the minds of the American Christians to the power of missions, and how that mind-opening experience emboldened and inspired them to become further engaged in world evangelism.

Back in the States I was wondering if I could possibly lead such trips—especially to Norway or Germany—when Scott, during a debrief, sat across from me and uttered softly, "You know, if you're going to buy a house here in Georgia and settle down for awhile to take care of your mom, you might want to consider the possibility of leading short-term teams all across Europe on a regular basis. That could be a win-win for both you and your supporters. It would be a valid and worthwhile ministry that could fill the gap between now and the time you move back to Europe long term. I mean, you love Europe. That's where your heart is. Why not assist the churches there with skilled mission teams and at the same time help raise up new missionaries from the U.S.?"

I was mesmerized by the thought. I had already visited most of my supporting churches. And there was still no indication of how long we would remain in the States. So, the more I thought about the idea of leading short-term teams, the more I was drawn to it. I blitzed Scott with question after question. I finally decided to plan two trips. I would first see if this approach to ministry would fit my skill set and be consistently fruitful. Then I would decide what I wanted to do going forward.

So I approached the worship band at Spivey Community, our new home church, and asked if they would like to take a ten-day mission trip to Berlin. Billy Lord, the leader of the group, grilled me for detailed information. He then discussed the proposition with his six musicians and reported back to me with a resounding "Yes!"

While I was prepping and training the musicians for the European adventure, Sherri and I one day received a call from Heidi in Florida humbly reporting how much healing—psychologically, emotionally, and spiritually—she was experiencing on a weekly basis. "I think I need to continue the program," she conveyed, "but to go to the next level, I'll need to move to Phoenix where the program is headquartered. It would be a twelve-month commitment. But I would be assigned a female mentor that I would live with and be accountable to. She would lead me through the next steps. It would be a holistic approach, focusing on my mental, emotional, physical, and spiritual well-being. I think this is what I need right now. I believe it would be life changing for me."

Sherri and I immediately researched the organization that was running the program. We even spoke to a few of the leaders there in Phoenix. When convinced that the place was legit and safe we didn't waste an additional minute. We urged Heidi to go for it, to not lose her momentum. We would help her financially as much as possible. She immediately started making plans to head in that direction.

Not long after, Sherri drove with her across country to help her settle in at her new Arizona address. As a broken and self-deprecating nineteen-year-old, Heidi adapted quickly to her new setting. She was thankful for the daily regiment of discipline, study, therapy, and accountability. We were equally thankful for the setup.

Back in Atlanta, Sherri joined me as we fought for our daughter everyday in prayer.

And then the time rolled around for me to lead my short-term mission team to Berlin. When the departure date arrived and everyone on the team rendezvoused at the Atlanta airport, the anticipation among the group had reached a joyous high. Everyone was thoroughly prepared and "chomping at the bit."

Once we touched down on German soil, the week of ministry could not have unfolded in a more beautiful fashion. As planned, the band gave worship concerts, outreach concerts; led church services; and shared personal testimonies about their journeys of faith. The impact of the group was visible and immediate. Two teenage girls from the former East Berlin district yielded their hearts to Christ, to follow Him as their Savior and teacher. One of the girls later wrote:

> "Here is one of the things that made this year special. I was experiencing major doubts, confusions, and fears that were almost killing me. This is when I encountered the Atlanta gang. They got me in touch with God! I mean, in final touch! In mid September I took the final step and accepted Jesus as my Savior. All my doubts and confusions immediately left me. Although so much crazy stuff happened this year, I will always remember it as the year I found God."

And that was just the beginning. I was so excited to be back in the city, especially with such skilled musicians who were so wonderfully engaging, that I'm sure my exuberance bubbled over onto everybody. As an extra bonus, we were able to lead a Vacation Bible School and present a moving concert at Gateway International, the church Sherri and I had planted and pastored. I was still exuberant about the potential of the church. The complete CAI team—the four couples and two singles—were now on site at Gateway and settling into their various leadership roles. I was pumped.

But in no time, it seemed, the week was behind us and our mission team was boarding the plane to return to Georgia. And then I had to ask; could I see myself replicating this kind of trip five or six times a year—all across Europe—during our prolonged stay in America? I had never felt stronger about any decision I had ever made. The answer was a resounding "Yes!" Absolutely. The glowing and heartfelt post-trip reports from the band members proved the absolute effectiveness of the adventure.

> "The trip to Berlin was truly one of the greatest experiences of my life. I now have more of a heart for missions than I've ever had." T.W.

> "What I saw the first night, second night, and the rest of the week was really a miracle. I saw the believers hungry to be with us. I feel we should not look at this as a passing phase, but prepare for another trip." R.C.

> "I may never know the impact I had on anyone by going on the trip. But I am certain of the impact it has had on me. The reservations I had before going were quickly transformed into amazement at what God could do with a few people who were 5,000 miles from home. I

shared my life with others for only a week, but in return I was given a lifetime of memories." J.L.

I realized the guys had penned their words in a heightened state of emotion. But nothing they declared was an exaggeration. I concurred with every one of their deep and passionate expressions, so much so, that I was now eager to plan a second and third trip.

But first, Sherri and I needed to find a house of our own, a more permanent place to live.

Chapter 75

One afternoon when I was exploring a dead-end street in the center of Stockbridge I saw a "For Sale By Owner" sign posted in a well-manicured yard. The house was a large two-story structure with a two-car garage and an above-ground pool. I promptly parked the motorcycle and knocked on the front door.

"How can I help you?" a middle-aged gentleman asked when the door opened.

"I'm interested in the house. Is it possible for me to come inside and look around?"

"Hold on just a minute." The man retreated to another room. I overheard him saying something to another person, presumably his wife. The man quickly returned, accompanied by a lady. "Sure, we'll be glad to show you around." He introduced his wife. I introduced myself. We all shook hands.

As I was led throughout the various rooms, I learned the couple had just posted the "For Sale" sign the day before. I was the first person to call or stop by and inquire about the property. As much as I despised the idea of purchasing Stockbridge real estate and settling indefinitely in the area, the house—as a straightforward dwelling place—had a long list of pluses. Located inside a mile and a half of the address was the post office, the tag office, the city hall, the police department, the public library, the fire department, a city park, an auto mechanic, several banks, multiple restaurants and gas stations, and a plurality of grocery stores. My mother's place was only seven miles away. Spivey Community Church was four miles away. Interstate 75 was accessible within three miles. The house was on a dead-end street which meant there was no through-traffic. The house sat on a full acre plot with acres of undeveloped land abutting the back property line. The house to the right of the property had no side windows facing the to-be-sold house. The house to the left didn't have side windows either, thus granting a bit of privacy from both neighbors. The house was seventeen years old with three bedrooms and two and a half bathrooms. With 2,100 square feet, the custom built home had been constructed with three walk-in closets and over fifty cabinets and drawers in the kitchen and laundry room. There was even a beautiful fireplace in the living room. I had to admit the place was more than adequate for our needs. And if we were going to live in Stockbridge, the location was ideal. Plus, there was an above ground pool that the kids would absolutely love. I quickly felt that Sherri would cast a positive vote for the place. But before asking if I could bring her and the kids to tour the property, I first inquired about the sales price.

"A-hundred and twenty-five thousand," the man stated decisively.

I was somewhat shocked. I wondered why the price was so low compared to all the other similar-sized houses we had seen. *Obviously, there must be something wrong with the place.* "So, I'm curious; what's your reason for selling?" I asked outright.

"We're moving to Israel in a few weeks, because of my work," the husband said.

Ah...that explains it, I thought. He has no choice but to sell the house and to sell it in a hurry. Thus, the low market price. "Well, I'm definitely interested. Is it okay if I bring my wife later this afternoon, and maybe a couple of friends who are carpenters? I would like for them to walk through the house, take a close look at everything, and give me their feedback."

"Of course," the man conceded.

Before nightfall, Sherri had given a strong thumbs-up for the entire property. So had my carpenter buddies. "It's a beautifully built home," was the consensus. The men had examined the attic, the crawl space, the flooring, the windows, the AC/heating unit, and all the visible plumbing. Everything they saw impressed them.

So, I gave the owner an offer. "We'll take it for a hundred and twenty thousand if you'll include all the appliances and the Snapper riding mower."

By the next day, after consulting at length with his wife, the husband accepted our offer.

Knowing the family wanted to finalize the deal as hurriedly as possible, we sought to secure a mortgage the following morning. The mortgage lender at our bank, however, showed extreme pessimism at our request. We couldn't produce the needed documents to prove we were a worthy credit risk. We had never had a credit card and thus had no credit history. We owned no property as collateral. And, of course, we had lived outside the United States most of our lives. So the banker assertively, but kindly, turned us down. He did, however, offer the name of a different bank he thought we should try.

At the other bank that was recommended, the mortgage lender who was working that day put forth extra effort to help us. "Are you currently paying rent," the man questioned, assuming we were. "If so, can you bring the cancelled rent checks that cover the last twelve months?"

Sherri and I stared at each other. This wasn't good. We explained that rather than renting, we were actively housesitting for a family and were paying only $50 a month for the owner's homeowner's insurance.

"Well, can you bring the cancelled checks for the utility bills you're paying?" came the follow-up question.

Sherri and I looked at each other again. This was going from bad to worse. "We do pay the utility bills," I declared. "But...the bills are still in the name of the older lady who lived in the house before us. She's currently in a nursing home."

At that point, the banker lifted his eyebrows. His countenance started to express serious doubt about our credibility. He squinted as he brainstormed. "Okay...let's try one more thing. Can you produce the cancelled checks for all the utility bills you've paid in the lady's name over the last year, and match those cancelled checks to copies of the bills?"

I paused. "Yes. It might take a day or two, but I'm sure we can manage that."

We produced those records two days later. A mortgage was granted. Using some of my book royalties I made a downpayment, and borrowed the remaining amount that was due. So we signed the contract and bought our first house. With the help of new friends at Spivey Community Church we repainted every room in the house, replaced every stitch of carpet, built a bonus room over the garage, and bought furniture, a lot of it custom made.

Once we were settled into the house, with a new excitement lifting the morale of our family, I started planning my next overseas trips. We even started hosting and leading a weekly Bible study in our home for young singles. It felt like we had embarked on a new season. I wondered at that juncture if I would ever write again. Perhaps my writing days were behind me. After all, my three novels—*Wisdom Hunter, Jordan's Crossing,* and *Brotherhood of Betrayal*—had all been birthed out of personal pain inflicted while living overseas. And I felt that I had squeezed every last bit of insight that I possibly could from those struggles, heartaches, failures, and disillusionments.

My mind stopped even trying to come up with a new story. So we plunged headlong into the new and unchartered waters before us.

PART IV

FORGOTTEN ROAD

Chapter 76

The next few mission trips that I planned and coordinated were as productive as I could have imagined. A young American guy on one of my teams, for example, was so deeply influenced by all that he heard and experienced that he felt God "call" him into full-time ministry. He enrolled in a Bible college for theological and pastoral training shortly after returning to the States.

On a different trip, again with Billy Lord and his band to Berlin, the drummer in the group engaged a young German man on a crowded city bus one afternoon and invited him to attend one of the week's multiple concerts. We did not know that the young fellow had just returned from America where he had spent a full school year as an exchange student and was sorely missing the optimistic and friendly American spirit. He gladly showed up, not at just one, but at three of the concerts. He heard several band members, between song sets, share their stories of reconciling to God and experiencing the Heavenly Father's undying love, miraculous support, and providential guidance. Those seeds of Truth took root in the German's heart. A few months later he let us know that he had humbled his heart and made peace with his Creator. He joined an international church and became a serious disciple of Christ.

Another person influenced on a different trip to Germany, with a different music group, was a Christian teenage girl. She wrote in her own words how our group had emboldened her in her faith.

> "Because of the team's influence in my life I took my cousin Sabrina to church for the first time. She was curious, but in the end very much confused. She had never even thought about God before. She literally said to me, 'Do you really believe all this stuff?' A week later, we started talking about God again. We probably talked for three or four hours. We then watched a movie about the last days. Last Sunday, Sabrina laid on my sofa reading the New Testament and liking it. We then went for a walk. She said her whole idea of the world was changing. She added, 'I think I believe a little bit more in God since last week."

A pastor sent me a note, referring to the affect the same team had within his congregation.

> "I can assure you that more than a few lives were changed. CJ wants to be recommitted in his marriage. PM came to know the Lord from a Catholic background. HC came to the Lord. Seeing JM grow in the faith over the weekend brings me to tears. This weekend solidified his

new commitment to the Lord. His wife says he is a new man."

The stories of changed lives continued to pour in from each trip. I was hooked. And deeply satisfied in my soul that I was investing my time and energy in the right direction. And I was delighted beyond measure that our financial backers wholeheartedly remained steadfast as I transitioned to this alternative and thrilling course of ministry.

It was around this same period that something else surfaced that was equally as fascinating. It was the realization of our five-year-old son's brainpower. Indications had been forthcoming for some time that he was unusually intelligent, but we were absolutely bamboozled by his thinking and the articulation that emerged behind that thinking. A few weeks before Christmas, for example, Sherri pulled from storage all our holiday decorations. One of those items was from Germany and required assembly. It was a three-tiered, rotating nativity set called a Pyramid. Ten blades, or impellers, were mounted at the top. Six candles and candle holders were put in place around the base. Mary, Joseph, and the baby Jesus occupied the first tier, the shepherds the second tier, and the angels the third tier. As Sherri erected the set piece by piece, Cayden sat at the table silently watching. It was obvious from his wide-eyed focus that his mind was churning. When Sherri lit the candles, and the rising heat moved the blades and rotated all the tiers, the first words that came out of Cayden's mouth were, "Mother, if you want to make the shepherds go backward, wouldn't you have to shift the angle of the blades?" For a five-year-old, the question was prophetic of amazing perceptions to come. And come they did. One right after the other.

A few weeks later, when Georgia schools were back in

session following the Christmas break, one of the single females attending our home Bible study arrived at our house looking dejected. She was a new-to-the-field fifth-grade teacher at a Christian elementary school. We asked if she was okay. "I feel like a failure," she lamented. "No matter how hard I try, I can't get a lot of my fifth graders to grasp double-digit division. It's downright discouraging. Maybe I'm just not cut out to be an elementary teacher."

I had an idea. "Maybe it's not the teacher," I speculated out loud. Maybe it's the students. I walked to the foot of the hall stairway and called Cayden who had been assigned, as usual, to his room during the adult Bible study time. I asked him to come to the kitchen where the early comers to the meeting were seated around the table. At that juncture in life, Cayden had never been taught the mathematical systems of multiplication or division. The concepts and terms were alien to him. "Hey, bud," I said when he entered the room, "Can you tell Miss Dawn what is two times five?"

"What does *times* mean?" was the immediate response.

"It means sets of. Two times five means two sets of five."

He looked at me as if I might be trying to trick him. "Ten," he said cautiously.

"That's correct," I confirmed. "So, what is three times five?"

He paused for only a second. "Fifteen."

"Correct again. Two times ten?"

"Twenty."

"Here's a hard one. Ten times ten?"

He closed his eyes for a moment. "One-hundred," he finally declared.

"Wow! You're right again. Okay, let's do something different. What is ten divided by two?"

"What does *divided by* mean?"

"It means, if you divide ten into sets of two, how many sets of two will there be?"

He scrunched his nose and thought. "Five," he said softly.

"Gosh, you've got this, kid! What about twenty divided by ten?"

He closed his eyes again, obviously replaying the instructions. "Two," came the reply.

"Dang, you're good." I glanced over at Dawn and winked. "Okay, here's the hardest one yet. What is one-hundred divided by fifty?"

"Two."

In less than five minutes, our five-year-old had been introduced to multiplication and division, had comprehended the formulas, and had correctly calculated double-digit division. "So, there you go, Dawn. Maybe it's not the teacher. Maybe it's the students. So, don't beat yourself up."

Not long afterward, Cayden was eating bite-size pieces of watermelon with extended family members. One of the adults told him to be careful not to swallow any of the small black seeds lest a watermelon grow in his stomach. I immediately paused my conversation with a different individual. I wanted to hear Cayden's response because when I was thirteen I was told the same thing by an elderly aunt. Sadly I blindly believed the lady and for several years afterwards tediously picked out every seed while trying to enjoy the southern-grown fruit. Cayden, in a contrasting move, confidently spoke up and said, "I don't think so." The adult chuckled and asked him to explain. "For a seed to germinate," Cayden stressed, "it has to have dirt, sunshine, and water. There's no sunshine in my stomach. And there's no dirt. So, the seed can't germinate. It's not possible." I just shook my head. I wasn't able to reason that out when I was thirteen. Cayden's extreme mental acuity demonstrated again that he was not an average kid.

One of our friends, a female psychologist, was so impressed with Cayden during that season of life that she asked if she could meet with him in her office and administer an IQ test. She explained that the test was designed for those five to sixteen years of age. "The test typically takes two hours," she told us. "And I charge a fee of four-hundred dollars. But I'll give the test this time for free." On the afternoon of the exam, Cayden was irritably tired. He cooperated unwillingly. Yet, later that evening the psychologist called the house after we had tucked Cayden into bed and said, "You might want to sit down. Your son at five has an IQ of a hundred-and-thirty-seven. He asked questions throughout the testing that I've never heard a sixteen-year-old ask. You've got to make sure from now on that he receives top notch mental stimulation. You need to know that you've been given a heavy God-given responsibility here." Going forth from that moment, Sherri and I regularly carried that responsibility in the forefront of our thinking. That burden, that duty, that drive would soon lead to a showdown with the Henry County Board of Education.

Chapter 77

Cayden had thrived in kindergarten intellectually, socially, and emotionally. His teachers at a private Methodist facility had understood his uniqueness and had worked with him accordingly. But now it was time for him to enter the first grade. We didn't have the finances to place him in a private elementary school. And in the area where we lived there were no charter schools or co-op schools. And Sherri was immersed in a new ministry that she had founded and was unable to give the unrestricted time that homeschooling would require. Plus, she felt that professional teachers would be better equipped to speak to Cayden's mind with a greater variety of approaches and resources. So, the only option, it seemed, was the local public school, Stockbridge Elementary.

I questioned a few people in the community about the quality of the first-grade teachers and the overall environment and morale at the school. I even interviewed a couple of the teachers. The answers I received provided enough hope for Sherri and me to enroll Cayden at the school. We were excited for him. He was equally excited.

But our dreams that his experience at the school would

be moderately good, along with his own dream that the experience would be an enhanced version of his kindergarten year, all crumbled within the first two weeks of the school calendar.

Every afternoon when Cayden returned home on the school bus, his spirit was totally deflated. He was eventually able to articulate the reason. "The teacher just screams most of the day at the kids who are not obeying."

He even started having ongoing nightmares about the stress of the milieu.

I had been led to believe that the teachers at Stockbridge Elementary did a decent job of maintaining discipline in the classroom. But after hearing Cayden's report I needed to see the situation with my own eyes. Thankfully, I was permitted to sit in his class for a full day as a guest. What I witnessed was upsetting even to me. The lady teacher had little, if any, control of her students. Cayden had not misspoken. The teacher spent at least seventy-five percent of her classroom time yelling and threatening. A handful of the kids were terribly disruptive and were not intimidated in the least by the teacher's warnings. The educational environment was truly miserable for anyone wanting to learn. Surely this couldn't be the everyday scene. Yet, the teacher of this class was supposedly the best of the first-grade educators at the school.

At my urgent request, Sherri visited the class as a guest two days later. We needed her assessment as well. She was so disturbed by the overall classroom chaos that she cut her visit short and took Cayden home with her. "We've got to get him out of that school," she insisted. I agreed a hundred percent.

I heard there was another public elementary school in our area—though out of our assigned district—that had a stellar reputation for all things educational. The next day I visited the school—Cotton Indian Elementary—and managed to speak to the principal, Mrs. Felicia Spicer. The lady's seriousness as an educator, and as a manager of teachers, was displayed immediately. The hallways were quiet. And the interactions I witnessed in the office areas between staff members and between staff and students were respectful and honorable. Felicia Spicer seemed to be adored by everyone around her, especially the kids.

I told Mrs. Spicer about Cayden and his unpleasant situation at Stockbridge Elementary. "I hear the school here is a lot different," I disclosed. "I need to find out if that's so. If it is, then I want to seek permission from the county to move Cayden from Stockbridge Elementary to here. So, is it okay if I walk the halls and peek into some of the classrooms? I want to see how the two schools compare."

"Sure," Spicer gladly conceded. "If the opportunity presents itself, even speak to one or two of the teachers. Here, I'll give you this clip-on badge that shows you're an approved visitor. Go for it."

Impressed with Spicer's confident demeanor I took a thirty-minute excursion through the maze of hallways. I looked through the door windows of at least ten classrooms where class was in session. In doing so, my respect for Spicer and her ensemble of teachers was clinched. Every single teacher was supervising her bevy of young students with grace and style. I honestly didn't see one child misbehaving. I looked in some of the door windows more than once. The teachers were lecturing, marking on the white boards, answering questions, and interacting with students one-on-one. Not one of the teachers was yelling or calling out troublemakers. The contrast between the two schools couldn't have been more stark. I even managed to talk to one of the teachers who was in the hallway, having shepherded her kids to the restrooms. The young lady absolutely loved the school and Felicia Spicer. "It's a dream team here. The teachers are all fantastic and love what they do. And Mrs. Spicer provides the ultimate in leadership. I can't imagine teaching at a better school."

I was completely mesmerized. This was a school where Cayden would thrive. I was convinced of it. I wanted it for him so badly that the next day I drove to the office of the Henry County Board of Education and spoke to the head guy, a Mr. *Baker. I told him about Cayden's extraordinary mind and about the toxic environment at Stockbridge Elementary's first grade and how it was failing miserably to advance Cayden academically. And not just Cayden, but probably all the kids. I told him about the glowing difference at Cotton Indian. "I'm requesting permission to move my son to that school," I announced decisively.

Baker listened patiently. "I hear you," he assured me after I made my pitch, "But that would be crossing attendance lines. So I'm sorry. I really am. I just can't honor the request. I'm not allowed."

"Of course you can," I retorted. "You're the Superintendent. There's got to be a legitimate loophole somewhere in the system."

Baker appeared to be shocked by my comeback. He rose higher in his seat. "Like I said, Mr. Dodd. It's not possible. Besides, even if I could make an exception and give you permission, I'd have to do the same for all the other parents. And that's just not going to happen."

I'd heard this argument before. "I don't see any other parents here," I remarked flatly.

Baker scowled. "I'll remind you again, Mr. Dodd, that Georgia is not a school-choice state. The final answer is, I can't do it."

I had fought for Shanda in Berlin during her sixth grade year at JFK. It looked like I would now have to fight for Cayden as well. I rubbed the bridge of my nose. "Well, you're the top educator in Henry County. And your aim should be for every student to receive a comprehensive education. My son is not even receiving a mediocre education. Actually, his attendance at Stockbridge Elementary is a waste of time. He's not learning anything there academically. So...I'm going to keep showing up here at your office on a regular basis with my request. I'm going to become a pest until you decide to give us some help.

As promised, I showed up at Baker's office the next day and the next. I spoke repeatedly to Baker, to his office staff, and to anyone around. I would even just sit and allow my presence to be a nuisance. At some point on the third day, when the office personnel understood I wasn't going to drop the matter, one of the side-office secretaries called me aside as I was leaving for the day. "Psst...," she whispered. She looked around to make sure no one else was watching, "There is a loophole that no one has told you about. If you can get a psychiatrist to sign off on the fact that your son is being mentally handicapped at Stockbridge Elementary, the Board of Education will then be obligated to let him cross attendance lines and attend a better school." The lady's tone was one of empathy. But her eyes said *Now, will you please leave us alone?*

I went straight home and called the psychologist who had given Cayden his IQ test, and asked if she could talk to Cayden and issue an official statement—if she felt it was accurate—saying Cayden needed to be transferred to a less turbulent school for psychological reasons.

"Of course, I'll be glad to sit down with him," she assured me. And she did, the very next day. Within twenty-four hours

I hand delivered her official assessment to Mr. Baker's office. Baker read the letter that stated in no uncertain terms that our son was clinically disturbed because of the undue anxiety he was forced to endure everyday at Stockbridge Elementary.

"I'm sorry. This letter carries no weight," Baker nearly growled.

At that point, I felt he was resisting my plea simply because of pride. I argued with him, making it clear that I did not understand his lack of concern as a so-called educator. I then took the letter to the helpful secretary and showed it to her. "If Baker says he's going to disregard the document, can I take it to someone over his head, someone at the State level?"

The lady, looking nervous, perused the piece of paper. "This assessment is not from a psychiatrist," she muttered. "It's from a psychologist. Plus, it's not notarized." Jittery, she then waved me away.

The next day, Cayden was sitting in the office of a certified psychiatrist and being talked through a litany of evaluation questions. We paid two-hundred dollars for the man's services. Like the psychologist, the psychiatrist perceived quickly that Cayden was suffering psychologically, emotionally, and socially as a result of the volatile environment at his school. The psychiatrist's letter was even more damning. I promptly had it notarized.

I delivered it in person to Baker the following morning. He reluctantly read the evaluation and became mildly enraged. "Who told you to get this letter?" he wanted to know.

"It doesn't matter. Now give me permission to move my son across attendance lines or I'll take the matter to the governor's office."

Baker, I was certain, never wanted to see me again. The

sentiment was plastered in his eyes. "There will be NO bus service. Period! I promise you that!" he lambasted. "You will have to sacrifice your time and money everyday to chauffeur your precious son to and from the school! And that's final! Now, get out of my office!"

Two days later, after Felicia Spicer received a communique from Baker's office saying Cayden had permission to attend Cotton Indian, Cayden was introduced to his new school, his new principal, and his new teacher. The change in his after-school demeanor was immediate. He loved the new setting and started looking forward to classes. He finally started thriving again.

For me and Sherri both, his excited and relieved spirit was worth every push and every sacrifice. We could now rest, knowing that in the hands of Felicia Spicer and her well-trained teachers, Cayden would finally receive the education he needed. We earnestly thanked God for the victory.

Chapter 78

With Cayden set up in such an excellent educational framework Sherri could relax and readily devote more attention to the young, budding ministry she had founded, called Treasured By God. She had felt strongly all along that there must be a way she could use her china collection to bless others. The first opportunity had come when a pastor's wife, who Sherri met at a Bible Study Fellowship gathering, asked if Sherri could conduct a tea party for the ladies at her Christian Church. The lady had heard Sherri talk about her collection and her love of hot tea. Sherri accepted the honor and had become so enthralled by the idea of a fancy tea party for a large group of ladies that her preparations for the event had taken on serious proportions. She divided the necessary preparations into eight different categories: Designing and making the table decorations. Planning the finger-food menu. Marketing the event and selling tickets. Praying for the affair. Setting up and taking down the table and chairs. Preparing the tea. Serving the tea. And washing and repacking the china.

She recruited eight ladies, each one to chair a category and pull together a team to carry out the responsibilities. She met with the eight ladies multiple times before the event in order to cast her vision and give them guidance for their tasks at hand. The overall plan was to invite a limited number of women (dictated by the number of three-piece china settings Sherri had in her possession at the time) to a relaxed, elegant tea party, lavished with beautiful table cloths, table decorations, and flowers. Sherri's highly-prized three-piece collections—the dessert plates, cups, and saucers, along with her bank of exquisite tea pots—from all across Europe would serve as the place settings. The ladies attending the party would be waited on by men in the church who, nicely dressed, would prepare and serve the tea. Following the lovely experience Sherri would present a message titled Treasured By God. She would tell the story of her collection: the searching, the selecting (even the pieces that were flawed), the valuing, along with learning everything possible about the age and history of each piece. In the presentation, she would highlight a few of the pieces that she had set aside on a stage table. She would then use her story as an analogy of how God is searching for us, choosing us (even with all our faults), valuing us, and redeeming us for his glory and purpose. *We're all treasured by God* would be her primary message.

The party was such a talked-about, successful occasion that one of the invited guests inquired eagerly about Sherri possibly giving a tea party at her church.

Sherri said, "Yes."

Birthed out of that second tea party were more invitations. And soon the invitations were coming nonstop. Sherri's calendar was quickly booked with a tea party every other month. She even corralled me to bring home additional settings from the European flea markets when I traveled on my mission trips. I had learned her preference in style and age, so I started returning with two or three new sets from each venture. The collection became so vast that Sherri's car—each time she departed for a tea party destination—was filled with large rubber containers holding the china. Each china piece was wrapped in a towel for protection. Soon the trunk was filled, along with the back seat and passenger seat. It was definitely a labor-intensive ministry. But the churches loved her. Some even started using her approach of training women as a template for building their own in-house ladies' ministries. Sherri loved it. And I cheered her on.

So...Sherri had found a fulfilling stateside niche.

Cayden was settled in school and infatuated with the new start.

Heidi was falling head over heels for a guy in Phoenix and talking about marriage.

Shanda was tolerating American high school the best she could.

Ministry wise, my heart as always burned for Europe. So I continued excitedly to lead mission trips and continued to see life-changing fruit.

If something more miraculous could happen on an overseas trip than what I had already witnessed, it soon transpired on a trip to France with another music team. An outdoor concert had been preplanned for the band to give in downtown Lyon on midsummer's eve, a big night of celebration for the French. At the host pastor's direction, the band set up late that evening on a cobblestone plaza—an island of relaxation that included an array of benches and a quaint cafe—surrounded by streets and six-story apartment buildings. Balconies jutted off the apartments, overlooking the beautiful plaza.

When the band finally launched into their music, the ring of listeners—from the benches, cafe, and apartment balconies—were most likely for the first time in their lives hearing the positive and uplifting beats and lyrics of contemporary Christian music. Two of the band members, between song sets, went to the main microphone with an interpreter at their side and shared their testimonies of being rescued from the emptiness of life by the sacrificial and unconditional love of God. They assured the listeners that God, with His incomparable love, could rescue them as well.

Following lots of music and the two testimonies, the host pastor stood at the mic and started presenting the story of the Gospel. He was five or six minutes into his delivery when a disturbance occurred. Out of nowhere, it seemed, a middle-aged man was marching across the cobblestones straight toward the pastor. The stranger's body was rigid. Anger blitzed his countenance. The whole scene shouted Red Flag. I was sitting on the cobblestones alongside the band members. I coiled, ready to jump up and try to stop the man. So were several of the musicians.

The French pastor saw the man huffing toward him. But he kept speaking into the mic.

Pausing no longer, I stood up, took two or three steps, ready to intervene. Just then, the charging man stopped a foot or two from the pastor, raised a finger and shouted something in French. The pastor stepped to the side and gave the intruder his attention. Within a couple of minutes, the pastor and the guy walked over to an empty bench and sat down. They carried on an intense dialogue for at least thirty minutes. The members of the band resumed playing, all the time wondering what was happening. Sometime after midnight when the band was ready to pack up and head back to the hotel, the pastor pulled us aside and revealed what had unfolded.

The stranger in question lived on the sixth floor in one

of the apartments across the street. From his balcony he had heard the music through the band's outdoor speaker system. He had also heard, with rapt interest, the testimonials of the two musicians. The words he heard were absolutely new to him and had highjacked his full attention. The man's wife and daughter—the loves of his life—had two years earlier been killed in an automobile accident. He had tried to medicate his overwhelming grief with alcohol and therapy. But the unrelenting pain, guilt, and sorrow had simply refused to vacate his soul, even for a moment. He had decided a week ago that he couldn't endure any longer. That he didn't even want to. So he planned his suicide. He had planned it for that evening, midsummer's eve. He had laid out his loaded handgun. Before he took the deadly shot, he had decided to stand on his balcony for a few minutes, bask in all the memories of his wife and daughter, stare at all the happy people on the plaza and remind himself of what he didn't have. He would then go and sit on the edge of the bed and with one carefully aimed bullet bring his misery to an end.

But...when he was standing on the balcony, he heard for the first time in his life that God actually loved all of mankind and wanted personal relationships with us. The man had never denied God's existence, but had always accepted that God was distant, cold, and demanding as had been modeled by the country's Catholic Church.

"When he marched across the plaza," the pastor explained, "he came right up to me and said, 'I need to talk to you now!' I asked him what about. He told me. So, we sat down. I answered his questions, and in those answers I told him about God's gracious, loving, and personal nature. I especially let him read a variety of Bible verses underlining those truths. He started to weep. 'Why have I never heard any of this before?' he wanted to know. I then shared the Gospel with him, step by step. I clarified that the deadness of life that he felt was due to the fact that he'd never been reconciled to his Creator through Christ's work on the cross. He wept again. He then wanted to know if he could be reconciled to God, if that was really possible. I shared God's invitation with him again. I even shared with him my story and the difference God has made in my life. He broke down again. He asked me to pray with him that God would rescue his soul and, if possible, give him peace. So I prayed aloud. I then encouraged him to talk to God himself. And he did. With tears. He now wants me to meet with him on a regularly basis to teach him more about the love of God. So, we've already planned to meet later this week. So, my friends, tonight you've helped save a man's life. And his soul!"

What a divine appointment! The bliss of what happened made it difficult to go to sleep that night.

The incident stoked the desire inside me to pick up my pen and write again. My first novel *Wisdom Hunter* had taught the intricacies and dangers of hardline legalism. *Jordan's Crossing* had revealed the slippery slopes of liberalism, of trying to be one's own master. *Brotherhood of Betrayal* had pinpointed the putridness of self-righteous and unforgiving attitudes. I wanted my next book to illustrate some other relevant and important truth that would touch hearts and change lives. That was my style.

Almost more than anything, I found that I now wanted to write another rousing narrative. I just had to.

Chapter 79

On my next trip to Europe, again to Berlin but with an entirely new team, I learned the shocking and heartbreaking news that the CAI team that took over the leadership at Gateway International Church had imploded. The various team members, having undergone no team training whatsoever in the States, simply butted heads once on site. There were disagreements about leadership, direction, and responsibilities. Two of the couples were so confused, angry, and frustrated that they were already packing to return to America. Sherri and I, as founders of the church, were devastated. But there was nothing we could do at that juncture to salvage the situation. The church's destiny looked totally bleak. We were crushed. For therapeutic relief, I reminded myself that everything that exists in the physical world—people, animals, plants, organizations, companies, governments, nations, local churches, and whatever else—has a definitive lifespan, an expiration date. Gateway, though its years were few, had without question been an effective tool to advance God's kingdom. That much we could rejoice in.

We could also celebrate the fact that the Christian

Women of Berlin ministry had become its own official organization and was still very much alive and fruitful. Plus, Ricky Allen, the young man who had surrendered at Gateway to preach and had received theological training at Columbia Bible College, was now back in Berlin with his bride with the goal of planting a strong evangelical church for the younger generation in the northeast quadrant of the city. I was definitely cheering him on.

Life was still good. And, besides, it was best to keep looking forward.

Before my next overseas trip I was cruising around my neighborhood on my motorcycle one afternoon and enjoying the ride when I was walloped out of the blue with a long-time, but never forgotten, fantasy. Memories of my two-wheeled adventure on the island of Cyprus nearly twenty years earlier resurfaced with a punch. I had promised myself following that adrenalin-filled group ride that I would one day plan another such escapade. So what was I waiting for? I owned a great motorcycle and I was already organizing and leading group trips. Why not coordinate a motorcycle trip somewhere inside the U.S.? I could sandwich the exploit between two of my transatlantic jaunts. Before I parked my bike in the garage that evening I enthusiastically determined, God willing, that I would bring the dream to life.

Once I was back in my home office I examined my yearly calendar. I daringly selected a date six months out. The motorcycle trip, I quickly decided, would be ten days in length, would be for men only, and not just for fun. Rather, it would be centered around ministry objectives - leading church services, doing home-repair projects for needy families, and creating a forum where men could dare open up and encourage one another. Those initial action steps generated such excitement for me that I could hardly sleep that night.

Within forty-eight hours, I had picked up the phone and called six or so Stockbridge churches. "Hello, my name is Randy Dodd. I'm a missionary who lives here in town. I'm in the process of planning a unique motorcycle mission trip for men. Do you know of any men in your church who ride motorcycles? If so, could I possibly have their names and phone numbers? I would like to extend a personal invitation to them to be part of this upcoming adventure." I naturally answered questions and offered references.

In less than a month's time I had a commitment from five men to join me on the two-wheeled odyssey. Tommy Brewer was a bounty hunter and bail bondsman. He invited Geoff Marott, the founder and CEO of a multimillion-dollar company, who had not ridden a bike in seventeen years but would purchase one for the trip. Cornel Unteanu was a Romanian who earned his livelihood as a web-developer and photographer. He had fled his country following the 1989 revolution that left his nation in shambles and ended up first in Washington State with his Romanian wife, then in Georgia with a new wife from America. He made plans to purchase a pre-owned, inexpensive bike for the trip. Derek Arwood was a freelance film maker, the youngest of the five. He had never ridden a motorcycle, but guaranteed he would have one in time for the big trip. Kent Kelsoe, a retiree, didn't own a motorcycle but volunteered to drive a truck and pull a motorcycle trailer as a support vehicle. Each of the men were believers but were at drastically different places in their faith journey. The first time I sat down with all five men in the same room, there was such an obvious dissimilarity in personalities, backgrounds, and tastes that I felt I had made a colossal blunder. I was convinced from the start that the longed-for trip would be a total disappointment, if not a complete failure.

The days and hours leading up to the August trip were definitely interesting, though. Cornel bought an old Honda 750 Nighthawk. Tommy prepped his Yamaha 750 Virago. Geoff bought a brand new Honda 1100 Shadow. Derek, one week before our departure, purchased a Yamaha VStar cruiser and procured his motorcycle license just one hour before we all rendezvoused at Tommy's church—Community Bible—for our big send-off. The wives were there. The pastor and associate pastor of Community Bible were there. Some friends were there. I had painstakingly scoured road maps for months and laid out a fifteen-hundred-mile circuit that would take us through Dahlonega, Georgia; Blueridge, Georgia; Gatlinburg, Tennessee; Kingsport, Tennessee; Winston-Salem, North Carolina; Mt. Airy, North Carolina; Galax, Virginia; Myrtle Beach, South Carolina; Charleston, South Carolina; Savannah, Georgia; and Macon, Georgia. We were scheduled to lead a Sunday worship service at First Baptist Kingsport, lead a Wednesday evening Bible study at a church in Mt. Airy, do a home-repair project for an impoverished minority family outside Charleston, and interact with a large group of foster kids in Savannah.

When we were packed and ready to leave, the wives and pastors encircled us and offered up heartfelt prayers for safety and fruitfulness. With the sight of duffel bags, tents, and sleeping bags strapped to the back of our bikes, I felt adrenalin flood my system as we pulled out of the parking lot. *Yes! It was finally happening! After nearly twenty years of dreaming!* I couldn't have made space for another ounce of exhilaration. I wasn't just grinning beneath my helmet, I was hooting and hollering, literally.

And then, in fifteen minutes time, our group of six rolled up behind a serious traffic jam in downtown Atlanta on the I-75/I-85 connector. It was a little before 9:00 AM. This was Derek's first time riding a motorcycle on an Interstate. It was Geoff's first time straddling a bike in seventeen years. And suddenly we were surrounded by eighteen-wheelers, massive pickups, and overheating autos. Drivers all around were impatiently trying to switch lanes and were honking horns. It was a tense situation for our group, with no margin for error. Wearing protective gear, we were sweating profusely in the August heat and humidity which only added to the discomfort.

Geoff crept up alongside me at one point when traffic was at a dead stop and raised his voice above the rumble of his v-twin. "I can't take this, man! It's too nerve-wracking! I think I'll get off at the next exit and call it quits."

Really? Are you kidding me? I was certain if he dropped out that his friend, Tommy the bounty hunter, would feel obligated to join him in a gesture of support. The morale of the group, already tentative, would completely vanish into the summer heat. The trip would be over before we had traversed thirty miles.

"Let's stop and talk when we get out of this mess," I shouted back at him. "I'll find a safe exit." I was intentionally delaying his decision. I figured he wouldn't just bolt at the next exit without offering an explanation to the group. I knew also that he would remain on pins and needles until I found a comfortable place for the whole group—including Kent driving the support truck—to pull over. But I intended for the stop to be six or seven miles further up the Interstate once we had cleared the worst of the traffic. Hopefully by then Geoff would feel differently, hopefully a little less uptight. It was a gamble.

When we did manage to stop, we got off our bikes and assessed the state of everyone's nerves. Geoff definitely was not shy or silent about the uncomfortableness he was feeling. Fortunately, he was the only one in the group thinking seriously about dropping out. Everyone else could unquestionably relate to his feelings, but begged him to remain for at least one more leg of the journey, especially since downtown Atlanta was behind us.

"Besides," one of the guys pointed out, "if you turn back now you'll have to immediately face the same horrible chaos in reverse order."

I think it was those words that detonated in Geoff's brain and coaxed him to say, "All right, I'll try for one more stretch."

By the time we reached Dahlonega, eighty miles northeast of Stockbridge, Geoff and everyone else was feeling less panicky and a bit more confident. To my great relief, Geoff decided at that moment to not give up. The group would remain unbroken. My spirit was instantly rejuvenated.

The odd mixture of personalities—all alpha males with polarizing preferences; a fact that kept me on pins and needles—was somewhat leveled the first night after dinner when Cornel asked the group to pray for the welfare of his marriage. The topic struck a cord that every one in the group—except for Derek who was single—knew far too well. The motorcycles had brought us together physically. But the topic of marriage it so happened started weaving our group together mentally and spiritually. In the process of giving counsel to Cornel we all ended up over the course of the week sharing the difficulties in our own marriages and accepting prayers and homespun advice.

Of course the hours were also filled with lightheartedness and laughter. One such instance was when Tommy told us about a telephone call he received one evening from 'Whitney Houston' asking him to help get Bobby Brown out of the Fulton County Jail. Believing the call was a hoax, Tommy hung up on the lady. She called back. It really was Whitney Houston.

Even though I was the only one in the pack experienced at public speaking, I was able to cajole three of the men to share their testimonies on Sunday morning in Kingsport. I figured raw testimonies shared from the heart with a trace of nervousness would be just as impactful as polished orations. When the men stood at the podium on the church's raised platform they bravely fought their nerves. Following the service, the men were approached by an array of individuals who told how the stories had spoken inspirationally to their hearts. As always, I enjoyed nudging passive believers into various types of ministerial action. Nearly always the results were positive.

By the time we arrived in Myrtle Beach, over halfway through our trip, Geoff decided the Honda Shadow wasn't a bike that really fit him. So he went to a motorcycle shop on the Grand Strand and traded the Shadow for a VTX 1300. Tommy was in the mood for a more powerful bike as well, so he turned around and traded his 750cc for Geoff's 1100cc. *Millionaires!*

The men gained riding confidence exponentially day by day. Scooting across the country's two-lane highways and experiencing the grass-roots life of America became genuinely fun, fun, fun.

On James Island, outside Charleston, the guys used their handyman skills to replace the drywall in a dining room ceiling for a low-income black family. Not gifted as an engineer or builder I became the token 'go fetch' and 'hold this' assistant. Helping the needy family with such a legitimate and dire need spread unusual satisfaction throughout the group of men. As we were prepared to leave Charleston in the late afternoon, I asked the elderly owner of the property if he knew of a campsite anywhere along the coast before we reached Savannah.

"Yassuh," he said in his deeply southern accent. "When you sees Eddie's sto, turn left. You kun pitch a tent rat thair on the wadder."

Leading the pack down the coastal highway, I was straining to spot 'Eddie's Store.' When I sensed we had maybe traveled too far and missed the turn, I stopped and asked a mechanic if he knew where I could find Eddie's Store.

"Do you mean Edisto?"

"Edisto?" I quizzed.

"I don't know of an Eddie's Store. But Edisto Beach is a little town about a mile back up the highway."

I just shook my head and laughed. "Thank you, man."

Finding the campsite, we pitched our tents on the leeward side of a beach dune, then took a dip in the Atlantic before dinner.

In Savannah the next day we were allowed to give inspirational talks to the teens at the state foster home. The bounty hunter went out of his way to scare them straight with his "jail" stories. Afterward I asked the house parents if our men could offer the guys and girls free motorcycle rides around the block. Assuring the directors we would be extremely careful and ride slowly, we were given permission. At least fifteen teenagers signed up and formed a line. Most had never been on a motorcycle before. Understandably they were both excited and nervous. As soon as the first ones returned from their circuit, they were unabashedly singing the praises of two-wheel exhilaration. "That was awesome!" "I never dreamed it would be so much fun!" "Can I do it again?" "You guys are awesome!"

After personally giving rides to three of the youngsters, amidst the other guys coming and going with their passengers, I made my way back to the parking lot to offer one final ride. Standing in line waiting for me was an African American female who weighed at least 250 pounds. I became nervous when I saw her heading my way. I wanted to say *I'm sorry, but a passenger, for a variety of reasons, can determine the safety factor of a ride, and you my dear are going to make it dangerous.* But I didn't have the heart to tell her. It took three people to help the girl onto my pillion seat. All the while I was fighting mightily to keep the bike balanced. When the girl finally rested her feet on the foot pegs, the rear suspension nearly bottomed out. This wasn't good. She then threw her arms around my chest and squeezed like an industrial vice grip.

"Ready?" I bellowed, barely able to breathe.

She only nodded.

I throttled slowly away. She started to relax after the first quarter mile. By the time we circled the block she was completely at ease. As I slowed to make the turn back onto the foster-home property, the girl in a violent movement jerked her arms from around me and started flailing. Sensing I might lose control and drop the bike I naturally accelerated to maintain equilibrium. Instantly the big gal started to fall backward. On my sport bike there was no sissy bar or backrest to catch her. I cringed. I just knew she was going to fall off, bang her head on the pavement, and die on the spot. At the last possible second, though, she grabbed my shoulders with a death grip that automatically pulled me with her. Gripping the handle bars with all my strength I honestly thought my arms were going to be pulled from their sockets. Somehow—and I've never understood the physics—I managed to keep us upright and deliver the girl safely back to the drop-off spot. Three people helped her dismount. Having seen what had happened, they were all laughing. A hornet had buzzed the girl's head and that's the reason she had wildly swiped at the air. Imagining the worse-case scenario I was only able to laugh a little later.

Our men's last night on the road was in Macon. It was difficult to believe the adventure had come to an end. Despite the upfront odds against a harmonious trip, our group had bonded. Together, as one unit, we had explored, camped, cooked, laughed, ministered, labored, prayed, cried, and especially conversed about deep issues. We had created memories that would endure for a lifetime. We instinctively understood that we had gloriously partook of something that most men would never experience. We all choked up. We didn't want it to end.

Tommy, the bounty hunter, blurted, "We've got to do this again! You can't let this die!"

The feeling was unanimous.

By the time we got back to Community Bible Church and into the arms of our waiting wives and friends, I had already started thinking about our next great ride.

Chapter 80

Back home for a few weeks with a pinch of free time on my hands I decided to teach Cayden a bit about American sports. I took him to the backyard one evening and brought a baseball and two mitts. I helped him position his hand properly in the glove.

"Before I explain the rules of the game," I told him, "I first want you to get a feel for the ball and what it's like to catch it in your glove." I back stepped about twelve feet and told him I was going to toss the ball to him and that he should try to catch it in the mitt before it hit the ground. He just stared at me like I was a farmer asking him to ingest cow dung. Not sure exactly what was churning in his mind, I lobbed a slow pitch underhanded, a pitch that could have easily been pulled from the air by anyone with the slightest bit of physical dexterity.

Cayden made no movement, whatsoever, to connect with the ball. The stitched American icon fell to the ground with a thud and rolled to a stop behind him. Cayden's eyes never followed the ball. Instead, he gaped at me carefully and asked, "And why do I want to do this?"

So much for teaching my son American sports. He had

rather take the ball apart and deduce how it was engineered. I huffed, then realized I was actually okay with that truth. My boy, the scientist! The description had a substantial and hopeful probability behind it.

So did Heidi's description as a newly engaged woman. The man who had captured her heart was an African American named Jarrett with family roots in Indiana.

Sherri and I had known about Jarrett for several months and had suspected the relationship was headed toward marriage vows. So we weren't surprised by the big announcement. And we weren't surprised by Heidi's interracial choice. She had told us years earlier that she was more attracted to men with darker skin. She had even asked as a sixteen-year-old if that was all right. Sherri's response had been, *If the man loves God and loves you, we don't care if he's purple.* We still felt the same. Plus, we liked Jarrett. He was a gentle spirit who was a member of a strong intact family; loved his mom, dad, and siblings; had a college degree; and had a strong work ethic. Our only concern was that he had been married before and had a daughter. The silver lining, though, was that he was a very engaged and devoted father, extremely so.

When Heidi announced the engagement to my mother, she heard her granny giggle with excitement on the other end of the line.

"Tell me all about him," my mom beseeched with more giggles.

"Well," Heidi said, "First of all, he's black."

"No, no, Heidi. I'm serious. Don't kid with me. I really want to know who the lucky man is."

"I'm serious, granny. He's a black gentlemen who's a mortgage underwriter." Heidi was met with an elongated silence. The phone call ended shortly thereafter.

My mother knew none of the facts about Jarrett's

background or character and hadn't afforded Heidi the opportunity to tell her. From her not-knowing point of view, she wrote a note to Heidi and dropped it at the post office. Included in the note were these words: *I will not be attending your wedding. I had rather die than to see you marry a black man.*

Heidi, always shameless, with only a minute measure of social tact, promptly called her granny and said, "Okay then, would you like for me to preach your funeral?"

My mom, to her credit—as a deeply southern segregationist—eventually calmed down, reexamined her heart, and reversed her decision about flying out to Arizona for the ceremony.

The church wedding was creatively unique and special, and well attended. I met Jarrett in person for the first time and welcomed him into our family. I did remind him that, going forward, his life as Heidi's husband would be a roller coaster ride, and never boring. He smiled, already understanding my words.

Years ago I had been genuinely sad and reflective when Heidi left our family nest. I experienced the same emotions on the day of her wedding when I saw her walk away under the care of another man. Sherri was equally, if not more, emotional. *Oh God,* I prayed, *Reinforce Heidi and Jarrett as newlyweds. Sustain them. May they never lose their heart for one another. Or for you.*

My mother grew to understand that Jarrett was a good man. As a Christian woman, she slowly started to deal with her culturally-induced prejudices, even at the age of eighty-four.

Back in Atlanta for a few weeks and trying to catch up on work that had been postponed I was greeted with the unsettling report that the director of our small mission board was deciding for personal reasons to close down the agency. "You need to start looking for another organization," the director broke the news to me. "Let me recommend PRO missions. PRO stands for Projects Reaching Others. I know the founder and leader. He's a great man. He and his agency will serve you well."

I was crestfallen at the decision. Scott, the founder and leader of EPM—European Partnership Ministries—had become a welcomed friend. As a mission director, he had been gracious, helpful, and communicative. He had never felt pressured to be my judge, unlike the leaders at IBWO. He had never postured himself as a 'superior.' He had never hidden behind a mask of self-righteousness. He had acted as an equal, a normal human being who tried to love God and love people the best he could. It had been a genuine pleasure serving beneath him. I would always be indebted to him for providing me with an alternative to IBWO at a crucial time in my life. Sherri was equally grateful.

But now, at Scott's persuasion, I leaned into PRO Missions, headquartered in Memphis, as a replacement board. It was a slightly larger mission board, but possessed the same corporate personality as EPM, gracious and freeing. I would miss Scott's personal touch and his geographical proximity, but PRO, I was convinced, would be a good mission agency for us. We officially applied at PRO and were accepted. I announced the change in one of our newsletters. And thankfully our supporters understood and accepted the transition.

In the mix of shifting to a new employer, planning overseas trips, and regularly serving as a missionary speaker, I was additionally laying out details for a second big motorcycle bonanza. I was also spending mental energy trying to generate a worthwhile storyline for a new and thought-provoking novel. No solid ideas, however, had taken root, and that empty palette of creative thought was a cause of frustration. Yet, I constantly felt compelled to continue as a writer-on-the-side. The desire was a fire that burned inside me, and wouldn't be quenched. I somehow felt that God was behind this drive. Plus, the unremitting impact of my first three novels inspired me to keep searching, fighting, and pushing for another effectual, universal story.

My first novel *Wisdom Hunter* was still churning waves after ten years on the market. I continually received letters testifying to the impact of its message. The head of Ministry Ventures in Atlanta, Boyd Bailey, for example, even wanted to name a branch of his ministry after the book. With my blessing, he went with the name Wisdom Hunters. An entrepreneur, starting a new mom-and-pop Christian bookstore, asked and received permission to brand their business as Wisdom Hunter. Sherri and I, at a personal invitation, even attended a stage play of *Wisdom Hunter* performed by a full cast of characters. The fruit borne from the book was showing up in all kinds of unexpected places. This was true of my other two novels as well. So, yes, I was determined—no matter how long it took—to come up with a new riveting story with a message that was relevant to a mass audience.

Little did I know that my motorcycle and the adventures it produced would become the springboard for my next faith-based tome. It started to happen bit by bit.

Chapter 81

"Can someone help me, please!" *Tyler raised his voice in frustration. Tyler was the support vehicle driver for our second motorcycle mission trip. Kent, the driver for our maiden trip, was now on a motorcycle.

We were pitching tents at the T.W.O.—Two Wheels Only—campground in Suches, Georgia.

Having never owned a tent before, Tyler had swung by Walmart a day earlier and hurriedly picked up a 'tent' from the camping-supplies aisle. For twenty minutes now he had been laying the various parts across the grass and scrutinizing the sheet of assembly instructions. The other twelve men in our group had already erected their tents and were arranging their accessories inside. Tyler was still fiddling with the 'tent' poles. "I'm serious," he blurted a little louder. "I need some help here!"

A couple of the men went over to offer assistance. In less than two minutes, knee-slapping laughter from the two guys ripped across the campsite. Tyler just stood there looking embarrassed and befuddled. The 'tent' he had purchased was actually a portable garden-gazebo.

Such spirit-lifting fun, in various forms, cropped up

daily, intermingled with relationship building, personal growth, and unforgettable ministry.

When we wrapped up that second trip I instinctively understood that the event, more than just special, was a viable life changer. It was decided soon thereafter that I would, without exception, include the motorcycle mission trip in my yearly itinerary. The men even wanted a name for the group. Since the bulk of our outreach was doing home-repair projects for the needy, the name that pushed its way to the forefront and stuck was AOK Bikers Fellowship, AOK standing for Acts Of Kindness.

Seventeen men joined us for the third trip. One man even flew in from Arizona. Once on the road, we were again amazed beyond words by the unexpected.

Bonnie—though we didn't know her name yet—sat in a darkened corner with her boyfriend quietly eating an evening meal, overhearing our group. That couple and my group of seventeen men were the only people utilizing the rustic barn-like facility. Our group had just finished dining. The campground owner, a huge dirt-covered Appalachian with only a few teeth, had prepared a massive succotash cooked in a homemade wok. Our group, with our tummies satisfied, entered into a share time. We were in Damascus, Virginia at the Iron Horse campground. Bill, a retired airline pilot, had asked an hour earlier if he could share his story. I gladly obliged.

"I was lying on the hospital bed dying," Bill explained tearfully halfway through his story. "The next thing I remember, I was hovering above the bed in an out-of-body experience. The doctors, against my will, were battling in a heroic effort to resuscitate me. And they achieved the miraculous. But when I regained consciousness and woke up in the bed, I wasn't pleased. Far from it. The very reason I'd overdosed in the first place is because I wanted to die. My struggle with chronic depression had simply robbed me of perspective, purpose, and any and all will power.

Since there was no microphone for Bill to use, and since our men were sitting around an array of tables, Bill was speaking loud enough for everyone to hear. We weren't aware that the couple in the far corner might be listening.

As Bill poured out his soul, several of the guys were wiping at tears. This type of heart-to-heart sharing among men was stereotypically unusual. But it was a phenomenon that more and more of our guys were becoming accustomed to.

Bill's heart-wrenching story captivated everyone's attention for a solid forty minutes. When he brought his talk to a conclusion, he asked the circle of men if they would gather around him and petition the Heavenly Father to sustain him in his current state of affairs, especially for his marriage that was regularly, for a host of reasons, carrying an overload of stress.

The men stood and placed hands on Bill's shoulders. The spontaneous pleas to the Creator from myriad male voices was enough in itself to make men all throughout the circle weep. Bill just sobbed. God's presence permeated the place. Before we officially dispersed, Bill proclaimed for all to hear, "This trip has been the highlight of my life! Thank you! Thank you! Thank you!"

We had only been dismissed a minute or two when one of the guys in my group approached me. A young lady was at his side. The girl, appearing to be in her late twenties, reflected a lifetime of unwise and pain-ridden choices across her eyes and face.

"The lady asked if she could speak to the leader of the group," the man stated.

"Hi, my name is Randy," I said to the lady, extending my hand. "How can I help you?"

The girl shook my hand with a weak and pulpy grip. "My name is Bonnie," she stated flatly. "Would you happen to have a few minutes,?" I realized she was the one who had been sitting in the corner.

"Absolutely."

"You guys are obviously Christians, right? I couldn't help but overhear your meeting."

I nodded. "Yes. Yes we are."

"And you're a pastor?"

I nodded again. "An ordained pastor. But currently serving as a missionary."

"Will you be around on Sunday?"

I squinted with curiosity. It was Friday night. "Nope. We're pulling out tomorrow morning."

A veil of vivid disappointment descended across the lady's countenance. She let out a deep breath as her shoulders sagged.

"Why?" I queried. "Why do you want to know if we'll be here on Sunday?"

"I was going to ask if you could possibly baptize me," she grunted.

Wow! That was not a question I was expecting. But I gladly went along. "Is Sunday the specific day you want to be baptized?"

"Isn't Sunday the only day a person can be rightly baptized?"

I smiled at the lady's spiritual innocence. "No. A person who chooses to be a follower of Christ can be baptized on Sunday, Monday, or any other day. The day of the week doesn't matter."

"Really? I didn't know that," she confessed with an air of self-consciousness. "Anyway, I chose to be a follower of Christ about a year ago. I've wanted to be baptized ever since. I've tried to be baptized several times, but the churches I've attended have made it really difficult."

"Why is that?" I fished for more enlightenment.

She pointed to the man she had just eaten dinner with. He was still sitting quietly in the dimly lit corner. "That's my boyfriend. We've been together for three years. He's a heavy equipment operator. So we move from construction site to construction site about every three months. He's working here in the area right now, so we're living here at the campground. I've asked the pastor in town to baptize me, but he refuses because I'm not going to be here long enough to be a member of his church. The pastor of the last church I attended wouldn't baptize me because I couldn't commit to a six-week course for new believers. The pastor before that refused because I'm living with a man out of wedlock. I don't know; maybe God is punishing me."

Hearing the girl's heart, I tried to absorb and decipher everything she was saying. "Tell me how you became a follower of Christ," I gently probed.

As the lady described her conversion experience, she gave too much detail for the spiritual awakening not to be genuine. Plus, the fact that she was regularly attending church searching for spiritual food was additional evidence of a new birth. So I felt comfortable with what I was going to propose.

"You do know that baptism itself doesn't transform the human heart, right? Rather, a transformed heart chooses to show itself to the world through the act of baptism." When I was convinced she understood the meaning and purpose of the sacrament, I said, "Why don't I baptize you tonight, right here in the river?"

"In the river? And that's okay?"

"Absolutely. As a matter of fact, most Christian baptisms throughout history have taken place in rivers, lakes, and oceans." That one tidbit of information made her face light up. She became almost instantly giddy. But before she could answer my question, I threw in something else. "Why don't we do this. There are two other men in my group who are ordained ministers. Why don't we all three go down into the river with you. As a show of support we can all baptize you in one beautiful act of immersion."

Sheer joy exploded across the lady's entire demeanor. If a face could become more radiant, hers did. It was as if God, his angels, and his people finally validated the groaning of her heart. "Yes! Yes! Yes! Let's do it now! Tonight!" She took a giant breath. "I can hardly believe this is happening!" she enthused over and over with the beauty of a trusting child.

I introduced Bonnie to the two other ordained men and explained to them what was unfolding. Like me, the men sensed something divine. Word quickly spread through our group about Bonnie and the impending baptism. A special excitement filled the ranks.

In order for everyone to savor the occasion, I slowed everything down a bit. "We'll gather at the river in thirty minutes," I announced. This gave me, Bonnie, and the two other baptizers time to mentally weigh the moment as well as prepare for the water by removing belts, wallets, keys, and shoes.

Since the sun had long since made its descent below the hilly horizon, someone in the group arranged for ten of the motorcycles to be parked side by side on the riverbank with headlights burning, spotlighting the river.

When Bonnie and I, and the two men entered the water, our breaths were hijacked by the harsh bite of the cold. But even the gasps to refill our lungs added to the commemoration of the night. The lights of the two-wheeled machines illuminated the area for all to see. Once chest deep in the water, we stopped. I and the two men with me shared privately with Bonnie a few words of encouragement and affirmation. Bonnie, so appreciative, was focused like a laser on everything we said, even as we were all shivering. The rest of the men were standing along the bank, watching. I then quietly prayed for Bonnie that God would grow her into a strong and faithful disciple.

When the moment arrived for the baptism—as had already been discussed and planned—I stood on Bonnie's left side. One of the men stood on her right side. The other stood behind her. I then lifted my voice and introduced the baptism for everyone to hear. And then at my behest, Bonnie loudly confessed her saving faith in Christ. I and my other two comrades then placed our hands on Bonnie's shoulders and the back of her head.

"And now, my sister," I declared, "we baptize you in the name of the Father."

My bud standing behind Bonnie continued, "In the name of the Son."

The other brother concluded, "And in the name of the Holy Spirit."

Together, the three of us leaned Bonnie back into the water until she disappeared beneath the surface of the cold Virginian river.

When we raised her upright, all the men on the bank were boisterously singing *How Great Thou Art*, like a choral group of stout and mighty angels. The sound of the chorus gloriously drowned out all other noises. It was surreal. Before I could fully grasp the awesomeness of what transpired,

Bonnie pushed water aside and lunged into my arms with the most heartfelt hug I've ever received. She was overcome with jubilation. She was bawling, smiling, and thanking us over and over for walking with her through this red-letter celebration.

When we teetered out of the river, some of the men helped Bonnie climb the bank. They allowed her straightway to return to her cabin to change into dry clothes. Then they swarmed her. With hugs. High fives. And congratulations. Sensing Bonnie was hungry for God, several of the guys rotated in and out of her presence teaching her important Bible truths. They earnestly wanted to help her in her faith journey. Several prayed with her. One of the men, so caught up in the euphoria, even gifted Bonnie with his own expensive leather-bound study Bible.

Bonnie seemed to be transfixed by all the attention and expressed her appreciation over and over. The interaction with her carried on for at least two more hours, until after midnight.

Before our team broke camp the next morning, Bonnie was up and giving hugs. She intentionally sought me out and let me and a couple of the other men know, "I told my boyfriend last night that I want him to marry me, or I'll move out. I just don't think it's right for us to continue living together without being married." I had not said a single word to her about her marital status or living arrangement. Interesting.

We finally all said goodbye, knowing that the last fifteen hours would remain in our treasure chest of memories for a lifetime.

And for me personally, Bonnie's baptism—out of the many I've performed over a forty-nine year stretch—will always be one of my favorites.

Chapter 82

The AOK bunch made it clear to me that our annual ten-day trip was so meaningful that they wanted more. Needed more. So I started adding a couple of weekend rides to the mix every year.

One of those initial mini adventures took place in Blue Ridge, Georgia. One of our guys secured cabins for the weekend. The cabins were spacious with three bedrooms each and included a giant hot tub that could seat six. There were no sleeping assignments. So upon our arrival on a Friday afternoon, the group scattered and everyone claimed a bedroom. A new guy, Todd Hughes, wound up in the same cabin as me. I had never met Todd prior to that day. He only knew me as the founder and leader of the motorcycle group. That was the extent of his knowledge of me.

Shortly after settling into the accommodations, I decided to don my bathing suit and enjoy twenty or thirty minutes soaking in the hot tub. Todd asked if he could join me. The third guy in our cabin left with a few others to make a grocery store run.

I had just switched on the hot tub jets and sunk into the

rippling, bubbling water when Todd climbed in. On opposite ends of the tub, facing each other, we commenced our very first conversation. In a non-hurried setting we learned about each other's work, family, faith, and riding history.

Fifteen minutes into our exchange, Todd said, "I see you have a book with you. What are you reading?"

I had indeed brought along a historical novel. I had left it lying outside the tub. I gave Todd a brief synopsis of the storyline, and asked if he enjoyed reading.

"I love to read," he answered with a lift in his voice. "I'm always reading, always trying to learn, always trying to gain knowledge on how to improve in life."

I was impressed with his answer. I knew, both from experience and observation, that it required a special humility for an adult male to admit out loud that he still had room for learning. "Have you read anything recently you would recommend?" I posed. Not only did the man appear to be humble, but he was obviously articulate and self-confident. So I was genuinely curious.

"I don't normally read fiction," he stressed, "but I just finished reading a novel that honestly has forced me to rethink a lot of things about organized religion and even about my own Christian walk. I've been recommending it to everybody. I believe it would actually change the American church for the better if every pastor and ministry leader would read it."

"Wow, that's quite a statement. What's the title? You've definitely piqued my interest."

"*Wisdom Hunter*," he stated with a punch. "I even like the name. Have you heard about it?"

Caught truly off guard, my mind instantly seesawed with a whomp. This couldn't be real, could it? Had I been set up on candid camera? I mean, the odds of this being a spontaneous and authentic encounter were nearly infinitesimal. Before I answered, I tried to inconspicuously look to the sides to see if there were cameramen hiding behind the windows or doors. "Uh...yeah, I've read it," I stammered. "Actually many times."

"Really? You've read it many times?" Todd scrunched his brows. "Obviously then, it's really spoken to you. I'd be curious to know how it's challenged you. I'd like to compare notes."

Again, I slowly looked for cameras. "Do you remember the name of the author?" I redirected.

"Yeah, the guy's name is Randall Arthur."

"What do you know about him?"

"Actually, I don't know much at all. I just know he's a dang good writer. Why do you ask? It sounds like you might have some information about him. Is there something I should know before I keep recommending his book?"

"Actually I do have information about him. Probably more than you would ever want to know."

Now Todd looked puzzled. His voice went silent as his brain wondered where to go next. While he paused I leaned forward and extended my hand across the water. Todd was totally confused.

"Meet Randall Arthur," I dared to say out loud, still suspecting I was being filmed.

Instantly Todd issued a bewildering smile as if he was now the target of a joke. "What do you mean?" he questioned, the awkward grin pasted across his face.

"I'm Randall Arthur," I repeated while shaking his hand, "the real live author of *Wisdom Hunter*."

Todd sloshed back in his seat. "No way!" he rebutted in

disbelief. "Your name is Randy....what; Dodd, or something like that?"

"Randy Arthur Dodd," I filled in the blank.

"No...this can't be real!" Now HE looked around the room to see if he was being spoofed.

"Yeah, I was thinking the same thing."

"For real? Are you kidding me? You, the guy sitting here in the hot tub with me in a cabin in the middle of nowhere, are the author of *Wisdom Hunter*?"

I laughed. "I'm afraid so."

When Todd was convinced I wasn't lying, he immediately got out of the tub and called his wife. "Hi honey! You're not going to believe what just happened!"

It became clear to me that night that there were just too many great stories birthed out of these road trips to let languish in the attic of boxed-up memories. I somehow needed to find a way to incorporate them into my next novel. But how? I was determined to find a creative solution.

Chapter 83

"Please, I can't stay here in the south!" had been Shanda's cry for five years. Since returning from Berlin she had never fully readjusted to the culture of Georgia with its absence of European safety, culture, and mystique. She had only endured it, simply biding her time. And now as a high school senior she was holding steadfast to her dream of beginning college life far from the deep south, preferably back in Europe.

During her Spring break, she and Sherri flew to London to scout out a university of interest. The dreaded take-away was that the cost of living in the British capital—for lodging, food, and transportation—was simply beyond the reach of our financial pockets...unless we surrendered my royalty savings which had become Sherri's and my old-age fund; a fund we could realistically never replenish. Besides, what if at some point Shanda dropped out? The money would simply vanish into someone else's coffers. Plus, if we used our retirement money to cover the cost of her college years, there wouldn't be enough left to fairly compensate for Cayden's university endeavors. So, we vetoed the option.

Shanda begged to apply for a student loan as an

alternative. London, as she had imagined, captured the full scope of everything she coveted at that stage of life. Sherri and I, however, were so opposed to debt that we refused, albeit gently, to co-sign for a loan. We trusted that Shanda would one day understand how we were sparing her from a ball-and-chain that would adversely restrict her flexibility in life for years to come. But at the moment, she was exasperated to the point of tears. To her utter dismay, we had to eliminate all European countries from her list of possibilities as well, due to the high price of basic necessities. The poor exchange rates between the U.S. dollar and European currencies only blackened the financial picture. This was almost more than Shanda could bear.

To reassure Shanda that we were still loving parents, Sherri made a promise to her. "If we can find a college on this side of the Atlantic that you like, one that offers the art major you're wanting, I'll use my Treasured By God tea party earnings to help pay your tuition."

The search was on.

In a completely different context I remembered hearing someone one day refer to McGill University in Montreal, Canada as a superb institution for higher learning. I remembered that Montreal was in the French province of Quebec. I didn't know much about that part of the world. But I surmised that the school and the city were probably endowed with at least some element of European flair. I knew that Canada was a cold climate territory. And I knew that Shanda preferred cold climates. So, on my own, I delved into information about the school that was available online. My positive interest in the university, though, was squashed when I learned it offered no art majors. But in my research I stumbled across the names of other universities in the city. Concordia

University was one of those schools, and it did offer an art major.

Concordia's size, reputation, and surprisingly low tuition—even for Americans who were granted a foreign-student visa and charged fifty percent more than the locals—placed the school dead center in the range of possibilities. An additional bonus was that one American dollar that year would purchase 1.40 Canadian dollars, a magnanimous plus for those of us paid in U.S. currency.

The city itself, with a population of three and a half million residents, was accessible all around by an efficient network of buses, subways, and trains. And for socializing, there were more university students per capita in Montreal than in any other city in North America.

When I laid out all this information for Shanda to review, she warmed up to the idea rather quickly. She decided to at least submit an application. I was excited for her. If she was accepted, she and I would take an exploratory trip to the campus and check it out in person.

She received an official acceptance in the mail a few weeks later. Next, she obtained a new passport.

We flew into Montreal for a first visit, not knowing a single soul in the city. But within a handful of hours, the feel, the vibrancy, the layout, and the amenities of the town had worked their magic on us. There was definitely a European flavor with most public signs in both French and English. And unlike American cities, the commercial and residential aspects of the city were not zoned separately. They were fused and layered in such a way that it filled the city with life at all times of day and night. Subways and buses were available everywhere, providing connections to every corner of the municipality. From the onset, the city seemed to combine the best of Canada, Europe, and the U.S. all in one territory. It was wonderful.

The Concordia facilities were a smattering of low and high rises in the middle of downtown. There was no dedicated campus with visible property lines. But it was safe. The city's crime rate was the lowest of all the big cities in North America.

We talked to professors and toured some of the classrooms. We were sold.

Even though Shanda had also been accepted at a prestigious university in Virginia, Concordia was now her choice. The most important question that remained was, where would Shanda reside? The university had precious few dormitory rooms, and all those rooms were already claimed.

After consulting local newspaper ads, internet postings, and people in the know, we found one single female art teacher who was willing to rent out an extra bedroom in her apartment. After speaking with the lady, I sensed she possessed no conservative values. As a father I had to ask, what kind of degrading impact would such a liberal and progressive lady have on my daughter? The risk of Shanda plopping down in an unhealthy lodging situation seemed too great to jump at, just for the sake of convenience. If we waited, would we find a more suitable setup? Of course, waiting for another door to open would also be risky. What if another door didn't open?

As we continued to walk and familiarize ourselves with the downtown area, consistently becoming more and more fond of the place, I noticed a blockish brick building with the name Peoples Church highlighted in large white lettering across the side. I had an immediate flashback to my Tennessee Temple years. The Peoples Church in Canada had been hawked as one of the strongest evangelical churches north of the U.S. border. This particular property that I was staring at, though, appeared to be too small to measure up to such grandiose hype. Nevertheless, I knocked on the office door with Shanda at my side. I wanted to find out if there was a student ministry in town that Shanda could possibly connect with. The pastor answered my knock. He was the only person in the building. He invited us in. He patiently let me explain who we were and why we were in the city. In addition to learning that his church was not the famous Peoples Church—the pastor reminded me that said church was located in Toronto—Shanda and I were given a list of worthwhile student ministries that we could investigate, including one led by his church. We thanked him effusively and headed toward the exit when I was pinged by an impromptu thought.

"Excuse me, pastor," I blurted as I whirled around, "Would you happen to know if there's an older Christian couple in town that rents out rooms to Christian students?" I had not mentioned that, while acquainting ourselves with the city, we were also searching for a residency for Shanda. When I posed the question, the pastor glared at me as if my request was somewhat serendipitous.

"Why, has someone told you about Warren and Lois Gamble?" he queried slowly.

"No, I've never heard those names before."

"Really? Well, it's strange you should ask, because it so happens that an older couple in our church has been hosting female students in their home for years."

"Really?" I echoed the pastor's exclamation.

He nodded and fanned out his palm. "Yeah...but I suspect by this time they're fully booked for the upcoming school year. I can give you their phone number, though."

"Would it be an imposition if I called them now? From the church?"

"No, no. Feel free."

He wrote down Warren and Lois's number and let me use his office phone.

In less than fifteen minutes, Shanda and I were on a metro bus headed to Warren and Lois's home in a western suburb. Lois had given me their address, and the bus route from the church to their home. She welcomed us to come on by. Yes, they rented out rooms to Christian girls, primarily university students. They did charge a small monthly rent, but from their point of view their hosting was a ministry that had engaged them for fifteen years. They had five rooms. Four of the rooms were already reserved for the fall semester. The remaining room was tentatively spoken for. They would know definitely in a week's time. But if we wanted, we could stop by, meet them, see the house, and hear the in-house rules. If there was no room for Shanda this time, perhaps there would be the following year.

When Shanda and I stepped off the bus at the designated stop in Westmount, we found ourselves in a clean, well-established neighborhood. Mature trees gave abundant shade to the sidewalks and small yards of the well-maintained duplexes, quadriplexes, and single-family homes that lined the quiet avenues.

The area instantly felt safe.

We found Warren and Lois's house on the corner of a quaint intersection, and knocked at the front door.

Lois, with a grandmotherly smile, welcomed us in. She gave us a tour of the aged two-story abode, a place that oozed wonderful character and homeyness. The girls who lived with them enjoyed their own private bedrooms, but shared a bathroom. Each girl, as part of the rental agreement, rotated with the household chores of cooking, cleaning, and doing the laundry. And everybody in the house sat together for the evening meal during the week nights.

The elderly couple, I realized, had honestly created an idyllic 'home away from home' for the young ladies. As a father, I had never even imagined such an environment of Christian influence and protection for Shanda's debut at college. But having seen it and realizing it was available, I now desired nothing less for my soon-to-be eighteen-year-old. Even Shanda was drawn to the arrangement.

Lois strongly reminded us, though, that the fifth room in question was being temporarily held for a girl named Rebecca, a missionary kid—an MK—who had grown up in Africa. "Of course, I'll add Shanda's name to the waiting list," Lois assured us. "She will be first in line if Rebecca cancels."

Back in Atlanta, we only had to wait three days.

"I'm really sorry," Lois essayed in a mild matter-of-fact tone from Montreal. "But Rebecca, the MK from Africa, has confirmed she will be moving in with us. But if you want, I can leave Shanda's name on the waiting list for next year."

We were crushed by the news. We had built up immense hope, perhaps unrealistically so. And hope deferred, as King Solomon avowed, makes the heart sick. We felt the sudden reality of that sickness.

"Yes, of course, Lois. Keep her on the waiting list," I muttered.

So, what now?

The female art teacher was still holding a room for Shanda, waiting for our final answer.

Oh, God, help us to know what to do! I agonized.

Neither Sherri nor I felt at ease about letting Shanda

move in with a progressive left-wing feminist who would not insist on any moral guidelines. There were just too many scenarios that could go awry. But if Shanda was going to attend Concordia, and by now she was too emotionally committed to voluntarily change directions, she only had the one, solitary offer for a room.

A day later, when we were just minutes away from securing the art teacher's available space, we received a second call from Lois Gamble. "I've got news that you'll appreciate hearing," she chirped. "When Rebecca, the incoming MK, learned that Shanda had been turned away because of a lack of bedrooms, she made a decision that amazed everyone in the house and brought us all to tears. She said if she can help it, she will not just stand by and let another MK miss out on such a great opportunity. So, with happy tears, she announced she would set up a makeshift room for herself in the basement and let Shanda have the other bedroom. Warren and I have talked it over, and we think we can handle one extra person in the house. So...if Shanda is still interested, she's..."

"Yes! Yes! We'll take it," I blubbered an emphatic interruption.

With tears of our own, Sherri and I conveyed endless thank-yous to Lois, Warren, and especially Rebecca. The young lady's decision, alone, was beyond remarkable. She had taken the character trait of thoughtfulness to a whole new level. And we did not for one second take it for granted.

As Shanda prepared for the move to Quebec, it was a heart-wrenching few days for us as parents, in the sense that Shanda's years as a youngster were suddenly over, but a glorious moment, in the sense that she was about to be elevated to a family of five beautiful sisters who loved Jesus, and a set of loving house parents who modeled Jesus with remarkable devotion. We couldn't have conjured up a better setting for her.

Of course, we knew with every ounce of perception that all of this was a gift. We just didn't know how profound and enduring that gift would be.

Chapter 84

In Phoenix, Heidi had jumped into her role as a stepmother with an enduring zest. Meikayla, her stepdaughter, was the beautiful progeny of Jarrett and his previous wife, also a caucasian. Jarrett had been awarded joint custody. So the little girl rotated between her birth mom's house and Jarrett's house. When she was in Jarrett's care, Heidi engaged fully as a stepmom, loving the precious caramel-colored, hazel-eyed darling unconditionally. Heidi merged into the role like a natural. Sherri and I were extremely proud of her.

And then Heidi announced her own pregnancy.

Sherri flew out to sweltering Arizona at the time of delivery. With Sherri and Jarrett present at Heidi's side in the hospital, coaching and encouraging her every step of the way, Heidi managed the exhausting labor with aplomb and gave birth to an eight-pound, healthy girl named Sidney.

Heidi was now a stepmother and a biological mother. And we were joyous grandparents. But the geographical distance between Phoenix and Atlanta was just too great for us to engage with the two little girls in any ongoing manner that felt significant and influential. We tried over and over, but could never find a satisfactory way to work around the geographical spread. My regular in-country and overseas mission trips and Sherri's thriving *Treasured By God* tea party ministry only added to the scheduling complexity.

And then Heidi and Jarrett hit all the family members with another big surprise. They were adopting a one-year-old girl from a local foster home. The biological mother—an African American drug addict—was serving substantial time behind bars for a variety of drug-related crimes. When Heidi and Jarrett brought the docile toddler home as their legally adopted child, Sherri and I made another trek to Phoenix and were introduced to Latavia, the adorable newcomer to the family. Latavia, with her delicate and confused-looking soul, won our hearts immediately.

Heidi was now a step mom, a biological mom, and an adoptive mom. She would later tell people, "I have three daughters, and they each have a different mother."

Heidi's world has never been labeled *boring* by anyone.

Of course, Heidi would say the same about Sherri's and my world. Because of Sherri's and my vast and ever growing network of friends, and our prolific number of yearly trips and adventures, it was only natural that big surprises and milestones—both exhilarating and dreaded—were a regular occurrence for us.

Todd, the *Wisdom Hunter* fan, for example, who discovered my identity as Randall Arthur on the North Georgia AOK ride, was the conveyor of another one of those surprises, one that honestly left us slack-jawed. He called me out of the blue one afternoon and asked if he could stop by the house for a few minutes. He wanted to talk in person.

At that point, he had journeyed with the AOK guys on several trips. He had met Sherri and learned about her nonprofit. Sherri and I had been in his home for a couple of home-cooked meals and had enjoyed meeting his lovely wife. When I heard him say over the phone that he wanted to speak face to face, I wondered if I had unknowingly been the cause of some grievous offense or if Todd simply needed to confide in someone he trusted regarding a personal matter.

"Yes, absolutely," I told him. "Come on over."

Thirty minutes later, he pulled into the driveway. Without customary chitchat or southern pleasantries, he moved straight to the purpose for his visit. He insisted Sherri be present for what he was about to share. So Sherri joined us.

"Sherri," Todd began in a semi-nervous tone. "I'm really impressed with your tea-party ministry. The more I learn about it, the more I want to encourage you. I know you often travel long distances. And most of the time you can't take anyone along to help because your trunk, back seat, and front passenger seat are stacked to the roof with tubs of china. For some reason that bothers me; the fact that you have to travel those distances alone. It's dangerous. So I would like to help." Todd paused to harness his emotions. "Yesterday I was on my way to Tennessee to purchase a new truck for my company when God spoke to my spirit and said, Sherri needs a newer, bigger vehicle more than you do." Todd had seen Sherri's compact car loaded to the gills, to the point that her lines of sight through the rearview mirror and passenger side mirror were dangerously blocked by rubber containers. "I couldn't shrug off the voice. So I'm here to say, I'd like to buy you a new Honda Element, just like my wife's." He pointed to the vehicle he had parked in the driveway just minutes before, a shiny red Element. "With a vehicle that size, someone can always travel with you. What do you think?"

What did we think? Was he kidding?

Sherri and I had a month earlier, unbeknownst to Todd, gone window shopping for a used van that could adequately service Sherri's ministry needs. We had, with wild dreams, test driven and assessed a Nissan, a Chevrolet, a Kia, and a Toyota. Sherri had fallen in car-love with the Toyota Sienna. It was markedly more powerful and more solid-feeling than the others. And the rear seats uniquely folded down flush into a floor compartment. It would be a fabulous vehicle for accommodating all the china and allowing room for a helper to boot. There would even be sufficient space for all the additional exquisite china pieces I was regularly bringing home from my European trips. But the window shopping and test driving were more of a tease. The Sienna was the only van on the market with the fold-away rear seats, a new feature introduced that market year, but the price was simply too costly...unless we were willing to procure a car loan and incur massive debt—which we weren't—or unless we were willing to splurge and tap into our retirement fund—which we weren't. So Sherri had been left drooling and dreaming.

And then Todd appeared.

"Before you answer," Todd said excitedly, "Why don't we load all the china into the vehicle and see how it fits."

Dazed in near unbelief, Sherri and I—with Todd at our side—hand toted the hefty plastic tubs, stuffed with the delicate china pieces wrapped in bath towels, from an indoor storage area to the SUV. When the last container was placed inside the vehicle, the passenger seat was indeed empty and available for a teammate, but the rear section of the car was completely filled from seat to ceiling and from door to door. And, as in Sherri's car, the huge plastic tubs rendered the rearview mirror useless and impeded visibility through all the rear windows.

Todd was the first to interject, "This isn't going to work.

It's not what I thought. There's not even enough room to expand your collection." Before Sherri and I could process disappointment, Todd continued, "So, let's take out all the tubs and go shopping. Surely, there's a vehicle out there somewhere that will work. Any thoughts?"

Sherri dared to mention the Toyota Sienna.

Without further discussion, we hauled the tubs back into the house and Todd drove us directly to the Toyota dealer in nearby Southlake. When he saw the spacious interior of the Sienna enhanced by the fold-away rear-bench, he declared. "Yeah, I can see it! This is it! It has way more space than the Element. So what color do you want?"

Sherri pointed to a light gray.

Todd paid $23,000 in cash and, with my solicited approval, dictated the title to Sherri's name. Nothing quite like this had ever happened to us before. We were still in blissful shock, thinking Todd at any second might halt the process and reverse his decision. I mean...$23,000! Who gives away $23,000? Todd was a custom-home builder, a husband, a father, and a son with a tapestry of financial responsibilities, including upcoming college tuitions.

Why would he do this?

And why were we in particular the chosen recipients of this rarest of rare honorariums? It was a God thing; that was for certain. Still, we were some of the least deserving of HIS little ones. We wept, still wondering if it was all real.

A week later Sherri drove the van, this time loaded with family members, to Virginia to visit her dad who was dying with cancer. It would be one of the last times she would see her dad alive. As a proud and caring father, Mr. Wehunt was able to see in his final weeks, again, just how God was continuing to miraculously provide for his daughter, a daughter he had surrendered to missions a lifetime ago.

Back in Atlanta, with the new van parked in the carport, we bequeathed Sherri's compact Infinity G20 to our daughter, Heidi. Heidi had flown to Atlanta to make the visit with us to Virginia. She drove the Infinity, elated in her own right, to her in-law's home in Indianapolis. A few days later, Jarrett made a visit to see his mom and dad, and drove the car back to Phoenix.

Todd's magnanimous gift had unquestionably been a godsend. Within months, the Sienna had made multiple Treasured by God trips in state and out of state as the tea-party ministry grew in popularity and as Sherri continued to minister to thousands of women. And to the relief of everyone in the family, a lady friend, serving as a helper, was able to travel with her on each trip.

Surpassing all attainment markers we could have ever imagined, our lives continued to amass surprise after surprise, adventure after adventure, and open door after open door.

Chapter 85

Some basic thoughts started to take shape for the content of my next book. As our stay in the U.S. was prolonged, due to my mother's fight to stay alive, I noticed a constant increase in televised religious programming. And most of the featured pastors and evangelists—charismatic men who looked like slick, upscale car salesmen—were regularly preaching a Prosperity Gospel, claiming it was never God's will for any of His children to be physically sick, financially handicapped, or mentally depressed; that any Christian who followed the correct formula of sowing financial seeds and exercising a pure, childlike faith would be guaranteed God's irrevocable blessings of health, happiness, and riches.

I kept scratching my head. Did these self-proclaimed theology experts really believe their own message? Or were they simply tickling the ears of gullible people and soliciting "seed" monies in order to finance their highfalutin lifestyles and stroke their egos?

I had to believe the latter. I mean—in the light of both Scripture and reality—how could they sincerely believe the Prosperity thesis? If they were indeed students of God's

Word, how could they outright dismiss Bible truths like Hebrews 11:36 that emphatically states:

> "Some (followers of God) were jeered at, and their backs were cut open with whips. Others were chained in prisons. Some died by stoning, some were sawed in half, and others were killed with the sword. Some went about wearing skins of sheep and goats, destitute and oppressed and mistreated. They were too good for this world, wandering over deserts and mountains, hiding in caves and holes in the ground. All of these people earned a good reputation because of their faith, yet none of them received all that God had promised."

Or the Apostle Paul's résumé of suffering recorded in II Corinthians 11:23:

> "I know I sound like a madman, but I have served him far more! I have worked harder, been put in prison more often, been whipped times without number, and faced death again and again. Five different times the Jewish leaders gave me thirty-nine lashes. Three times I was beaten with rods. Once I was stoned. Three times I was shipwrecked. Once I spent a whole night and a day adrift at sea. I have traveled on many long journeys. I have faced danger from rivers and from robbers. I have faced danger from my own people, the Jews, as well as from the Gentiles. I have faced danger in the cities, in the deserts, and

on the seas. And I have faced danger from men who claim to be believers but are not. I have worked hard and long, enduring many sleepless nights. I have been hungry and thirsty and have often gone without food. I have shivered in the cold, without enough clothing to keep me warm."

Or the Apostle James' urging in James 1:2:

"Dear brothers and sisters, when troubles of any kind come your way, consider it an opportunity for great joy. For you know that when your faith is tested, your endurance has a chance to grow."

Or the hundreds of Psalms where the writers lay bare their disillusionment, depression, and anger. There is simply no way hermeneutically to interpret these texts figuratively or metaphorically.

Plus, life from the dawn of recorded history has broadcasted on an hourly basis the brutal truth that everybody in life struggles—everybody—including ALL Christians. No amount of financial "seed sowing" or childlike faith will manipulate God to exempt anyone from the reality of this cursed world by wrapping them in a protective and exclusive cocoon of prosperity and happiness. Never. Period. That will occur only in heaven when all creation has been redeemed. Not here in a fallen world. To teach otherwise is an absolute perversion of the Gospel. And of reality.

Besides, and this is noteworthy data, anyone who owns two or more vehicles; who has earned a college degree; who owns land; and who owns their own free-standing house with two or more bedrooms, hot-and-cold running water, around-the-clock electricity, central heating and air, a refrigerator and freezer, and a bathroom with a flushing toilet is already in the top 5% of the most fortunate people on the planet. And it's a fact that most of the U.S. audiences listening to the Prosperity-Gospel teachers are in this top 5%. For a Prosperity-Gospel teacher to dare look this audience in the eye and claim it's God's will for them here and now to have MORE, and that they actually deserve MORE, is beyond the apex of ingratitude.

Still, the brassy evangelistic voices continued to scream this incessant, addlebrained message from the rooftops. And it ruffled me every time I heard it. So I decided my fourth novel would present a narrative that would illustrate the blatant absurdity of this so-called Prosperity Gospel; this perverted gospel.

But, I wasn't sure how I could plausibly work that fact into my ever expanding list of motorcycle adventures. I convinced myself, though, that there had to be a creative solution. I even toyed around with the notion of interweaving 'human trafficking' into the mix. The trafficking of human flesh was a burgeoning industry in Europe and wreaking havoc in hundreds of thousands of lives. Europeans were keenly aware of this blight on humanity. Beautiful Russian girls in particular—in the crumbling Russian economy—were being lured daily into Western Europe under the false pretense of being hired as high-wage fashion models, secretaries, makeup artists, and hair stylists, only to have their passports locked away upon arrival and forced to work in the slave dens of prostitution. It was more than a serious issue, and I wanted American Christians to know about it. I wanted to coax people to pray and to ask how they could get involved in the ever growing campaign to slow the tide of such human travesty.

So. Human trafficking. The Prosperity Gospel. Motorcycle trips. Mission adventures. How could I possibly concoct a workable recipe, using all four ingredients, that would produce an exotic and palatable read that would make people hunger for more? I invested mental energy on a regular basis trying to solve the puzzle. All the while, more and more material was being stockpiled in my source file.

For example...

When one of my mission teams first arrived at our hotel in downtown Madrid, we were taken aback by the melee of prostitutes loitering up and down the pedestrian-only avenue. One of the young streetwalkers even tried to solicit one of the men in our group. When we checked into our rooms, three of the ladies on my team hurriedly made their way to me and declared, "We're not comfortable with this location. Is there any way we can move to a different hotel?

"I apologize," I explained. "I wasn't aware, and I wasn't told, when I booked our rooms that there were prostitutes in the area. Believe me, I understand your uneasiness. I really do. But before we make a knee-jerk decision, we need to consider a couple of things. Number one, the hotel here has a forty-eight-hour cancellation policy which means if we cancel our reservations immediately, we will still have to pay for the next two nights. So, is everybody on the team prepared to pay out an extra hundred-and-twenty dollars without knowing if we can even find another hotel with available rooms at the price we're paying here? And number two, will it make a difference if you know that many of the girls out there have probably been trafficked and are prisoners to some dark-hearted pimp who's watching their every move and forcing them to turn a certain number of tricks every day or face a savage beating?"

The three women went instantly silent. Their eyes—the lift, the squint, the consternation—revealed immediate shock. "You really think so; I mean, that the ladies are trafficked?" one of them questioned with a disconcerted whisper.

"I do," I answered in truth.

There was a heavier silence this time accompanied by some kind of emotional shift. "Then what can we do to help?" The question was delivered with nervousness, but desirous of a serious and sober answer.

Caught off guard by the unexpected initiative, I pondered for a moment and said, "I don't know exactly. But give me some time to think about it. And I'll see if I can come up with any ideas." I was now the one who was nervous.

In the meantime, it was a group decision to not relocate. We would settle in at the hotel and ask God to turn an uncomfortable situation into a ministry opportunity, and show us how to reflect His compassion, grace, mercy, and love right where we were.

"All right," I announced to the team after dinner that evening, "everybody now understands that a lot of the girls working the streets are very likely prisoners. And some of you have asked if we can do anything to help them. So, here's what I've decided. For those interested, we can go out in pairs. We can approach the girls and ask if they understand English. If they do, we can ask outright if they are being held against their will. If they indicate they are, we can tell them we're willing to pass along their name, description, and location to the police or to their family. But I will remind you that the girls who are trafficked will have watchers. So, this could be dangerous; I'm just not sure to what extent."

The contemplation that filled the room was perceptible. No one spoke for thirty seconds or more.

"So," I finally amended, "how many of you want to do this?"

One man and two women volunteered. They were emotionally charged, not with bravado, but with brokenhearted eagerness to reach out to sister human beings who were hurting.

Within the hour, we were on the street. Instead of dividing into two teams, we went as a group of four. The two ladies felt safer that way. We petitioned God for His wisdom and protection, then approached the first prostitute we saw and asked if she could understand English. Unaccustomed, probably, to being approached by a group of both men and women, the young girl hesitantly replied "yes" as her eyes darted suspiciously from person to person.

I quickly blurted, "If you're here against your will, we would like to help by contacting your family and letting them know where you are."

Panic instantly raked the girl's whole being, from head to toe. She jerked her head to one direction, looking for someone unknown to us, most likely a watcher or a pimp. She looked back at me, her eyes flush with fear. "NO! NO! NO!" she hawked, gesturing with her hands as if pushing us away. "Leave! Now! Now! Pleasssseee!"

The girl's arrant fright was so physical it raised the hair on our arms. I so badly at that point wanted to be the 6'5" 280 lb seasoned street fighter who could stand there and pummel the girl's captor to the very edge of his life and set the girl free. But not being that man and not knowing what we could possibly do or say in response, we backed away and left the area. I felt ashamed. And angry.

Stunned by the dark reality of what we had just witnessed,

but not giving up, we walked around the corner, took a deep breath, and introduced ourselves to another lady of the night. The girl, standing in an inset doorway, appeared to be slightly older. Like the first girl, she looked somewhat uncertain when she saw two females and two males walk intentionally into her space. When queried if she could speak English, she shook her head no. Nevertheless, her eyes were opened extra wide, projecting a brain on high alert. One of our ladies spontaneously touched her own heart, then transferred her hand to the girl's heart. She then put her hands together in a sign of prayer, nodded at the girl, then opened her arms to offer a comforting hug. To our group's utter surprise, the street walker threw herself into the embrace and cried. It was a heaving, soulish cry of misery and pain that lasted at least five minutes. The second lady in our group joined that simple but profound human act of sharing the pain. I kept an eye open for any angry men coming our way. I was now ready to fight if I had to, regardless of my 5'7" stature. When the hug finally ended and tears were being smeared away, we gave the girl a Spanish Bible pre-marked with special verses telling of God's grace and love for broken and wrecked lives.

The girl pulled the Bible to her bosom as if it was the greatest gift she had ever received. We prayed for the girl out loud in her presence. Even though she didn't understand our words, she understood we were interceding to God Almighty on her behalf. She wept some more and in her language thanked us profusely, then gave us each a beautiful, unforgettable hug.

We interacted with three more streetwalkers that night.

Throughout the remainder of the week, our team of staunch conservatives from rural America went out of their way to smile at the hookers every day, communicate a non-judgmental hand sign of prayer, and occasionally give a rose here and there along with a pre-marked Spanish Bible. The females on our team also made sure our team prayed together every evening for the girls.

I absolutely had to weave an element of these experiences into my next novel. I was resolute about it.

Chapter 86

In the meantime, the Monte Carlo SS I was driving while stateside started to become a burden. It was a highly coveted car in the African American community. Nearly every time I stopped—at a traffic light, gas station, restaurant, grocery store, post office, any place really—a young African American man would approach me. "You want to sell your car?"

The vehicle simply garnered too much attention. I couldn't commute in peace. The number of waylays and interruptions over a week's time was so predictable that I discouraged Sherri from driving the vehicle when alone. Being car jacked—a growing criminal encounter in Atlanta—was always a looming threat. To go anywhere in the Monte Carlo was no longer a pleasant experience. So, sadly, after owning the vehicle for multiple years, I marked it "For Sale." I included the sales ad, along with my phone number, on a few websites. I listed the car at a premium price.

There was a proliferation of phone calls. But most of the callers were young men who wanted to know if I would sell the car at a discounted price. I held steady at my offer. And then I received a call from an older African American gentleman. He explained that he was looking for a muscle car like the Monte Carlo as a high school graduation gift for his son. His voice was calm and respectful. He raised a few questions about the vehicle's maintenance history, then asked if he and his son could drive down from the other side of Atlanta and take the car for a test drive.

Refusing to give out my home address, I arranged for the pair to meet me the next afternoon near my home at a Walmart parking lot. At the appointed time Sherri followed me in her van to the outer edge of the Walmart property. When the two men showed up, I was surprised to see they both looked to be in their early-to-mid twenties. Both were absolutely too young to be the father of a high school graduate. I introduced myself to the pair and said, "Where is the dad?"

The older of the two identified himself as the big brother and explained that their dad had been rendered immobile with a fever. So, the big brother had assumed the responsible role for the day.

"Would you like a test drive?" I offered the younger of the two, hoping the sale would be finalized within the hour. He nodded yes. He seemed rather preoccupied, though, for a young man on the verge of receiving such a grand graduation gift. When we took a seat in the SS, I told him to simply drive around the Walmart building. "There's plenty of room on the backside of the store to accelerate and brake. You'll know quickly if the car is everything I say it is."

Throughout the ride around the property, the young man never accelerated above 25 mph. He seemed to be intimidated by the car. I kept wondering if he had ever driven before.

Back with his brother, he told him, "I like it. I really do."

The older brother interjected, "I believe the Mustang we looked at yesterday is a better fit for you. That's what I'm telling you."

"No, this one!" the younger guy insisted.

The older brother looked at me. "Is there any way you'll come off the price?"

"Can't do it. Sorry."

"I'm a thousand short in cash, then. So if this is the one he wants, I'll go across the road to the bank and get the rest."

I was wholeheartedly convinced the sales transaction was underway.

"Can I drive it around the building one more time?" the younger guy asked when the big brother headed for the bank.

Locked in a seller's fever, I consented. Believing the sale was a done deal, I revealed to the young African American that the car was equipped with a LoJack tracking device. I assumed this bit of information would add to his enthusiasm about the vehicle. Plus, if he was going to become the new owner, he needed to be aware of the aftermarket apparatus.

As he took another turn at the wheel, he was more assertive with the accelerator and brakes. On the backside of Walmart he said, "What's causing the wobble in the front end?"

"Wobble?" I had maintained the car meticulously. I had always been keenly aware of any drive-train issues, even the slightest ones. And I had certainly not detected any tire or alignment problems.

"I feel something," the guy insisted. "And it's definitely in the front end."

Could I have really missed such a problem?

When the guy reached the far side of the building, he

stopped the car. "Why don't you drive? I'll explain what I'm feeling."

Still enmeshed in the heat of the sale, I jumped out of the passenger's side, assuming the young guy would exit the driver's seat. The moment I was completely out of the car, though, and on the asphalt, the high-pitched squeal of the spinning rear tires pierced the air. And the car sped away. Knowing instantly I had been played, I slumped my shoulders and ran a two-hundred-yard dash to where Sherri was relaxing in the van. "Quick!" I yelled breathlessly. "Call 911! The car's been stolen!"

Two patrol cars were on site in less than ten minutes. I spewed a quick version of what had transpired. I stated emphatically that the car was equipped with a LoJack transmitter. I begged the officers to hurriedly contact whoever was necessary to track the car before the thief pulled over and ransacked the vehicle to find and remove the hidden device. The cops told me the county's police force had only one car equipped with a LoJack transponder and that the car was momentarily out of commission. *What? Really? Are you kidding me?* I kicked the asphalt and said a few harsh words under my breath. I immediately abandoned any hope of ever seeing the Monte Carlo again.

That night around 10:00 PM, however, I received a call from the local police station. The SS had been found. It was parked in a yard under a tarp in the adjacent county. A Dekalb County law-enforcement copter equipped with a transponder had picked up the LoJack signal. The dispatched cops not only found my automobile; they found three or four other tarp-covered cars on the same property, all stolen. The thief was arrested, and my car was returned undamaged.

Having believed the LoJack on the SS was powered by

the car battery, the young thief had disconnected the battery cables. He was unaware that the LoJack transmitted a signal through its own battery pack.

When the defendant was found guilty on multiple charges in a court of law, the county's DA office called and said, "We're just curious; what kind of sentence would you like to see imposed?"

I huffed. "I want the judge to sentence the man to a forty-hour-a-week real job until he earns the exact amount of money I was asking for the car. I then want the crook, under court order, to purchase the car in a legal transaction like a decent human being. But not just my car. I would like for this sentence to be meted out for every stolen car that's ever been linked to the man!"

The caller from the DA office chuckled and said, "I hear you. Unfortunately the judge isn't going to trust that the man would abide by those conditions if he was released."

Following the whole stressful ordeal, I yearned to take Sherri and Cayden and move back to Europe. But my mother, now 88, was showing no signs of weakening, contrary to what all the medical experts had predicted. Realizing we would be residing in the States a while longer, I promptly traded the prized SS for a small nondescript Toyota Tacoma pickup truck, title for title. And I was grateful for the relief.

Chapter 87

A few years earlier—immediately after we had returned to the States—Sherri and I met a man who worked as a life coach. It was the first time Sherri and I had heard this particular job title. Sherri had been absolutely intrigued. When she listened to the man explain the function of a life coach, she said, "This is what I've been doing all my years as a missionary. You mean, with certification, I can do this going forward and get paid for it?"

And now, years later, the idea of serving as a life coach had never left her. She was subdued more and more by the feeling that missionaries could thrive better on the mission field if they, of all people, could be regularly assisted by a life coach— a life coach that was certified, that was pledged to confidentiality, and that had cross-cultural experience, especially a life coach not connected to their sending agency or sending church. Sherri and I knew from years of personal experience and private conversations with others that the mission board and the home church were the last people missionaries would reach out to for help when they were struggling with their marriage, their teammates, their faith, their kids, etc. To divulge too much personal information to the mission board or home church could easily jeopardize their financial support, reputation, or career. Thus, an objective, third-party life coach pledged to confidentiality would be ideal. Sherri was sure missionaries would talk if this safe guard was in place.

Sherri mentioned her idea to the founder and president of an organization called Global Focus. The man stared at Sherri as if she were a Victorian scholar. "This is the missing link in missions!" he declared. "I've heard a lot of ideas over the years as to how missionaries could be better served. But you, my dear, are the one who's just pioneered a concept that could truly revolutionize the world of missions."

Sherri researched day after day and could find no organization anywhere in the world that was bringing life coaching exclusively to the world of missions. This reframed her whole burden. She prayed incessantly and fervently, "Lord, this type of help for missionaries is so obvious. Why won't you raise up an agency somewhere that employs a bevy of coaches who can give missionaries all over the world this kind of assistance?" She heard in her spirit the stringent response, *That's exactly what I'm doing. Through you.*

Like Moses of old, Sherri fought the calling. "You've made a mistake. I'm not a business woman. You know that!" She argued with God in dead seriousness and trepidation. "I'm not the right choice. Something like this is way too big for me!" None of her pretexts, however, weakened the calling she felt. Not even a whit. She finally relented. "All right! All right! But if I mess this up, don't blame me! I'm serious!"

Shortly, thereafter, she was introduced to an organization called Ministry Ventures. MV's exclusive focus was to coach ministry founders step by step through the process of establishing strong and successful nonprofits. Sherri signed up. Several interested parties covered the cost for her to begin the two-year Master's program. She would be coached by five individuals who would coach her around the needs and strategies of developing (1) a sound ministry model, (2) an engaging board of directors, (3) a faithful prayer team, (4) an efficient and legal administrative structure, and (5) an optimal fundraising program.

Sherri decided at the offset that the name of her nonprofit would be Advance Global Coaching. AGC would provide a team of well-trained, highly-skilled coaches who would help ADVANCE God's kingdom by coming alongside evangelical missionaries of all denominations and coaching them online around issues unique to their cross-cultural work. Certainly, such a prized resource would help reduce the escalating number of missionary casualties.

Having always been an A student, Sherri launched into the program with a rabid dedication to listening and learning. If she was going to pioneer a totally new type of ministry structure, she without a doubt wanted to lay a foundation that was big enough and strong enough for future generations to build on.

As she submersed herself in the Ministry Ventures program, she still carried on with her Treasured By God tea-party ministry. At her request, I had continued to bring home additional tea-cup sets from my European trips. She could now give parties for over two-hundred ladies and each lady would have a matching cup, saucer, and desert plate that was distinct from all the others. Most of the china was at least seventy years old and was visually striking. The various churches that hosted the event were enraptured by the novelty and quality of the presentation. The party was so much in demand that Sherri wasn't able to honor all the invitations that came her way. She had already addressed nearly 8,000 women. At a friend's suggestion, Sherri hired a professional videographer to film one of the parties. The film footage was then edited and used to produce a high-quality DVD that was made available for purchase.

Along with the *Treasured By God* DVDs, Sherri added handmade jewelry crafted from broken china, copies of my novels, and a few pieces of intact china to her sales table. She used most of her earnings from the events to offset Shanda's college tuition and cost of living. Because of this injection of monetary assistance, Shanda graduated from Concordia University with her Bachelor's degree without any financial debt.

With Sherri's tea parties and schooling, and my motorcycle ventures and overseas trips filling our schedules to the limit, we decided to allow Cayden to knock out his middle-school studies from home via online classes. Permitting him to study from home would spare us a lot of hours of chauffeuring to and from a brick-and-mortar facility. Thankfully, the state of Georgia offered a reputable and cost-free digital curriculum that was quite impressive. Nevertheless, the adjustment—from a thriving elementary school to a bedroom desk all alone, especially at his age—wasn't easy for Cayden. Academically, though, the online school was superior to the local middle school that had a tenuous reputation.

Around that time, Shanda—now 21—announced her intention of traveling around the planet on the World Race. We learned that a Georgia-based ministry called Adventure In Missions had just a year earlier inaugurated a signature program called the World Race. The Race was an eleven-month-long mission trip that literally circumnavigated the globe. Two teams were launched each year. The mission teams, composed of young singles between the ages of 21 and 25, would live and minister in a different country each month. They would work their way around the planet from continent to continent, from select country to select country. AIM had even developed a dedicated website where every team member was allotted pages to post their stories, insights, and itineraries for the contentment and inspiration of their parents, friends, and supporters. It all sounded fantastic.

And then Shanda announced the price - $14,000 per-person. $10,000 had to be submitted up front. Our coffer of expendable income was depleted. So, in order to secure a place on the next trip, our 21-year-old had about four months to raise the funds. I personally doubted she would be able to procure the money in time. But, due to her hyper-energetic and tireless efforts, the dollars in vast amounts started to accumulate. Remarkably she had all the required money in hand the day before the deadline. When the fundraising and training had ultimately purged many of the World Race applicants, there were just thirty young people left who made the upcoming team. Shanda was one of them.

She would be in AIM's third pod ever sent out.

As her father, I was thrilled. Then, a few weeks before the team's departure, I saw the movie *Taken* in a local theater. I would be fibbing if I claimed the intense, frightening storyline didn't cajole me to nearly ask Shanda to cancel out of the trip. The unforeseen risks of such a lengthy and porous itinerary in distant lands—especially Central America, Asia, and Africa—suddenly seemed too dangerous. But how could I, of all people, tell my daughter we couldn't, or shouldn't, trust God for her well-being, even in a world gone mad with human trafficking? Was God not trustworthy any longer?

Did He not love Shanda more than I could ever possibly love her? I had to resolve all over again that my daughter's life, journey, and path were watched over by the Sovereign God who ruled the universe. So, Sherri and I cheered her on with our parental blessing when she and her teammates departed from the Atlanta airport.

Within weeks, newsworthy stories from the group began to surface via the internet and phone. I'll never forget the story that came out of month four when she and her team were living in Thailand. They were approaching a ten-day period when their schedule was free of commitments. They had started calling these stretches of free time ATL weeks, ATL standing for Ask The Lord. Their group of thirty had split into six small teams of five. Managing meals, lodging, and even ministering was logistically easier for only five people when moving about. The six pods normally stayed and worked in the same vicinity for support and safety, but as they approached this particular ATL week, Shanda's team sensed God's Spirit leading them to the northern part of the country. The five other pods felt impressed to remain in the south.

Living on a budget of $7.00 a day at that point, Shanda and her crew—three females and two males—stood on the side of a major road one morning and extended their thumbs to hitchhike northward. A man in an open-bed truck stopped and let them pile in the back. They traveled for four or five hours into a remote region. They were totally ignorant of the territory, didn't know a single soul in that part of the country, and had very little money. When their ride was over, they found themselves in a small, quaint village. They found a tiny cafe where they promptly quenched their thirst and brainstormed openly about their next move. Did God have a ministry role for them in this village, they wondered aloud. To help a church somehow? An individual? A family? Maybe the whole community?

As they were talking, a tall Caucasian man walked up to their table. "Excuse me," he interrupted in British English. "I couldn't help but overhear your conversation. I understand you're wanting to do some volunteer work in the area. Is that correct?"

Shanda and her team, somewhat surprised, nodded that the man had heard correctly.

The man introduced himself as a missionary, then said, "My wife and I run a safe house for Thai kids about an hour north of here. We provide a secure home for boys and girls between the ages of seven and fifteen, when they're the most susceptible to being kidnapped out of their villages and being trafficked into the sex industry of Bangkok. Parents bring them to us where we feed, clothe, and educate them for free, and, of course, keep them safe. But it's just me and my wife that run the place. We could certainly use some extra help if you don't mind traveling another hour to the north." One of the young men on Shanda's team started to ask how they might assist when the older man proceeded. "We can always use help with general maintenance or just interacting with the kids. But we do have two or three special projects that I especially need help with." Shanda and her team remained silent and let the man elaborate. "A lot of our little girls are from villages in the far northern parts of the country where the landscape is covered with hills, forests, waterfalls, exotic animals, and such. Our safe-house property is in an area that for them is flat and boring. I've often thought it would be great if someone could come along one day and help paint a beautiful mural on their bunk-room wall, a mural that highlights a dense forest with hills, water, animals, and flowers. It would make the girls feel so much more at home. But I'm guessing that none of you would feel capable of designing and painting something like that." The man's last words were more of a question.

Instant silence blanketed Shanda's team as her mates stared at her with looks of wonderment.

Shanda raised her hand. "Uh...I just graduated with a bachelor's degree in painting and drawing. And one of my last projects was a mural." Her voice oozed amazement. "So, yes, I'd be able to design and paint a forest scene in the girl's bunk room for you."

"Really?" the man questioned with tempered exuberance as if he might be dreaming. "Wow! Wow! That would mean more to us than you can even begin to imagine."

Everybody smiled and for a few seconds basked in the infinite odds of what had just happened.

"What are the other special projects?" one of the young men on Shanda's team finally spoke up.

"Well, we have about eighteen bicycles on our property. But only three of them are functional. The kids are always fighting over those three bikes. It would be a huge blessing if some of you could help me figure out how to get two or three of the other bikes working. The kids would feel like it was a big New Year's Eve party."

At those words, Shanda's group was rendered speechless. God's presence overcame them.

"Are you serious?" the boys asked.

The man responded with a look of mild confusion.

"We just left our jobs as bike repairmen to come on this trip. Not only can we fix two or three, we'll repair every bike you have."

Tears rolled down several cheeks at the mutual understanding that God in real time was orchestrating what was tantamount to a miracle. That He was answering the prayers of everyone in the mix.

The missionary wiped his eyes. He looked at the two remaining girls in this mystifying group that had just appeared out of the blue. "So," he posited slowly, "I guess the two of you have business degrees?"

There were more tears.

"Uh...yes...that would be our skill set," the girls confirmed.

Everybody just shook their heads at the inexplicable.

"Then you can help my wife in the office with correspondence, filing, and maybe a little accounting?"

"It would be our privilege," the girls enthused.

Over the following week, Shanda was able to paint the mural. The boys were able to repair all the bikes. And the other two girls were able to help the missionary wife get the office in tip-top shape. It was a week the group would never forget.

And the stories from Shanda's trips—from Cambodia, Vietnam, Mozambique, Zimbabwe, South Africa, Romania, Hungary, and England—and my trips—across Europe and the Eastern United States—just kept coming.

Chapter 88

Yet, contrary to our family's hoped-for plans of moving back to Europe, our stint in the U.S. was looking more and more like it might be indefinite. Mother celebrated her 90th birthday and appeared stronger than ever.

At the same time, Sherri graduated from her Ministry Ventures program and launched her eagerly anticipated nonprofit—Advance Global Coaching—the first ever organization in America to bring life coaching exclusively to cross-cultural missionaries.

And after finally managing to create a complex plot that wove together the topics of motorcycling, human trafficking, cross-cultural missions, and the prosperity gospel, I started my fourth novel, *Forgotten Road*.

The opening paragraphs of the story were finally typed into my word processor and saved.

> Nearly breathless after performing for an hour and a half, he tucked the fiddle beneath his chin and raised the bow for one final song. He closed his eyes and waited until the crowd quieted.
>
> Slowly, he drove the bow into the first notes

of Soul Dreamer, an original ballad that had climbed the pop chart to number eleven and the country chart to number eight.

There was an immediate outburst of cheers and hollers.

"We love you, Cole Michaels!" someone near the stage shouted.

He smiled.

Mindful of his every move, he worked the bow with total passion, then sang his heart out. The audience loved him. He could see it in their posture. Their attentiveness. Their faces—especially their faces.

The faces of his beautiful raven-haired wife and his three-year-old son were glowing as well. They sat just a few yards away on the front row. He smiled again.

He could hardly believe the moment. His pastor had assured him just under a year ago that if he would choose God, that God would in return give him everything he wanted. "It's never God's will," were the pastor's precise words, "that any of His children be financially poor, physically ill, mentally distraught, or socially uncomfortable. Give Him your life and trust Him. And He'll prosper you beyond measure."

And now here he was—Cole Michaels, a follower of God—standing at the brink of stardom, poised to make millions.

As he looked out over the packed three-thousand-seat Nashville auditorium, he shook his long blonde hair and interjected a giant 'Thank you!' to all his new fans.

The people roared their pleasure.

Absolutely overjoyed, he turned his 6'2" frame and nodded his approval to his accompanying musicians. His lifelong dream of becoming famous and wealthy was finally, after so many discouraging years, coming true. And to think—less than twelve months ago, he had tried to accept the likelihood that his dream would over time become nothing more than the over-indulged fantasy of an old man.

He was sure the critics would rave about this particular concert. He could feel it in his bones.

***

After the minutes-long explosion of final applause, Cole—bursting with euphoria—bowed and exited the stage. Amidst the high fives, slaps on the back, and shouts of congratulations from the offstage crew, he grabbed a rag to wipe the sweat from his face just as his wife Jana—with their son Shay in tow—rushed toward him. She threw herself into his embrace. "Oh my gosh, I'm so proud of you!" she laughed, pushing herself onto her toes. "I've got goose bumps all over!" She extended her forearms for him to see.

He laughed with her. "It's unreal!" He scooped up Shay, squeezing him in a giant hug and kissing his forehead.

But, as a celebrity in demand, he was quickly

pulled away. The next forty minutes presented a nonstop barrage of accolades—from the production team, the hired musicians, the lucky fans who had won backstage passes, and the journalists from a half-dozen newspapers and magazines.

This was show business. And Cole loved it!

He signed autographs, gave high-fives, granted a couple dozen photographs, and answered questions from the journalists. As a twenty-nine year old living out his childhood dream, he shamelessly enjoyed every second of it.

***

A few hours later, alone with Jana and Shay in the peace of their newly purchased home in Nashville's posh suburb of Brentwood, Cole was still pumped with adrenaline. Dancing and singing, he helped put his son to bed with another round of hugs and kisses. Before leaving the bedroom, he pulled the sheet up to the three-year-old's chin. "I love you, buddy. You're my favorite boy in the whole world." He watched the little eyes close and the little lips curl into a half smile. He kissed the tip of his own finger and placed the finger on the bridge of the boy's nose. "Sleep tight. We'll see you in the morning."

He waited for Jana in the outdoor hot tub. She slid into the water beside him, wearing a red bikini and clutching a magazine. "Before we do or say anything else, I've got to read this to you."

He put his arm around her, drew her close, and inhaled the fading aroma of her expensive perfume.

With barely controlled giddiness, she folded a page backward and read. "As recently as eleven months ago, very few people in the American music industry—producers and consumers alike—had ever heard the name Cole Michaels. Today, however, thanks to the hit single *Soul Dreamer* from the Sweet Manipulations album that has sold over a half-million units and has received more radio air time than most fast-food commercials, there are only a few people left who have not heard of the man and his music."

She turned, looked intently into his eyes, and gave him a quick kiss. Then she continued reading. "Blonde, rugged, and good looking, the man captures the eye as strongly as his music captures the ear and the soul. Cole Michaels quite simply is the new man in town. Single-handedly, this 29-year-old Tennessee native has created a new mixture of music that is a genre unto itself. With his trademark golden fiddle and his rich baritone vocals, he has given birth to a style of soul-stirring music that is one part country, one part light rock, one part Celtic, and one part new age. It is mood music so emotional that it makes the heart beat fast. And in a strange way, his minimal lyrics—typical for his songs—fill the mind with the reminder of all that is good in life."

She rubbed her thigh against his and gave him a sexy wink.

"With his shoulder-length hair, his facial stubble, his leather trench coat, and his powerful charisma, this handsome musician has undeniably won our hearts and our pocketbooks. Ten months ago, when a prominent Nashville radio station gave *Soul Dreamer* its first airtime, the crossover single rocketed onto the charts and has continued to climb ever since. Hopefully, for the pleasure and inspiration of thousands of music lovers, Cole and his music are here for the long haul."

Cole thrust his hands into the air. "Yes!" He took the two glasses of wine sitting on the edge of the hot tub and gave one to his wife. "To you, me, and Shay! To a life of never-ending bliss and happiness!"

"And God's favor!" she said. "Let's not leave Him out of the picture."

And God's favor," he smiled. He hoisted his glass. They toasted. Then sipped.

Under a full moon, the night could not have been more momentous. When they had drained their glasses, Cole reached for his wife and drew his fingers through the softness of her hair. He pulled her onto his lap and into a smoldering kiss.

They were still lost in passion when a single word intruded: "Mommy!"

Simultaneously, they turned and saw Shay standing a few feet away in his pajamas, seemingly frozen to the floor of the deck, a look of painful confusion etched on his face. Cole and his wife looked at each other with alarm. Something was not right.

The outline for the full story was already completed. It was typed and lying on my desk. Through a hefty amount of brainstorming I had managed to create a plot line that brought all my desired elements together in a plausible and intriguing saga. I had even found a way to once again bring Pastor Jason Faircloth—the legalistic dictator turned gracious mentor from *Wisdom Hunter*—seamlessly into the narrative. Satisfied with the tempo of the opening pages, I felt extremely optimistic about the book. Once again, it was now simply a matter of pulling the 130,000-word-story out of my head one word at a time.

As I continued to lead mission trips, I devoted a fair bit of time each week to the *Forgotten Road* manuscript. The chapters started to materialize at a nice pace.

Chapter 89

In the meantime, Advance Global Coaching—with an established group of board members, a team of certified life coaches, and a roster of missionary clients—had earned a nonprofit status. The ministry, according to the testimonials of the missionaries being coached, was filling a capacious void in the world of missions, and was proving to be so effective that Sherri felt compelled to terminate her Treasured By God tea-party ministry and devote herself full time to AGC and its ongoing expansion. She believed in AGC's ultimate potential so deeply that in the midst of a fundraising spree she dared to pitch her young ministry and its financial needs to the GlobalX missions staff at North Point Community Church, the famed mega church in Atlanta. One of Sherri's Ministry Venture coaches was a high profile member of the church and helped her gain access to a GlobalX staff meeting, not an easy feat.

When Sherri stood in the presence of the staff—two powerful men—she understood that she was facing a duo who stewarded enormous amounts of money. She zealously shared the story of AGC—its birth, its function, and its vitalness. "Will you partner with us?" she implored after emptying her heart.

The two men for a few seconds were rendered speechless.

"In all truth, this sounds like a pivotal resource you're providing," one of the men eventually conceded. "It really does. And it makes so much sense. We both know about life coaching. We just never thought of it as a personal ministry to missionaries." Captivated by the thought that a new missionary transitioning to a foreign culture could have the assistance of a certified life coach who possessed years of cross-cultural experience, or that a veteran missionary struggling with personal issues could have the needed support of a one-on-one coach, the two men enthusiastically, but carefully, presented question after question.

Sherri answered every inquiry with her special poise.

The GlobalX staff were unable to dismiss what they heard. "To be honest, we love this whole idea. We truly do. But...we've never seen it in action with missionaries. We don't know how readily it'll be received. Or what impact it'll actually have. So here's our proposal. We have three single women we've recently started supporting. One has been on the field for just six months in South America. The other two—one preparing to move to South Asia, the other to Southeast Asia—are still raising funds here in the U.S. as we speak. We'll pay you to coach these ladies, let's say for six months or so. We would like to hear and see their response. If it's favorable, we'll meet with you again and possibly establish some kind of partnership."

Over the following months, Sherri—via Skype—coached each of the ladies once every two weeks. The sessions lasted about ninety minutes each.

From the beginning of the trial run, all the way through

to the projected end, the missionary ladies unanimously proclaimed the helpfulness of having a coach come alongside them. The one-on-one assistance was so profitable and so appreciated that near the end of the scheduled trial, all three ladies beseeched the GlobalX staff to extend the coaching relationship indefinitely. "I can't imagine being on the field at this point without my life coach," the ladies heralded their heartfelt sentiment.

After debriefing the ladies on the various ways coaching had helped them, the leaders of GlobalX immediately understood the far-reaching value of what AGC was providing. The GlobalX staff not only voted to extend the coaching agreement with the ladies, they also made another decision—a decision that was bold and daring. They rewrote the church's mission policy specifying that North Point, going forward, would require all their supported missionaries to have a life coach. And that AGC, as long as it was in good standing, would be hired to provide the coaching.

And thus began a partnership that blossomed beyond everyone's expectations.

As North Point funneled dozens of their missionaries to AGC, they encouraged the missionaries to choose the eighteen-month program from the menu of packages. Some of the missionaries were dubious about the whole ordeal, but nevertheless complied in order to remain in the good graces of their biggest supporter.

And then the magic happened.

The missionaries discerned quickly that the AGC coaches were serious professionals who truly cared for them. That the coaches understood their world. That the coaches were trustworthy, even with the most sensitive and personal issues. Subsequently, the missionaries—both men and women alike—spilled their hearts to the coaches. They talked about matters they would never divulge to their sending church or sending agency. They had found a safe place where they could be real without the risk of being judged.

After the eighteen months of opening their hearts and lives to their coach, and being genuinely helped—in some cases to avoid serious mistakes—they all, like the original beta group, earnestly requested that North Point renew their coaching packages. Again, the collective mantra was, "I can't imagine being out here without a coach."

Sherri's vision was consistently validated by missionary after missionary. At some unseen milestone, the GlobalX staff markedly declared, "The money we give to AGC is the best investment we make in our missions program."

As AGC grew, along with its stellar reputation, new partnerships formed with numerous mission agencies and local churches around the nation. AGC soon became the premiere organization for connecting missionaries with life coaches.

Chapter 90

I finished the manuscript for *Forgotten Road* in 2012. I was absolutely elated. As an author, I had been out of the market—as far as producing new material was concerned—for thirteen long years. And I was more than ready to make a comeback. But the publishing industry had changed dramatically.

One of the principal changes was that most of the independent mom-and-pop Christian bookstores around the country had been driven out of business by the big corporate chains like Family and LifeWay. For many authors like myself, this was not a good thing. At the mom-and-pop bookstore there had typically been one or two staff members—often the store owners—who regularly perused new books on the market, by known and unknown authors alike. The books they purchased to fill the bookstores' shelves were handpicked by staff who personally knew their community and customer base. Others on staff would often read the books in full once they were catalogued and on the racks. When a book struck a heart cord with several of the staff, they would enthusiastically recommend the book to their shoppers. And the shoppers would respond favorably. As a result, some books were rocketed into bestsellers, at least locally. And the ripple effect would spread outward geographically from there. This is what had happened with *Wisdom Hunter, Jordan's Crossing,* and *Brotherhood of Betrayal.*

But when the big chains became dominate in the industry, the book buyers for those conglomerates sat far away in high-rise corporate offices and, at least in the beginning, cherry picked the books that were selling well in the mom-and-pop stores. My novels at the time had dropped in sales and were, therefore, not part of the selection process. As an author, I missed the "pick up" wave. So my books were absent in the Family and LifeWay stores during the 2000s.

My books were still selling, but almost exclusively online.

Another pivotal change in the industry was the growing use of online social-media platforms. In the 60s, 70s, and 80s—before the internet—the major publishing houses budgeted big money to market their forthcoming books via magazines, newspapers, posters, radio blurbs, and even fancy floor displays. But once social media platforms like Facebook, Twitter, and Instagram grew a strong user base, the publishing houses saw a way to trim their marketing budgets. They simply transferred the bulk of the marketing to their authors. "You need to set up a Facebook page; create a Youtube channel; start a podcast; or better yet, do all three," they said to the authors. "You can do a much better job at marketing your books than we can."

Personally, however—and there are many authors who share my standpoint—I had rather be writing, researching, studying, conversing, traveling, or teaching than sitting at a computer screen creating social media content.

So, I struggled with a big decision. Should I sign a

contract with a big publishing house to publish *Forgotten Road*, or should I self-publish the book? If the task of marketing would be my responsibility regardless, what would be the advantage of having the logo of Tyndale, Bethany House, Harvest House, Zondervan, Word, or Multnomah imprinted on the spine? Yes, a book from a major publishing house might stand a better chance of finding its way onto a bookstore shelf. But I personally had not known of a single novel that had become a good seller because of the name of the publishing house highlighted on the cover. A book either earned a following or it didn't, based solely on the merit of its content. Or on the name of the author.

I did have a bit of name recognition, and this provided a little advantage. So I opted to self-publish. In doing so, I would have total control of the production process, and I wouldn't be required to give up most of the sales profits in perpetuity to a company to help cover their huge salaries and massive overhead.

I was then faced with a follow-up decision. Should I pay a flat fee up front to a self-publishing service that would do all the work of a publishing house—the editing, formatting, printing, and binding, along with designing the cover art—but would not manage the inventory or the sales of the book? Or should I do it all myself—editing, formatting, creating a cover, and finding a local printer to do the printing and binding? And then keep a well-stocked inventory and make sure Amazon was supplied with a sufficient number of copies.

To better understand the intricacies of the publishing world, I chose—for better or worse—to plan and manage every aspect of the process myself.

I began with the editing. As I had done with my previous novels, I chose twenty to twenty-five people who represented the general reading market to first read the story and offer editing suggestions. The people I selected represented a variety of careers, races, degrees, ages, and beliefs. I wanted a brigade of critical eyes scrutinizing every page before I took the book to press. I had learned long ago that some test readers had a natural proclivity for finding grammatical mistakes. Others, typos. Others, plausibility issues. Others, character development problems. Others, pacing hiccups. And others, contradictory statements. And I naturally wanted all these elements to be as flawless as possible.

When the feedback started getting back to me, as always I stood amazed at the number of needed corrections the readers spotted. One, for example, was found on the last page of Chapter 51 where it was said about Cole Michaels the main character; 'He came home to glimmering windows, shining floors, polished furniture, and sparkling countertops and cabinets—and a thank you note for the laptop.' The 'polished furniture' was a glaring error. In chapter 47, Cole had already sold all the furniture in his house and it had been removed. Only one of the test readers pinpointed this slip-up on my part.

After addressing all the legitimate issues that the test readers highlighted, I sent a cleaned-up digital copy of the novel to a renowned Christian-fiction editor for one final sweep.

When I was finally satisfied with the editing, I set about the task of formatting the book for the printing press. I chose the size of the pages, the size of the margins, the style and size of the font, the spacing between the letters and the lines, the location of the page numbers, the style of the chapter markings, and the layout of the copyright page. I didn't have the appropriate software on my computer at the time, however, to allow for all these implementations. But my home church did. We were members at the time at Eagle's Landing First Baptist. And thanks to two long-time friends who were part of the Eagle's Landing media department, I was given permission to use a church computer. For several weeks, I sat at a cubicle and meticulously formatted the layout of my new creation.

At the same time, I hired Heidi, my oldest daughter, to compose the cover art and provide a press-ready version for the printer. Of course, I had to purchase an ISBN number and a barcode.

When the novel was finally ready to print and bind, it took me an unexpected amount of effort to find a print shop in Atlanta that had both an offset press and binding equipment. But I did find one, about an hour away. I negotiated a price per thousand copies and submitted my files. The print shop first printed two sample copies, for my approval, on a simple copy machine using standard white copy paper. They bound the pages without the cover. They printed the cover separately on the same machine for me to see.

I was thrilled with the size and look of the bound pages. I knew the paper that would be used on the offset press would be creamier in color, thinner, and more flexible. And that it would be more enjoyable to hold. So I gave an enthusiastic thumbs up. Plus, the cover was everything I had hoped for. The design was unique and the colors popped. And across the spine was featured the name of my new LLC—Life Image Publishers. So I signed off on the cover as well. I ordered 5,000 copies of the book, and took the two sample copies home. I mailed one to the copyright office in D.C., filing for the registration that would prove I was the owner of the material. I safely stored the other copy for posterity.

I then built a 'Randall Arthur' website and announced

the forth-coming novel. Amazon would be the primary retailer.

The whole beginning-to-end process had been labor intensive, so I was thrilled the afternoon I drove to take delivery of the first print run. The books were secured in stacks of boxes ready for pick up. I eagerly opened a carton just to gaze at one of the completed volumes. But when the novel was in my grip I felt an emotional punch to the gut.

How could this be!

I closed and reopened my eyes, hoping I was only imagining things. I removed three or four additional copies from the box. My heart sank. The cover, instead of popping with color, looked washed out, dull, and totally vague. It looked nothing like the vibrant sample I had approved earlier.

With *Jordan's Crossing* there had been the editing fiasco. With *Brotherhood of Betrayal* there had been the romance cover and the poorly selected release date. And now, with *Forgotten Road*, there was a printing blunder. I was now staring at a pallet of boxes holding 5,000 copies. And I had already paid for the product in full.

I felt truly sick!

It was finally acknowledged that the individual who set up and operated the press for the print run had used too much black ink. But what was done, was done. The printer, of course, could run a new batch. But it would cost. And because of a backlog of orders for other materials, it would be weeks before they could attend to the matter. And I had already publicly announced the release date of the book—just a few days away.

I didn't have the extra money or time to order a reprint. So, once again—embarrassed—I hauled the books home and fed them to Amazon as orders were placed. The only consolation, in my opinion, was that the book felt great in the hands. The cover, though a disappointment to the eyes, felt smooth and almost powdery to the touch. And it flexed beautifully due to the quality of paper. It was one of my favorite books ever touch-wise. But if books were judged by their cover—and they were—then the first print run of *Forgotten Road* was probably not worthy of the professional marketplace.

PART V

A QUIET ROAR

Chapter 91

As the orders started streaming in for *Forgotten Road*. I was certain it was because of the name recognition that I'd established years earlier, or what bit of recognition was left after a thirteen year hiatus.

My long-ago fans who had somehow discovered the book were obviously overlooking the defective cover. But what about potential first-time buyers? I suspected they were indeed judging the book by its cover and passing it by. Or was I too harsh a critic?

The *Forgotten Road* reviews quickly followed—via newspapers, websites, emails, and letters—in the wave of the book's release. And again I was gobsmacked.

> "How does one proof a masterpiece? Randall has a commanding voice in his writing. Few books on faith can keep a man's interest as well as a woman's, and Randall has managed to cross that barrier. The book is a tear-jerker of major proportions. It should become the 'Gone With the Wind' of religious tomes."- PJ, Founder of a writers group

"I have to say, this is one of the BEST books I have ever read! This is a book you will NOT want to miss. I just can't stop thinking about it."- National reviewer

Back in the public eye and receiving such a positive reception, I decided to do something that for me was completely atypical. I decided to take sway of my rejuvenated success in the industry and rush two additional books to the marketplace—a children's book and a work of nonfiction.

I had already written the text for the children's book, a progressive reader highlighting the ABCs along with corresponding animals and machinery. So I hired a young man who lived locally to hand-draw the accompanying illustrations. We started meeting regularly for me to review and edit his work. In the meantime, I leveraged years of sermon, meditation, and study notes and compiled a list of forty-six common notions, tendencies, and beliefs in the evangelical world that I believed were actual stumbling blocks to one's spiritual and mental health. I titled the work *46 Stones*. As the young illustrator created the colorful drawings for my children's book titled *ABCs On The Move* I labored in my spare time—between overseas trips, motorcycle adventures, speaking engagements, and home responsibilities—to flesh out the nearly four dozen chapters of 46 Stones. Months later I was proud to self-publish both titles under my Life Image Publishers label.

Initially, both books were met with encouraging reviews.

"46 Stones is a home run! Prepare to be convicted, challenged, and inspired to look closer at the true nature of the Christian Gospel." - JM, Senior Pastor

"I gave my grandnephew a copy of ABCs—the book is now his favorite! His parents have had to read the book to him a kazillion times this weekend."- DH, Publisher

But to my befuddlement, neither of the volumes garnered any widespread interest. For example, I preordered 500 copies of *ABCs On The Move* for my inventory. Boxed copies were still stored in my closet months after the book's release. *46 Stones* was ignored almost to the same extent.

I could only conclude that my public persona as an author was codified strictly as a novelist. So, I mentally returned to the drawing board of fiction. I had a couple of vague ideas for new storylines, but nothing anywhere near satisfactory. I knew according to my personal track record that it would take several years for me to assemble a medley of characters, plots, and life lessons that would prove to be intriguing, pertinent, and memorable. As I had done regarding my previous novels, I again would extract storyline ideas from real-life experiences. The drive to put prose to paper still burned inside me. In due time I was sure I would witness something, contemplate something, learn something, or undergo something that would give birth to a new novel. I would simply have to exercise patience as my mind strove on-and-off to weave a story worthy of a reader's precious time.

So I carried on in life with a watchful eye and an alert mind.

It was only a little while later that an invitation came my way from a German pastor in Berlin to fill in for him for six weeks while he and his family took a well-needed sabbatical. The six-week stretch would fall during the upcoming summer. I could bring Sherri and Cayden, and we could live in the pastor's three-bedroom apartment for the full six weeks.

For many reasons, Berlin had become my favorite city in the world. It would be a thrill to spend time there again. Pragmatically, it would be an easy ministerial assignment. Sherri and I knew the city. And we wouldn't need an automobile. The pastor's residence was located just a five-minute walk from an inner-city train station. The expansive train system—combined with subways, street cars, and buses—would be able to transport us to any place in the city we needed to go. Plus, the apartment was in walking distance to grocery stores, restaurants, and parks.

Since our calendars were free of any unalterable plans for the days in question, we gladly accepted the invitation. Having been out of the pastorate for many years, I was excited by the prospect of immersing myself in that role again, even if it would only be for six weeks. We were definitely giddy over the prospect.

My expectations were matched by reality when we eventually arrived in the German capital and settled in. Berlin felt as comfortable as Stockbridge and Atlanta. And the small congregation of forty or so people was more than welcoming. Sherri was especially pleased to be back in the city where our family had created so many great memories. Nearly a decade had elapsed since her last visit. I could read the rich nostalgia in her eyes as she introduced herself to the German congregation on our first Sunday there and invited the people to approach her as a minister's wife at anytime for fellowship, prayer, counsel, or as a needed sympathetic listener.

Sherri had always been an exceptional upfront communicator. But as she spoke to the congregation that day, I was struck for the first time ever by the mental image of her serving side by side with me one day as a co-pastor and teacher. It was odd that I would have such a thought. The idea, of course, was anathema in our patriarchal-led Baptist denomination. I couldn't even guess why the notion had arisen. Yet, the imagery was somehow pleasing. It was an impulsive whim that to my surprise actually took root in my subconscious. Little did I know that the subject of 'female pastors' would one day resurface in my life as a poignant topic and lay the groundwork for my next novel.

In the meantime, my son and I were about to descend into the darkness of Berlin's insidious history.

Chapter 92

"Dad, come here! You need to see this!" Cayden enthused one afternoon from the apartment's dining room table.

"What is it?" I quizzed. When I approached, he was sitting and staring at his laptop.

"It's this article written by an Irishman," he said, pointing to his computer. "The man says he was here in Berlin a few weeks ago and that he explored an abandoned bunker deep in the woods an hour or so north of the city. He claims it's where the German Navy, under Admiral Dönitz, moved their headquarters when the allies started bombing Berlin. He even gives the coordinates. He says you can enter through a weed-covered hatch." Cayden paused and looked at me, his eyes and face begging me to say *Let's go check it out*.

"Let me take a look." I took Cayden's seat and read the article. Oddly, the write-up was void of details about the layout and size of the underground facility, only that it was there and abandoned. "All right," I smiled. "Let's get an early start tomorrow morning and see if we can find it."

Cayden pumped his fist in a show of excitement. He had recently immersed himself in the world of GeoCaching, an outdoor activity using a portable GPS to find containers hidden everywhere around the world by members of the GeoCaching community. If the Irishman's account was true, Cayden's GPS that he had brought to Berlin could be instrumental in helping us locate one of the underground lairs of the German war machine, a lair that had reputedly been consigned to oblivion. We would definitely find out.

The next morning Cayden and I used a regional map of Germany and plotted our course. When we finally reached the specified coordinates—by train, taxi, and foot—we trudged around an empty forest for three hours and didn't find anything resembling a bunker entrance. We were ready to give up and call off the search when, to our surprise, we came across a set of rusty, substantial double gates from the WWII era that barred the entry to some kind of compound, a compound overrun by the forest. The outer gate was still locked. Barbed-wire strung on concrete-pillars extended into the distance on both sides.

Cayden and I looked at each other. There was simply no turning back now. So we scaled the gate. Once inside the perimeter, we were pressed by an uncanny silence. It was as if ghosts of stern officers from the third reich were suddenly standing still, questioning our presence. It felt for a moment that we were trespassing history itself and should leave. But our adventurous spirits simply wouldn't let us. So we carefully pressed onward. After another forty yards or so, we suddenly spotted a metal hatch, an underground entrance with a rust-covered dome. It appeared off to our left, on a slight knoll. We slowly ascended the rise, gawking at the hatch, almost in disbelief. Was this the hatch the Irishman had written about? Was it the hatch that led into a WWII bunker?

But, more importantly, was it unlocked?

Yes! It was unsecured. It lifted with a measure of resistance and a muted screech. I took a deep breath and peered into the hole. Pitch darkness stared back at me. It was then that I realized Cayden and I were totally unprepared for what we were about to do. We had no proper flashlights, no helmets, no boots, no ropes, and no water. Cayden had his mobile phone which had a tiny flashlight and a battery charge of only 65%. And I had a cheap, compact camera with a built-in flash. That was the extent of our 'equipment.'

I stared into the hole again. I saw the top of a wall-mounted steel ladder that was textured with rust. Was the metal structure still trustworthy? Were all the rungs intact and able to bear weight? How deep was the descent anyway? Was this even the same bunker the Irishman had written about? We didn't know any of the answers. If we dared attempt an entry and somehow got injured, how long would it take for a rescue party to respond to a phone call, even with the coordinates? But we had come this far. And the site, with all of its mysteries, was so intriguing, how could we walk away?

"All right," I told Cayden, "I'll check out the ladder and see if it's secure. If I'm able to reach the bottom, you can follow."

Cayden, wearing an expression of anxiety layered with excitement, nodded.

I carefully negotiated my way onto the ladder, lightly applying pressure to every place my hands and feet touched. Within seconds I was standing in partial darkness, my full weight on one of the rungs. The ladder felt thoroughly solid in every way, so I began a slow and steady descent into the unknown. I covered at least twenty feet and was still going down.

After what seemed like thirty feet—or three stories—I lowered my foot to reach the floor. I called up to Cayden. "Come on down, bud! Just take it slow and steady."

As Cayden lowered himself rung by rung I suddenly realized that nobody in the world knew where we were. In my mind I could hear Sherri saying, *That was stupid!*

When Cayden reached the floor, he pulled out his mobile phone and switched on its diminutive light. He pointed it into the chamber. The spacious enclosure was about a thousand square feet with an extremely high ceiling. The floor on the left side of the cavern was piled high with concrete and metal debris. But at the back, and to the far right, there was a distinct silhouette of an opening—a normal-size doorway. With nothing of interest to occupy us in the big room, we negotiated our way over to the thru-passage.

As we grew closer to the opening—with the miniature flashlight leading the way—it became visually apparent that we were about to enter a hallway.

When we stepped through the door and shone the light to our left, our hearts skipped a beat. As far as our eyes could see, the hallway disappeared into the distant darkness, with dozens of doorways leading off to the right and the left. I felt like we had stepped into the twilight zone. I had never stood in a place that equaled the abandoned bunker's outright tone of spookiness. It was the sheer darkness combined with the unexpected expansiveness that provoked an air of fear.

Nevertheless, we carefully marked our location at every turn and ultimately searched every nook and cranny of the hidden facility, including a 'basement' level with six inches of rancid water covering the floor. When we made our way back to the entry/exit ladder two and a half hours later, Cayden's iphone showed 10% battery life remaining. We had explored a labyrinth of forty rooms. As a father and son, it was a two and a half hour stretch of time we would never forget.

Our hunger to know the identity of the overall location just wasn't going to fade. So, back in Berlin, we set about doing serious research via the internet. What we finally learned was that the bunker indeed had served for awhile as the command center for the Germany navy. A couple of handpicked souvenirs we collected were, in a fashion, now priceless.

The successful ploy into the bunker became another great addition to our résumé of adventures.

Plus, the audacious outing was special in another manner. Cayden was only weeks away from beginning a new chapter in his life, a chapter that would keep him from engaging in such family events for quite some time.

After two years of studying at a top-notch co-op school in the Atlanta area, Cayden would soon be leaving the nest and moving two hours from home to Cochran, Georgia where he would commence two years of duel enrollment at G.A.M.E.S.—the Georgia Academy for Math, Engineering, and Science. The academy was hosted at the Middle Georgia State College. For his junior and senior years of high school, he would attend college classes with college students and do college work. Upon graduating, he would receive his high school diploma along with an associate's degree in biology.

As our family's wonderful summer in Berlin eventually came to a close, I had no earthly idea that it would be Cayden's stint at G.A.M.E.S. that would indirectly give birth to my next novel. I had already toyed with a creative storyline that I thought would be utterly unique and captivating. But a trip at a later date to visit Cayden would change all that.

In the meantime, Shanda was in the process of relocating from Mijas, Spain where she had been serving on staff at a Christian-leadership school following the World Race. She and her best friend were moving to the coastal city of Malaga where they were planning to pioneer a new ministry called The Dwelling House. The aim was to rent an apartment in the middle of town and make the place a center for a whole host of outreach activities—mini concerts, art shows, poetry readings, book discussions, photography lessons, baking classes, prayer meetings, worship sessions, Bible studies, and a place of refuge for individual souls that were burned out or hurting. Sherri and I were, of course, cheering her on.

Chapter 93

The Georgia Academy for Math, Engineering, and Science was an elite program. A mere seventy-five teens, handpicked from across the state, filled out the roster. Cayden was one of those minors. He and his G.A.M.E.S. classmates were so advanced academically that the college students hired them as tutors in the various sciences.

One of the Middle Georgia College professors badly wanted to establish the school's first ever science-bowl competition team. So—using only G.A.M.E.S. students—he built two competitive teams, an A team and a B team. Over a period of time he trained the groups, then bussed them to Savannah on the Atlantic coast to compete in the state's annual championship. Cayden was one of the four minors on the A team.

Parents were invited to attend the one-day event. Sherri and I, barring any sicknesses, wouldn't have missed the occasion. We actually decided to make the four-hour trip a day in advance. Knowing that the three-hour stretch of I-16 approaching Savannah claimed only a few exits with even fewer places of commerce, we chose to travel the back roads that were dotted with small, charming townships. The two-lane route would offer an assortment of options for fuel and food, and would allow us to enjoy the scenic farmland that covered the moderately rolling landscape.

En route to the coastal town, Sherri and I settled in to enjoy the alone time as a couple. We talked seriously for awhile about a few family matters. And then, as we oftentimes did when traveling back roads, we played a few car games that we made up when our girls were teenagers.

For example, "The twelfth house on the left will be your new address for the next two years. You get the cars that go with it."

"The third business on the right will be your business and your only source of income. How will you adjust?"

"You will be the mayor of the next town we pass through. Based on a visual assessment and nothing more, what elements of the town would you try to improve, and how would you go about it?"

These *pretend* games always kept us in suspense. What kind of house would we get—a mansion with a manicured lawn or a mobile home falling apart from age and neglect? What kind of business—a bank or a tire-repair shop?

We had just passed through the town of Vidalia—a town known for its sweet onions exported to all fifty states and Canada—when I added a fresh twist to our game. "The next church we see," I said to Sherri, "you'll have to serve as their new pastor." Mentally, I was spring-boarding off the eruptive thought that had swept through my mind a few months earlier in Berlin.

Instantly, though, Sherri looked genuinely interested as if she had just been handed a for-real contract from the church's pastoral search committee. For the next few miles, we drove while gazing ahead in the distance for the next church. Would it be a small cinder-block Primitive Baptist Church? A nondescript metal building hailing a Pentecostal name marker? Or something completely different?

As it so happened, it was something completely different.

We didn't see another church property until we entered the town limits of Lyons. And there, standing tall and graceful, was a steeple towering over a beautiful brick sanctuary with stained-glass windows. A portico highlighted four white columns. And on the red-brick marque—on the front lawn—were the words Lyons First Baptist in bold black letters. Sherri and I laughed. We knew that many Christian denominations permitted women to serve in the role of senior pastor. But the Southern Baptist Convention was one of the few that opposed the notion with the utmost conviction. And we knew instinctively that Lyons First Baptist was a member of that group. So we wondered out loud what would actually happen if the church's deacon board officially announced they were bringing in a lady missionary to pastor the congregation. We were sure we knew the answer. For the next forty minutes or so, we had an absolute blast voicing that visualization. Based only on what was typical of south Georgia churches, we surmised that the congregation was all white and conservative. A female pastor alone, with no added baggage, would be enough in itself to split the church and its households right down the middle, and maybe even the whole town. But what if, as a missionary, the new lady pastor began inviting Hispanics, Blacks, and Asians into the church services? Sherri and I were certain that all hell would break loose. It would be a tsunami of destruction. We painted a verbal picture of the fallout that was so real and so detailed—encompassing the deacons, the wives, the young people, and the community—that right there in the car, the story became nearly a fully written novel, a novel so rich that it begged to be written. I knew immediately that it wasn't going to sit patiently or quietly under any circumstance. It was spastically jumping up and down like an irresistible puppy demanding attention. And it just felt right to afford it the priority it wanted. In a strange way I almost felt obligated, in a joyous manner, to address the project pronto. So I did. On the stretch of two-lane highway between Lyons and Savannah I dictated to Sherri a basic outline for the new story, a story that would have its setting in Lyons and Vidalia. With a few sufficient notes on paper I was momentarily satisfied.

When Sherri and I checked into a Savannah hotel I was able to shift my focus to Cayden and the science-bowl event. Over the course of the elimination rounds, the G.A.M.E.S. teams quickly scored several wins, carrying them to the finals. Sherri and I were astounded at the complexity of the questions and the breathtaking speed at which the young students responded with detailed answers. Sherri and I heard the individual words that made up the questions, but most of the science-related nouns and verbs were foreign to us. In a dash to our pride we honestly didn't understand the meaning of 95% of the questions. Cayden and his mates, however, had no such problem. Though they didn't walk away with a trophy, they performed shockingly well considering they were neophytes in the competitive arena. They were only beaten by a couple of schools that had been fielding and grooming science-bowl teams year after year after year.

After a well-earned celebration with Cayden and a couple of his team members, Sherri and I headed back to Atlanta.

Once on the road, the potential story of the female pastor in Lyons reclaimed my attention. I was now so captivated by the narrative that I swung back through the small town. I needed to confirm something. I stopped five or six shoppers on Broad Street, introduced myself as Randall Arthur a bestselling novelist, explained that I was working on a new book with its setting in Lyons, and asked if I could pose a quick research question.

"Sure, go ahead," was everyone's response.

"Hypothetically," I tendered, "if the First Baptist Church here in town announced they were bringing in a lady pastor, how do you think the people in the church, and in the town, would respond?"

"I've lived here all my life, and I can guarantee that a decision like that would break the church into pieces," was the unanimous sentiment expressed in slight variations.

Of course, that was the certainty I expected to hear. And it was that exact certainty among the townspeople that sealed my commitment to write the story. Quite frankly, I wanted to tell a story that would provoke controversy, and debate, along with a deeper study. Plus, the creation of the story's details would require extensive research on my part. And I've always wanted to be in a constant state of learning.

So, the first task I assigned myself regarding the story was to select a name for the female pastor. I felt that a strong and memorable name would give her 'real-life' legitimacy in my mind and would cajole me to treat her right away with serious respect. After all, I wanted her in the end to be an inspiration to me. And my readers.

After much thought, I gave her the name Kathleen Rose. I was already looking forward to meeting her.

Chapter 94

I slowly started fleshing out the outline for the new novel, creating a full range of characters, plot twists, and sideline issues. I grew more excited about the story with each new development. I felt the book would simply flow from my pen once I started writing.

I already knew that the main female character, the pastor, was going to be a person who wielded explosive influence but was known for her brokenness and meekness. So, I decided after immense brainstorming that the working title would be *A Quiet Roar*. I just needed to put pen to paper and begin.

Around that time, Amazon—the digital online bookstore—was becoming one of the top players in the world of commerce. The company's book-review feature became more and more popular. It was so user friendly that both seasoned and tyro critics by the thousands doled out declarations of praise for selected volumes and pronouncements of mediocrity and mockery for others. The countless reviews, like the sun and moon, were for the first time in publishing history permanently visible twenty-four hours a day from every place on the planet.

As a montage of faceless readers uploaded their honest

remarks about *Wisdom Hunter, Jordan's Crossing, Brotherhood of Betrayal,* and *Forgotten Road,* I was fortunate that all four volumes received a high portion of positive accolades. The uplifting reviews inspired me anew as a part-time writer. Consequently, I was motivated to commence *A Quiet Roar* with no further delays.

With a detailed outline already in hand to guide me, I was soon reading my freshly written prologue. I was pleased with what I had constructed. I especially felt that this latter part of the prologue that unfolds in Mali, Africa would hook the reader from the onset.

> Staring out the car window at the great Niger River Jake tried to gear his mind up for the cello lesson. It would be his next to last lesson for the school year. He would then enjoy a much-appreciated break. He started taking cello lessons almost two years ago, right before his dad died with malaria. Following the loss of his dad, he clung to the instrument as an outlet for his anger and grief. At that time, the weekly lessons couldn't come soon enough. The instrument still provided a therapeutic release, but the lessons themselves were no longer part of that therapy. He had now reached a level of dexterity that allowed him—to varying degrees—to play pretty much any music he wanted to play to pacify his moods of melancholy, joy, or sadness. As his mom turned south onto the ten-mile-long dirt road leading to the music teacher's house, Jake once again thought of his dad, Scott Nicholas Carter. Jake still missed him, more than anyone

would ever know. He missed the nightly father-son prayer time. He missed the hiking expeditions. He missed the movie nights. He missed the optimistic spirit his dad exhibited in everything he did. He missed the logical way his dad thought about things, and explained things. He missed the heartfelt father-son conversations. To Jake, the man had been bigger than life. He had been his hero. Jake stared quietly ahead as the Toyota approached a washboard curve. The thoughts of his dad yielded a fresh cloud of sorrow.

He started to ask his mom if the clouds of grief would ever go away, but was distracted when he saw a young teenage boy on bended knees, leaning over a goat, in the middle of the road. The boy was just on the other side of a short concrete bridge. Was the goat dead? The boy was dressed in a dirty brown tunic and dirty trousers. The boy looked up when he heard the Toyota coming and tried to lift the goat off the road. Did Jake see tears reflecting off the boy's black face? Had his goat been run over? There didn't seem to be anyone else around to lend a hand.

Jake's mom immediately slowed the Land Cruiser to a crawl, the dust from the road whirling to the front of the vehicle.

Jake looked at his mother. "Should I try to help?" Because of the controversial and high-profile work his mom did, she often received threats on her life. Jake knew she always tried to exercise caution when in public.

His mom, looking tentative about the situation, slowly pulled over onto the shoulder of the road—close to a field of tall, thick shrubs—and nodded that it was okay.

As Jake reached for the door handle, he saw his mother out of his peripheral vision reach under the seat to retrieve her 9mm Glock. Just in case.

Jake jumped out of the car, in the sweltering heat, and moved toward the boy. "Do you need help?" he asked in French, the national language of Mali.

The Muslim teenager looked in Jake's direction and nodded.

When Jake walked up to the boy, he bent over and lifted the back end of the goat while the boy lifted the front end. Jake was nearly overcome at the moment by an unexpected stench. He did not know if the odor came from the boy or the animal. He tried not to wince.

The black teen nodded for Jake to reverse direction and head toward the bridge embankment.

Not exactly sure what the boy was doing, Jake complied, trying all the while not to inhale deeply. With the goat in their arms, they sidestepped their way toward the bank leading down to a dry creek bed. Jake struggled to not slip on the dirt as they carried the goat down the bank.

He was caught totally off guard, and momentarily froze, when seven or eight men in tunics and head scarves rushed from beneath the bridge and grabbed him. He was instantly overpowered. The goat was shoved from his arms. Fear blitzed his body. Flushed with adrenalin, he started thrashing, and screaming for his mom. His hands were quickly twisted and tied behind his back. Before he knew what was happening, his head was stretched backward and the blade of a razor-sharp machete was pressed against his neck.

On his tiptoes, Jake closed his eyes and sucked air frantically through his nose. His pants were already being ripped off by the time he heard his mother rushing down the bank, screaming his name. Jake managed to look in her direction. Her eyes carried the flames of panic.

"Let him go!" she screamed, sweeping the Glock from man to man. "Let him go NOW!"

The man holding the machete to Jake's throat swung Jake to face the gun. "Drop the gun or I'll cut his throat!" the man shouted in the indigenous Bambara language.

Jake emitted a ghostly, high-pitched cry.

Another man stepped out of the shadow, aiming a rifle at Angela's head. "Put the gun down!" he repeated the feverish demand.

Jake suddenly realized he was naked from the waist down. His eyes rolled back in his head as he breathed his next breath in absolute terror.

In chapter one that followed, I introduced the centerpiece of my story—the most prominent church in Lyons, Georgia. I so badly wanted to identify the entity as the First Baptist

Church, the church that inspired the story. But...because of litigious tendencies in the U.S., an attorney friend strongly advised me to not use the name "First Baptist" since there was a real First Baptist in town, especially if I was planning to manufacture controversies surrounding my fictitious church's history, mission, and reputation.

"It could be a lawsuit waiting to happen if you go that route. So, don't do it," the attorney warned.

I reluctantly agreed.

So, based on the attorney's urging, I decided on an alternative name for the church. Searching town records online and finding no church in or around Lyons bearing the name "Central Baptist," I opted for that identifier. That particular marker, Central Baptist, highlighted the prominence of the congregation in the county, along with its unmistakable denominational affiliation. And I definitely wanted the church to be Baptist. The Baptists were one of the few denominations across America that vehemently stood in opposition to female pastors. Thus, the tension in my story would ooze a sense of in-your-face realism.

So, from a blank slate, I would create a fictitious congregation that mirrored a Southern Baptist assembly. Additionally I would fabricate a national church convention that mirrored the Southern Baptist Convention with its doctrines, policies, and polity. I would call it the Evangelical Baptist Alliance.

With all my characters and entities in place—including a Muslim terrorist group—I fell into a nice rhythm of churning out an average of four pages a week.

I was experiencing a writer's high.

Chapter 95

As I continued to plan new mission trips, both domestic and foreign, I maintained a bit of rhythm as I worked on *A Quiet Roar* in my spare time. I actually couldn't pull myself away from the project. It was the first of my novels that was not birthed out of personal pain or some level of personal experience. It was purely a creative work. Enchanted by the story, I naturally had to give the female pastor a voice. And in the making of such, I had to equip her with a strong and viable Christian defense. This required hours of research and study. But I kept asking myself *Could I realistically support her position as a lead pastor with Scriptural fidelity?* I would have to learn the answer for myself. Additionally, because of the bent of the story, I felt compelled to produce exceptional sermons for the lady; sermons that were original, substantial, and thought-provoking; sermons that would justify the strength of her mind and integrity of her heart.

The headway that I made from month to month regularly blessed me with an unforgettable sense of satisfaction and achievement. I could hardly wait for my fans to enjoy the full story. It would be controversial, I knew. But it would be inspiring, I was sure of it.

One of my most ardent fans was definitely eager to get her hands on a published copy. That fan was my mother. She knew it would be a lengthy wait of twelve months or more, but she never failed to inquire about my progress when I was in her presence. She was now 97 and living healthily at The Palms, a five-star home for seniors on the outskirts of Stockbridge. Residing in independent living, she was enjoying all the in-house activities as much as anyone—the competitive card games, food-laden birthday celebrations, festooned holiday parties, free movie nights, summer pool aerobics, varied church services, and lazy garden jaunts on her nearly-worn-out four-wheel scooter.

Sherri and I, in the midst of our sundry ministries, reminded ourselves regularly that we had now delayed our return to Europe as church planters by sixteen years for the sole purpose of honoring my word to my mom that we would remain in the States for her final years. We never imagined for a second, though, that our street address after so much time would still be in Stockbridge. And mother didn't appear in any fashion to be languishing or "on her last leg." It was quite remarkable really.

My mother was soon privileged to witness Cayden, her first grandson, graduate from the Georgia Academy of Math, Engineering, and Science with his associate's degree in biology. Cheered on by his grandmother, Cayden promptly began his university studies at Georgia Tech in downtown Atlanta.

Yes, Granny was a serious cheerleader for everybody in the family—for me, my books, my trips, Sherri's nonprofit, Shanda's ministry in Spain, Heidi's mothering, and Cayden's educational pursuit—and incessantly didn't hesitate to broadcast her feelings about it.

Unfortunately, Cayden's entry into the world of academia at Georgia Tech was fraught with culture shock so severe that it temporarily derailed him. At G.A.M.E.S. he had sailed through the two years of educational rigor as part of a cohesive team. The seventy-five kids in the elite program had bonded quickly. Because of their high IQs and their proximity inside one dormitory building, they studied, researched, brainstormed, and prepped for exams as a family. Those who were strong in physics tutored those who needed extra lessons. Those who were strong in biology, chemistry, calculus, and engineering did the same. The team approach became a standard for Cayden. Georgia Tech, however, was everything but a team effort. It was every one for himself. Not expecting the individualistic ethos to be the norm at the famous institute, Cayden selected bio chemistry—one of the most demanding fields of study in the school's curriculum—as his major. And feeling confident as an incoming junior, he registered for a maximum number of class hours.

But to his dismay, not only did Tech students struggle independently with their onerous workloads, but most of the professors, instead of leading their classes, utilized student teachers who were earning their doctorates. So, the professors were almost never accessible. And in classes with a hundred-and-fifty competitive peers, Cayden simply became a disposable number. Homework assignments—major papers and projects—that realistically required weeks of devoted labor were given short deadlines that bordered on the unreasonable.

In an attempt to stay out in front of the academic demands, Cayden regularly found himself reading and studying at the local Waffle House at 3:00 in the morning. Afraid to go back to his dorm and crawl into bed, lest he oversleep and miss his first-period class, he would lay down in the hallway outside the classroom where, if he was lucky, he might manage three or four hours of sleep. So sleep deprivation quickly became an issue. So did despondency. Sleeping through a few classes because of his inability to ignore utter fatigue, he fell behind in his note taking and class requirements. It became impossible at that point grade-wise to rebound to a level playing field. He sought help from an on-campus psychiatrist who prescribed an antidepressant. Sadly, the medication played havoc with his biology and bludgeoned his despondency to despair and then to depression. The depression became so severe that it sucked all hope and purpose from his psyche. He started skipping classes.

Around that time I saw a question-provoking photo he had taken, a nighttime aerial photo looking down on many of the lighted Atlanta skyscrapers in midtown. *How in the world?* Cayden confessed to me that he had trespassed onto a construction site and climbed a towering construction crane where he had snapped the picture with his phone. It was only then that Sherri and I learned of his state of affairs and his depth of lassitude. I urgently arranged for the three of us to meet with a couple of the school's academic advisors. Their urgings, though, were void of any apparent sympathy or understanding.

"Get a grip," was pretty much a summation of their counsel. "If you can just hold on to a three-point-o grade average, your HOPE scholarship will remain intact. If you can just survive this year and the next, you'll be able to go anywhere in the country tuition free to pursue your Masters."

Those were not the words Cayden needed to hear. Nevertheless, he fought valiantly for his academic survival. A different antidepressant was even prescribed by the school's psychiatrist. But as before, the panacea backfired and drove his brain into an even deeper and thicker depression. At that point, Cayden threw up his hands.

Someone in the finance office—after hearing Cayden's story—told us Cayden could possibly salvage his allotted HOPE scholarship hours if he immediately withdrew from the school with a medical release. So, with the psychiatrist's notarized authorization, Cayden made the humiliating and guilt-ridden decision to leave the school.

With no certain direction in life at that point, he buried himself as a server at a Stockbridge Waffle House and battled his depression.

He was stoic, but pitiful.

The following semester, however—after extensive self analysis and determination—he decided to reenter Tech with fewer class hours this time and make a second attempt at consummating his junior year. But no matter his gallant efforts, his unique temperament just wouldn't synch with the school's machine-like tenor. Again, because of mounting anxiety, he fell behind in his studies. Far sooner than he liked, he surrendered a second time to the uncaring spirit of the place, and—as disheartening as it was—officially withdrew and walked away for good.

"I'm convinced something is not right in my brain," he surmised, utterly dejected. "Chemically, I mean." He slowly shook his head like a grief victim in shock. He was terribly concerned about his proclivity toward depression. "I think I need to try something out of the ordinary, something that could potentially stimulate the chemicals in my brain to surge in new ways, maybe coerce it to make necessary corrections, to find a better measure of equilibrium."

A few weeks later he announced a life-altering decision.

"I'm going to hike the entirety of the Appalachian Trail, starting at Springer Mountain. And I'm going to do it solo."

The A.T., as the trail is commonly called, is an earthen footpath that stretches 2,200 miles across the valleys and ridges of the Appalachian Mountain range, from Georgia to Maine, traversing fourteen states. Those who hike the route carry their own supplies and sleep in tents or in wooden shelters located at designated campsites. Rattle snakes and black bears are not an uncommon sight. Most hikers who set out to conquer the full length of the artery in a single season give up after a few days or a few weeks. Painful foot blisters, due to ill-fitting shoes and individual walking styles, are a typical malady forcing many people to quit. Other factors are overweight gear or just the harsh reality of the commitment.

Cayden's decision to challenge the A.T., though unexpected for us, didn't surprise me. I knew he now needed to demonstrate to himself that he still possessed value as a human being and as a man. So I cheered him on as a proud father.

Following maniacal research and the purchase of carefully selected equipment, he set out early one morning weeks later to begin the big adventure. Wanting his trek to be as pure as possible, he hitchhiked from our front door. The hitchhiking element, however—with its hits and misses—constrained him to spend his first night tented in a church parking lot north of Atlanta in a torrential downpour. It was a good first test of his staying power in the great outdoors.

The next afternoon, he was proudly making his ascent up Springer Mountain, the A.T.'s trailhead, that rises above Amicalola Falls State Park.

He promised to update us once a week.

Go for it, bud, I hailed.

While Sherri and I rooted for Cayden as he plodded northward, Sherri—since there was an opening in her schedule—decided to take advantage of the opportunity and head westward to visit Heidi and our three granddaughters in Arizona.

Anticipating the reunion, Sherri contacted Heidi and the girls by phone several times prior to the flight. They caught up with each other's lives and, of course, talked about possible activities they might enjoy during Sherri's stay.

In one of her private conversations with Sidney—Heidi's only biological child—Sherri listened to the young teenager rave about a new Netflix series she was "addicted" to. It was a Netflix original called *Stranger Things*. Sidney was so captivated by the production that Sherri decided in the following days to watch two or three episodes. As a caring and engaging grandmother she wanted to be able to converse intelligently with Sidney about the characters, the storyline, the cinematography, etc. So she sat down one evening and began watching the first episode of Season One.

She was about fifteen minutes into the program when she clicked the pause button on the remote and summoned me to the living room where a puzzled look contorted her eyes.

"Look at this," she entreated. "Am I crazy? Or do you see the same thing I see?" She then played a three minute segment for me.

"You're not crazy," I assured her. "That's definitely Stockbridge High School."

The stranger thing about *Stranger Things* was that the fictitious Hawkins Middle School scenes were apparently filmed at the old Stockbridge High School where both Sherri and I had attended for four years. Bug-eyed, we gaped at the

TV screen. We were viewing the same parking lot, same front entrance, same hallway, same lockers, and same restroom where she and I had traipsed thousands of times as high school students.

"Really!" we questioned out loud. Within minutes we were in the car driving over to the old campus, a campus that had long ago been a public courtyard for our evangelistic fervor. As we approached the school property, we immediately saw the giant words plastered across the front of the old gymnasium, Hawkins Middle School. The Netflix sensation was actually being filmed in Stockbridge. "You've got to be kidding! What are the odds?" We looked at each other with a weird smile, and agreed, "Sidney is never going to believe this!"

And at first, she didn't.

"You're teasing me! she volleyed over the phone with a smirk in her voice. "I'm not falling for it." She honestly didn't take us seriously, not until I emailed a picture of the Hawkins Middle School building with Sherri in the frame, waving and smiling. And then Sidney became ecstatic. "This is sick!" she howled. "It's almost unreal! I can't stop smiling! You've got to take me there the next time I come to visit! My friends are going to be so jealous!"

It was one of those rare moments when our cool factor as grandparents took a strong uptick.

Chapter 96

Because of a stress fracture in his right foot occurring on the trail, Cayden was forced to abort his hike after only two-hundred miles. With no paucity of grit, though, he immediately outlined his plans to start over again from Springer Mountain. While he waited for his foot to heal, he pared down the collective weight of his equipment and acquired an expensive pair of Red Wing hiking boots. The moment a series of x-rays showed that the fractured bones had stoutly fused, he was out the door again. School was not even in his line of sight at that juncture, only the trail.

After lifting one foot in front of the other across 1,025 mountainous miles, he came off the trail at Harper's Ferry, West Virginia to honor a commitment he had made to a friend back in Atlanta. During this parenthetical break, he dared follow through with a request that Sherri and I presented.

I had recently researched colleges and universities in the state, beyond Georgia Tech, that offered a strong major in bio-chemistry. One name that repeatedly surfaced as a highly touted school for bio-chem majors was Berry College in Rome, Georgia. The school, in its marketing materials, even boasted of (1) its supportive community of professors, staff, alumni, and career advisors that served as personal mentors to every student, (2) its restricted enrollment numbers, maintaining small-size classes with a relaxed, family atmosphere, and (3) its eighty-eight miles of hiking, biking, and horseback riding trails on its 27,000-acre property, the world's largest college campus.

It was everything Georgia Tech was not. It sounded like an ideal learning environment for Cayden.

But...it was one of the most expensive colleges in the state, with a yearly tuition three times that of Georgia Tech's. So, how could we realistically even consider the school as a possible option?

To see for myself if the place was as marvelous as portrayed and even worthy of exceptional pursuit, I had made a special trip to the campus. Following a tour of the property and multiple conversations with professors and students, I had walked away so impressed that I seriously wanted Cayden to see the environment and experience it for himself. If he was mesmerized like I was, maybe there were scholarships and grants he could procure.

Cayden agreed to visit the campus. So we made an appointment for a guided tour.

On the day of our walk-through, Cayden was able to observe science labs; interact with professors; talk to students; and scope out facilities such as the student center, cafeteria, and dormitories. He was definitely intrigued, so much so that we promptly visited the financial aid office to inquire about possible scholarships and grants. What we heard was promising enough that within days Cayden submitted his academic records and applied for enrollment.

He then returned to the A.T. at Harper's Ferry.

At some point, Sherri and I happily notified Cayden that he had been accepted at Berry. The financial impact would be softened by his remaining H.O.P.E. hours, available scholarships, and a significant grant.

Cayden managed to clock six-hundred more miles on the A.T. before he had to once again break away, this time for his orientation at Berry. Overall, he had walked 1,600 miles from Georgia to Vermont, just 600 miles shy of the trail's terminus at Mount Katahdin, Maine's tallest peak. He promised himself he would one day conquer those remaining miles.

With both excitement and trepidation, Cayden in the fall of 2018 launched into his studies at the famous Berry College and immediately loved everything about the experience. The milieu suited his temperament perfectly. He started thriving again. We could hear it in his voice. Sherri and I, with thanksgiving on our lips, breathed giant sighs of relief.

One of the blessings—and there were plenty—of our extended time in the States was to be present for Cayden during his tumultuous four-year stumble. We now felt confident that he was finally going to be okay.

Yet, we still weren't in a position to move back to Europe full time. It was the same refrain; my mother, still spritely, was approaching a new birthday, her 100th.

Right before my mom's landmark celebration, Shanda handed The Dwelling House ministry in Malaga over to a new team and moved back to the U.S. She had ministered overseas for eleven years. At 33, she was at a crossroad in her life, and needed a stretch of down time to think through her next season. Plus, the timing of the move would allow her to participate in her granny's 100th birthday bash.

And what a hoopla it was!

Mom's home church at the time, the First Baptist of

Stockbridge, permitted us to use their massive fellowship hall for the big gala. Sherri and I—along with my sister and her family, Heidi and her family, Shanda, and Cayden—spent a day and a half setting up chairs for three-hundred guests; preparing the stage and sound system for musicians and speakers; stringing up a menagerie of special-made decorations, including clusters of helium-filled balloons; creating a sleek photo area with a decorative and well-lit backdrop; and preparing nicely-set tables for finger foods, drinks, and three giant birthday cakes.

On the big day, an invited journalist arrived early to interview people and shoot photos for the county paper.

To add an element of unforgettable surprise to the event, we hid the birthday lady out of sight until the official welcoming. After a few introductory words and a prayer, I gave the signal to one of my AOK buddies.

He rode slowly into the building on his Harley Davidson trike. On the passenger seat was my 100-year-old mother adorned in a white dress suit and grinning and waving like the queen of England. She looked elegant. The crowd of three-hundred people—relatives, friends, neighbors, church buddies, and pastors—erupted with laughter and applause, and of course the 'happy birthday' song. It was a moment that no one present would soon forget.

The program that ensued was equally inspirational in its content and more than worthy of a life well lived. The lineup of events included a professionally-made video about mom's life, scores of planned and impromptu testimonials regarding her impact on individual lives, an original light-hearted song about the resilience of her earthly existence, and several heartfelt prayers of thanksgiving for her legacy.

Following the program, people eagerly formed a long

line to have their picture taken with the centenarian while standing beside or behind her. All the while, mom sat upright in a throne-like chair looking like a royal. She sat patiently for more than an hour and a half as individual after individual, and family after family, looked into the camera lens with her, and then whispered endearing words to her before heading off to the food line.

During the fellowship time, several people approached me and asked, "What do you think is the secret to her longevity; is it a special diet of some kind?"

I laughed and told them, "Well, she's eaten at least two dump truck loads of lard in her life." And then I assured them that her long life was not credited to anything resembling a healthy diet. "She eats mainly processed and fried foods, cooks her vegetables to mush, and smothers everything with tons of salt. And I think I've seen her eat fruit maybe four or five times in my life." We would then all just smile and shake our heads in wonderment.

I did share with serious inquisitors, though, that there WERE at least three character traits that were likely the mainspring of her extended years. The first was that she had learned early in life to let go of losses. She had lost her mom at fourteen and her first husband in her twenties. Those losses nearly killed her. She even underwent shock therapy to recover mental stability. At some point shortly afterward, she understood that if she was ever going to survive life with any sense of happiness, she couldn't allow her losses to keep beating her down like a cruel schoolmaster. She would have to let them go. And that had been her very practice for the last eight decades. I had never one time heard her play the 'pity-me' card. Not once. Yet, because of her age, she had lost more in life than most, and could have easily and justifiably sought bucket loads of pity from those around her. But she never did. Secondly, she had likewise learned to let go of offenses. Like everybody on the planet, she had at moments been the target of abusive, hurtful, and damning words and actions. But she had chosen—at my father's conversion twenty-seven years earlier—to never again let the negative words or actions of others throw her into a state of despondency, bitterness, or vindictiveness. She had chosen instead to love her enemies. Thus, she had never played the 'victim' card either. Thirdly, the one thing she had never let go of was her faith in the Heavenly Father's trustworthiness. God had proven his lovingkindness to her far too abundantly for her to ever doubt His sovereign presence and undergirding hand. So she trusted Him explicitly. Those three practices, along with the fact that she had always been surrounded by friends and had always stayed active, had undoubtedly been some of the reasons she had enjoyed a multitude of extra days on our great planet.

At 100, she had seen the passing of literally hundreds of relatives, friends, and acquaintances. Yet, there were still over three-hundred people—young and old—who felt a strong enough connection with her to attend the 100th birthday gathering. And that in itself was a testament of her widespread influence.

If she made it to additional birthdays, I couldn't conceive of a grander celebration than what we witnessed on that amazing day.

Yet, mother didn't look to be anywhere near her final days.

Chapter 97

Interspersed with overseas mission trips to Greece, Germany, Portugal, and the Czech Republic; and in-country AOK trips to Tennessee, Florida, North Carolina, and Alabama, I found time to finally complete the manuscript for my fifth novel *A Quiet Roar*.

Following my usual protocol, I distributed copies of the manuscript to a host of test readers, twenty-one to be exact. "Don't hold back with your critiques," I urged. "Be brutal. Tear it apart. Pinpoint every weakness you can find—in the pacing, the grammar, the vocabulary, the character development, the interest level, and the plausibility effect. Make a note of every inconsistency, every mistake, and every oversight on my part. I'm not loaning out the manuscript for you to tell me I have a great story. I'm loaning it out for you to read with a critical eye, to help me turn a good novel into a better novel. I assure you, I will not be offended by anything you communicate."

As prompted, the readers—representing a variety of ages, races, backgrounds, and careers—unearthed a cornucopia of flaws that had slipped passed me. I expressed my utmost thanks to the readers for their pugnacious scrutiny, and reminded myself that it always requires dozens of eyes to spot the areas of a book that need repairing.

I wasted no time making all the necessary edits. I then asked three other people to read the updated version. Other than finding one or two typos that all the other readers had missed, they declared I had a winner on my hands.

I then hired a girl in Pakistan—via Fiverr, an online marketing place for graphic designers—to create the cover art. She took the photos I forwarded to her and pieced together a beautiful bit of artwork. It was one of my favorite Randall Arthur book covers to date. And it cost less than a hundred dollars. The world-wide-web of marketing proved to be a fantastic resource.

I then contacted an acquaintance in Nashville, Tennessee who was the long-time manager of Michael W. Smith, Amy Grant, and Frank Peretti. "I have a big question for you," I posed. "I have a new novel that's ready for publication. Based on all the changes you've seen in the industry over the past fifteen years, would you recommend I submit the manuscript to a big publishing house, or just self-publish it? I'm curious to hear your answer and the reason behind it."

It was the same question I had asked a few years earlier when *Forgotten Road* had been ready for the press.

Without fumbling even a bit, the man asserted, "Either a book has the X factor or it doesn't. If it does, then word-of-mouth will push the book through the marketplace regardless of the publisher."

It was the truthfulness of those words—illustrated by the success of William Young's *The Shack*—that convinced me to go the route of self-publishing once again. I had already self-published *Forgotten Road, 46 Stones, and ABCs On The Move* under my own label, Life Image Publishers LLC. So the setup and procedure was already in place to simply add one more title to the list.

But first I revamped my Randall Arthur website, then announced on the website the forthcoming book and its release date. I, of course, promoted the novel on my Randall Arthur Facebook page as well.

At the appropriate time, I uploaded the *Quiet Roar* text and cover files to Amazon's affiliate, Ingram Spark, to become a Print-On-Demand title. I clocked in the release date. And the countdown began.

As always, introducing my readership to a new book loosened a torrent of emotions inside me: immense liberation, euphoric hope, and genuine thankfulness.

On the day *A Quiet Roar* was finally available for purchase as a finished product, I felt genuinely lighter, as if my brain had won a long, hard-earned vacation. For awhile, I didn't have to think one iota about writing. And I relished the break, a stupendous feeling that only a published writer can understand.

One of the first big reviews of *A Quiet Roar* came from the pastor of a mega church, a Southern Baptist Church. Pastor Wade Burleson, as a top 100 Christian blogger, wrote:

> "I picked it up on Christmas Day and began reading it. I didn't put it down until I finished. Then I gave it to my wife and said, 'Here, read this. I want your opinion when you're done.' When it was all said and done, my wife looked at me and said, 'Wade, the author has done Christianity a service. He has taken what you write about in theological terms and put it in a gripping narrative that makes one understand

how silly it is to frame ministry around gender rather than giftings.' My wife is correct. Randall Arthur has hit a home run. With keen insight into multi-faceted issues, Randall Arthur has done a huge service for the reader. He has the unique ability to heal wounds through a quiet roar."

I was absolutely tickled that the book hit the reading community with such a weighty endorsement. My own pastor at the time even devoured the book with interest. He too was a Southern Baptist. He later told me that the morning he finished the novel, he was driving to a funeral home to officiate a burial, and that he had asked himself *What would Kathleen Rose*—the female pastor in my novel—*say at such an occasion?* It was his way of saying how much the book had provoked his thinking and inspired him.

Indeed, one of my targeted audiences for the book was the Southern Baptist Convention, a denomination that was furiously debating the controversial issue of female pastors. Across the nation, almost all SBC leaders were staunch complementarians who believed according to their interpretation of the Bible that women could never serve as senior pastors, but were only permitted to complement male pastors with other positions of less authoritative leadership. The few SBC leaders who became egalitarians—who believed that women could equally serve as senior pastors, just like men—were typically thrown out of the convention.

I even wrote in the Final Notes of my book:

"Some protestant denominations, such as the Methodists and Presbyterians, commonly allow ladies to serve as senior pastors in their congregations. In order to create a sense of realistic tension and controversy in this story, I needed to select a denomination that typically does not permit ladies to serve as pastors. I could have chosen the Evangelical Free Church, the Missouri Synod Lutheran Church, or others. Instead, I opted to use the Baptist denomination simply because it has a larger footprint in society and has a larger audience. With that said, the Baptist denomination is not a target in this narrative. I have no personal agenda to undermine Baptist Churches. As a matter of fact, I believe that the tens of thousands of Baptist Churches across our nation have through the years—with their belief in the authority of Scripture—been a pillar of moral strength in our culture."

Of course, reviews of the novel started appearing online from non-Baptists as well. The Book Club Network Blog wrote:

"Randall Arthur rocked the Christian world with his first novel *Wisdom Hunter*. This was a ground breaking book because nobody had written a novel like he did about legalism. He was transparent and brutally honest of its affects on a community and the world. It was a wild ride that wasn't preachy. He gave the circumstances and let the readers make up their own mind. Randall Arthur is back with a novel that has blown me away even more than his first novel. Again he brings up a subject and lets readers decide for themselves. I'm thrilled to introduce this new novel *A Quiet Roar; Sometimes Disruption Is Overdue*. It gives a peek into a congregation's experience through a change of pastors, traditions, and a brutal look at what missionaries can get caught up in as they share the good news of Jesus. This is a book I couldn't put down and one that will rock your book club meetings." - President, BCN

Another said:

"Over the years I have read a ton-and I mean a ton!-of books. After all, my work as a pastor requires I read, read, and read some more. If you read no other novel this coming year, please please please read *A Quiet Roar*. I guarantee your life and faith will no longer be the same." - B. G., Senior Pastor.

As the novel continued to generate interest locally and nationally, I received another bit of exciting news regarding something totally different.

Penguin RandomHouse—now the publishing-rights holder of *Wisdom Hunter*—announced they were making plans for the first ever audio edition of the twenty-eight-year-old novel. The book was still a good seller. As they say in the industry, "it's a book with legs." The volume had been classified by many as a classic. The hope now was that the audio version would give the book a fresh new pair of legs.

Penguin RandomHouse, to my surprise, allowed me to handpick the voiceover artist. I chose Scott Pollack, a proven narrator—and a brother motorcyclist—recommended by a long-time Atlanta friend. Scott's sample narrations satisfied my demand for excellence.

Within weeks, the novel that was over a quarter century old and that had won so many accolades became accessible for the ears as well as the eyes. Scott's storytelling skills introduced the book to a whole new audience.

The audio rendition was so fresh and so impactful that I now wanted a professional audio recording for each of my stories.

But suddenly, everything in life was placed on hold.

Not just for me.

But for the whole world.

Chapter 98

I'm not a so-called conspiracy theorist, but I do believe there WAS a conspiracy regarding COVID, but only spiritually speaking. I believe the forces of darkness—Satan and all his demonic cohorts—orchestrated the viral devastation in order to kill, steal, destroy, and devour on a massive scale. The fear, the confusion, the panic, the tension, the isolation, the hopelessness, and the hate-filled divisiveness that saturated the entirety of the human race were all hallmarks of Satan's ways of operating.

Contrary to basic human nature and historical norms, nearly all governmental leaders around the planet surrendered their human reasoning when confronted by the hysteria. For such a staggering number of national and regional officials to take the same inexplicable stance regarding a single issue was unprecedented in our lifetime. There indeed seemed to be evil forces pulling levers behind the curtain.

In the face of such immense world pressure, only a minimal number of leaders maintained a semblance of common sense. And those gallant few were maligned incessantly by the media, by the masses, and by all other authority figures. Fortunately,

Georgia—our home state—was governed by one of those brave few. That was Brian Kemp. He closed our state's schools and commerce for only about three weeks. After that minimal shutdown, he pretty much said to the state, and I paraphrase with latitude, *Look, everyone here in the room is an adult. Be wise. Protect the elderly. But make your own decisions. Keep your businesses open, or close them, depending on what you deem is best for you and your customers. If you choose to stay open, implement a six-foot-separation rule for the time being. Wear a mask if you feel it's safer for you. If you are a business owner, you have the right to ask your customers to wear a mask while on your property. All I ask is that everyone try to get along and respect everyone else's choices.*

And with that proclamation, Governor Kemp set the residents of Georgia free to live and work as they wished. While most of the world's businesses, churches, and schools were forced—under the threat of legal prosecution, or even the threat of jail time—to keep their doors locked, we in Georgia were at liberty to live relatively normal lives. Yes, most business owners in the state imposed a mask-wearing regulation for customers. Yes, most business owners set up a six-foot-separation policy for their customers. BUT, the majority of the stores, churches, and places of commerce did not lock their doors. Georgia's economy did not suffer a catastrophic setback like many other states.

As I listened with amazement at how officials in places like California, New York, Australia, and Malaysia, assumed the role of potentates and coerced their populations hour after hour, month after month, to submit to their extreme ideas of safety, I woke up each morning in Georgia saying, "Thank you, Brian Kemp. Thank you. Thank you. Thank you."

While people in other states and countries were forced

to remain inside their homes, I began serving as a fill-in speaker at a small church. The congregation had suspended its weekly worship service for a grand total of just three Sundays. When the group resumed Sunday services, I accepted an invitation to fill their pulpit for about three months until they found a new full-time pastor. And I was honored to do so.

Sherri and her team of life coaches continued to serve missionaries around the world via Zoom. There was virtually no interruption in her rhythm of life.

Cayden's life, however, was sidetracked. Because of COVID concerns, the campus at Berry was closed throughout his final semester as a senior. Consequently, he completed his academic work online from our home in Stockbridge and earned his Bachelor of Chemistry. Sadly, there was no graduation ceremony. His diploma was simply sent to our address through the United States Postal Service.

But before his classes had been relegated to online streaming, one of his Berry professors had approached him. "Look, I know you haven't had a lot of free time to contemplate where you might pursue your doctorate. And I know you don't make decisions quickly. So why don't I help you a bit. I know the lead research scientist at one of the Vanderbilt labs in Nashville. The man's name is Craig Lindsley. He was one of the chief researchers at Merck. But he was too much of a curious and creative thinker to stay in the lane they assigned him. He wanted the freedom to think and experiment outside the box. But Merck simply refused to give him that kind of license. Vanderbilt, on the other hand, recognized his genius. So they hired him to lead their neuroscience lab and set him free to run with his imagination. And I got to tell you, you and Craig are cut from a similar mold. Let me talk to him and see if he will interview you for a job as a Research Assistant. If he'd be willing to do that...and if he chose to hire you for a year or two, that would give you plenty of time to think about your doctorate. And the experience, of course, at the world-class lab would be invaluable for you."

Cayden humbly said, "Yes" to the offer.

Craig Lindsley eventually agreed to the interview and had set up the phone call from his office at the Neuroscience Drug Discovery Research Lab.

On the day and hour of the call, Sherri and I were praying that God would open or close doors according to what would be best for our son's destiny. When the phone call ended, Cayden walked into the room with a dazed expression. "Uh...well...they want to know if I can start on Monday."

"They?" I asked.

"Yeah...I thought the conversation would be between just me and Dr. Lindsley. But he'd invited three postdocs, some of his top scientists, to join the call. They...uh...peppered me with questions to discern my level of knowledge regarding the basics of their research. The call was scheduled to last forty-five minutes. But at about the twenty-minute mark, they asked if I could start on Monday."

Sherri and I were two proud parents.

Extra time for Cayden to make the move from Atlanta to Nashville was requested, and granted. And within two weeks Cayden was moving into a third-floor apartment in Brentwood, a suburb of Nashville. A day or two later, he began his stint as a Research Assistant at the Warren Center, working with teams of chemists searching for ways to cure Alzheimers, Parkinson's, and Schizophrenia. At 24, Cayden was given his own research portal at a renowned lab, working for some of the top scientists in the world.

And within months, he dared challenge Craig Lindsley with a new out-of-the-box method of attaching synthetic compounds to human brain receptors. Intrigued by the visionary idea, Craig asked why his postdocs had never thought of it. He soon assigned one of his teams to implement Cayden's concept, and allowed Cayden to help guide the process. Cayden was now on his way to building a good reputation for himself in the world of chemistry.

As he was thriving in his discipline, Shanda announced that she was purchasing a franchise on the north side of Nashville. Tapping into her art skills, she had earlier found work at a DIY barnwood-decor studio called Board and Brush. She started as an assistant instructor. Within three months she had scaled the ranks to full-fledged instructor, assistant manager, and eventually manager. And then, because of the negative effect on the business caused by COVID, the owners wanted to offload the studio, one of five they owned. The initial asking price was $120,000. Because of the mounting debt the owners were incurring, however, they eventually out of desperation offered the studio for $25,000. Shanda accepted the offer. She had secured a loan and was now in the process of closing the deal.

In just a matter of a few days, she was the sole owner of the Hendersonville Board and Brush studio, complete with thousands of dollars of inventory and office equipment. She also divulged that she had met a Nashville musician she had fallen for. There was even mention of a likely wedding.

Around the same time, Heidi in Arizona secured a full-time job as a teacher of photography at a prestigious high school.

With the kids thriving in their different sectors of life, I continued to coordinate and lead overseas and in-country mission trips, and make sure my mother was taken care of. I also started to think seriously about writing another book. The drive inside my spirit to pen thought-provoking and inspiring stories just wouldn't go away. And it happened to be a personal study of the Old Testament book of Proverbs that solidified my plans for my next book.

We know that every Old and New Testament book was written with a specific recipient in mind—a nation, a king, a pastor, a congregation, etc. So, I asked myself *Who was Solomon's targeted audience when he compiled his litany of Proverbs? Who was he writing to?*

What I learned is that over twenty times throughout the first twenty-seven chapters, Solomon directs his words to "my son," "my sons," "my child," "my children." Many theologians claim Solomon was speaking figuratively when he used those words, that he was referring to those in the world of politics, religion, and academia who sought after his sagacious insights, to those who considered themselves his students—his classroom children per se. But I could find no hermeneutical reason to interpret his words figuratively. The Hebrew word that Solomon uses for child, and all the variations thereof, is the word *ben*, which means human offspring. This word as it's used throughout the entirety of the Old Testament is clearly denoting a biological progeny.

So Solomon, I'm convinced, is certainly addressing his biological children, which forces the question; How many sons and daughters did Solomon have? The Bible doesn't reveal an exact number, not even an estimate. But the Scripture does tell us the precise number of women that were joined with him in matrimony, along with the number of women who were part of his harem. I Kings 11:3 reads, "He had seven-hundred wives of royal birth and three-hundred concubines." And we know according to I Kings 11:42 that Solomon reigned as Israel's king for forty years. So, one man times one-thousand women times forty years equals how many children? The answer is certainly hundreds, if not thousands. Solomon even hints in Ecclesiastes 6:3 and Psalm 127:3-5 that this truth could definitely have been his norm.

So, if the book of Proverbs was indeed Solomon's catalog of fatherly precepts for his biological sons and daughters, what would have inspired him to take on such a laborious project? I believe the answer is found in Proverbs 4:3-9:

> "For I too was once my father's son, tenderly loved as my mother's only child. My father taught me, 'Take my words to heart. Follow my commands, and you will live. Get wisdom; develop good judgment. Don't forget my words or turn away from them. Don't turn your back on wisdom, for she will protect you. Love her, and she will guard you. Getting wisdom is the wisest thing you can do! And whatever else you do, develop good judgment. If you prize wisdom, she will make you great. Embrace her, and she will honor you. She will place a lovely wreath on your head; she will present you with a beautiful crown.'" (NLT)

We discover here that Solomon, the offspring of David and Bathsheba, thoroughly understood the impact of a loving dad. The one-on-one exchanges that his father had shared with him irrevocably changed his life.

Solomon now wanted to love his kids in the same manner.

But with his never ending responsibilities as a mighty king, there was no way he could interact one-on-one with hundreds of kids in a quality fashion. But, what he could do—and did do—was communicate in handwriting his fatherly intuitions regarding life's most important issues and made sure each of his children received a copy.

What a priceless gift!

It was this Bible study that roused me to temporarily set aside my plans to write a new novel and instead write a volume specifically devoted to my three children—Heidi, Shanda, and Cayden—along with my three grandchildren—Meikayla, Sidney, and Latavia. As the patriarch of my family, I decided I wanted to leave behind a written chronicle of my life—an integral part of my family's history, their heritage—hopefully to enlighten, teach, and inspire each of them.

The fulfillment of that dream is the book you're now reading.

Chapter 99

In early fall of 2020 I constituted a detailed outline for the autobiography you're holding in your hand. I knew immediately the book was going to be a lengthy one. But I placed the writing on pause until after Shanda's wedding. She married in November in a fabulous three-day extravaganza in Chattanooga, Tennessee. Her artistic flare shone brilliantly in the venue, the parties, and the official ceremony itself. The decor, the music, the events, the speeches all unfolded with a mythical feel. Everybody who attended raved about it.

A week or so following the wedding, I was ready to begin scripting chapter one of my new book. Using an e-ink pad as a paper substitute and blank canvas, I focused and soon completed the first few pages of - *The Real Wisdom Hunter Story*. In light of my daily, primary tasks of arranging and planning the details of mission trips, I was making decent progress with the book on the side.

Unfortunately, that progress was waylaid by a motorcycle accident.

Late one morning, my best friend and I loaded our motorcycles into his toy-hauler-RV and headed north to spend a couple of days exploring country roads around the Tennessee River.

By the time we finished setting up the RV on our first evening out—leveling the rig and connecting to the water, electricity, and sewage lines—there was maybe forty minutes of sunlight left in the day. I jumped on my bike—a Royal Enfield Himalayan that had been gifted to me—for an evening ride before dinner. Immediately outside the RV park was a small one-lane earthen road covered in a bit of gravel. The track disappeared into the forest. It looked as if it had not been used in quite a while. What really piqued my interest, though, was the old road sign that said *Cottonport Ferry Road*. Specifically, it was the word ferry that stoked my curiosity. I assumed that at the end of the lane was an old abandoned ferry landing where ferries once transported wagons and cars across the Tennessee River. It would be just the type of place I enjoyed investigating.

Except...I never got to see it.

Within a hundred yards, the path made a descent. Rumbling the Himalayan carefully down the hill, I could see that the track ahead swept left through the trees. As I approached the bend at 20 mph, I positioned the bike in the middle of the restricted lane and looked through the cluster of oaks to see if I could see anyone or anything coming from the opposite direction. But, right as I entered the sweeping curve a four-wheeler came sliding around the apex at 30 mph, spraying gravel into the air. I looked at the driver, a young teenage boy. He looked at me. He was on my side of the path, so I cut sharply to the inside of the curve to avoid a collision.

He swerved to the inside of the bend at the same time.

The pre-collision moment is still a vivid snapshot in my head. The two vehicles facing each other just twelve inches a part, with an immutable destiny. The two operators with a look of unexpected chaos and doom frozen on their faces.

And then...BAM!

I was squeezing the handlebars so tightly that the explosive impact of the head-on collision splintered my forearm just above the wrist. As I was launched over the bike into the woods, I don't know if I flipped, twisted, or rolled. All I remember is that within seconds I was back on my feet, pacing in shock, and holding my right arm.

My friend, not far behind, rode up and saw the mayhem.

"I broke my arm!" I bemoaned in a high pitch, still cradling the injured limb in my left hand.

"Are you sure?"

"I'm positive!" I groaned as the pain intensified.

We then noticed the young teenage driver of the four-wheeler. He too was injured. He was hobbling, frantically massaging his thigh, "My leg! My leg!" he kept shouting.

My friend immediately went into action. He called 911 and gave our location. He helped the teen summon his dad. He then contacted a tow company to fetch the Himalayan.

In a daze and unable to stand still I shuffled the two-hundred yards back to the RV, waiting desperately for the paramedics to hurry.

Within forty-eight hours a sports-medicine orthopedic surgeon at a hospital in Cleveland, Tennessee had realigned the broken bones in my arm with a titanium splint and stitched me up. The post-surgery x-ray showed the exquisite nature of his work. I couldn't have been more pleased with the surgeon, the hospital, or the staff. They were all a godsend.

As my arm healed, I took the motorcycle insurance money that came my way and bought another Himalayan. I was soon riding again.

"Why in the world do you keep riding those things?" a

few people wanted to know. "If you don't give it up, you're going to get killed one day!"

Of course, they were accurate in their assessment. Sherri had resigned herself to that possibility a long time ago, but had entrusted me into God's sovereign hands. And I had told her on more than one occasion, "If you get a call one day, saying, 'Randy has been killed in a motorcycle accident,' just know that you might find my corpse with an expression of shock or pain, but on the inside I was smiling."

Truly though, the motorcycle—at least for me—has always been a source of therapy unlike any other. Plus, with grand testimonies like the following from the AOK motorcycle guys, how could I not keep leading them on mission trips?

> "These mission trips have encouraged me to speak in front of congregations. I remember when I spoke to over 300 people one Sunday. Hopefully it touched others in the room, but it sure touched me. The trips have helped stretch my faith and my outreach to others."

> "This group is far and away the most important community in my life. It's a brotherhood that makes us better for the ones we love. We men desperately need each other. Riding motorcycles is just the forum in which vital things happen to us as we engage with one another's lives at an intimate level. The value of our rides is categorically unimpeachable."

> "Dave had given up on life. But God. We showed up with servants' hearts and worked on his roof. He and Ron shared about their love of music.

Bam! That afternoon he sat on the porch as it rained and restarted playing his guitar, and continued until he died. I can't forget the lady in the shotgun house in coal country where the TV crew came and filmed us. We can't leave out the lady who watched us cut over 20 cords of firewood to get her and her granddaughter through the winter, or the beautiful black lady who cried as she walked safely across her new porch. Each year is filled with stories of changed hearts and lives - a pastor in Williamsburg, Virginia; an inn keeper at Harpers Ferry; a young man that came to our campfire each night in New Hampshire; a judge and mayor in Arkansas."

Again, how could I so easily terminate this life-changing ministry when I could still ride and still loved it so much? After all, it's not just motorcycles that pose a dangerous risk in life. It's actually a dangerous planet we live on. We risk our lives everyday just by getting up and moving. Or not moving.

Every individual chooses their level of risk-taking and their level of caution. But regardless, in the end we're all going to die. Somehow.

Or as Sherri says, "We're all in line marching toward our deaths over the edge of the cliff. We just don't know where we are in line. Near the back? Near the front? Or next in line over the precipice?"

Of course, practicing safety is important. But more important is making sure our souls are eternally secure in God's gift of righteousness through Christ. Making sure we've actually readied ourselves for the inevitable. For our earthly exit, however and whenever that might be.

Chapter 100

Because of my age, and because of the fact I have served in full-time ministry for nearly five decades, I've been customarily asked by friends, relatives, and acquaintances, "When are you going to retire?"

"I'm not even thinking about retirement," has always been my response. I'm still as passionate about teaching, leading, and discipling as I've ever been. Maybe more so. Life is still far too interesting, still overflowing with new places to explore, people to befriend, and truths to learn. Every mission trip I coordinate and lead provokes me to think new thoughts, ask new questions, and learn new lessons. The idea of retiring is simply incongruous with my perspective of being a lifetime student and explorer. I'm still determined to live life to the fullest, to the last possible moment; not sit in a rocking chair somewhere and watch life go by. I'm still bedazzled by the universe around me. I'm still hungering for added wisdom, understanding, knowledge, and insight.

I'm even still growing in my faith as a believer. This fact was underscored recently on an AOK mission trip to Nashville, Tennessee.

I decided to leave three days before the official start date, and rendezvous with the men at our designated campsite at Percy Priest Lake three days hence. I simply needed some time alone before engaging with the men and shouldering the responsibility for the group's adventure.

As I left the house I noticed the ZRX engine—the ZRX is my go-to bike—was emitting an excessive amount of heat. The heat was transferring through the frame and seat, making the ride extremely unpleasant. I was carrying a digital infrared thermometer in my tank bag. So I stopped and gauged the engine temperature. The digital readout showed the engine was indeed running hot, extremely hot. And I couldn't determine a reason. I knew that all the air in the coolant system had been flushed out during the last coolant change. And since then, the bike had been operating at its standard temperature. So, why now would the motor be generating abnormally high temps?

I actually resorted to prayer.

Oh Father, you know more than anyone how much I and my men need this getaway. Already, we have too many things on our plates that distract us from you and from trouble-free rest. So, can you please give me, as the leader of the group, a break? I really don't want this heat issue to consume my focus or to ruin the week ahead. I want to relax, get lost in my meditations, and concentrate on meaningful interactions with my brothers. Please, as pitiful and trivial as it sounds, can you somehow just make this heat problem go away!

The prayer was heartfelt but somewhat dismissive. After all, would God honestly give a second's worth of His attention to such a universally insignificant matter?

Well...

Within a few miles, I realized—almost in passing—that my legs didn't feel like they were walking at the edge of a brush fire anymore. The change was so noticeable that I pulled to the side of the road, removed the digital thermometer, pointed it at the engine, and took a new reading. Mechanically, it didn't make sense. The temperature was now in the normal range. The pervasive skepticism of my depraved heart sought for a logical explanation. There must be one. I thanked God, nevertheless. But throughout the remainder of the day, I stopped every twenty miles and took a new reading. And each time, the display showed a normal-operating temperature. I started to relax, but kept wondering if the heat reduction might only be temporary.

The next day I regularly monitored the situation, using the digital infrared. The engine heat continued to hold steady, within the proper parameters. And I was so grateful. What a relief!

But then I made a brief stop at the Alpine Resort in Burkesville, Kentucky. I knew the owner. I wanted to reconnect. Plus, I needed to take a few minutes to stretch my back, shoulders, and legs.

Even though I hadn't experienced any heat management issues for a day and a half, I still—for some reason—felt compelled to remove the infrared thermometer and collect another reading from the ZRX engine. While I was doing so, the owner of the resort—who was standing and conversing with me at the bike—said, "Do you know you have a nail in your rear tire?"

What?

I was sure he was teasing.

But...he wasn't.

The man directed my sight to the intruder, actually the shiny head of a Phillips-head screw, just off center on the wide, tubeless rear tire.

"Let me pull it out," the man volunteered. "The tire's

not flat, so maybe it's just a broken-off screw head that's barely hanging on."

"No! No! No!," I countered. "If it's the whole screw and we remove it, there's no place here in Burkesville to buy a new tire or to get this one patched." I knelt and positioned my ear near the screw head. I didn't hear the hiss of any air escaping. I squinted and tried to assess my options.

"Surely you're not going to keep traveling like this, though," my friend remarked.

I didn't see any other option. There were no rental companies, like U-Haul, in the area that had trucks and trailers available. I stood and shook my head. "I'll just cut my plans short and start heading slowly back toward Nashville. Hopefully, I'll find a tire shop, or maybe even a motorcycle shop, along the way."

To the man's amazement, I soon mounted the bike, said my goodbye, and slowly left the parking lot.

And, of course, I prayed. *Oh God, I need your help again! As you know, I'm in the middle of nowhere Kentucky. My guys will be expecting me tomorrow evening in Nashville. Some of them have taken vacation time to be part of this upcoming adventure. So for their sake, and for mine as their leader for the week, will you providentially guide me safely to a place where I can find help? And can you make it sooner than later, so that by tomorrow afternoon I can be at the campsite and in a relaxed state of mind when the men start arriving? Please! Please! I beg you!*

No more than five miles down the road, I stopped and checked the air pressure in the rear tire. The psi had not dropped a single digit. Maybe the tire is not actually punctured, I reminded myself. Maybe the screw head was indeed nothing more than a piece of road debris sticking to the surface of the tire. Yet, I dared not pull at it. While on the side of the road,

I checked the engine temperature again. Thankfully, all was good at the moment.

To be as safe as possible, I rode slowly and stopped every ten miles to recheck the tire pressure. The psi continued to hold. After an hour or so of traveling on back roads to avoid traffic, I spotted a small independent mom-and-pop tire shop.

"We only have automobile tires," the owner informed me.

"Then, can we find out if the screw is penetrating the tire? And if it is, can you get your technician to seal the hole with a tire-plug kit?"

The man threw up his hands. "No sir. Plugging a motorcycle tire is something we will not do. It's for liability reasons."

I tried at another tire shop further down the road and was given the same answer.

At a town called Tompkinsville, I stopped and refueled. When I placed the dispenser nozzle back into its cradle, I heard a distinct hissing sound. I traced the noise right to the head of the Phillips-head screw, visible near the top of the tire, hissing almost mockingly so, like a defiant teenage princess. I knew then that the tire was definitely punctured. Crazily, I removed a Phillips-head screwdriver from the tiny toolkit beneath my seat and used it to turn the screw in a tightening direction. The hiss stopped.

Really?

But for how long?

I decided that the risk of an accident, or becoming stranded with no one around, was now too great to keep pushing. Businesses were closing for the day, so I checked into a hotel a few blocks away.

The next morning, the tire was still sufficiently inflated to ride the bike inside the town limits. I quickly found a tire shop. One of the bays was unoccupied, so I rode the bike inside.

A young man who looked to be eighteen or nineteen greeted me before I could get my kickstand down. "How can I help you?" he asked in an upbeat voice.

I removed my helmet and told him my story. I rolled the bike until the head of the screw came into view.

The young man examined it. "Sure, I can plug that. It's not a problem." He mentioned nothing about liability. Before I could say anything, he went to a shelf and returned with a tire-plug kit. In less than ten minutes, he had removed the screw, inserted and trimmed the plug, and added air according to my specification. "That'll be seven dollars," he said, wrapping up the transaction.

Wow! I had expected him to say twenty-five or thirty dollars.

"How long have you worked here," I asked while removing my debit card, hoping I wasn't going to hear something like; Oh...just a couple of weeks.

"A year and a half," he offered cheerfully.

"So, I imagine you've plugged quite a few tires, for cars and motorcycles?"

"Oh yeah...all the time."

"So, do you think I should take it easy? Or just ride like normal?"

"Well, I wouldn't race across the country at a hundred miles an hour."

"Gotcha," I replied, and genuinely thanked him for his service.

Leaving the shop, I prayed again. *Oh Father, thank you, thank you, thank you! You got me safely to this town and led me to this shop where someone was willing to help. And just for seven dollars.* I grinned. *Again, thank you, thank you! Now, will you supernaturally secure this plug for my ride to Nashville? I trust that you will. In Jesus' name.*

Ten miles out of Tompkinsville I stopped and checked the air pressure and engine temperature. Everything was good. I repeated the checks multiple times along the route with no further alarms.

That evening in Nashville I excitedly greeted all my AOK men as they arrived. I was hoping so much for a problem-free week during which everyone would feel thoroughly rejuvenated in mind, body, and spirit.

Let it be, Oh God.

"All right," I reminded the men after welcoming them with a few words and settling in, "one of the first things on the agenda tomorrow morning, per your request, is our visit to the Vanderbilt lab where my son works. He has been given special permission to give us an insider's tour." Several of the men had known Cayden for years. We were all excited about this rare opportunity that had been extended to us.

The following morning, I awoke fully rested. One of my first actions, though, was to pull out the tire-pressure gauge and find out if the plug was still being effective. The psi was firm. So, would I stop dwelling on the issue, I pondered. Or would I exercise common sense and buy a new tire in the next day or two?

By midmorning, the men were lined up on their bikes, ready to make the thirty-minute trip to Cayden's lab in Cool Springs. I asked one of my great friends in life, Joe Watkins, to lead the way, using his GPS app. I would help bring up the rear.

I prayed aloud for our group, and we departed the campsite.

We had ridden less than one mile when the one brother

behind me raced up beside my bike and motioned for me to pull over.

Oh no, what was wrong?

"Something fell off your bike!" the man shouted over the noise of the engine when we were stopped on the shoulder of the road.

I switched off the ZRX's motor.

"I'm telling you; something fell off your bike," the man repeated.

"There's no way!" I clamored. The only two accessories on my bike were my tank bag and a strap-on trunk secured to the passenger seat behind me. And both items were in place.

"Yes," the guy rebutted. "There is a way! A piece of hardware, something relatively small, flew off your bike and ricocheted off the pavement into the grass!"

My heart rate accelerated. *God, why? I begged you to let this be a trouble-free week!*

I dismounted the bike and circled it, scanning all the hardware—mirrors, pegs, levers, brackets, cables, chain, and pipe. Nothing was missing or out of place. "Maybe my tire kicked up something off the street," I muttered to my bud. "I don't see that anything has come apart from the bike."

"All right. But I'm telling you; what I saw was not some figment of my imagination."

The guy and I rendezvoused thirty minutes later with the rest of the men at the Cool Springs lab parking lot. We were on site ten minutes before our scheduled appointment with Cayden. As I swung my leg to get off my bike, I noticed that the small pocket on the top of the tank bag was unzipped. That was strange. I had never, not one time, left the pocket unzipped in all the years I had owned and used the bag. Inside the pocket, I regularly stored several ink pens, two compasses, a kickstand pad, the tire-pressure gauge, and the digital infrared thermometer.

I looked inside.

Everything was there. Except two things.

Two things were missing. Only two.

The tire-pressure gauge and the infrared thermometer.

It hit me like a ton of bricks that one of those was the item my buddy had seen fly off my bike.

And as certain as I've ever been about anything, I sensed God's Spirit say to me, *You prayed to me with your requests. I answered both your prayers. And yet, for the last three days you have refused to trust me. You've shown your doubt every time you've stopped to check your engine temperature and tire pressure. And that has been constantly. I've now thrown those instruments away. SO TRUST ME, RANDY!*

I had wanted to believe all along. And should have. But to my shame, I hadn't. It was as if an angel, at God's beckon, had literally unzipped the tank bag while I was riding, yanked the two items out of the bag, and hurled them to the side. I was stunned.

A day later, one of my men asked when I was planning to replace the plugged tire.

"Not until it has completely worn out," I informed him.

The man raised his eyebrows at my seeming unconcern and lack of precaution.

Over the next few months, I rode on that tire—I admit with childish glee—for an additional thousand miles or more, even at interstate speeds. And never one time did I check the air pressure again. I never checked the engine temperature again either. And I never felt unsafe or uncomfortable. Not for a second.

That stark lesson about God's trustworthiness was as

significant for me as Peter's lesson was for him when, at Jesus' promise, he miraculously pulled the silver coin from the mouth of the fish he caught, the exact amount of money needed to cover his tax payment.

Even at my age I am still learning the meaning of childlike faith. Nevertheless, I know that my journey has been an anomaly, and has contributed to five impactful novels. But I also know that in the big picture my story is no more special than anyone else's. It's just that my story has been emblazoned and widely circulated in crafted fictitious narratives.

And now, with this volume, I have added a portion of my real story to my overall collection of work. And it's my deepest hope that what I have shared will be a new source of entertainment, reflection, and provocation.

As a matter of fact, I believe that the world—because of such widespread darkness and lostness—needs a steady flow of good redemptive stories that graciously and boldly point readers to the magnificent Creator who stands ready with open arms to redeem.

So now, as I bring this volume to a close, I feel impressed to encourage you to tell your story as well. Yes...even in a well-crafted, written format. If I have been able to achieve such a feat, you probably can as well. I dare you—double dog dare you—to go for it. As I have proclaimed in writers' workshops, "Great authors like Shakespeare, JR Tolkien, Walter Isaacson, and Ken Follett are really just ordinary men who had a burning desire to write, had something to say, and had the willingness to hone their craft through countless hours of practice—along with a willingness to welcome brutal critiques over and over and over."

Again, if you possess the burning desire to write, I encourage you to go for it!

EPILOGUE

I began writing this manuscript in my spare time in December 2020. It is now four years later.

Flora Dodd, my mother, is now 106. Recently her vital signs were: Blood pressure=128/70. Oxygen intake=95%. Standing heart rate=70. She has now lost most of her hearing, most of her sight, and most of her mobility. But her mind is still sharp. And she only takes one prescription med a day, a sleeping pill. Since giving up her driver's license at the age of 90, she has worn out four battery operated mobility scooters.

Sherri continues to serve as the CEO of her nonprofit, Advance Global Coaching. She and her coaches have now coached ministry leaders across 72 different countries. She recently earned her Master Certified Coach credential from the International Coach Federation, a credential that requires 2,500 hours of coaching and 240 hours of classroom training. I couldn't be more proud of her. Over her lifetime, she has touched the lives of thousands.

Heidi, as an award winning photographer and teacher, continues to teach photography to high school students in Arizona. She has even created her own spectacular curriculum. Her students love her. She lives life without shame and without a filter.

Shanda recently sold her Board and Brush franchise for a nice profit. She is now at a crossroad in life trying to figure out her next big move. All the traveling she has done in life has imbued her spirit with wanderlust, which makes it difficult for her to ever feel "at home." She is a beautiful soul with a self-confidence that undeniably shines.

Cayden, after three years of working at the Vanderbilt drug discovery research lab, enrolled last fall in a doctorate program at the University of Michigan in Ann Arbor. His doctorate, of course, will be in Chemistry. Some of his work can already be found on the internet under Cayden J. Dodd. His intelligence is off the charts. I can read the individual words of his research papers, but I don't understand the meaning of any of them. His discipline in life is truly inspiring. Oh...and he still plans to complete the Appalachian Trail one day.

My dad—Toy Arthur Dodd, who died thirty-three years ago—is buried at Fairview Memorial Gardens in Ellenwood, Georgia. I occasionally visit the gravesite, sit in the grass, and talk to the man who called me son. I've come to realize that my dad, considering his hapless upbringing, did the best he could as a father. I've thanked him multiple times for loving me in his own way.

I have now served as a full time missionary, with Sherri at my side, for 49 years. I've planted and pastored three international churches; written five novels (four of these now available as audio books), one work of non-fiction, one children's book, and this autobiography. I've led over 85 foreign mission trips, having taken teams to Scotland, Iceland, Norway, Sweden, Denmark, Poland, Germany, Belgium, the Czech Republic, Austria, France, Luxembourg, Spain, Portugal, Italy, Greece, Croatia, Serbia, Cypress, Canada, Chile, St. Kitts, and Puerto Rico. And I've led over 45 AOK motorcycle mission trips here in America. I've also filled in periodically for a few European and American pastors when they've embarked on a vacation or sabbatical.

Wanting and needing to keep our financial supporters regularly updated through the years, I've printed and mailed a newsletter about every six weeks, which means I've written close to 380 of those briefs. For posterity I've archived a copy of every one I've written. The other day while reminiscing about the many seasons represented by those newsletters, I suddenly caught myself staring at my bare toes. I humbly realized that those ten small digits—without me ever thinking about them—have traversed Norwegian glaciers, Alaskan tundras, Scottish castles, German bunkers, Canadian ports, Chilean markets, Austrian cathedrals, Mexican deserts, French restaurants, the Mediterranean seafloor, American crime scenes, Roman alleyways, and countless other places.

I recently reached that Biblical milestone of 70 (Psalm 90:10), something I don't like to admit. I actually stopped celebrating birthdays thirty years ago. Sherri claims I am in denial about growing old. I keep telling her, "No, I'm not in denial; it's just that I do not want to think old, talk old, or walk old. As long as I'm physically fit and mentally sharp, I do not want to play the "old age" card.

I'm fully aware that I've been blessed beyond measure. My kids are also aware of this. Thus, I've written this autobiography for them as a reminder that one's life—when seeking God and seeking wisdom—is a life filled with fearless anticipation, joyous learning, and unspeakable forgiveness. So again, this volume is dedicated to Heidi, Shanda, and Cayden. And also to my three grandchildren—Meikayla, Sidney, and Latavia.

And at the rowdy request of some of my fans, I've also made it available to you, the public.

And this is the real *Wisdom Hunter* story.

Psalm 39:4-7

"Lord, remind me how brief my time on earth will be. Remind me that my days are numbered—how fleeting my life is. You have made my life no longer than the width of my hand. My entire lifetime is just a moment to you; at best, each of us is but a breath."

ACKNOWLEDGMENTS

This volume was written primarily for my kids and grandkids. The uncut manuscript that I gave to my family was twice the size of the volume you're holding in your hand. Yes, twice the size. With the help of the following individuals—Heidi Mixon, Janie Dunn, Terry Day, Rhetta Duren, Angie Vittur, Linda Foltz, Terry Hawkins, Julie Beacham, Brenda Bair, Gene Ross, Jan Williams, TJ Hedges, Carolyn Haldeman, and Sherri Dodd—I progressively managed to trim the size of the manuscript until it was suitable for the marketplace. The above-mentioned individuals, with their exceptionally sharp minds and keen eyes, not only helped decide which parts could be cut, they also helped identify spelling and grammatical errors, along with many other contextual mistakes. And I want to thank them profusely, a-thousand-times-over, for their time, interest, and focus. If you, as a reader, have found any lingering mistakes, I am the one responsible. I am the one who typed all the final changes.

My mother, who was looking forward to this volume, passed away during its lengthy editing phase. She was 106 years, 7 months, and 5 days old.

You can correspond with Randall at
LifeImagePublishers@gmail.com

www.ingramcontent.com/pod-product-compliance
Lightning Source LLC
Chambersburg PA
CBHW031357290426
44110CB00011B/194